PRAISE FOR *NEW WORLDS: AN INTRODUCTION TO COLLEGE READING*

"The text is what it says it is—a book that gives students the skills to enter a new world of reading/literacy."

Helen E. Woodman, Ferris State University

"The readings are wonderful in this text. The wide variety as well as the high interest of the readings are appealing to me as an instructor, and I believe that the readings would appeal to students of all ages."

Marian Helms, College of Southern Idaho

"This text contains all the skills necessary for college reading. It is clear, concise, and to the point."

Barbara Geoffrion, North Shore Community College

"There are many features of *New Worlds* that make it an excellent teaching tool. . . . Serious attention has been given to the development and refinement of basic skills while offering an abundance of readings. . . ."

Susan Brandt, Volunteer State Community College

"*New Worlds* presents an intelligent, systematic approach to developing reading skills."

Christine Evans Carter, St. Louis Community College at Meramec

"I appreciate the practical, hands-on approach of the authors in preparing developmental-level students for college-level readings."

Carol Perdue, Green River Community College

"I particularly like the end-of-chapter review cards, the type of questions used with reading selections, and the application exercises. Content-wise this is one of the most comprehensive textbooks I have seen for this English level."

Maureen Cahill, Tidewater Community College

"*New Worlds* is a well-organized and well-written text that presents the material wonderfully for developmental students. It not only tells the student what the skill is, but it also tells why [the student] is learning it and how to apply it step-by-step in his [or her] reading."

Lori Partlow, Chesapeake College

"I am exhilarated by *New Worlds*."

Ellen McMurdie, Montgomery College

SECOND EDITION

New Worlds

An Introduction to College Reading

Joe Cortina and Janet Elder

Richland College
Dallas County Community College District

Boston   Burr Ridge, IL   Dubuque, IA   Madison, WI   New York   San Francisco   St. Louis
Bangkok   Bogotá   Caracas   Kuala Lumpur   Lisbon   London   Madrid   Mexico City
Milan   Montreal   New Delhi   Santiago   Seoul   Singapore   Sydney   Taipei   Toronto

Higher Education

NEW WORLDS: AN INTRODUCTION TO COLLEGE READING
Published by McGraw-Hill, a business unit of The McGraw-Hill Companies, Inc.,
1221 Avenue of the Americas, New York, NY, 10020. Copyright © 2004, 2000 by The McGraw-Hill
Companies, Inc. All rights reserved. No part of this publication may be reproduced or distributed
in any form or by any means, or stored in a database or retrieval system, without the prior written
consent of The McGraw-Hill Companies, Inc., including, but not limited to, in any network or
other electronic storage or transmission, or broadcast for distance learning.
Some ancillaries, including electronic and print components, may not be available to customers
outside the United States.

This book is printed on acid-free paper.

3 4 5 6 7 8 9 0 VNH/VNH 0 9 8 7 6 5 4

ISBN 0-07-255213-1 (student edition)
ISBN 0-07-285839-7 (annotated instructor's edition)

President of McGraw-Hill Humanities/Social Sciences: *Steve Debow*
Senior sponsoring editor: *Alexis Walker*
Senior developmental editor: *Jane Carter*
Executive marketing manager: *David S. Patterson*
Senior media producer: *Todd Vaccaro*
Senior project manager: *Rebecca Nordbrock*
Production supervisor: *Enboge Chong*
Coordinator of freelance design: *Mary E. Kazak*
Supplement associate: *Kathleen Boylan*
Associate photo research coordinator: *Holly Rudelitsch*
Cover design: *Jenny El-Shamy*
Interior/Cover photo: *© Howard Davis/GreatBuildings.com*
Typeface: *10.5/12 Times Roman*
Compositor: *Shepherd-Imagineering Media Services Inc.*
Printer: *Von Hoffmann Press*

Library of Congress Cataloging In-Publication Data

Cortina, Joe.
   New worlds : an introduction to college reading / Joe Cortina, Janet Elder.—2nd ed.,
Annotated instructor's ed.
     p. cm.
   Includes index.
   ISBN 0-07-255213-1 (soft cover : alk. paper)—ISBN 0-07-285839-7
   1. Reading (Higher education) 2. College readers. I. Elder, Janet. II. Title.
LB2395.3 .C68 2004
428.4'071'1—dc21   2002043241

www.mhhe.com

About the Authors

(John Pollock)

(John Pollock)

Joe Cortina and Janet Elder are reading professors in the Human and Academic Development Division of Richland College, a member of the Dallas County Community College District. Both are trained reading specialists, and both teach basic and advanced reading improvement and study skills courses. Their combined teaching experience spans elementary, secondary, and undergraduate levels, as well as clinical remediation.

Dr. Cortina and Dr. Elder began collaborating in 1985. Their first textbook was *Comprehending College Textbooks: Steps to Understanding and Remembering What You Read.* Their intermediate-level textbook, *Opening Doors: Understanding College Reading,* is now in its third edition. Dr. Elder is also the author of another college reading improvement textbook, *Exercise Your College Reading Skills: Developing More Powerful Comprehension.* In addition, she co-authored the reading section of *How to Prepare for the TASP,* a study guide for students entering public colleges and universities who must take the Texas Academic Skills Program Test.

Both authors are longstanding members of the College Reading and Learning Association (CRLA) and the National Association for Developmental Education (NADE), as well as the Texas counterparts of these national organizations, Texas-CRLA and TADE.

Joe Cortina earned his bachelor of arts degree in English from San Diego State University and his master's degree and doctoral degree in curriculum and instruction in reading from the University of North Texas. He has taught undergraduate teacher education courses in reading at the University of North Texas and Texas Woman's University. In 1981 he was selected to represent the Dallas County Community College District as a nominee for the Piper Award for Teaching Excellence. In addition, Dr. Cortina was selected as his division's nominee for Richland's Excellence in Teaching Award in 1987, 1988, and 1993.

In 1992 he was selected as an honored alumnus by the Department of Elementary, Early Childhood, and Reading Education, of the University of North Texas, and in 1994 he was a recipient of an Excellence Award given by the National Institute for Staff and Organizational Development. In addition to teaching reading courses at Richland College, he has served on interdisciplinary teaching teams for honors English courses and has served as a faculty leader of Richland's writing-across-the-curriculum program. Dr. Cortina has served as a member of the editorial advisory board of *The Journal of Adolescent and Adult Literacy*. He is a frequent speaker at professional meetings and in-service workshops.

Janet Elder graduated summa cum laude from the University of Texas in Austin with a B.A. in English and Latin. She is a member of Phi Beta Kappa. She was the recipient of a government fellowship for Southern Methodist University's Reading Research Program, which resulted in a master's degree. Her Ph.D. in curriculum and instruction in reading is from Texas Woman's University, where the College of Education presented her the Outstanding Dissertation Award. She established the first comprehensive secondary reading program in the Dallas Independent School District and conducted extensive staff development training for Dallas area teachers. After teaching reading and study skills courses at Richland for several years, she was asked to develop and implement an honors program for the college. After coordinating the honors program during its first six years, she resumed teaching full-time. In addition to teaching reading courses, Dr. Elder periodically serves on interdisciplinary teaching teams for honors English and humanities courses. She has served on a task force that reevaluated Richland's program in writing-across-the-curriculum program. She used a sabbatical to create multimedia instructional materials in reading. She has received the Extra Mile Award from special services students, has twice been her division's Piper Award nominee for excellence in teaching, and in 1993 received an Excellence Award from the National Institute for Staff and Organizational Development. In 1999 she was one of three nominees for Richland's Excellence in Teaching Award. Dr. Elder often conducts in service workshops and makes presentations at professional conferences.

OTHER BOOKS BY THE AUTHORS

Opening Doors: Understanding College Reading, Third Edition, by Joe Cortina and Janet Elder

Comprehending College Textbooks: Steps to Understanding and Remembering What You Read, Third Edition, by Joe Cortina and Janet Elder

Exercise Your College Reading Skills: Developing More Powerful Comprehension, by Janet Elder

Brief Contents

Contents

PART 2

A New World of Understanding: *Using Core Comprehension Skills When You Read College Textbooks*   117

CHAPTER 3

Determining the Topic   119

CHAPTER 4

Locating the Stated Main Idea　167

CHAPTER 5

Formulating an Implied Main Idea   219

What You Need to Learn   221

What Is an Implied Main Idea Sentence, and Why Is It Important to Be Able to Formulate One?   221
What Are Three Methods for Formulating an Implied Main Idea Sentence?   222

> *Formula 1: Add an Essential Word or Phrase to a Sentence in the Paragraph That Almost States the Main Idea   222*

> *Formula 2: Combine Two Sentences That Each Tell Part of the Main Idea   224*

> *Formula 3: Summarize Important Ideas into One Sentence or Write One Sentence That Gives a General Inference Based on the Details   226*

Other Things to Keep in Mind When Formulating an Implied Main Idea Sentence   230

- *You must always use a sentence—not just a phrase—to express a formulated main idea.   230*
- *All formulated (implied) main idea sentences must have certain characteristics.   231*
- *A longer passage often has an implied overall main idea that you must formulate.   231*

Creating Your Summary   233

Developing Chapter Review Cards   233

Comprehension Practice: Formulating Implied Main Idea Exercises (1)   235

Comprehension Practice: Formulating Implied Main Idea Exercises (2)   239

Readings

CHAPTER 6

Identifying Supporting Details   277

What You Need to Learn   279

What Are Supporting Details, and Why Is It Important to Be Able to Identify Them?   279
What Is the Method for Identifying Supporting Details?   280
Major and Minor Details and How to Tell the Difference   283

CHAPTER 7

Recognizing Authors' Writing Patterns   331

PART 3

A New World of Reading and Thinking Critically   389

CHAPTER 8

Reading Critically   391

CHAPTER 9

Thinking Critically   451

What You Need to Learn   453

What Is Thinking Critically, and Why Is It Important?   453
What Are Facts and Opinions, and Why Is It Important to Be Able to Distinguish Between Them?   453
What Are Inferences, and Why Is It Important to Make Them?   459
Other Things to Keep in Mind When Thinking Critically   466

- *Facts and opinions may or may not appear together.*   466
- *Authors sometimes present opinions in such a way that they appear to be facts.*   466
- *There are other critical thinking skills that can also be used to evaluate written material.*   466

Creating Your Summary   467

Developing Chapter Review Cards   467

Critical Thinking Practice: Fact and Opinion Exercises   471

Critical Thinking Practice: Making Logical Inferences Exercises   474

Readings

PART 4   A New World of Studying   507

CHAPTER 10

Approaching College Reading and Studying   509

What You Need to Learn   511

What Are the Keys to Studying College Textbooks?   511
What Is Comprehension Monitoring and Why Is It Important?   512
How Can You Be Selective as You Read and Study?   514

CHAPTER 11

Applying Core Comprehension Skills as You Study   557

What You Need to Learn   559

To the Instructor: Getting Started in *New Worlds*

Welcome to the second edition of *New Worlds: An Introduction to College Reading.* This text is designed to help students move toward a college reading level. It presents a systematic way of approaching college textbook material that can make students more efficient in their reading and studying. The heart of the text is Part Two, *"A New World of Understanding: Using Core Comprehension Skills When You Read College Textbooks"* (Chapters 3 through 7).

The scope of this book is broad, but the focus is always on comprehension. Moreover, the skills are integrated, and there is continual application of skills once they have been introduced. Although this text emphasizes essential main ideas and supporting details (Part Two, "Comprehension"), it includes skills that range from being successful in college and developing a college-level vocabulary (Part One, "A New World of Learning: Getting Started in College"), to reading critically and evaluating material you are reading (Part Three, "A New World of Reading and Thinking Critically"), to selecting, organizing and rehearsing textbook material to be learned for a test (Part Four, "A New World of Studying"). In Part Four, students learn to use textbook features to full advantage, to underline and annotate textbook material, and to organize material several ways in writing so that it can be mastered for tests.

Although *New Worlds* is designed for developing readers, we have chosen to use only college textbook excerpts and other materials students would be likely to encounter in college. The reading selections were chosen on the basis of field-testing with hundreds of our students in order to identify selections that are interesting, informative, and appropriate. Field-testing also revealed that *with coaching and guidance from the instructor, students can readily comprehend all of the selections.* Equally important is the fact that students like dealing with "the real thing"—actual college textbook material—since that is what they will encounter in other college courses. This type of practice enables them to transfer skills to other courses and avoid the frustration and disappointment of discovering that their reading improvement course did not prepare them for "real" college reading. Finally, these passages help students acquire and extend their background knowledge in a variety of subjects.

College textbook material contains many words students do not know, but need to learn. However, underprepared students and English-as-a-second-language students tend to focus on *words* rather than ideas. Therefore, we present vocabulary-in-context exercises. It will also be important for you, the instructor, to help students view words as a means of accessing content rather than as ends unto themselves. We hope *New Worlds* will help you accomplish this.

Vocabulary words are from the chapter reading selections and are, as noted above, presented in context. The practice exercises in *New Worlds* are extensive. Comprehension questions are the same type that content-area teachers ask on tests (rather than "The main idea of the selection is . . ." etc.). There are also word-structure questions and reading skill application questions. Single paragraphs and short excerpts are used to introduce and illustrate skills; however, students *apply* these skills to *full-length* selections. Exercises include both objective and short-answer questions. Despite our continued, long-held belief that having students "write out" their responses to questions over a selection is the most complete way to assess their comprehension, we realize that students need practice with traditional multiple-choice items as well.

PROVEN FEATURES

- An extensive "comprehension core" as the heart of the text (Part Two).
- Clear explanations and understandable examples of each essential comprehension skill.
- Numerous textbook passages for application of reading and study skills.
- Three full-length reading selections in each of the first nine chapters. Chapters 10 and 11 each present a single but longer reading selection.
- Exercises that integrate writing and reading and call for both objective and essay responses.
- Cumulative review and continued application of skills taught in the comprehension core.
- Presentation of vocabulary and study skills as they relate to learning from college textbooks and other college-level materials.
- Flexibility, allowing instructors to adapt assignments to the specific needs of their own students.
- Skills typically included on state-mandated reading competency tests are addressed, as well as tips for scoring well on standardized reading tests.
- Consistency in philosophy and approach with *Opening Doors: Understanding College Reading* and *Comprehending College Textbooks,* our other reading comprehension textbooks, as well as *Exercise Your College Reading Skills: Developing More Powerful Comprehension* (Elder).
- An extensive online *Instructor's Manual and Test Bank* that contains supplemental materials, answer keys, and pages that can be used to make transparency masters.

ENHANCEMENTS AND NEW FEATURES IN THE SECOND EDITION

- Ten new reading selections with accompanying activities and exercises:

    1-3: "Wise Up! The When and How of Preparing for Tests" *(Study Skills)*
    2-2: "McDonaldization: The Sun Never Sets on the Golden Arches" *(Business)*

3-3: "Giving a Speech? If You're Nervous, You're Normal!"
(Speech Communication)

4-3: "Engagement and Marriage: The Same—Yet Different—Worldwide"
(Human Development)

5-2: "Causes of Cancer" *(Biology)*

5-3: "Why Relationships Develop and What Makes Them Last" *(Psychology)*

6-3: "Learn to Control Your Assets—and You May Become
a Millionaire" *(Business)*

7-3: "The Right to Vote: Valued but Under Utilized" *(Government)*

8-1: "Ticket Scalping: A Bum Rap?" *(Economics)*

9-2: "Whose Grave Is This Anyway?" *(Art Appreciation)*

- Comprehension and Vocabulary Quizzes are now included for all 29 reading selections. These 20-question quizzes contain four parts: *Comprehension, Vocabulary in Context, Word Structure, and Readings Skills Application.*

    Comprehension   This part of the Comprehension and Vocabulary Quiz contains five questions much like those that a content area instructor (such as a psychology professor) would expect students to know after reading this selection.

    Vocabulary in Context   This part of the Comprehension and Vocabulary Quiz contains five questions that test the ability to determine the meaning of a word by using context clues.

    Word Structure   This part of the Comprehension and Vocabulary Quiz contains five questions that test the ability to use word-structure clues to help determine a word's meaning. In these exercises, students will learn the meaning of a word part (root) and use it to determine the meaning of the several other words that have the same root.

    Reading Skills Application   This part of the Comprehension and Vocabulary Quiz contains five questions to test the student's ability to apply certain reading skills to the material in this selection. These are the types of questions that appear on standardized reading tests, exit tests, and state-mandated basic skills tests.

- Comprehension monitoring questions (for reading comprehension and critical reading and thinking) featured throughout the book in the margins and are now summarized inside the front cover of the book as well.

- Many new photographs, cartoons, graphic materials, and other visual aids.

- Websites for each reading selection so that students can read more about the topic or the author of the selection.

- New section on major versus minor supporting details (accompanied by diagrams) in Chapter 6.

- A new Online Learning Center that offers a review of skills in each chapter and additional exercises to reinforce those skills; also contains journal writing prompts.

While many instructors will choose to use the 11 chapters in *New Worlds* in the order in which they are presented, others may choose an alternative sequence (three possible sequences are included in the Instructor's Guide in the Annotated Instructor's Edition) that suits their specific course. For this reason, the instructions for completing Chapter Review Cards are deliberately repeated in each chapter. Similarly, the instructions for the practice exercises that accompany each reading selection are included with each selection so that instructors may assign the reading selections in any order (although the instructions are somewhat abbreviated in the second and third readings in Chapters 3–7).

We hope that you, along with your students, will learn new and interesting things from the selections in this book. Your enthusiasm for acquiring new information, your willingness to become engaged with the material, and your pleasure in learning will serve as a model for your students.

We wish you success in using *New Worlds* to prepare your students to read textbooks effectively and to be successful in college. We hope the endeavor will be enjoyable and rewarding for both you and your students.

SUPPLEMENTS TO *NEW WORLDS*

Print Resources

- Annotated Instructor's Edition (AIE) (0-07-285839-7)

  The AIE contains the full text of the student edition of the book with answers as well as marginal notes that provide a rich variety of teaching tips and related information.

Digital Resources

- *New Worlds* Online Learning Center (OLC)

  A new OLC for students offers a review of the skills in the text and additional exercises to reinforce those skills such as: for chapter tests presented in each chapter; journal writing prompts; additional websites for each reading selection; and Internet exercises. *Take a tour of this website's rich offerings at:* www.mhhe.com/newworlds.

- Instructor's Manual and Test Bank (www.mhhe.com/newworlds)

  This manual provides specific suggestions for teaching each topic in the text. In this edition of the *IM/TB* we have added reading selections (with accompanying quizzes) from the previous edition of *New Worlds* that can be used in a variety of ways, including as additional classroom tests or quizzes.

- PageOut: The Course Website Development Center

  PageOut lets you build your own course website, offering students instant access to your syllabus and lecture notes, original material, recommended website addresses, and related material from the *P.O.W.E.R. Learning* website. Students can even check their grades online. PageOut also provides a discussion board where you and your students can exchange questions and post announcements, as well as an area for students to build personal Web pages.

To find out more about PageOut: The Course Website Development Center, ask your McGraw-Hill representative for details, or fill out the form at www.mhhe.com/pageout.

- *Study Smart* (0-07-552888-6)

  This innovative study skills tutorial for students is an excellent resource for the learning lab. Teaching students note-taking methods, test-taking strategies, and time-management secrets, Study Smart operates with a sophisticated answer analysis that students will find motivational. Available as a free CD-ROM and online with adoption of *New Worlds*.

Additional Value-Added Packaging Options

- *Random House Webster's College Dictionary* (0-07-240011-0) and *Student Notebook* (0-07-243099-0).

  Updated for the 21st century, the dictionary is available at a nominal cost when packaged with the text.

- The Paperback Deal

  A number of Random House and HarperCollins paperbacks are available at minimal cost when shrink-wrapped with *New Worlds*. Titles include: Cisneros's *The House on Mango Street* (0-07-243517-8), Hurston's *Their Eyes Were Watching God* (0-07-243422-8), Achebe's *Things Fall Apart* (0-07-243518-6), Tan's *The Joy Luck Club* (0-07-243509-7), and many more. For a complete list of titles please contact your local McGraw-Hill sales representative, or visit www.mhhe.com/english.

ACKNOWLEDGMENTS

We are grateful to Sarah Touborg, formerly Executive Editor of Developmental English and Literature and cherished friend, for her guidance and support through the initial stages of this edition of *New Worlds*. We are grateful to Alexis Walker, Senior Sponsoring Editor for Developmental English, Composition, and Literature, for seeing the project to completion. We are especially indebted to Jane Carter, Senior Development Editor, and to Becky Nordbrock, Senior Project Manager. We also appreciate the expertise of Gillian Cook, Review Coordinator; Marty Granahan, Permissions Editor; Mary Kazak, Coordinator of Freelance Design; David S. Patterson, Executive Marketing Manager; Holly Rudelitsch, Associate Photo Research Coordinator; Heather Severson, Online Learning Center Content Specialist; and Anne Stameshkin, formerly Assistant to the Editor. Each has contributed in his or her own way to the success of this project.

We have benefited from feedback provided by our Richland College adjunct faculty who teach our introductory-level developmental reading course: Deborah Atchley, Patricia Bowman, Lajuana Buescher, Jane Buxton, Erlann Clark, Virginia Friend, Carole Howe, and Margaret Riley. We thank you all. Our dean, Mary Darin, has been unfailingly supportive in our efforts to help our students. Amela Tufina assisted us with the typing and Web research. Finally, we thank our students for participating in the field testing of the new material in this edition and for their helpful suggestions and encouraging comments. We dedicate this book to all of them.

Our reviewers also served us well with their constructive criticism, suggestions and supportive comments. We are grateful them:

Lori Pangborn	*Saddleback College*
Susan Brandt	*Volunteer State Community College*
Carol Perdue	*Green River Community College*
Barbara Geoffrion	*North Shore Community College*
Jan Sutherland	*Pasadena City College*
Helen E. Woodman	*Ferris State University*
Janet L. Brotherton	*Cedar Valley College*
Christine Evans Carter	*St. Louis Community College at Meramec*
Maureen Cahill	*Tidewater Community College*
Sharon H. Bernthal	*Delta College*
Diana I. Stafford	*Utah Valley State College*
Marian Helms	*College of Southern Idaho*
Robin Redman Wright	*Stephen F. Austin State University*

Joe Cortina   **Janet Elder**

To the Student

*"Didn't I realize that reading would open up whole new worlds?
A book could open doors for me. It could introduce me to people
and show me places I never imagined existed."*

Richard Rodriguez, *Hunger of Memory*

Welcome to *New Worlds*. We hope that this reading improvement textbook will lead you to "new worlds" of success.

New Worlds is designed to help you acquire and polish the reading and study skills that will make you a success in college. Described below are the special features that will help you learn efficiently from this book.

SPECIAL FEATURES OF OPENING DOORS

New Worlds is organized into three parts. Each part focuses on skills that are essential to your success.

Part 1   A New World of Learning: Getting Started in College (Chapters 1–2)

This section includes information on goal-setting, motivation, time management, learning styles, making sense of college reading, and developing vocabulary.

Part 2   A New World of Understanding: Using Core Comprehension Skills When You Read College Textbooks (Chapters 3–7)

Comprehending what you read is vital to your success as a college student. This section will help you:

- Determine the topic.
- Locate the stated main idea.
- Formulate an implied main idea sentence.
- Identify supporting details.
- Recognize authors' writing patterns.

Part 3   A New World of Reading and Thinking Critically (Chapters 8–9)

This section will help you:

- Read critically
- Think critically

Part 4   A New World of Studying

This section will help you:

- Select and organize essential textbook information to prepare for a test

---

BUILT-IN LEARNING AIDS

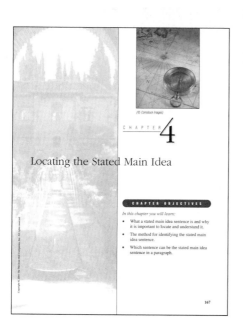

Chapter Introduction

These pages contain chapter objectives to focus your learning.

Chapter Table of Contents

These pages list the skills presented in the chapter. They show the material in the chapter and how it is organized. They also list the chapter reading selections.

Chapter Opening Page

Each chapter has major headings and subheadings that make the chapter's organization clear.

Key Terms

Important terms appear in the margins so that the terms and their definitions are easy to locate.

Stop and Annotate Exercises

These exercises give you the opportunity to stop and annotate actual college textbook excerpts. You will learn actively by underlining or highlighting stated main idea sentences, writing formulated main ideas in the margin, or numbering the important supporting details in a passage, for example.

Chapter Review Cards

These simulated index cards allow you to create your own summary of the important points in the chapter. Each card includes questions and initially prompts with page numbers to direct you to the significant information.

CREATING YOUR SUMMARY

DEVELOPING CHAPTER REVIEW CARDS

Chapter review cards are a way to select, organize, and review the important information in a textbook chapter. Preparing chapter review cards helps you organize the information so that you can learn and memorize it more easily. In other words, chapter review cards are an effective study tool.

Preparing chapter review cards for each chapter of this book will give you practice in creating these valuable study tools. Once you have learned how to make chapter review cards, you can use actual index cards to create them for textbook material in any of your courses and use them when you study for tests.

Now, complete the chapter review cards for this chapter by answering the questions or following the directions on each "card" below. (The boxes below represent index cards.) Beginning with this chapter, the page numbers are omitted on the chapter review cards.

Supporting Details

1. What is the definition of *supporting details*?

2. List three reasons why it is important to identify supporting details.

3. What question should you ask yourself in order to identify supporting details? Be sure you write a question.

Card 1   Chapter 6: Identifying Supporting Details

287

288   PART **2** A New World of Understanding

The Method for Identifying Supporting Details

1. What can be done to a main idea sentence of a paragraph to help you identify details that support it?

2. List some signal words and other clues an author may provide to help you identify a list of supporting details.

Card 2   Chapter 6: Identifying Supporting Details

When Identifying Supporting Details, Keep in Mind . . .

Write the three things you should remember about identifying supporting details.

1.

2.

3.

Card 3   Chapter 6: Identifying Supporting Details

CHAPTER READING SELECTIONS FOR CHAPTERS 1 TO 11

All the reading selections in Chapters 1 through 11 are excerpts taken from widely used introductory-level college textbooks, news magazines, and literary selections of the type you are likely to encounter in college. These selections provide important practice, and they will increase your background knowledge in a variety of interesting subjects. They were chosen to give you the practice, skill, and confidence you need to handle subsequent college courses successfully.

Each reading selection is accompanied by annotation exercises and follow-up exercises. In order, the exercises are:

Introduction to the Selection and Annotation Practice Exercises

Each selection begins with an introduction that provides helpful background information about the selection's topic. The Annotation Practice Exercises give you the opportunity to apply to the selection the reading skills you are learning.

READING

SELECTION 6-1   WHO NEEDS CASH WHEN YOU'VE GOT A SMART CARD?

INFORMATION TECHNOLOGY   From *Information Technology*
By Dennis P. Curtain, *et al.*

Imagine yourself at a shopping mall where you make several small purchases, use a pay phone, and have lunch—all without using a single credit card, writing a single check, or even using any cash. In the near future, all of us will be able to do this—if we have smart cards. A smart card student ID could replace multiple cards students now carry—ATM cards, prepaid phone cards, and credit cards—as well as contain a transcript, résumé, medical record, and other useful information. This selection from an information technology textbook explains how smart cards will be used in the future.

1   The typical smart card contains a printed image and message, usually an advertisement from the issuer or information about the user, such as a photo and name.
2   Embedded in the smart card is a special type of integrated circuit that stores information in electronic form. It controls who uses this information and how it is used. The smart card chip holds about 16 kilobytes of information and that is expected to increase to 32K within a few years. That's enough to store up to 3,200 words of text or a digital snapshot of your finger print, palm print, or retinal scan.

Applications

3   The most common smart card is the prepaid phone card. In France almost all public telephones accept prepaid smart cards. Over 100 million are used annually. As calls are made, their cost is deducted from the card and a display on the telephone indicates how many units are left on the card. When no units are left, a new card must be procured. It is expected that smart cards will be used for pay phones in over 100 countries by the end of the century with over 1 billion cards used annually. However, smart cards are also used as cash cards, ID cards, medical record storage, and cellular phone activators.
4   In many parts of Europe and Asia, smart phone cards store account and PIN numbers (personal account and ID number) so that the same cellular phone can be used by different people who simply insert or swipe through their smart card to activate the phone. Airlines and hotel chains are using smart cards to store passenger frequent flyer and frequent guest credits. And smart cards are in wide distribution in the trucking industry where they are used as debit cards for tolls and transit fees, and to keep track of records such as weigh station reports, bills of lading, and state registrations. MasterCard International is

Annotation Practice Exercises

Directions: For each exercise below, write the topic and the main idea of the paragraph on the lines beside the paragraph. (You may need to formulate the main idea.) Then, identify the supporting details and list them *separately* on the lines provided.

Annotation Exercise

Topic of paragraph 2:
_____

Main idea sentence:
_____
_____
_____
_____

List the supporting details on separate lines:
_____
_____
_____
_____
_____
_____
_____
_____
_____
_____
_____

299

---

300   PART 2   A New World of Understanding

committed to the use of smart card technology because this innovation will offer enhanced card security and provide you with faster and safer ways to use your Master-Card to make purchases and payments. Smart cards bring banks as close as your computer. Virtual banking can offer many services over the Internet or specially equipped phones.

Adding Money to a Card

5   Some cards are fixed in value. You purchase them from vending machines, banks, or other outlets in amounts of $1 and up. As you use the card to make purchases, the balance falls. When it's zero, you recycle it or even sell it to a collector. (With billions in use, just throwing them away would create a major environmental problem.) Other cards are more like an electronic purse or wallet that you can spend from and add to. You can insert the card into ATM machines, phones, or card readers next to your PC to have them refilled. Basically, you would just have funds transferred to your card from a credit card or bank account.

Examples of smart cards. (Gemplus)

The Retailer's Machine

6   To make a purchase, you hand the retailer the smart card and he inserts it into a machine, much like credit cards today. The big difference is that the machine doesn't have to dial into a central computer to find account information because it's stored right in the card. The retailer's machine deducts the amount of the purchase from the card right in the store. The retailer then collects from the bank or other organization that sold you the card. You are not involved because you have already paid for it. For security, new smart cards are virtually impossible to steal and use because they require the entry of a PIN (personal ID number). The retailer cannot deduct funds from the card unless you first key in a PIN.

Security

7   Some smart cards are smarter than others. The simplest cards, such as phone cards, are virtually impossible to copy or falsify, but offer no protection in case of loss. If you lose one, anyone can use it. Other smart cards have one password to restrict its use to one person or machine, and the most sophisticated cards manage several passwords and can use authentication and ciphering techniques to combine total freedom with total security.

Annotation Exercise

Topic of paragraph 7:
_____
_____

Main idea sentence:
_____
_____
_____
_____

List the supporting details on separate lines:
_____
_____
_____
_____
_____
_____
_____

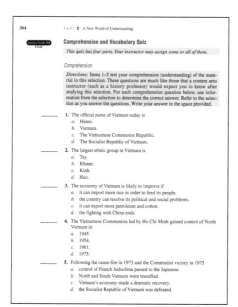

Comprehension and Vocabulary Quiz

This 20-question quiz contains four parts: Comprehension, Vocabulary in Context, Word Structure, and Reading Skills Application.

Comprehension

This part of the Comprehension and Vocabulary Quiz contains five questions much like those that a content area instructor (such as a psychology professor) would expect you to know after reading the selection.

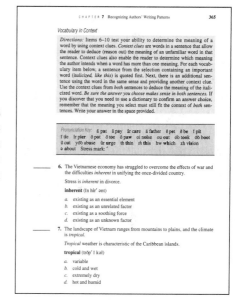

Vocabulary in Context

This part of the Comprehension and Vocabulary Quiz contains five questions that test your ability to determine the meaning of a word by using context clues. *Context clues* are words in a sentence that allow you to deduce (reason out) the meaning of an unfamiliar word in that sentence. Context clues also enable you to determine which meaning the author intends when a word has more than one meaning.

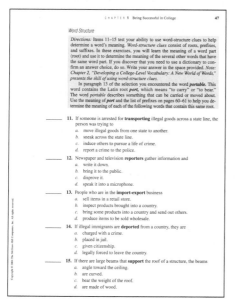

Word Structure

This part of the Comprehension and Vocabulary Quiz contains five questions that test your ability to use word structure clues to help determine a word's meaning. *Word structure clues* consist of roots, prefixes, and suffixes. In these exercises, you will learn the meaning of a word part (root) and use it to determine the meaning of the several other words that have the same root.

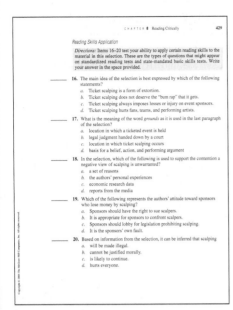

Reading Skills Application

This part of the Comprehension and Vocabulary Quiz contains five questions to test your ability to apply certain reading skills to the material in this selection. These are the types of questions that appear on standardized reading tests and state-mandated basic skills tests.

Writing and Collaborating to Enhance Your Understanding

These short-answer and essay-type exercises ask you to write about the selection. They will help you relate the material to your own experiences. They will also give you practice in thinking critically and determining the overall main idea of the selection.

Read More about It on the World Wide Web

This list of websites related to the topic or author of the selection gives you an opportunity to explore the topic further.

SPECIAL LEARNING AIDS

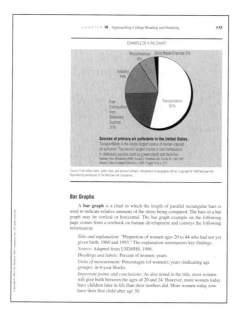

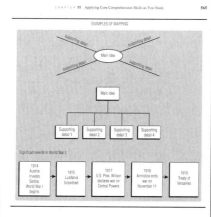

As you work through this book, we hope that you will take advantage of all of its features and that you will discover that you are becoming a better reader. Not only will you have a clearer understanding of the reading comprehension skills, but you also will have had a great deal of practice with them, so that you are able to use these skills in your other college courses.

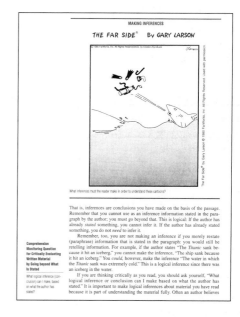

In addition to the built-in learning aids that occur in each chapter, *New Worlds* offers you summary charts, diagrams, photos, cartoons, study maps, and outlines.

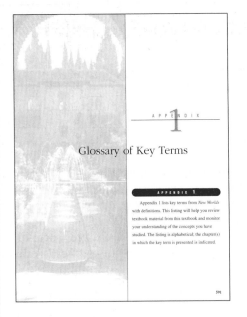

A P P E N D I X

1

Glossary of Key Terms

APPENDIX 1

Appendix 1 lists key terms from *New Worlds*
with definitions. This listing will help you review
textbook material from this textbook and monitor
your understanding of the concepts you have
studied. The listing is alphabetical; the chapter(s)
in which the key term is presented is indicated.

591

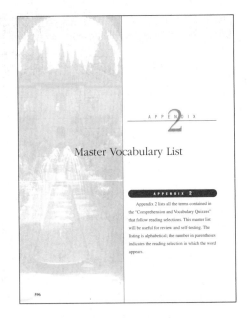

A P P E N D I X

2

Master Vocabulary List

APPENDIX 2

Appendix 2 lists all the terms contained in
the "Comprehension and Vocabulary Quizzes"
that follow reading selections. This master list
will be useful for review and self-testing. The
listing is alphabetical; the number in parentheses
indicates the reading selection in which the word
appears.

596

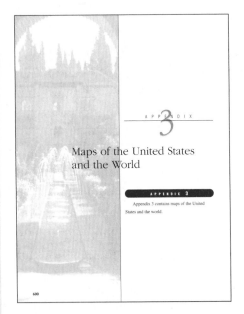

A P P E N D I X

3

Maps of the United States
and the World

APPENDIX 3

Appendix 3 contains maps of the United
States and the world.

600

There are three appendices. Appendix 1 is a glossary of important reading and study skills terms that appear in the text. Appendix 2 lists the vocabulary words from the "Comprehension and Vocabulary Quizzes" and the reading selections in which each appears. Appendix 3 consists of a U.S. map and a world map so that you can look up place references that occur in the reading slections.

We welcome you to *New Worlds*. We hope your journey through this textbook is an enjoyable and rewarding experience.

Joe Cortina   Janet Elder

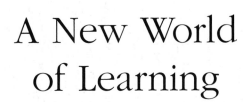

PART ONE

A New World of Learning

Getting Started in College

CHAPTERS IN PART ONE

(Myrleen Ferguson Cate/PhotoEdit)

CHAPTER 1

Being Successful in College

A New World of Reading and Studying

CHAPTER OBJECTIVES

In this chapter you will learn:

- What you need to do to be successful.

- How to set goals.

- What the process of reading and studying involves.

- What learning styles are.

4

WHAT DO YOU NEED TO DO TO BE SUCCESSFUL?

Welcome to the new world of college reading and studying. It's a world in which you can be successful—if you do certain things. Most students want to be successful, of course, but not every college student knows what to do in order to succeed. One way is simply to examine what successful students do and then make sure you do the same things yourself.

What characterizes students who are successful? According to a study in the *Journal of College Reading and Learning,* there seem to be at least six important factors for success. What is interesting about these factors is that they are so obvious and logical. Yes, they require some self-discipline, but so do most things in life that are worthwhile and lead to a feeling of accomplishment. These "success" behaviors and attitudes are within the reach of nearly all students. In fact, you may already do several of them. Keep doing them! However, there may still be ones that you can improve upon or do more consistently. They are all strategies you can begin using today, and if you use them consistently, semester by semester, you will become an even more effective and successful student. In short, anyone who wants to be a successful student must do the things successful students do.

The six characteristics are:

1. **Successful students are prepared for class.** Preparing for class includes reading the textbook assignment and taking notes from the text. Successful students complete their homework assignments. They also look over the information again before class so that they can understand what the instructor is talking about and so that they can do a better job of taking notes in class. Being prepared for class also enables them to enter class discussions when appropriate and to ask questions that help them understand the material and keep their attention focused.

2. **Successful students attend every class.** Not only do they attend every class, they arrive early. They sit where the instructor can see them and where they can see the instructor. They participate in class discussions, even if their participation is limited at first to asking questions. They know that going to class gives them the opportunity to hear more about the important information in their homework assignments. They know that identifying the material the instructor considers important is especially helpful when it is time to study for a test on the material. These students do more than just attend class: They "attend" in the sense that they are "attentive." They are attentive in class and they participate in the discussions. They view attending class as an opportunity to learn rather than as an occasion for socializing with friends.

3. **Successful students perceive instructors as experts.** Successful students know that their instructors are expert resources and that instructors want their students to do well. Because successful students are always prepared for class and always attend class, they feel more comfortable

approaching the instructor when they need assistance. They do not wait until they need a favor or need help to establish rapport with the instructor. More importantly, they do not wait until failure is inevitable before they ask for help. Some students perceive asking for help as showing their ignorance. Successful students, however, view this action as a positive one. (And most instructors are very pleased when a student is interested enough to seek help.)

4. **Successful students follow an organized study routine.**   Organized students regularly take time to think about (*a*) what they need to complete, (*b*) what they need to start, (*c*) what they can do at a later date, and (*d*) what they can ignore. They are aware of when they are using their time well and when they are wasting time. They routinely establish daily objectives that will help them fulfill both short- and long-term goals. (Goal setting is discussed later in this chapter.) Successful students who have learning differences know that it is particularly important for them to take time to consider and plan their intended academic activities on a daily basis. Successful students work ahead so that work does not pile up and so that tests and deadlines do not cause them undue stress.

5. **Successful students develop a set of study skills strategies.**   Successful students constantly review course information. To help them do this, they develop creative ways to reorganize course information. For example, they might put the material in the form of review cards, summary notes, charts, or diagrams. Depending on their learning style, some students find that making tape recordings is helpful. (Ways of organizing information are discussed in Chapter 11; learning styles are discussed later in this chapter.) Reorganizing information requires that students work actively with the information to make sense of it and then organize it in a way that they can remember it. When preparing for exams, successful students isolate themselves. They start early, review all the assignments, and reread all the important points. They rewrite their notes. They ask for help on material they still do not understand.

6. **Successful students take responsibility for their own success.**   Successful students are realistic about the amount of time they need to study. Moreover, they will continue to study during their study time even when an unexpected opportunity arises for them to socialize or to entertain themselves instead of study. They place a higher priority on their schoolwork than on their social life. Successful students are more willing to make sacrifices in order to keep up their grades because they value the long-term rewards associated with completing a college education. They have a clear idea of why they want to complete college (and it is not simply to make money), and they often know what they want to do once they have completed college.

The *Journal of College Reading and Learning* article concludes: Most students attain the maturity to balance their academic and social life. Those who do not know where to draw the line often drop out or fail out of college. The good news, as noted at the beginning of this chapter, though, is that the characteristics described above are ones that almost any student can acquire and use.

Source: Robert Nelson, "Using a Student Performance Framework to Analyze Success and Failure," *Journal of College Reading and Learning* 29, no. 1, Fall 1998, pp. 82–89.

WHY IS IT IMPORTANT TO SET GOALS?

As noted above, successful students have a clear idea of why they want to complete college and what they want to do once they finish college. In other words, they have specific goals they want to achieve. Setting goals is a factor that distinguishes not just successful students, but successful people.

Setting goals involves identifying things that you would like to accomplish, writing them down, and making a commitment to achieve them.

There are several benefits from setting goals. Three important ones are:

- **Having goals keeps you motivated.**   The reason is that when you set goals, you identify future achievements that are important and meaningful to you.

- **Having goals enables you to make good decisions about how you use your time and energy.**   At any given moment, you can ask yourself whether what you are doing is moving you toward achieving one of your goals or whether it is moving you away from it.

- **Having clear, written goals enables you to measure your progress toward achieving them.**   It is satisfying to accomplish goals and to look back on ones you have achieved.

To be useful, goals should be specific and clear. They should also be realistic, that is, things that you can actually achieve (even though some may require considerable effort). An example of a clear, specific, and realistic goal is: "I will complete all of my courses this semester and make at least a B average." (An example of a vague goal is, "I'll do better this semester." An example of an unrealistic one is, "I'll work 40 hours a week, take five courses this semester, and make all As.")

It is also important to put your goals in writing. Otherwise, they are no better than wishes. Writing them down helps you make a commitment to them. Keep a copy of them on your desk or some other place where you will see them daily. Read them often and visualize yourself achieving them. Be sure, too, that you review your goals on a regular basis, perhaps at the beginning of each month. Update them as needed by modifying them, adding new ones, and removing ones you have attained.

You should list your goals according to whether they are short-term goals, intermediate goals, or long-term goals. These designations refer to the amount of time in which you intend to accomplish the goals.

KEY TERM
short-term goal

Goal you want to accomplish during the next 3 to 6 months.

- **Short-term goals** are goals that you want to accomplish during the next three to six months (or during a semester). Examples would be, "To learn to use a word-processing program," "To find a part-time job," and "To earn enough money to take a ski trip during the semester break."

KEY TERMS
intermediate goal

Goal you want to accomplish
during the next 3 to 5 years.

long-term goal

Goal you want to accomplish
during your lifetime.

- **Intermediate goals** are those you want to accomplish during the next three to five years. Examples are, "To attain my undergraduate degree," "To gain an entry-level job in my career field," and "To complete a marathon."

- **Long-term goals** are large, often more complex goals that you want to accomplish during your lifetime. Examples are, "To establish and run my own software company," "To get married and have a family," and "To travel to all 50 states."

Finally, you may find it helpful to categorize your goals such as personal, financial, health, educational, travel, career, spiritual, and so forth.

WRITING OUT YOUR GOALS

Take a few minutes to write out your goals. Write at least three goals for each category. (These are personal and private, and they do not have to be shared with anyone.)

What are my short-term goals?

On the lines below, write three things you want to accomplish this semester.

1. _____
2. _____
3. _____

What are my intermediate goals?

On the lines below, write three things you want to accomplish during the next three to five years.

1. _____
2. _____
3. _____

What are my long-term goals?

On the lines below, write three things you want to accomplish and achieve during your lifetime.

1. _____
2. _____
3. _____

WHAT DO YOU NEED TO KNOW ABOUT THE READING AND STUDYING PROCESS?

KEY TERM
prior knowledge

What you already know about a topic.

Prior knowledge is also known as *background knowledge.*

KEY TERM
previewing

Examining material to determine its topic and organization before actually reading it.

KEY TERM
predicting

Making educated guesses about what is coming next.

In addition to doing what successful students do, including setting goals, you will find that knowing more about the reading process can make your studying more effective.

Did you know that reading is more than just decoding and pronouncing words, or moving your eyes in a certain way? Reading is a form of the *thinking* process; the goal is to comprehend the author's message. To do this, you must "think along" with the author; that is, you must follow and understand his or her train of thought. Further, you must make connections between what you are reading and knowledge you already have, which is called **prior knowledge:** what you already know about a topic.

How can you activate your prior knowledge when you begin reading an assignment? One way is to preview the assignment. Successful college students know they benefit from previewing an assignment before they actually begin reading it. **Previewing** means examining material to determine its topic and organization before actually reading it. These successful students look it over to see what it is about and how it is organized. They think about the information they are likely to learn and what they already know (their prior knowledge) about the subject or topic. If they do not know very much about a subject, they may need to learn more about it first. To accomplish this, they might read simpler explanations, talk with a knowledgeable classmate, or talk to their instructor. After they have finished reading, they take a few minutes to reflect on what they have read and, often, to take notes on it or make review cards for the material.

Good readers are active readers. They know that, as they read, they must constantly ask questions and think about how the material is organized. In addition, good readers use the skill of **predicting** to make educated guesses about what is coming next. Predicting helps readers to concentrate on what they are reading.

Did you know that even good readers have to reread certain things, especially if the material is complicated or the topic is unfamiliar to them? Moreover, good readers take specific steps to fix the problem whenever they realize they are not comprehending. The box on pages 10–11 gives a summary of the process of reading and studying college textbooks. (Chapter 11, "Applying Core Comprehension Skills as You Study," explains these study-reading strategies in depth.)

Skillful readers also adjust their reading strategies and their reading rate according to the *type* of material they are reading (such as a textbook, a newspaper, a book of poems, a comic strip) and their *purpose* for reading (to gain information, to entertain themselves, to receive inspiration or comfort, and so forth). You will learn more about all of these skills in *New Worlds.*

SUMMARY OF THE THREE-STEP PROCESS FOR READING AND STUDYING COLLEGE TEXTBOOKS

Step 1: Prepare to Read

Preview the selection to see what it contains and how it is organized.

- Read the title.
- Read the introduction.
- Read headings and subheadings in each section.
- Read words in italics, bold print, or color.
- Look over illustrations, charts, and diagrams.
- Read any questions that are included in the chapter or a study guide.
- Read the summary.

Ask Yourself:

- "What topics does the author seem to be emphasizing?"
- "How are the topics organized?"

Assess your prior knowledge.

Ask Yourself:

- "What do I already know about the topic?"
- "How familiar am I with this topic?"

Plan your reading and study time.

Ask Yourself:

- "How can I best allot my time for this assignment?"
- "Do I need to divide the assignment into smaller units?"

Step 2: Ask and Answer Questions as You Read

Guide your reading by asking and answering questions.

- Turn chapter headings into questions.
- Create questions based on what the paragraphs or sections appear to be about.
- If the author has included questions, use them.
- Use questions in a study guide, if there is one.
- Use questions given out by the instructor.

Read actively.

- Look for answers to questions.

Record the answers to the questions.

- Write the answers on notebook paper or in the margins of the textbook.
- Take notes on the material on notebook paper.
- Emphasize the answers by highlighting or underlining them in the text or in your notes.

Step 3: Review by Rehearsing the Answers to Your Questions

Review the material to transfer it into long-term memory by rehearsing.

- Recite (say aloud) the answers to the questions.
- Try to write the important points from memory.

WHAT ARE LEARNING STYLES?

KEY TERM

learning style

The modality—visual, auditory, tactile—through which an individual learns best.

Being aware of learning styles can help you become a more successful student. The term **learning style** refers to the modality through which an individual learns best. The modalities are visual, auditory, and tactile. A person's learning style may be visual (prefers reading or seeing), auditory (prefers hearing information), or tactile (prefers touching or manipulating materials). Take a moment at this point to complete the brief learning styles assessment below.

Most students are capable of learning in any of these ways, yet most people have a preferred style, that is, one that they prefer to use because it makes learning more effective for them. For example, one student may prefer to look at a map, while another may prefer to listen to directions for reaching the same destination; still another student might find it helpful to actually draw the map or trace the route with a finger tip. Some students might be comfortable with any of these ways or a particular combination.

Some students are primarily *visual learners* who learn best when they see or read the material to be learned. They benefit from books, class notes, review cards, test review sheets, and the like. Other students are primarily *auditory learners* who learn best when they hear the material one or more times. They benefit from classes that feature lectures and discussions. Auditory learners also benefit from reciting material or reading it aloud to themselves, making audio tapes, and participating in study groups. Still other students are primarily *tactile learners* who benefit from writing information down or manipulating materials physically. These students learn best from laboratory work and other types of hands-on activities. The box on page 13 summarizes this information on learning styles. Once you have identified your preferred learning style, you can choose classroom settings and study techniques that let you use it to full advantage.

As noted, most students have a learning style that they *prefer* to use. However, all students will find themselves in situations that require them to utilize the other learning styles. For this reason, it is important to develop a range of study and learning skills.

IDENTIFYING YOUR LEARNING STYLE

Answering the following questions can help you identify your learning style. For each item, circle all the answers that describe you.

1. When I go someplace new, I usually
   a. trust my intuition about the right direction or route to take.
   b. ask someone for directions.
   c. look at a map or printed directions.

2. I like to go to places where
   a. there is a lot of space to move around.
   b. people are talking or there is music that matches my mood.
   c. there is good "people watching" or there is something interesting to watch.

3. If I have many things to do, I generally
   a. feel anxious until I get most of them done.
   b. repeat them over and over to myself so I won't forget to do them.
   c. make a list of them or write them on a calendar or organizer.

4. When I have free time, I like to
   a. work on a hobby or do crafts, or do an activity such as play a sport or exercise.
   b. listen to a tape, a CD, or the radio, or talk on the phone.
   c. watch television, play a video game, go online, or see a movie.

5. When I am talking with other people, I usually
   a. move close to them so I can get a feel for what they are telling me.
   b. listen carefully so I can hear what they are saying.
   c. watch them closely so that I can see what they are saying.

6. When I meet someone new, I usually pay most attention to
   a. the way the person walks or moves, or to the gestures the person makes.
   b. the way the person speaks and how his or her voice sounds.
   c. the way the person looks (appearance, clothes, etc.).

7. When I choose a book or article to read, I typically choose one that
   a. deals with sports or fitness, hobbies and crafts, or other activities.
   b. tells me about a topic of particular interest to me.
   c. includes a lot of photos, pictures, or illustrations.

8. Learning about something is easier for me when I can
   a. use a hands-on approach.
   b. have someone explain it to me.
   c. watch someone show me how to do it.

Total up your As, Bs, and Cs:

_____As _____Bs _____Cs

If your highest total consists of As, you are a *tactile* or *kinesthetic* learner.
If your highest total consists of Bs, you are an *auditory* learner.
If your highest total consists of Cs, you are a *visual* learner.

In addition to knowing your learning style, you should think about whether you prefer to work by yourself or with others. If you are a person who studies more effectively alone, you may need to take steps to "protect" your study time and your study space. If you are a person who finds it helpful to study with others, you may want to find a serious study partner or form a small study group. Of course, you will want to select study-group members who are motivated. And remember that being part of a study group does not automatically mean you will be successful. To benefit fully from participating in a group, every member must prepare by reading and studying alone first.

THREE LEARNING STYLES

If This Is Your Learning Style . . .	Then These Are Helpful Activities for Learning:
Visual Learner (prefers to read or see information)	Reading textbooks Rereading class notes Reading your chapter review cards Studying test review sheets
Auditory Learner (prefers to hear information)	Listening to class lectures and discussions Reciting material (saying it out loud) Reading aloud to oneself Listening to audio tapes Participating in study groups
Tactile Learner (prefers to write material down or to manipulate materials physically)	Taking notes from lectures and from your textbooks Doing laboratory work (science labs, computer labs, etc.) Taking hands-on classes (science, engineering, computer science, and other technical or vocational subjects)

DEVELOPING CHAPTER REVIEW CARDS

Chapter review cards are a way to select, organize, and review the important information in a textbook chapter. Preparing summary review cards helps you organize the information so that you can learn and memorize it more easily. In other words, chapter review cards are an effective study tool.

Preparing chapter review cards for each chapter of this book will give you practice in creating these valuable study tools. Once you have learned how to make chapter review cards, you can use actual index cards to create them for textbook material in any of your courses and use them when you study for tests.

Now complete the chapter review cards for this chapter by answering the questions or following the directions on each "card" below. (The boxes below represent index cards.) The page numbers indicate the place in the chapter the information can be found.

Doing What Successful Students Do

List the six characteristics of successful students. (See pages 5–7.)

1. _____

2. _____

3. _____

4. _____

5. _____

6. _____

Card 1   Chapter 1: Being Successful in College

Setting Goals

List three reasons it is useful to set goals. (See pages 7–8.)

1. _____
   _____
   _____

2. _____
   _____
   _____

3. _____
   _____
   _____

Card 2   Chapter 1: Being Successful in College

Three Types of Goals

Describe these three types of goals: (See page 8.)

Short-term goals: _____
_____
_____

Intermediate goals: _____
_____
_____

Long-term goals: _____
_____
_____

Card 3   Chapter 1: Being Successful in College

The Reading Process

What is *reading?* (See page 9.)

_____

_____

_____

What is *prior knowledge?* (See page 9.)

_____

_____

What do readers do when they *predict?* (See page 10.)

_____

What is *previewing?* (See page 10.)

_____

_____

Card 4   Chapter 1: Being Successful in College

Three Learning Styles

Describe these three learning styles and the most helpful activities for learning. (See pages 12–14.)

Visual learners: _____

Most helpful activities for learning: _____

_____

Auditory learners: _____

Most helpful activities for learning: _____

_____

Tactile learners: _____

Most helpful activities for learning: _____

_____

Card 5   Chapter 1: Being Successful in College

SELECTION 1-1
NONFICTION

A MOTHER'S ANSWER

From *The Big Picture: Getting Perspective on What's Really Important*
By Ben Carson with Gregg Lewis

Ben Carson is the director of pediatric neurosurgery at the Johns Hopkins Hospital in Baltimore, MD. At Hopkins, where he received his training in neurosurgery, this handsome, calm, soft-spoken man with the "gifted hands" was only 33 when he was appointed the director of his department, the youngest person in the United States to be appointed to such a position. He is internationally known for his success in the intricate, delicate surgeries for separating conjoined twins who are born joined at the head and for hemispherectomies, removing one side of the brain to treat those with extreme seizure disorders.

Carson also specializes in giving young people an inspirational boost. Despite his demanding schedule, he goes out of his way to address groups of school children. In 1994 Carson and his wife, who have three sons of their own, established the Carson Scholars Fund by earmarking half a million dollars of their own money for it. Their ultimate goal is to give a $1,000 college scholarship to a student in each public school in the nation.

When Carson was a child, no one ever would have predicted that he would become a world-famous brain surgeon. He grew up in an inner-city in extreme poverty, came from a broken home, and had a hot, hair-trigger temper. By the middle of fifth grade, he was failing every subject. What changed his life and started him on a path that eventually led to a scholarship to Yale University and then on to the University of Michigan School of Medicine?

Looking back at his childhood, Carson says, "My poor mother was mortified. Here she was with a third-grade education, working two or three jobs as a domestic, cleaning other people's houses, knowing that life didn't hold much for her, and seeing my brother and me going down the same road. She didn't know what to do, so she prayed and asked God to give her wisdom. What could she do to get her two young sons to understand the importance of education so that they could determine their own destiny?" In the selection below, Carson tells about the answer his mother found that helped him and his brother—and ultimately changed his life forever.

1   God gave her the wisdom—though my brother and I didn't think it was all that wise. It was to turn off the television. From that point on she would let us watch our choice of only two or three television programs during the week. With all that spare time, we were to read two books a week from the Detroit Public Library.

2   I was extraordinarily unhappy about this new arrangement. All my friends were outside, having a good time. I remember my mother's friends coming to her and saying, "You can't keep boys in the house reading. Boys are supposed to be outside playing and developing their muscles. When they grow up, they'll hate you. They will be sissies. You can't do that!"

3   Sometimes I would overhear this and I would say, "Listen to them, Mother." But she would never listen. We were going to have to read those books.

4   Sometimes, when I tell this story, people come up to me afterwards and ask, "How was your mother able to

Prediction Exercises

Directions: Use the skill of predicting to anticipate what certain paragraphs will be about. At each of the points indicated below, answer the question, "What do you predict will happen next?"

Prediction Exercise

What do you predict will happen next?

_____

_____

get you to read those books? I can't get my kids to read or even turn off the television or Nintendo."

5   I just have to chuckle and say, "Well, back in those days, the parents ran the house. They didn't have to get permission from the kids." That seems to be a novel concept to a lot of people these days.

6   At any rate, I started reading. The nice thing was my mother did not dictate what we had to read. I loved animals, so I read every animal book in the Detroit Public Library. And when I finished those, I went on to plants. When I finished those, I went on to rocks because we lived in a dilapidated section of the city near the railroad tracks. And what is there along railroad tracks, but rocks? I would collect little boxes of rocks and take them home and get out my geology book. I would study until I could name virtually every rock, tell how it was formed, and identify where it came from.

7   Months passed. I was still in fifth grade. Still the dummy in the class. Nobody knew about my reading project.

8   One day the fifth grade science teacher walked in and held up a big, shiny black rock. He asked, "Can anybody tell me what this is?"

9   Keep in mind that I never raised my hand. I never answered questions. So I waited for some of the smart kids to raise their hands. None of them did. So I waited for some of the dumb kids to raise their hands. When none of them did, I thought, *This is my big chance.* So I raised my hand . . . and everyone turned around to look. Some of my classmates were poking each other and whispering, "Look, look, Carson's got his hand up. This is gonna be good!"

10   They couldn't wait to see what was going to happen. And the teacher was shocked. He said, "Benjamin?"

11   I said, "Mr. Jaeck, that's obsidian." And there was silence in the room because it sounded good, but no one knew whether it was right or wrong. So the other kids didn't know if they should laugh or be impressed.

12   Finally the teacher broke the silence and said, "That's right! This is obsidian."

13   I went on to explain, "Obsidian is formed after a volcanic eruption. Lava flows down and when it hits water there is a super-cooling process. The elements coalesce, air is forced out, the surface glazes over, and . . ."

14   I suddenly realized everyone was staring at me in amazement. They couldn't believe all this geological information spewing from the mouth of a dummy. But you know, I was perhaps the most amazed person in the room, because it dawned on me in that moment that I was no dummy.

Prediction Exercise

What do you predict will happen next?

_____

_____

Prediction Exercise

What do you predict will happen next?

_____

_____

15   I thought, *Carson, the reason you knew the answer is because you were reading those books. What if you read books about all your subjects—science, math, history, geography, social studies? Couldn't you then know more than all these students who tease you and call you a dummy?* I must admit the idea appealed to me—to the extent that no book was safe from my grasp. I read everything I could get my hands on. If I had five minutes, I had a book. If I was in the bathroom, I was reading a book. If I was waiting for the bus, I was reading a book.

16   Within a year and a half, I went from the bottom of the class to the top of the class—much to the consternation of all those students who used to tease me and call me Dummy. The same ones would come to me in seventh grade to ask, "Hey, Benny, how do you work this problem?" And I would say, "Sit at my feet, youngster, while I instruct you."

17   I was perhaps a little bit obnoxious. But after all those years it felt so good to say that to those who had tormented me.

18   The important point here is that I had the same brain when I was still at the bottom of the class as I had when I reached the top of the class.

19   The difference was this: In the fifth grade, I thought I was dumb so I acted like I was dumb, and I achieved like a dumb person. As a seventh grader I thought I was smart, so I acted and achieved accordingly. So what does that say about what a person thinks about his own abilities? What does this say about the importance of our self-image? What does it say about the incredible potential of the human brain our Creator has given us?

Dr. Benjamin Carson has been director of the division of pediatric neurosurgery at Johns Hopkins since 1984. He is a professor of neurosurgery, plastic surgery, oncology, and pediatrics. He is also the co-director of the Johns Hopkins Craniofacial Center. His practice includes traumatic brain injuries, brain and spinal cord tumors, achondroplasia, neurological and congenital disorders, craniosynostosis, epilepsy, and trigeminal neuralgia. This work includes active research programs.

Dr. Carson has written over 90 neurosurgical publications. He has been awarded 24 honorary degrees and dozens of national citations of merit. He is the author of three best-selling books, *Gifted Hands, Think Big,* and *The Big Picture.* (© Keith Weller/Johns Hopkins)

Source: Ben Carson with Gregg Lewis, *The Big Picture: Getting Perspective on What's Really Important* (Grand Rapids, MI: 1999), Zondervan Publishing House, pp. 48–50. Copyright © 1999 by Benjamin Carson. Used by permission of the publisher.

Comprehension and Vocabulary Quiz

This quiz has four parts. Your instructor may assign some or all of them.

Comprehension

Directions: Items 1–5 test your comprehension (understanding) of the material in this selection. These questions are much like those that a content area instructor (such as a psychology professor) would expect you to know after reading this selection. For each comprehension question below, use information from the selection to determine the correct answer. Refer to the selection as you answer the questions. Write your answer in the space provided.

_____ **1.** The type of rock Ben identified was
    a. lava.
    b. obsidian.
    c. opal.
    d. onyx.

_____ **2.** Mr. Jaeck's reaction to Ben's correct answer was
    a. joy.
    b. anger.
    c. shock.
    d. disappointment.

_____ **3.** Before the event described in the passage, the reason Ben never raised his hand was
    a. he didn't want to show off.
    b. he didn't want to embarrass those who didn't know the answer.
    c. he was waiting for his big chance.
    d. he didn't know the answer.

_____ **4.** As an adult Ben Carson probably believes that
    a. parents should set the rules.
    b. children should set the rules.
    c. parents and children should set the rules together.
    d. there should be no rules.

_____ **5.** Ben Carson says that he realized that he "had the same brain" when he was still at the bottom of the class as he had when he reached the top. He mentions this to show that
    a. he did not expect his brain ever to change in any way.
    b. although he was intelligent, his perception of himself had caused him to act as if he were a "dummy."
    c. he did not have high enough expectations for himself when he was at the top of the class.
    d. more research needs to be done on the human brain.

Vocabulary in Context

Directions: Items 6–10 test your ability to determine the meaning of a word by using context clues. *Context clues* are words in a sentence that allow the reader to deduce (reason out) the meaning of an unfamiliar word in that sentence. Context clues also enable the reader to determine which meaning the author intends when a word has more than one meaning. For each vocabulary item below, a sentence from the selection containing an important word (*italicized, like this*) is quoted first. Next, there is an additional sentence using the word in the same sense and providing another context clue. Use the context clues from *both* sentences to deduce the meaning of the italicized word. *Be sure the answer you choose makes sense in both sentences.* If you discover that you need to use a dictionary to confirm an answer choice, remember that the meaning you select must still fit the context of *both* sentences. Write your answer in the space provided. *Note: Chapter 2, "Developing a College-Level Vocabulary: A New World of Words," presents the skill of using context clues.*

Pronunciation Key: ă pat ā pay âr care ä father ĕ pet ē be ĭ pit
ī tie îr pier ŏ pot ō toe ô paw oi noise ou out o͝o took o͞o boot
ŭ cut yo͞o abuse ûr urge th thin *th* this hw which zh vision
ə about   Stress mark: ′

6. The nice thing was my mother did not *dictate* what we had to read.

   Our company's dress code prohibits nose rings, brow rings, and other facial "jewelry," but otherwise does not *dictate* what we may wear at work.

   dictate (dĭk′ tāt)

   a. like
   b. say as an order or command
   c. say aloud in order to be written down
   d. understand

7. When I finished those, I went on to rocks because we lived in a *dilapidated* section of the city near the railroad tracks.

   The city refurbished the *dilapidated* Civil War mansion and turned it into a museum.

   dilapidated (dĭ lăp′ ĭ dāt əd)

   a. shabby; rundown
   b. historic
   c. fashionable; up-to-date
   d. dangerous

_____ **8.** The elements *coalesce,* air is forced out, the surface glazes over, and . . .

Scientists believe that planets may form because great heat and pressure cause particles to *coalesce.*

coalesce (kō ə lĕs′)

a. disintegrate; dissolve
b. disappear
c. fly apart
d. fuse; unite

_____ **9.** They couldn't believe all this geological information *spewing* from the mouth of a dummy.

My car's radiator hose broke, *spewing* hot water everywhere.

spewing (spyōo′ ĭng)

a. gushing forth; streaming out
b. sending
c. trickling; dribbling
d. gathering

_____ **10.** Within a year and a half, I went from the bottom of the class to the top of the class—much to the *consternation* of all those students who used to tease me and call me Dummy.

My brother's tattoos caused my conservative parents great *consternation.*

consternation (kŏn stər nā′ shən)

a. joy; happiness
b. relief
c. dismay; upset
d. pride

Word Structure

Directions: Items 11–15 test your ability to use word-structure clues to help determine a word's meaning. *Word-structure clues* consist of roots, prefixes, and suffixes. In these exercises, you will learn the meaning of a word part (root) and use it to determine the meaning of the several other words that have the same word part. If you discover that you need to use a dictionary to confirm an answer choice, do so. Write your answer in the space provided. *Note: Chapter 2, "Developing a College-Level Vocabulary: A New World of Words," presents the skill of using word-structure clues.*

In paragraph 6 of the selection you encountered the word **dictate.** This word contains the Latin root **dict,** which means "say" or "tell." The word *dictate* has several meanings, including "to *say* as an order or a command" and "to *say* aloud information that is to be written down." Use the meaning of *dict* and the list of prefixes on pages 60–61 to help you determine the meaning of each of the following words.

_____ 11. **Predictable** means

    a. able to explain what has happened.

    b. preventable; avoidable.

    c. able to say or tell ahead of time.

    d. not able to know in advance.

_____ 12. When one person **contradicts** another, it means that person is

    a. speaking with anger.

    b. saying something with impatience.

    c. speaking in defense of the other person.

    d. saying the opposite of what the other person has said.

_____ 13. Speech teachers help students with their **diction,** which means

    a. the quality of their speaking.

    b. stuttering.

    c. proper breathing.

    d. the ability to carry on a conversation.

_____ 14. A **dictator** is one who

    a. says the opposite of what others say.

    b. says what others want to hear.

    c. tells others what to do or say.

    d. tells interesting stories.

_____ 15. A religious **edict** is a

    a. ceremony; ritual.

    b. document that tells or proclaims a new law.

    c. follower of a religion; believer.

    d. place of worship.

Reading Skills Application

Directions: Items 16–20 test your ability to apply certain reading skills to the material in this selection. These are the types of questions that might appear on standardized reading tests and state-mandated basic skills tests. Write your answer in the space provided.

_____ 16. What is the author's primary purpose for writing this selection?

    a. to prove that self-image affects whether a person uses his or her potential

    b. to explain the important role reading can play in a person's life *c.*   to pay tribute to a mother's wisdom

    d.   to show that students can be wrong about a classmate they view as a "dummy"

17. Which of the following is the meaning of the word *novel* as it is used in paragraph 5?

    a.   frightening

    b.   unpleasant

    c.   familiar

    d.   new

18. Which pattern has been used to organize the information in paragraph 15 of the selection?

    a.   comparison-contrast

    b.   cause and effect

    c.   sequence

    d.   list

19. Which of the following statements best expresses the main idea of paragraph 16?

    a.   Within a year and a half, I went from the bottom of the class to the top of the class—much to the consternation of all the students who used to tease me and call me Dummy.

    b.   The same ones would come to me in the seventh grade to ask, "Hey, Benny, how do you work this problem?

    c.   And I would say, "Sit at my feet, youngster, while I instruct you."

    d.   Other students teased Ben and called him Dummy.

20. Based on the information in the selection, the author would most likely agree with which of the following statements?

    a.   Even slow learners can be successful.

    b.   Being a good reader is the one key to success.

    c.   Believing in yourself can be the key to success.

    d.   A person's mother is the key to his or her success.

NONFICTION

Collaboration Option

Writing and Collaborating to Enhance Your Understanding

Option for collaboration: Your instructor may direct you to work with other students or, in other words, to work *collaboratively.* In that case, you should form groups of three or four students as directed by your instructor and work together to complete the exercises. After your group discusses each item and agrees on the answer, have a group member record it. Every member of your group should be able to explain all of your group's answers.

1. **Reacting to What You Have Read:** Think of an experience in school—good or bad—that made you see yourself differently as a student. Describe the experience and explain how it changed the way you perceived yourself.

   _____

   _____

   _____

   _____

   _____

   _____

   _____

   _____

2. **Comprehending the Selection Further:** Even though she herself could not read, Ben Carson's mother required her young sons to read two books each week and write book reports. She pretended to read them and then put check marks on them. Based on her actions, what conclusions can you draw about the importance she placed on reading?

   _____

   _____

   _____

   _____

   _____

   _____

   _____

   _____

3. **Overall Main Idea of the Selection:** In one sentence tell what the authors want readers to understand about how seeing himself differently as a learner affected Ben Carson's success as a student. (Be sure you include Ben Carson's name in your overall main idea sentence.)

_____

_____

_____

_____

_____

Read More about It on the World Wide Web

To learn more about the topic of this selection, visit these websites or use your favorite search engine (such as Yahoo®) to discover more about this author and this topic on your own. Whenever you go to *any* website, it is a good idea to evaluate it critically. Are you getting good information—that is, information that is accurate, complete, and up-to-date? Who sponsors the website? How easy is it to use the features of the website?

http://www.carsonscholars.org

http://www.drbencarson.com/

http://www.cnn.com/SPECIALS/2001/americasbest/science.medicine/
pro.bcarson.html

http://www.usdreams.com/Carson.html

http://www.carolina.com/achievements/janapr/carson.htm

http://www.pbs.org/newshour/gergen/july-dec99/carson_9-7.html

http://myhero.com/hero.asp?hero=b_carson

http://www.takingfive.com/drbencarson.htm

http://www.amazon.com *(Type in the book title,* The Big Picture, *and then click on the word "Go.")*

SELECTION **1-2**

HEALTH

COPING WITH STRESS AND MAKING IT WORK *FOR* YOU

From *Targeting Wellness: The Core*
By Martin Levy, Mark Dignan, and Janet Shirreffs

Did you know that, in some cases, stress can be good for you? While sometimes it is best to avoid stressful situations, there are times when stress can be beneficial. This selection from a health textbook explains how people can deal with stress in two different ways.

1   Stress is a part of everyone's life, yet there are many different ways to view stressors and their effect on a healthy lifestyle. Health experts agree that a person's attitude toward stressful events has an effect on how that person will react. Two ways of coping with stress are presented below. The first point of view suggests making lifestyle changes to avoid some stressors and lessen the effect of others. The second point of view recommends viewing stress as a source of energy that can be channeled to help a person accomplish individual goals.

Find Ways to Avoid or Reduce the Effects of Stress

2   High levels of stress have been correlated with health problems. Stress has been suspected as a contributing factor in such illnesses as high blood pressure, heart disease, and ulcers. Too much stress may also compromise the immune system and make a person more susceptible to infection.

3   Coping with stress successfully means avoiding the damaging effects of stressors in one's life. One way to do this is to discover how certain stressors can be avoided. Suppose a student knows that sitting in traffic on his route to school makes him tense and irritable. Perhaps he can avoid this problem by finding an alternate route to school.

4   If stressors cannot be avoided, it is possible to lessen their negative effects by making other changes in one's life. Plenty of sleep and regular exercise are important. Eating a balanced diet and cutting down on alcohol and caffeine may also help. Many people find meditative and relaxation techniques help counteract the effects of stress. A network of positive relationships can also provide support and encouragement.

5   Overall, there are many ways to alleviate the stresses of modern life. Individuals must identify the causes of stress and find ways to avoid or reduce it.

Prediction Exercises

Directions: Use the skill of predicting to anticipate what each of the two sections of this selection will be about. After you read the heading of each section, answer the question, "What do you predict this section will be about?"

Prediction Exercise

What do you predict this section (paragraphs 2–5) will be about?

_____

_____

_____

Make Stress Work *for* You

6   Most people think of stress as a negative, damaging thing. Yet there is another way of looking at stress—as a form of energy.

7   Looked at in this way, stress is a challenge to be managed and used to enhance one's life. Dr. Robert Ritvo, dean of the University of New Hampshire's School of Health and Human Services, points out that stress can drive people to reach their goals. Dr. Peter G. Hanson notes that "students maximize their learning curves with the stress of an upcoming exam. Athletes set world records only with the stress of stiff competition."

8   In other words, stress can make people perform better. The key lies in a person's attitude toward stressful events. Is the end of a romantic relationship merely a loss? Or is it an opportunity to examine one's values and renew relationships that may have been neglected?

9   Stress can have its most devastating consequences when a person feels a sense of helplessness. Instead of identifying sources of stress as problems, individuals should strive to see them as challenges to be met. Finding ways to use stress to one's advantage gives a person more control over stressful situations, and this success boosts self-esteem and helps the individual face life's events with courage and confidence.

Practice Exercise

What do you predict this section (paragraphs 6–9) will be about?

_____

_____

Source: Marvin Levy, Mark Dignan, and Janet Shirreffs, *Targeting Wellness: The Core,* p. 117. Copyright © 1992 McGraw-Hill. Reprinted by permission of The McGraw-Hill Companies. Based on ideas in Paul Martin, "The Power of Positive Stress," *Better Homes and Gardens,* March 1990, and in Peter G. Hanson, *Stress for Success* (New York: Doubleday, 1989).

SELECTION **1-2**

HEALTH

Comprehension and Vocabulary Quiz

This quiz has four parts. Your instructor may assign some or all of them.

Comprehension

Directions: Items 1–5 test your comprehension (understanding) of the material in this selection. These questions are much like those that a content area instructor (such as a health professor) would expect you to know after studying this selection. For each comprehension question below, use information from the selection to determine the correct answer. Refer to the selection as you answer the questions. Write your answer in the space provided.

_____ 1. An example of a way to avoid a stressful situation would be

    a. using a relaxation technique in order to calm yourself down.

    b. taking an alternate route to avoid sitting in traffic.

    c. monitoring your blood pressure.

    d. doing deep breathing exercises.

_____ 2. You can lessen the negative effects of stress by

    a. exercising regularly and getting plenty of sleep.

    b. avoiding a sense of helplessness.

    c. thinking of stress as a negative, damaging thing.

    d. talking things over with a friend.

_____ 3. You can make stress work for you if you

    a. avoid difficult situations and cut back on your activities.

    b. think of it as a form of energy and a challenge.

    c. stay away from situations that make you tense and irritable.

    d. view it as an inescapable part of life.

_____ 4. If you view stress as a source of energy, it can

    a. contribute to health problems.

    b. help you avoid stressful situations in your daily life.

    c. drive you to reach your goals.

    d. cause physical and emotional problems.

_____ 5. Stress can make you perform better if you

    a. do what you can to avoid challenging situations.

    b. maintain a positive attitude toward stressful events.

    c. identify the sources of your stress.

    d. make the decision to ignore.

Vocabulary in Context

Directions: Items 6–10 test your ability to determine the meaning of a word by using context clues. *Context clues* are words in a sentence that allow the reader to deduce (reason out) the meaning of an unfamiliar word in that sentence. Context clues also enable the reader to determine which meaning the author intends when a word has more than one meaning. For each vocabulary item below, a sentence from the selection containing an important word (*italicized, like this*) is quoted first. Next, there is an additional sentence using the word in the same sense and providing another context clue. Use the context clues from *both* sentences to deduce the meaning of the italicized word. *Be sure the answer you choose makes sense in both sentences.* If you discover that you need to use a dictionary to confirm an answer choice, remember that the meaning you select must still fit the context of *both* sentences. Write your answer in the space provided. *Note: Chapter 2, "Developing a College-Level Vocabulary: A New World of Words," presents the skill of using context clues.*

Pronunciation Key: ă **pat**   ā **pay**   âr **care**   ä **father**   ĕ **pet**   ē **be**   ĭ **pit**
ī **tie**   îr **pier**   ŏ **pot**   ō **toe**   ô **paw**   oi **noise**   ou **out**   oŏ **took**   ōō **boot**
ŭ **cut**   yōō **abuse**   ûr **urge**   th **thin**   *th* **this**   hw **which**   zh **vision**
ə **about**   Stress mark: ʹ

_____   **6.** High levels of stress have been *correlated* with health problems.

   The number of years of education is *correlated* with the amount of income a person earns in a lifetime.

   correlated (kôrʹə lāt əd)

   a.   related to
   b.   caused by
   c.   determined by
   d.   prevented by

_____   **7.** Too much stress can *compromise* the immune system and make a person more susceptible to infection.

   If enemy agents are able to *compromise* our embassy's security by installing hidden surveillance equipment and listening devices, it will no longer be safe to hold meetings there.

   compromise (kŏmʹ prə mīz)

   a.   to weaken
   b.   to improve
   c.   to reach agreement
   d.   to defend

_____ **8.** Too much stress can compromise the immune system and make a person more *susceptible* to infection.

Children and elderly persons are more *susceptible* to flu than other groups in the population.

susceptible (sə sĕp′ tə bəl)

a. easily influenced
b. likely to be affected by
c. highly impressionable
d. resistant

_____ **9.** Overall, there are many ways to *alleviate* the stresses of modern life.

Although there is no cure for the common cold, there are medications that can *alleviate* its unpleasant symptoms.

alleviate (ə lē′ vē āt)

a. to remedy or cure
b. to lessen or make more bearable
c. to increase or enhance
d. to change the form of

_____ **10.** Looked at this way, stress is a challenge to be managed and used to *enhance* one's life.

An increasing number of men are having cosmetic surgery to *enhance* their appearance.

enhance (ən hănz′)

a. to improve
b. to diminish
c. to remain or keep the same
d. to spoil

Word Structure

Directions: Items 11–15 test your ability to use word-structure clues to help determine a word's meaning. *Word structure clues* consist of roots, prefixes, and suffixes. In these exercises, you will learn the meaning of a word part (root) and use it to determine the meaning of the several other words that have the same word part. If you discover that you need to use a dictionary to confirm an answer choice, do so. Write your answer in the space provided. *Note: Chapter 2, "Developing a College-Level Vocabulary: A New World of Words," presents the skill of using word-structure clues.*

> In paragraph 9 of the selection you encountered the word **confidence.** This word contains the Latin root **fid,** which means "faith" or "trust." The word *confidence* means "having *faith* or *trust* in someone or something." Use the meaning of **fid** and the list of prefixes on pages 60–61 to help you determine the meaning of each of the following words.

_____ 11. To **confide** means to

    a. instruct or explain to someone how to do something.

    b. give an excuse.

    c. tell someone information that you do not want repeated to others.

    d. consider various options.

_____ 12. **Infidelity** means

    a. inflexibility.

    b. impatience.

    c. lack of respect.

    d. unfaithfulness.

_____ 13. A **confidant** is a person

    a. to whom secrets or private matters are disclosed.

    b. you enjoy talking to.

    c. whom you do not know very well.

    d. who does not tell the truth.

_____ 14. **Bona fide** means

    a. genuine; authentic.

    b. sarcastic; cruel.

    c. insincere; false.

    d. like new; restored.

_____ 15. The U.S. Marine Corps motto "**Semper fidelis**" means

    a. always ready.

    b. always brave.

    c. always faithful.

    d. always strong.

Reading Skills Application

Directions: Items 16–20 test your ability to apply certain reading skills to the material in this selection. These are the types of questions that might appear on standardized reading tests and state-mandated basic skills tests. Write your answer in the space provided.

_____ **16.** Which of the following statements best expresses the main idea of the selection?

a. Health experts agree that a person's attitude toward stressful events has an effect on how that person will react.

b. Making lifestyle changes can enable you to avoid some stressors and lessen the effect of others.

c. Although stress is part of everyone's life, there are ways to avoid or reduce the effects of stress and make stress work for you.

d. Overall, there are many ways to alleviate the stresses of modern life.

_____ **17.** In paragraph 7 of this selection, the term *stiff* means which of the following?

a. rigid and unbending

b. highly challenging

c. very unpleasant

d. easily defeated

_____ **18.** According to the selection, stress appears to contribute to all of the following except

a. ulcers.

b. high blood pressure.

c. pneumonia.

d. heart disease.

_____ **19.** The authors' primary purpose for writing this selection is

a. to convince readers to avoid stress whenever possible.

b. to describe the major causes of stress.

c. to inform readers about the negative consequences of stress.

d. to present two ways to deal with stress more effectively.

_____ **20.** The information in paragraph 8 of the selection is organized using which of the following patterns?

a. cause-effect

b. list

c. sequence

d. comparison-contrast

HEALTH

Collaboration Option

Writing and Collaborating to Enhance Your Understanding

Option for collaboration: Your instructor may direct you to work with other students or, in other words, to work *collaboratively.* In that case, you should form groups of three or four students as directed by your instructor and work together to complete the exercises. After your group discusses each item and agrees on the answer, have a group member record it. Every member of your group should be able to explain all of your group's answers.

1. **Reacting to What You Have Read:** Do you tend to view stress as something negative and damaging or as a challenge that can be managed and used to enhance your life? Explain which point of view you have and why.

    _____

    _____

    _____

    _____

    _____

2. **Comprehending the Selection Further:** Suppose you discover that you are going to have three major tests within three days during the same week, and it is causing you a great deal of stress. How could viewing this as a challenge make stress work *for* you instead of *against* you?

    _____

    _____

    _____

    _____

    _____

3. **Overall Main Idea of the Selection:** In one sentence tell what the authors want readers to understand about coping with stress. (Be sure to include the word "stress" in your overall main idea sentence.)

    _____

    _____

    _____

    _____

    _____

Read More about It on the World Wide Web

To learn more about the topic of this selection, visit these websites or use your favorite search engine (such as Yahoo®) to discover more about these authors and this topic on your own. Whenever you go to *any* website, it is a good idea to evaluate it critically. Are you getting good information—that is, information that is accurate, complete, and up-to-date? Who sponsors the website? How easy is it to use the features of the website?

http://wellnessonline.com
http://stress.jrn.columbia.edu
http://www.calmcenter.com
http://www.hyperstress.com

WISE UP! THE WHEN AND HOW OF PREPARING FOR TESTS

From *P.O.W.E.R. Learning: Strategies for Success in College and Life*
By Robert S. Feldman

Do you feel uneasy whenever your instructor announces that there will be a test? Do you wait until the last minute to start preparing for tests? Are you usually surprised by the types of questions or type of material on tests? If you answered yes to any of these questions, then this selection is for you! The author, Dr. Robert Feldman, is a psychology professor who has extensive experience and expertise in the strategies students need for academic success.

As noted at the beginning of this chapter, you should start preparing for your final exams from the first day of the semester. In other words, you should learn as you go. In this selection, Dr. Feldman takes this a step further by giving specific strategies for preparing for various types of test questions and for dealing with test anxiety. This reading selection is presented in Chapter 1 of New Worlds *so that you can use the valuable techniques in it from the beginning of the semester. Chapter 11 presents valuable information about organizing textbook information so that you can learn it for tests.*

Ready Your Test-taking Skills

1   How much you reap the benefits of a test depends on a number of considerations: the kind of test it is, the subject matter involved, and above all how well you prepare for it. Preparation for tests requires a number of strategies. Among the most important are the following:

Remember Everything You Do in a Course Is Preparation for a Test

2   Completing a reading assignment. Writing a paper. Filling out a worksheet. Everything you do during a course helps to prepare you for a test. There is no surer way to get good grades on tests than to attend class faithfully and to complete all class assignments seriously and on time. Preparing for tests is a long-term proposition. It's not a matter of "giving your all" the night before the test. Instead, it's a matter of giving your all to every aspect of the course.

Know What You Are Preparing For

3   Determine as much as you can about the test before you begin to prepare for it. The more you know about the test, the better you'll be able to get ready. To find out about an upcoming test, ask these questions:

- Is the test called a "test," "exam," "quiz," or something else? As you can see in Table 1 on page 40, the names imply different things. For simplicity's sake, we'll use the term *test* throughout this selection, but know that these distinctions exist and they should affect the way you prepare.

Prediction Exercises

Directions: Use the skill of predicting to anticipate what certain sections will be about. At each of the points indicated below, answer the question, "What do you predict this section will be about?"

- What material will the test cover?
- How many questions will be on it?
- How much time is it expected to take? A full class period? Only part of the period?
- What kinds of questions will be on the test?
- How will it be graded?
- Will sample questions be provided?
- Are tests from previous terms available?

Form a Study Group

4   Study groups are small, informal groups of students who work together to learn the course material and study for a test. Forming such a group can be an excellent way to prepare. Some study groups are formed for particular tests, while others meet consistently throughout the term.

5   The typical study group meets a week or two before a test and plans a strategy for studying. Members share their understanding of what will be on the test, based on their own perceptions of what an instructor has said in class about the upcoming test. Together, they develop a list of review questions to guide their individual study. The group breaks up and the members study on their own.

6   A few days before the test, members of the study group meet again. They discuss answers to the review questions, go over the material, and share any new information they may have about the upcoming test. They may also quiz one another about the material to identify any weaknesses or gaps in their knowledge.

7   Study groups can be extremely powerful tools because they help accomplish several things:

- They help members to organize and structure the material, which forces members to approach the material in a systematic and logical way.
- They aid in the sharing of different perspectives on the material.
- They help prevent students from overlooking any potentially important information.
- They force their members to rethink the course material, explaining it in words that they and the other group members will understand. This helps both understanding and recall of the information when it is needed on the test.
- They also help motivate members to do their best. When you're part of a study group, you're no longer working just for yourself; your studying also benefits the other study-group members. Not wanting to let down your classmates in a study group may sometimes give more of a push to your study habits than you get from working only for yourself.

TABLE 1
QUIZZES, TESTS, EXAMS . . .
WHAT'S IN A NAME?

Although they may vary from one instructor to another, the following definitions are the ones most frequently used:

Quizzes. A **quiz** is a brief assessment, usually covering a relatively small amount of material. Some quizzes cover as little as one class's worth of reading. Although a single quiz usually doesn't count very much, instructors often add quiz scores together, and collectively they can become a significant part of your final course grade.

Tests. A **test** is a more extensive, more heavily weighted assessment than a quiz, covering more material. A test may come every few weeks of the term, often after each third or quarter of the term has passed, but this varies with the instructor and the course.

Exams. An **exam** is the most substantial kind of assessment. In many classes, just one exam is given—a *final exam* at the end of the term. Sometimes there are two exams, one at the midpoint of the term (called, of course, a midterm) and the other at the end. Exams are usually weighted quite heavily because they are meant to assess your knowledge of all the course material up to that point.

8   There are some potential drawbacks to keep in mind. Study groups don't always work well for students with certain kinds of learning styles in which they prefer to work independently. In addition, "problem" members, who don't pull their weight, may result in difficulties for the group. In general, though, the advantages of study groups usually far outweigh their possible disadvantages.

Match Test Preparation to Question Types

9   Test questions come in different types (see Table 1, page 40), and each requires a somewhat different style of preparation.

10   **Essay Questions**   Essay questions are meant to see if you have a broad knowledge of the material being tested. You'll need to know not just a series of facts, but also the connections between them, and you will have to be able to discuss these ideas in an organized and logical way. Essay exams focus on the ways in which the various pieces of information on a topic fit together. The best approach to studying for an essay exam involves four steps:

- Carefully read your class notes and any notes you've made on assigned readings that will be covered on the upcoming exam. Also go through the readings themselves, reviewing underlined or highlighted material and marginal notes.

- Play professor: Think of likely exam questions. To do this, you can use the key words, phrases, concepts, and questions you've earlier created in your notes. In addition, your class instructor may have given you a list of possible essay topics.

- Without looking at your notes or your readings, answer each potential essay question aloud. Don't feel embarrassed about doing this. Talking aloud is often more useful than answering the questions silently in your head. You can also write down the main points that any answer should cover. But you probably shouldn't write out complete and full answers to the questions, because your time is probably better spent learning the material you'll be tested on. The one exception: if your instructor tells you exactly what essay question is going to be on the exam. In that case, it pays to write out the answer.

- After you've answered the questions, check yourself by looking at the notes and readings once again. If you feel confident that you've answered particular questions adequately, check them off. You can go back later for a quick review. But if there are questions that you have trouble with, review that material immediately. Then repeat the third step above, answering the questions again.

Prediction Exercise

What do you predict this section (paragraphs 9–16) will be about?

_____

_____

Study groups, made up of a few students who study together for a test, can help organize material, provide new perspectives, and motivate members to do their best. *(Gary A. Conner/ PhotoEdit)*

11   **Multiple-Choice, True-False, and Matching Questions**
While the focus of review for essay questions should be on major issues and controversies, and on integration of the material—more of a "big picture" focus—studying for multiple-choice, true-false, and matching questions requires more attention to the details.

12   Almost anything is fair game for multiple-choice, true-false, and matching questions, and so you can't afford to overlook anything when studying. This means that your studying needs to be detail-oriented. And it means that you must put your memory into high gear and master a great many facts.

13   It's a particularly good idea to write down important facts on index cards like those shown on this page. Remember the advantages of these cards: They're portable and available all the time, and the act of creating them helps drive the material into your memory. Furthermore, you can shuffle them and test yourself repeatedly until you know you've mastered the material.

> Political reforms of progressive age:
> -direct primaries: people vote for whom they want to run; not appointed
> -initiative: people propose laws on their own
> -referendum: gov. proposes; people say yes or no
> -recall: people can remove politicans from office before they finish term

14   **Short-Answer and Fill-in Questions**   Short-answer and fill-in questions are similar to essays in that they require you to recall key pieces of information; that is, you have to dredge the information up from your memory rather than, as is the case with multiple-choice, true-false, and matching questions, finding it on the page in front of you. However, short-answer and fill-in questions—unlike essay questions—typically don't demand that you integrate or compare different types of information. Consequently, the focus of your study should be on the recall of specific, detailed information.

> Endoplasmic reticulum (ER):
> Smooth ER—makes fats (lipids)
> Rough ER—has ribosomes which make proteins
>
> Together, they make membranes for whole cell (for plasma membrane, mitochondrion, etc.)
> Also make more of themselves

15   **Test Yourself**   Once you feel you've mastered the material, test yourself on it. There are several ways to do this. One is to create a complete test for yourself in writing, making its form as close as possible to what you expect the actual test to be. For instance, if your instructor has told you the classroom test will be primarily made up of short-answer questions, your test should be too. One bonus: Constructing a test is actually an excellent way of studying the material and cementing it into memory.

16   You might also construct a test and administer it to a classmate or a member of your study group. In turn, you could take a test that someone else has constructed. The combined experience of making and taking a test on the same general subject matter is among the very best ways to prepare for the real thing.

17   **Deal with Test Anxiety**   What does the anticipation of a test do to you? Do you feel shaky? Frantic, like there's not enough time to get it all done? Do you feel as if there's a knot in your stomach? Do you grit your teeth? Fortunately, test anxiety is a temporary condition characterized by fears and concerns about test taking. Almost everyone experiences it to some degree, but if it is too great, it can make it harder for you to study and do your best on a test.

18   You'll never eliminate test anxiety completely, nor do you want to. A little bit of nervousness can energize us, making us more attentive and vigilant. Like any competitive event, testing can motivate us to do our best. So think of test anxiety as a desire to perform at your peak—an ally at test time.

19   On the other hand, for many, anxiety can spiral into the kind of paralyzing fear that makes your mind go blank. So you definitely want to keep it in its place. There are several ways to do this:

- *Prepare thoroughly.* The more you prepare, the less test anxiety you'll feel. Good preparation can give you a sense of control and mastery, and it will prevent test anxiety from overwhelming you.

- *Take a realistic view of the test.* Remember that no single test determines how you'll do for the rest of your life. Your future success does not hinge on your performance on any single exam.

- *Learn relaxation techniques.* You can learn to reduce or even eliminate the jittery physical symptoms of test anxiety by using relaxation techniques. The basic process is straightforward: You want to breathe evenly, gently inhaling and exhaling. Focus your mind on a pleasant, relaxing scene such as a beautiful forest or a peaceful spread of farmland, or on a sound such as ocean waves.

- *Visualize success.* Think of an image of your instructor handing back your test, on which you've received an A. Or imagine your instructor congratulating you on your fine performance the moment you walk into your classroom on the day after the test. Positive visualizations such as these, which highlight your potential success, can help replace negative images of failure that may be fueling your test anxiety.

Prediction Exercise

What do you predict this section (paragraphs 17–19) will be about?

_____

_____

_____

Source: Adapted from Robert S. Feldman, *P.O.W.E.R. Learning: Strategies for Success in College and Life,* pp. 142–148. Copyright © 2000 McGraw-Hill. Reprinted by permission of The McGraw-Hill Companies.

STUDY SKILLS

Comprehension and Vocabulary Quiz

This quiz has four parts. Your instructor may assign some or all of them.

Comprehension

Directions: Items 1–5 test your comprehension (understanding) of the material in this selection. These questions are much like those that a content area instructor (such as a human development professor) would expect you to know after studying this selection. For each comprehension question below, use information from the selection to determine the correct answer. Refer to the selection as you answer the questions. Write your answer in the space provided.

_____   **1.** A good strategy for preparing for a test is to
    a. find out as much as you can about the type of test, length, grading, etc.
    b. match your test preparation to the type of questions that will be on the test.
    c. form a small study group.
    d. all of the above

_____   **2.** Preparing study cards is an effective way to prepare for multiple-choice test questions because
    a. the very act of creating them helps drive the material into your memory.
    b. they allow you to discover different perspectives on the material.
    c. they allow you to "play professor."
    d. they help you "give your all" the night before the test.

_____   **3.** In order to prepare for any exam you should
    a. memorize as many specific details as possible in the order that they were presented in class.
    b. eliminate test anxiety completely.
    c. test yourself on the material once you feel you've mastered it.
    d. all of the above

_____   **4.** Essay questions are similar to short-answer and fill-in questions in that they both
    a. require you to integrate and compare different types of information.
    b. require more attention to details when you are studying.
    c. require you to put your memory in high gear and master a great many facts.
    d. require you to recall key pieces of information.

_____ **5.** Most students benefit from participating in a study group because it

    a. helps prevent students from overlooking any potentially important information.

    b. forces members to approach the material in a systematic and logical way.

    c. helps motivate members to do their best.

    d. all of the above

Vocabulary in Context

Directions: Items 6–10 test your ability to determine the meaning of a word by using context clues. *Context clues* are words in a sentence that allow the reader to deduce (reason out) the meaning of an unfamiliar word in that sentence. Context clues also enable the reader to determine which meaning the author intends when a word has more than one meaning. For each vocabulary item below, a sentence from the selection containing an important word (*italicized, like this*) is quoted first. Next, there is an additional sentence using the word in the same sense and providing another context clue. Use the context clues from *both* sentences to deduce the meaning of the italicized word. *Be sure the answer you choose makes sense in both sentences.* If you discover that you need to use a dictionary to confirm an answer choice, remember that the meaning you select must still fit the context of *both* sentences. Write your answer in the space provided.

Pronunciation Key: ă **pat** ā **pay** âr **care** ä **father** ĕ **pet** ē **be** ĭ **pit**
ī **tie** îr **pier** ŏ **pot** ō **toe** ô **paw** oi **noise** ou **out** oŏ **took** ōō **boot**
ŭ **cut** yōō **abuse** ûr **urge** th **thin** *th* **this** hw **which** zh **vision**
ə **about** Stress mark: ′

_____ **6.** They try to help members organize and structure the material, which forces members to approach the material in a *systematic* and logical way.

Using a *systematic* approach to managing your money can lead you to early financial freedom and security.

systematic (sĭs tə măt′ ĭk)

    a. related to money

    b. methodical in procedure or plan

    c. determined by a group rather than an individual

    d. difficult and unrewarding

_____   **7.** In general, though, the advantages of study groups usually *outweigh* their possible disadvantages.

Our company president took early retirement because he felt the stress of the job had begun to *outweigh* the benefits.

outweigh (out wā′)

   a. to cancel out

   b. to have greater importance than

   c. to weigh more than

   d. to decrease

_____   **8.** Short-answer and fill-in questions are similar to essays in that they require you to recall key pieces of information; that is, you have to *dredge* the information up from your memory rather than, as is the case with multiple-choice, true-false, and matching questions, finding it on the page in front of you.

My grandmother is remarkable: It takes her a few minutes, but she is always able to *dredge* up birthdates of all 16 of her grandchildren.

dredge (drĕj)

   a. to record in written form

   b. to forget

   c. to bring to light by deep searching

   d. to comment upon with insight

_____   **9.** A little bit of nervousness can energize us, making us more attentive and *vigilant.*

Vigilant parents would never allow their elementary-school age children to go to the mall unsupervised or alone.

vigilant (vĭj′ ə lənt)

   a. selfish and uncaring

   b. extremely immature

   c. highly emotional

   d. alertly watchful

_____   **10.** Positive visualizations such as these, which highlight your potential success, can help replace negative images of failure that may be *fueling* your test anxiety.

The actor and his wife were seen having a loud argument in public, thus *fueling* rumors of a possible divorce.

fueling (fyo̅o̅′ əl ĭng)

   a. supporting; stimulating

   b. diminishing; decreasing

   c. ending; stopping

   d. spreading

Word Structure

Directions: Items 11–15 test your ability to use word-structure clues to help determine a word's meaning. *Word-structure clues* consist of roots, prefixes, and suffixes. In these exercises, you will learn the meaning of a word part (root) and use it to determine the meaning of the several other words that have the same word part. If you discover that you need to use a dictionary to confirm an answer choice, do so. Write your answer in the space provided. *Note: Chapter 2, "Developing a College-Level Vocabulary: A New World of Words," presents the skill of using word-structure clues.*

In paragraph 13 of the selection you encountered the word ***portable.*** This word contains the Latin root ***port,*** which means "to carry" or "to bear." The word *portable* describes something that can be carried or moved about. Use the meaning of ***port*** and the list of prefixes on pages 60–61 to help you determine the meaning of each of the following words that contain this same root.

_____ **11.** If someone is arrested for **transporting** illegal goods across a state line, the person was trying to
   a.   move illegal goods from one state to another.
   b.   sneak across the state line.
   c.   induce others to pursue a life of crime.
   d.   report a crime to the police.

_____ **12.** Newspaper and television **reporters** gather information and
   a.   write it down.
   b.   bring it to the public.
   c.   disprove it.
   d.   speak it into a microphone.

_____ **13.** People who are in the **import-export** business
   a.   sell items in a retail store.
   b.   inspect products brought into a country.
   c.   bring some products into a country and send out others.
   d.   produce items to be sold wholesale.

_____ **14.** If illegal immigrants are **deported** from a country, they are
   a.   charged with a crime.
   b.   placed in jail.
   c.   given citizenship.
   d.   legally forced to leave the country.

_____ **15.** If there are large beams that **support** the roof of a structure, the beams
   a.   angle toward the ceiling.
   b.   are curved.
   c.   bear the weight of the roof.
   d.   are made of wood.

Reading Skills Application

_____ **16.** What is the author's primary purpose for writing this selection?

    a. to prove that test preparation and test grades are highly correlated

    b. to explain how to prepare for tests and deal with test anxiety

    c. to explain the different types of tests

    d. to prove that working with a study group can enhance test performance

_____ **17.** Which of the following is the meaning of *key* as it is used in the second bulleted item in paragraph 10?

    a. familiar

    b. confusing

    c. foreign

    d. important

_____ **18.** Which pattern has been used to organize the information in paragraph 7 of the selection?

    a. comparison and contrast

    b. cause and effect

    c. sequence

    d. list

_____ **19.** Based on the information in the selection, the author would most likely agree with which of the following statements?

    a. If students know more about test preparation, they can improve their performance on tests.

    b. Test anxiety is a fact of life and nothing can be done about it.

    c. There are test-taking techniques that can make every student successful in college.

    d. Study groups are the secret of success when preparing for tests in college.

_____ **20.** The author has credibility because he

    a. has had experience himself as a highly successful college student.

    b. presents the results of interviews with successful students.

    c. is an expert on learning and study skills.

    d. has conducted extensive research projects on study skills.

STUDY SKILLS

Collaboration Option

Writing and Collaborating to Enhance Your Understanding

Option for collaboration: Your instructor may direct you to work with other students or, in other words, to work *collaboratively*. In that case, you should form groups of three or four students as directed by your instructor and work together to complete the exercises. After your group discusses each item and agrees on the answer, have a group member record it. Every member of your group should be able to explain all of your group's answers.

1. **Reacting to What You Have Read:** "Know thyself," the old saying goes. Through experience, most college students discover techniques that prepare them to do well on tests. List at least three things that you have discovered that help *you* prepare effectively for tests.

    _____

    _____

    _____

    _____

    _____

    _____

    _____

2. **Comprehending the Selection Further:** List and explain the four ways to deal with test anxiety.

    _____

    _____

    _____

    _____

    _____

    _____

    _____

    _____

    _____

    _____

3. **Overall Main Idea of the Selection:** In one sentence tell what the author wants readers to understand about what you should do when preparing for tests. (Be sure to include the words "prepare" and "test" in your overall main idea sentence).

_____

_____

_____

_____

_____

Read More about It on the World Wide Web

To learn more about the topic of this selection, visit these websites or use your favorite search engine (such as Yahoo®) to discover more about this author and this topic on your own. Whenever you go to *any* website, it is a good idea to evaluate it critically. Are you getting good information—that is, information that is accurate, complete, and up-to-date? Who sponsors the website? How easy is it to use the features of the website?

http://www.mhhe.com/power
http://www.aboutcollege.com
http://ee.calpoly.edu/~jbreiten/htbas.html

(© Shannon Fagan/Taxi/Getty Images)

CHAPTER 2

Developing a College-Level Vocabulary

A New World of Words

CHAPTER OBJECTIVES

In this chapter you will learn:

- Why it is important to develop a college-level vocabulary.

- How to understand words according to the way they are used in context.

- What word-structure clues are and how to use them.

- How to use a dictionary pronunciation key.

- What figurative language is and how to interpret figures of speech.

51

WHAT YOU NEED TO LEARN

CREATING YOUR SUMMARY

READINGS

denotation = dictionary definition
connotation = emotional association

Selection 2-2 *(Business)*

"McDonaldization: The Sun Never Sets on the Golden Arches"
by William G. Nickels, James M. McHugh, and Susan McHugh

Selection 2-3 *(Health)*

"Rage on the Road: The Danger of Aggressive Driving"
by Wayne Payne and Dale Hahn

WHAT YOU NEED TO LEARN

WHY IS IT IMPORTANT TO DEVELOP A COLLEGE-LEVEL VOCABULARY?

The most important reason to develop a college-level vocabulary, of course, is so that you can understand your college textbooks. Increasing your vocabulary will also make your college work easier in other ways besides reading. Increasing your vocabulary will enable you to understand more of what others—especially professors—say. In addition, it will make your speaking and writing more precise and more interesting. If all that is not enough, your increased vocabulary may result in an increased salary. Research tells us that the size of a person's vocabulary correlates with how much money is earned: The larger your vocabulary, the larger your income is likely to be. Thinking of each word you learn as potential "money in the bank" may be an incentive for you to make the effort to add new words to your vocabulary! Indeed, developing a powerful vocabulary is a process that takes time and effort, it is an asset that will benefit you all your life.

How can you develop a strong vocabulary? Every time you read, you have an opportunity to expand your vocabulary. The more you read, the better your vocabulary can become—if you develop an interest in words and their meanings.

When you read there are four techniques you can use to develop and expand your understanding of words. The techniques are:

1. **Use context clues.** Figure out the likely meaning of a word from clues provided by the surrounding words and sentences. The word might be completely unfamiliar to you, or it might be a common word that has some other meanings you are unaware of.

2. **Use word-structure clues.** Determine a word's meaning by examining any prefix, root, or suffix it contains.

3. **Use a dictionary.** Determine a word's pronunciation and the precise meaning as it is used in the passage you are reading.

4. **Know how to interpret figurative language.** Understand the nonliteral meaning of words and phrases when they are used in figures of speech.

In this chapter, we will take a close look at each of these four skills for developing your vocabulary. (To give you ample practice applying these skills, there are extensive vocabulary exercises that accompany every reading selection in *New Worlds*.)

WHAT ARE CONTEXT CLUES AND HOW DO YOU USE THEM?

KEY TERM

context clues

Words in a sentence or paragraph that help the reader deduce (reason out) the meaning of an unfamiliar word.

Textbook authors want you to understand what they have written. When they use words that they think might be unfamiliar to the reader, they often help the reader by providing context clues. **Context clues** are words in a sentence or paragraph that help the reader deduce (reason out) the meaning of an unfamiliar word. Such clues are called "context" clues because *context* refers to the setting in which something occurs. In this case, it refers to the rest of the sentence and the paragraph in which the unfamiliar word appears.

Since context clues can help you figure out the meaning of an unfamiliar word, think of them as gifts the writer gives you to make your job easier. How can you take advantage of these "gifts"? Simply read the sentence carefully and pay attention to the words and other sentences surrounding the unfamiliar word. If you encounter an unfamiliar word when you are reading, ask yourself, "What would this word have to mean in order for it to make sense in this sentence?" For example, suppose you read this sentence: "My four-year-old nephew loves cookies, cakes, candy, *gurp,* and anything else that is sweet." *Gurp* is not a real word, of course. But if it were, you could deduce its meaning from the context: It is some type of dessert-like food. The context clues are the examples of "cookies, cakes, candy" and the words "and anything else that is sweet." To make sense in the sentence, *gurp* would have to refer to some type of sweet, sugary food.

For words with more than one meaning, context clues can also help you determine which meaning the author intends. You may know one meaning of the word *consume* is "to eat," as in this sentence: "Americans consume millions of hotdogs every year." Suppose, however, you encounter this sentence: "On average, Americans consume almost 19 million barrels of oil a day." "Eat" makes no sense in a sentence about consuming barrels of oil. You can deduce, therefore, that in this sentence, the word *consume* means "use." This is the meaning the author intends.

In the chart on page 55 are six very common types of context clues. The chart explains what to ask yourself and what to look for when you encounter each type of context clue. The chart also presents example sentences that illustrate each type of context clue. (You also have the opportunity to learn the meaning of any unfamiliar words in the example sentences.)

Using the context is the first strategy you should use when you encounter an unknown word. Remember, however, that even though context clues enable you to make an educated guess, they do not always allow you to determine the meaning of a word accurately. For example, you might read the sentence, "He spent the entire weekend visiting used car dealerships, but in spite of his *exhaustive* search he was unable to find a suitable car in his price range." Although *exhaustive* might appear from the context to mean "exhausting" or "tiring," it actually means "thorough" or "complete." (For example, a scientist might do exhaustive research about a particular subject.) In this case, the context is not sufficient to make the meaning of the word clear.

USING CONTEXT CLUES TO DETERMINE THE MEANING OF UNFAMILIAR WORDS

Type of Clue	What to Ask Yourself	What to Look For	Example
Definition clue	Are there *definition clues* and a definition?	Phrases that introduce a definition, such as: *is defined as, is called, is, is known as, that is, refers to, means, the term;* a term that is in bold print, italics, or color; certain punctuation marks that set off a definition or a term. (See page 68).	A ***panic attack*** *is defined as* a mood disorder that is characterized by sudden, unexpected feelings of fear.
Synonym clue	Is there a *synonym* for the unfamiliar word? That is, is the meaning explained by a word or phrase that has a *similar meaning?* The synonym may be set off by commas, parentheses, a colon, dashes, or brackets. (See page 68.)	Phrases that introduce synonyms, such as: *in other words, or, that is to say, also known as, by this we mean, that is.*	A ***puma,*** *or mountain lion,* has a large, powerful body.
Contrast clue	Is there an *antonym* for the unfamiliar word? That is, is the unfamiliar word explained by a contrasting word or phrase with the *opposite meaning?*	Words and phrases that indicate opposites: *instead of, but, in contrast, on the other hand, however, unlike, although, even though.*	*Unlike* his *talkative* older brother, Alvin is a ***taciturn*** person.
Experience clue	Can you draw on your *experience and background knowledge* to help you deduce the meaning of the unfamiliar word?	A sentence that includes *a familiar experience* (or information you already know) can help you figure out the meaning of the new word.	Because he prefers ***solitude,*** *he lives alone in an isolated mountain cabin with no telephone.*
Example clue	Are there *examples* that illustrate the meaning of the unfamiliar word?	Words that introduce examples of the meaning of the unfamiliar word: *for example, such as, to illustrate, like.*	He enjoys many types of ***cuisine,*** *such as Mexican, Italian, Chinese, Thai, and Indian foods.*
Clue from another sentence	Is there *another sentence* in the paragraph that explains the meaning of the unfamiliar word?	*Additional information in another sentence* that helps explain the unfamiliar word.	Her taste in music is very ***eclectic.*** *She likes opera, rock, hip-hop, classical, and country music.*

WHAT ARE WORD-STRUCTURE CLUES AND HOW DO YOU USE THEM?

KEY TERM
word-structure clues

Roots, prefixes, and suffixes
that help you determine a
word's meaning.

Word-structure clues are also
known as *word-part clues.*

Although context clues should be your first strategy in determining the meaning of unknown words, examining the structure of words can also be extremely helpful. **Word-structure clues,** or word-part clues, consist of roots, prefixes, and suffixes that help you determine a word's meaning. Affixes are word parts that are added to roots: Prefixes and suffixes are affixes. Word-structure clues can often be used to confirm the meaning suggested by the context of the sentence.

Word-structure clues can help you in other ways as well. First, they can help you remember the meaning of a word. Second, they allow you to enlarge your vocabulary by learning "families" of related words that come from the same root (called *cognates*). Finally, knowing prefixes, roots, and suffixes can help you improve your spelling. For instance, if you know the prefix *mis* (meaning "bad" or "wrong"), then you will understand why the word *misspell* has two s's: One is in the prefix and one is in the root word: mis + spell.

The more prefixes, roots, and suffixes you know, the more you will be able to utilize this vocabulary-building strategy. This means that it is well worth your time to memorize common word parts. Of these, roots and prefixes are by far the most helpful. (Lists of common roots, prefixes, and suffixes appear on pages 58–62.)

As you can tell, there are three categories of word parts—prefixes, roots, and suffixes. Each will be discussed in this chapter. Here are their definitions:

Root: Base word that has a meaning of its own.

Prefix: Word part attached to the beginning of a root that adds its meaning to the root or base word.

Suffix: Word part attached to the end of a root word that changes the word's part of speech or inflection.

To use word-structure clues, examine an unfamiliar word to see if it has a word part that you recognize that gives you a clue to its meaning. Think of roots and affixes as puzzle parts that can help you figure out the meaning of unfamiliar words. Keep in mind that, as noted above, you increase your chances of figuring out an unfamiliar word's meaning if you are able to use *both* context clues and word-structure clues together. Now, let's take a closer look at each of the three types of word parts.

A **root** is a base word that has a meaning of its own. Roots are powerful vocabulary-building tools, since entire families of words in English are based on the same root. For example, if you know that the root *aud* means "to hear," then you will understand the connection between *audience* (people who come to hear something or someone), *auditorium* (a place where people come to hear

KEY TERM
root

Base word that has a meaning
of its own.

something), *auditory* (pertaining to hearing, as in *auditory nerve*), and *audiologist* (a person specially trained to evaluate hearing). Knowing the meaning of a word's root makes it easier to remember the meaning of the word.

A **prefix** is a word part that is attached to the beginning of a word that adds its meaning to the meaning of the base word. For example, adding the prefix *tele* (meaning "distant" or "far") to the word *marketing* creates the word *telemarketing,* selling goods and services from a distance (in this case, over the telephone), rather than face-to-face. By adding the prefixes *pre* (meaning "before") and *re* (meaning "back" or "again") to the word *view,* you have the words *preview* (to view or see something ahead of time) and *review* (to see or look back at something again).

Remember, however, that just because a word begins with the same letters as a prefix, it does not necessarily contain that prefix. The prefix *mal* means "wrong" or "bad," as in *malnutrition* (bad nutrition). However, the words *mall* and *male* also begin with the letters *mal,* but they have no connection with the prefix *mal.* Nor does the word *rent,* for example, contain the prefix *re,* or the word *pressure* the prefix *pre.*

A **suffix** is a word part attached to the end of a root word. Some suffixes add their meaning to a root, but most suffixes simply change a word's part of speech or inflection. Inflectional endings include, for example, adding *-s* to make a word plural or *-ed* to make a verb past tense. Consider these other forms of *predict* (a verb) that are created by adding suffixes*: prediction* (a noun), *predictable* (an adjective), and *predictably* (an adverb).

Suffixes are not as helpful as roots or prefixes in determining the meaning of unfamiliar words because many suffixes have similar or even the same meanings. Also, some suffixes cause roots to change their spelling before the suffix is added. For instance, when certain suffixes are added to words that end in *y,* the *y* becomes an *i: sleepy* becomes *sleepier, sleepiness,* and *sleepily.*

A word may consist of one or more of the word parts. For example, the word *graph* consists of a root only. The word *telegraph* consists of a prefix *(tele)* and a root *(graph).* The word *graphic* consists of a root *(graph)* and a suffix *(ic). Telegraphic* consists of a prefix, a root, and a suffix.

It is unlikely that you or any other student will learn every Greek and Latin word part, but the more word parts you know, the easier it will be for you to use word-structure clues and, of course, the larger your vocabulary will become. A good place to begin is by familiarizing yourself with the common roots, prefixes, and suffixes on the lists that follow. (You probably already know many of the word parts on these lists.) Then watch for these word parts in new words you encounter. Use these word-structure clues whenever possible to help you confirm the "educated guess" you made about a word's meaning based on the context.

COMMON ROOTS

Root	Meaning	Examples
1. anthro	man, humankind	anthropology, misanthrope
2. aud	hear	audible, audience
3. auto	self	autobiography, automatic
4. bene	good, well	beneficial, benediction
5. biblio	book	bibliography, bibliophile
6. bio	life	biology
7. cede, ceed	go, move	precede, proceed
8. chron	time	chronology, chronic
9. cide	kill	homicide, suicide
10. clud, clus	close, shut	exclude, inclusive
11. corp, corpus	body	corporal, corps
12. cred	believe, belief	credible, credit
13. dic, dict	say, speak	predict, dictionary
14. duc, duct	lead	produce, conductor
15. fac	make, do	manufacture, factory
16. fid, fide	faith	fidelity, confidence
17. gam, gamy	marriage	bigamist, monogamy
18. gen	origin, birth, race	generation, genealogy
19. geo	earth	geology, geography
20. graph, gram	write	graphic, diagram
21. gress	go, move	progression, regress
22. ject	throw, hurl	reject, projection
23. mater, matri	mother	maternal, matricide
24. mem	memory	remember, commemorate
25. meter	measure	metric, thermometer
26. miss, mit	send, sent	mission, transmit

Root	Meaning	Examples
27. mor, mort	death	morgue, mortal
28. mot	move, go	motion, promote
29. nov	new	novelty, innovation
30. pater, patri	father	paternal, patriotic
31. pel	push, drive, thrust	repel, compel
32. pend	hang	pendulum, dependent
33. phil, phile	love	philosophy, bibliophile
34. phobia	fear	claustrophobia, phobic
35. phon	sound	telephone, phonics
36. photo	light	photograph, photosynthesis
37. pod, pedi	foot	podiatrist, pedestrian
38. port	carry	portable, import
39. pos	put, place	pose, position
40. psych, psycho	mind	psychic, psychology
41. rupt	break, burst	rupture; bankrupt
42. scribe, script	write	inscribe, prescription
43. sol	one, alone, only	solo, solitude
44. spec	see, look	spectacle, inspect
45. ten	grasp, hold, stretch	attention, retention
46. therm	heat	thermometer, thermal
47. tempor	time, occasion	temporary, contemporary
48. tort	twist, bend	tortuous, contort
49. tract	drag, pull	tractor, contract
50. ven, vene	come	convention, intervene
51. vers, vert	turn	reverse, convert
52. vid, vis	see	video, vision
53. viv, vive	live, living	vivid, survive
54. voc	call, say	vocal, invocation

COMMON PREFIXES

Prefix	Meaning	Examples
Prefixes That Mean "No" or "Not":		
1. a-	not	atypical, asocial
2. an-	not	anarchy, anaerobic
3. in-, il-, im-, ir-	not	insecure, illegal, immoral, irresponsible
4. non-	not	nonviolent, nonpoisonous
5. un-	not	unhappy, unkind
6. dis-	not, opposite of, undo	displease, disservice, disconnect
7. mis-	wrong, bad	mistreat, mistake
8. mal-	bad, evil	maladjusted, malevolent
9. anti-	against	antivirus, antithesis, antiwar
10. contra-	against	contradict, contrary
Prefixes That Relate to Time:		
11. ante-	before	antebellum, antechamber
12. ex-	former	ex-boss, ex-spouse
13. post-	after	posttest, posterior
14. pre-	before	predict, precede
15. re-	again	repeat, recycle
Prefixes That Show Placement:		
16. ab-	away, away from	absent, abnormal
17. circum-	around	circumference
18. co-, col-, com-	together or with	cooperate, colleague, community
19. de-	down from, away	descend, depart
20. dis-	away	displace, disappear
21. ex-	out	exit, export, exterior
22. in-	in	inside, interior, inhale
23. inter-	between, among	interstate, interrupt, interfere
24. intra-	within, inside	intrastate, intramural, intravenous
25. pro-	forward, ahead	progress, promote
26. re-	back	return, revert, report
27. sub-, sup-	down	submarine, suppress
28. tele-	far, distant	television, telepathy
29. trans-	across	transatlantic, transport

Prefix	Meaning	Examples
Prefixes That Indicate How Many or How Much:		
30. extra-	outside, beyond	exterior, extraordinary, extracurricular
31. hemi-	half	hemisphere
32. hyper-	too much, excessive	hyperactive
33. hypo-	under, too little	hypothermia, hypodermic
34. macro-	large	macroeconomics, macrobiotic
35. micro-	small	microscope, microorganisms
36. omni-	all, every	omnipotent, omniscient
37. poly-	many	polygamy, polygon
38. pseudo-	false	pseudonym
39. semi-	half	semiconscious, semiformal
40. super-	over, above	supervisor, superlative
Prefixes That Show Number or Quantity:		
41. uni-	one	united, unify, uniform
42. mono-	one	monopoly, monocle
43. bi-	two	bicycle, bisect
44. du-	two	duet, dual, duel
45. tri-	three	triangle, triplet, tripod
46. quad-, quar	four	quadrant, quarter, quart
47. quint-	five	quintet, quintuple
48. penta-	five	Pentagon, pentathlon
49. sex-	six	sextuplet
50. hex-	six	hexagon
51. sept-	seven	septuplets, septuagenarian, septet
52. octo-, oct-	eight	octagon, octopus
53. nov-	nine	novena, November, nonagenarian
54. dec-, deci-	ten	decimal, decade, decimate
55. cent-	hundred	century, cent
56. mill-, kilo-	thousand	millennium, kilowatts

COMMON SUFFIXES

Suffix	Meaning	Examples
Suffixes That Indicate a Person:		
1. -er, -or, -ist	one who (does what the root word indicates)	banker, inventor, scientist, pacifist
Suffixes That Indicate a Noun:		
2. -ance, -ence, -tion, -sion, -ment, -ness, -ity, -ty, -tude, -hood, -age	state of, quality of, condition of, act of	tolerance, permanence, retention, vision, government, happiness, maturity, beauty, gratitude, statehood, marriage
3. -itis	inflammation of (whatever the root indicates)	sinusitis, tonsillitis
4. -ology	study or science of (whatever the root indicates)	psychology, microbiology
5. -ism	philosophy of or belief in	terrorism, Buddhism, pacifism
Suffixes That Indicate an Adjective:		
6. -al, -ic, -ish, -ical, -ive	pertaining to (whatever the root indicates)	normal, hormonal, psychic, selfish, magical, defective, pacific
7. -less	without, lacking (whatever the root indicates)	homeless, toothless
8. -ous, -ful	full of (whatever the root indicates)	harmonious, colorful
9. -able, -ible	able to do or be (whatever the root indicates)	comfortable, comprehensible
Suffixes That Indicate a Verb:		
10. -ify, -ate, -ize, -en	to do (whatever the root indicates)	pacify, meditate, criticize, enlighten
Suffixes That Indicate an Adverb:		
11. -ly	in the manner (indicated by the root)	slowly, heavily, peacefully
12. -ward	in the direction of (whatever the root indicates)	eastward, homeward, backward

HOW DO YOU USE A DICTIONARY PRONUNCIATION KEY?

Most college students know how to locate a word in the dictionary and how to determine which definition pertains to what they are reading. But like many students, you still may not be skilled or confident in using a dictionary pronunciation key. Being able to use a pronunciation key is important because when you need to remember a word, one of the most helpful things you can do is learn its correct pronunciation and say it aloud. Checking and practicing a word's pronunciation takes only a moment or two.

Most dictionaries have an abridged (shortened) pronunciation key at or near the bottom of each page. This abridged key gives only vowel sounds and the less common consonant sounds. (A bridged pronunciation keys usually look similar to this one:

Pronunciation Key: ă **pat**   ā **pay**   âr **care**   ä **father**   ĕ **pet**   ē **be**   ĭ **pit**
ī **tie**   îr **pier**   ŏ **pot**   ō **toe**   ô **paw**   oi **noise**   ou **out**   o͝o **took**   o͞o **boot**
ŭ **cut**   yo͞o **abuse**   ûr **urge**   th **thin**   *th* **this**   hw **which**   zh **vision**
ə **about**   Stress mark: ′

Of course, a complete pronunciation key appears at the beginning of every dictionary. Typically, it looks similar to the example shown in the table on page 64. Notice that the complete pronunciation key gives a familiar word that contains a particular sound, accompanied by the symbol that dictionary uses to represent that sound. For example, the first word, *pat,* contains the sound of short *a.* That sound is represented in this dictionary by the symbol ă. The pronunciation of words in the dictionary will be written using these phonetic symbols. For example, suppose you read the sentence, "Marjorie is an *avid* football fan who hasn't missed a Dallas Cowboys home game in eight years." When you look up the word *avid,* you confirm what you suspect, that it means having a great interest and enthusiasm for something. You also see that the pronunciation for *avid* is written this way: ăv′ ĭd. To pronounce this word, you simply find the phonetic symbols for ă and ĭ in the pronunciation key and determine the way they sound in short, familiar words. The ă and the ĭ are pronounced the same as the *a* in the word *pat* and the *i* in the word *pit.* When you substitute those sounds in place of the symbols in the pronunciation, you will know how to say the word correctly.

As you work through *New Worlds,* you will have numerous opportunities to practice this skill, since the pronunciation is given for each vocabulary term in the quizzes that accompany the reading selections. To help you interpret the symbols, the sample pronunciation key is repeated in each of these exercises. Your instructor can give you further guidance and practice in using a dictionary pronunciation key, if you need it.

DICTIONARY PRONUNCIATION KEY

Examples	Symbols	Examples	Symbols
pat	ă	pop	p
pay	ā	roar	r
care	âr	sauce	s
father	ä	ship, dish	sh
bib	b	tight, stopped	t
church	ch	thin	th
deed, milled	d	this	*th*
pet	ĕ	cut	ŭ
bee	ē	urge, term, firm, word, heard	ûr
fife, phase, rough	f		
gag	g	valve	v
hat	h	with	w
which	hw	yes	y
pit	ĭ	abuse, sue	yōō
pie, by	ī	zebra, xylem	z
pier	î	vision, pleasure, garage	zh
judge	j		
kick, cat, pique	k	*a*bout, it*e*m, ed*i*ble, gall*o*p, circ*u*s	ə
lid, needle	l (nēd′l)		
mum	m	butter	ər
no, sudden	n (sŭd′n)		
thing	ng	FOREIGN	
pot	ŏ	*French* feu, *German* schōn	œ
toe, hose	ō		
caught, paw	ô	*French* tu, *German* über	ü
noise	oi		
took	ŏŏ	*German* ich, *Scottish* loch	KH
boot	ōō		
out	ou	*French* bon	N

STRESS

Primary stress ′   bi ol′ o gy (bī ŏl′ ə jē)

Secondary stress ′   bi′ o log′ ical (bī′ ə lŏj′ ĭ kəl)

WHAT IS FIGURATIVE LANGUAGE AND HOW DO YOU INTERPRET FIGURES OF SPEECH?

KEY TERM
figurative language

Words that present unusual comparisons or create vivid pictures in the reader's mind.

Figurative language is also called *figures of speech.*

KEY TERM
metaphor

Figure of speech suggesting a comparison between two seemingly dissimilar things, usually by saying that one of them *is* the other.

KEY TERM
simile

Figure of speech presenting a comparison between two seemingly dissimilar things by saying that one of them is *like* the other.

Knowing how to interpret figurative language is yet another way to develop your understanding of words' meanings and interpret an author's message correctly. **Figurative language** refers to words that present unusual comparisons or create vivid pictures in the reader's mind. Figurative expressions are also called *figures of speech.* Because figures of speech do not literally mean what they say, your job is to *interpret* their meaning. If you take the words literally, you will misunderstand the author's meaning. When you encounter figurative language, think about what the author is trying to convey by presenting a comparison or creating a vivid mental image.

You use figurative language every day, although you may not know it by this name. Whenever you say something such as, "That homework assignment was a killer!" you really mean, "That was a tough assignment!" When you say, "I made such a good grade on my test they'll probably hire me to *teach* the course next semester!" you really mean "I made an extremely high grade on the test."

Because figures of speech do not literally mean what the words say, the reader or listener must interpret their meaning. If you say, "I bombed my last math test," you do not literally mean that there was an actual bomb or any sort of explosion. You expect your listener to interpret your words to mean that you did not do well on your math test.

There are four very common types of figurative language. These figures of speech are *metaphor, simile, hyperbole,* and *personification.* Let's look at each of them.

A **metaphor** is a figure of speech suggesting a comparison between two seemingly dissimilar things, usually by saying that one of them *is* the other (rather than saying it is simply "like" something else). On the surface, the two things seem very different from each other, yet they are alike in some significant way. The reader must figure out the way in which they are similar.

The author assumes that readers will not take his or her words literally, but will understand that this is a figure of speech whose meaning must be interpreted. That is, the sentence is to be taken *figuratively,* not literally. For example, in the sentence "Becky *is a walking encyclopedia,*" the writer is making a comparison between Becky and an encyclopedia to suggest that Becky has a vast amount of knowledge. To interpret this metaphor correctly, the reader must compare Becky and an encyclopedia and think about the way in which they could be similar: Both have knowledge, a multitude of facts and information. The author, of course, does not mean that Becky is literally an encyclopedia.

A **simile** is a figure of speech presenting a comparison between two seemingly dissimilar things by saying that one of them is like the other. Whereas a metaphor makes comparisons using the words *is, are, was,* and *were,* a simile is usually introduced by the words *like* or *as.* An example of a simile is, "Becky is *like* an encyclopedia." The point is the same as in the metaphor: Becky has a vast amount of knowledge.

Here are some examples of similes: "David felt *like a king* when the company chose him as its new president" and "Alexis's mind is as fast and accurate with numbers *as a computer.*" In the first sentence, David's feeling about being chosen president of the company is compared to the feeling of being a king. The author wants us to understand that being chosen as president made David feel as important (and perhaps even as powerful!) as if he were a real king. In the second simile, Alexis's mind, because of her mental ability, is compared to a computer. In other words, Alexis's mind is *extremely* fast.

To repeat: A simile says that one thing is *like* another. (The word *sim*ile suggests a *sim*ilarity between two things.) When you encounter a simile, you must first determine which things are being compared. To interpret the author's meaning, you must determine the important way in which the author considers them to be similar.

KEY TERM
hyperbole

Figure of speech using obvious exaggeration for emphasis and effect.

Another type of figurative language is **hyperbole,** in which obvious exaggeration is used for emphasis and effect. (The prefix *hyper,* meaning "too much" or "excessive," will help you remember that a hyperbole is an obvious exaggeration. Note, too, that the word *hyperbole* has four syllables and is pronounced: hī pûr′ bə lē). "If I have to type one more paper this week, *my fingers will fall off!*" is an example of hyperbole. Of course, the student's fingers are not literally going to fall off. To interpret the hyperbole correctly, you must understand the point of the exaggeration: to convey that he or she has already had to type several papers this week and is extremely tired of typing.

Hyperboles can also be used to achieve a particular effect. For example, to achieve a comic effect, someone might write, "If I eat one more serving of fish on this diet, I'm going to grow fins!"

KEY TERM
personification

Figure of speech in which nonhuman or nonliving things are given human traits.

In **personification,** nonhuman or nonliving things are given human traits. (You can actually see the word *person* in *person*ification. Note, however, that the pronunciation is pər sŏn ə fĭ kā′ shən.) For example, consider the human characteristics or qualities used in this sentence about a vending machine: "The vending machine *swallowed* my money and then *refused* to give me my coffee." Swallowing and refusing to do something are human behaviors. Vending machines, of course, cannot do these things intentionally or in the same sense that a person would. The author wants the reader to make the correct interpretation that the machine accepted the money but did not produce any coffee in return. In other words, the machine is broken (it malfunctioned).

The box that follows summarizes metaphor, simile, hyperbole, and personification and gives additional examples of each.

Figures of Speech	Examples
Metaphor: Implied comparison between two dissimilar things using *is, are, was,* or *were.*	The old man's face was a *raisin.* Our apartment is a *disaster area.*
Simile: Stated comparison between two dissimilar things, usually introduced by the words *like* or *as.*	After being stranded in the airport for two days, she felt *as if her teeth had little sweaters on them.* After we had slept outside in tents for a week, the motel seemed *like a palace* to us.
Hyperbole: Obvious exaggeration for emphasis and effect.	I tried to get his attention, but he was *glued to the TV set.* The steak they served me at the restaurant *would have fed a dozen people!*
Personification: Giving human characteristics or qualities to nonhuman or nonliving things.	The *letters danced* on the page before my tired eyes. *Poverty stole* their childhood.

Careful readers ask themselves, "Is the author using figurative language?" If the answer is yes, they ask these additional questions:

- "Are two things being compared, and if so, how are they alike?" (metaphor and simile)
- "Is there an obvious exaggeration?" (hyperbole)
- "Are human traits being given to nonliving or nonhuman things?" (personification)

Understanding figurative language helps you interpret an author's message correctly, and it also makes material more interesting and enjoyable to read when you interpret figures of speech correctly.

OTHER THINGS TO KEEP IN MIND WHEN DEVELOPING YOUR COLLEGE-LEVEL VOCABULARY

Here are three helpful things you should keep in mind with regard to developing a college-level vocabulary:

1. Certain punctuation marks in a sentence can signal a definition.

Commas, parentheses, brackets, dashes, and colons can be used to set off definitions in sentences. Each of the sample sentences below presents the statement "Ayurveda is older than Chinese medicine." However, because the author knows that many readers may not be familiar with the term *ayurveda,* he includes the definition in the sentence as well. Notice how the punctuation marks in each example signal that a definition is being given. (The definition in each sentence appears in italics.)

- *Commas*   Ayurveda, *traditional Indian medicine based on herbal remedies,* is older than Chinese medicine.

    or

    A form of medicine that is older than Chinese medicine is ayurveda, *traditional Indian medicine based on herbal remedies.*

- *Parentheses*   Ayurveda (*traditional Indian medicine based on herbal remedies*) is older than Chinese medicine.

- *Brackets*   Ayurveda [*traditional Indian medicine based on herbal remedies*] is older than Chinese medicine.

- *Dash*   Ayurveda—*traditional Indian medicine based on herbal remedies*—is older than Chinese medicine.

- *Colon*   A form of medicine that is older than Chinese medicine is ayurveda: *traditional Indian medicine based on herbal remedies.*

As you can see, there are several ways an author can use punctuation marks to set off a definition.

2. The most common and helpful roots, prefixes, and suffixes in English come from Latin and ancient Greek.

Although English is a Germanic language, it has thousands of words derived from Latin and ancient Greek. Today, the English language contains a considerable number of technological, scientific, and medical terms that are derived from Latin and Greek. If you take college courses in any of these areas, you will benefit greatly from knowing common Latin and Greek word parts.

Incidentally, knowing common Latin word parts also makes it easier to learn Spanish, French, Italian, Portuguese, and Romanian. These languages are referred to as *romance languages,* not because they have anything to do with love, but because they all draw so heavily on Latin. Latin was the "Roman" language because it was spoken in ancient Rome. For that reason, languages derived from Latin came to be known as romance languages. Of course, many Spanish, French, and Italian words such as *rodeo, boutique,* and *galleria* have also become words in English.

3. A word's etymology (origin and history) indicates the word parts it was created from, including Latin or Greek ones.

A word's etymology is its origin and history. Dictionaries usually give the etymology of a word in brackets [ ] before or after the definition. An etymology can be helpful because it tells the meaning of the original word parts from which the current word was derived. This can enable you to understand and remember the word's meaning more easily. For example, the word part *re* means *back* and the root *ject* means to *throw*. The English word *reject* literally means to "to throw back" (that is, not accept) something.

When you look up a word in the dictionary, make it a habit to examine the word's etymology. See if the word contains familiar word parts. Over time, you will expand not only your vocabulary, but also your knowledge of word parts. And the more word parts you know, the easier it will be to develop your vocabulary. Below are some examples of interesting words that have come into English from other languages. Their etymologies are given in brackets after the definitions.

al•ge•bra	(ăl′ jĕ- brə) *n.* A generalization of arithmetic in which symbols represent members of a specified set of numbers and are related by operations that hold for all numbers in the set. [< Arabic: al - jabr, "the (science of) reuniting."] -al′ ge bra′ ic (-brā′ ik) adj.
bou•tique	(bōō tēk′) *n.* **1.** A small retail shop that specializes in gifts, fashionable clothes, and accessories. [French: from Old French, *botique,* small shop, from Old Provençal *botica,* from Latin *apothēca,* storehouse. See APOTHECARY.]
cor•ral	(kĕ răl′) *n.* **1.** An enclosure for confining livestock. **2.** An enclosure formed by a circle of wagons for defense against attack during an encampment. —*v.* -ralled, -ralling, -als. **1.** To drive into and hold in a corral. **2.** To arrange (wagons) in a corral. **3.** To take control or possession of. *Informal.* To seize; capture. [Spanish: from Vulgar Latin *currāle,* enclosure for carts, from Latin *currus,* cart, from *currere,* to run.]
gal•le•ri•a	(găl′ ə rē′ ə) *n.* A roofed passageway or indoor court usually containing a variety of shops or businesses. [Italian: from Old Italian. See GALLERY.]
ro•de•o	(rō′ dē ō, rō dā′ ō) *n., pl.* -os. **1.** A cattle roundup. **2.** A public exhibition of cowboy skills, including riding broncos, lassoing, etc. [Spanish: *rodear,* to surround.]
yen	(yĕn) *n. Informal.* A yearning; a longing. [Cantonese: *yan.*]

DEVELOPING CHAPTER REVIEW CARDS

Chapter review cards are a way to select, organize, and review the important information in a textbook chapter. Preparing summary review cards helps you organize the information so that you can learn and memorize it more easily. In other words, chapter review cards are an effective study tool.

Preparing chapter review cards for each chapter of this book will give you practice in creating these valuable study tools. Once you have learned how to make chapter review cards, you can use actual index cards to create them for textbook material in any of your courses and use them when you study for tests.

Now, complete the chapter review cards for this chapter by answering the questions or following the directions on each "card" below. (The boxes below represent index cards.) The page numbers indicate the place in the chapter the information can be found.

Context Clues

1. What are *context clues*? (See page 54.)

_____

_____

_____

2. List the six types of context clues. (See page 55.)

1. _____

2. _____

3. _____

4. _____

5. _____

6. _____

Card 1   Chapter 2: Developing a College-Level Vocabulary

Word-Structure Clues

1. What are *word-structure clues*? (See page 56.)

_____

_____

_____

2. Define each of these terms. (See pages 56–57.)

roots: _____

_____

prefixes: _____

_____

suffixes: _____

_____

Card 2　Chapter 2: Developing a College-Level Vocabulary

Figurative Language

1. What is *figurative language*? (See page 65.)

_____

_____

2. Define each of these figures of speech. (See pages 65–66.)

metaphor: _____

_____

simile: _____

_____

hyperbole: _____

_____

personification: _____

_____

Card 3　Chapter 2: Developing a College-Level Vocabulary

VOCABULARY PRACTICE: CONTEXT CLUE EXERCISES

Directions:

- Items 1–20 below present sentences primarily from college textbooks. Each contains an important word or term that is *italicized*. Next, there is an additional sentence that uses the word in the same sense. This sentence provides a second context clue. *Read both sentences.*

- *Next, use the context clues from both sentences to deduce the meaning of the italicized word.* Remember, the answer you choose must make sense in *both* sentences. Test each answer choice by substituting it in both sentences.

- *Write your answer in the space provided.*

Suggestion: You will find it helpful to mark context clues in the sentences before you select an answer choice and to identify the type of clue.

_____ **1.** Requirements for *naturalization* in the United States include several years' residency, the ability to communicate in English, demonstrated knowledge of American government and history, a commitment to American values, and no membership in any subversive organization.

Through *naturalization,* millions of immigrants to the United States have become American citizens.

naturalization

 a. process of becoming an immigrant
 b. process of making something more natural
 c. process by which a foreigner becomes a citizen of a different country
 d. process of establishing residency in a country

_____ **2.** *Tsunamis,* or seismic sea waves, are often incorrectly called tidal waves.

Tsunamis are produced by underwater earthquakes.

tsunamis

 a. underwater earthquakes
 b. seismic sea waves
 c. tidal waves
 d. earthquakes

_____ **3.** We harbor *stereotypes* or prejudgments of college professors, Asians, hairdressers, used car salespeople, the elderly, preachers, Southerners, Democrats, rock musicians, and countless other groups of people.

Stereotypes originally referred to a metal printing plate or mold, but now refers to long-standing, oversimplified, exaggerated, inflexible prejudgments about groups of people.

stereotype

a. printing done with a metal plate

b. numerous groups of people

c. oversimplification

d. prejudgment about a group of people

————   **4.** The blurring of gender roles is clearly evident in many of today's *androgynous* styles and fashions, such as wearing earrings or having tattoos.

Both the male and female employees protested their company's new uniforms of khaki slacks and blue shirts; they complained that the uniforms looked *androgynous.*

androgynous

a. not clearly masculine or feminine, as in dress, appearance, or behavior

b. wearing earrings or having long hair

c. wearing the styles and fashions of today

d. wearing a uniform

————   **5.** For a special promotion, many retail stores deliberately sell a product below its customary price, or even below cost, to attract attention to it. The purpose of this *loss-leader pricing* is not to sell more of that particular product, but to attract customers in hopes that they will buy other products as well.

Mass merchandisers, such as Target, often sell home videos at half their customary price because this *loss-leader pricing* draws so many customers to their stores.

loss-leader pricing

a. special promotions to sell videos

b. selling a product below its customary price, or even below cost, to attract customers in hopes that they will buy other products as well

c. retailing technique used by all mass merchandisers

d. attracting customers by selling things half price

————   **6.** *Blues* grew out of African American folk music, such as work songs, spirituals, and the field hollers of slaves.

It is uncertain exactly when *blues* originated, but by around the 1890s it was sung in rural areas in the South and was often performed with a guitar accompaniment.

blues

a. African American folk music that originated around the 1890s

b. work songs, spirituals, and field hollers of slaves

c. a form of vocal and instrumental music that grew out of African American folk music

d. music performed in the South

_____ **7.** A densely populated area containing two or more cities and their suburbs has become known as a *megalopolis*. Such areas exist not only in the United States, but in Great Britain, Germany, Italy, Egypt, India, Japan, and China.

An example of a *megalopolis* is the 500-mile corridor that stretches from Boston south to Washington, D.C., and includes New York City, Philadelphia, and Baltimore—one-sixth of the total population of the United States!

megalopolis

a. densely populated area containing two or more cities and their suburbs

b. areas existing in the United States, Great Britain, Germany, Italy, Egypt, India, Japan, and China

c. the 500-mile corridor that stretches from Boston south to Washington, D.C.

d. areas that equal one-sixth of the total population of the United States

_____ **8.** Motorists are aware of an increasing sense of aggression on America's *congested* highways.

The mall can become so *congested* with Christmas shoppers that potential buyers give up and go home.

congested

a. flowing freely

b. overfilled or overcrowded

c. hostile

d. filled with pollution

_____ **9.** New mothers seem more *susceptible* to stress and fatigue because they are now primary caregivers as well as wives, homemakers, and often employees as well.

Not eating a balanced diet or getting enough sleep can make you more *susceptible* to colds and other infections.

susceptible

a. having an unknown effect

b. unaffected by

c. having no effect upon

d. easily affected by

_____ **10.** Listing your qualifications on your résumé gives a prospective employer *tangible* clues about the type of person you are.

Many people enjoy volunteer work immensely even though they receive no pay or other *tangible* rewards for the hours they contribute.

tangible

   a. pertaining to an actual object or something real
   b. free; having no cost
   c. pertaining to a legal matter
   d. expensive; costly

_____ **11.** Many states have now prohibited *capital punishment,* but some states still execute those who are convicted of first-degree murder.

Opponents of *capital punishment* cite numerous deathrow inmates who have been cleared of crimes as a result of sophisticated DNA testing that is now available.

capital punishment

   a. severe punishment
   b. the penalty of death for a crime
   c. punishment decreed by the government
   d. life imprisonment

_____ **12.** The Mississippi River, the longest river in the United States, *meanders* from Minnesota to Louisiana before emptying into the Gulf of Mexico.

The writer was described as a vagabond who *meanders* through life, open to every new adventure and experience.

meander

   a. flows
   b. stays
   c. wanders
   d. visits

_____ **13.** The *façades* of art deco style buildings are characterized by the use of chrome, steel, glass and aluminum, geometric patterns, and a rich display of surface decoration.

Over time air pollution has eroded the *façade* of many ancient buildings in Venice, Italy.

façade

   a. building
   b. exterior
   c. interior
   d. windows

_____ **14.** "Ice cold," "little baby," and "old antique" are examples of *redundant* phrases.

To use time effectively, employees should avoid *redundant* activities such as writing an e-mail message and leaving the same message on voicemail.

redundant

a. needlessly repetitive; unnecessary

b. useful; helpful

c. exact; precise

d. boring; uninteresting

_____ **15.** Many art treasures exist today because rulers such as the Roman emperor Augustus and the Byzantine emperor Justinian chose to *glorify* themselves through art.

Throughout the ages cathedrals, hymns, and paintings have been created to *glorify* God.

glorify

a. to make larger

b. to give glory, honor, or praise

c. to hide weaknesses

d. to create a portrait of

_____ **16.** In their autobiography, sisters Sarah and Elizabeth Delany, who both lived more than 100 years, attributed their *longevity* to doing what they felt was right for them and to helping others.

Careful eating, regular exercise, sufficient rest, and a positive attitude contribute to a person's *longevity.*

longevity

a. intelligence

b. wealth

c. long length of life

d. physical endurance

_____ **17.** The *Middle Ages,* the period of European history between ancient times and modern times, began with the fall of Rome in the fifth century and ended with the Renaissance in the fourteenth century.

Back in the *Middle Ages,* life for peasants was difficult, harsh, and short.

Middle Ages

a. ancient times

b. the period of time when peasants lived

c. the period in a person's life between the ages of forty and sixty

d. the period of European history between ancient times and modern times

_____ **18.** The white marble Taj Mahal, a magnificent tomb built in the mid-seventeenth century by a Mogul emperor for his beloved wife, is perhaps the most famous *mausoleum* in the world.

In England, the ancestors of distinguished families are often buried in a *mausoleum* on the grounds of the family's estate.

mausoleum

a. a simple, unmarked grave

b. a building designed as a burial vault

c. a building constructed of stone

d. place where bodies are kept before burial

_____ **19.** By learning how to reduce conflict, managers and supervisors can help angry employees avoid an *altercation.*

To avoid danger to themselves, police officers receive training in how to break up violent *altercations.*

altercation

a. loud party

b. loud music

c. loud argument

d. loud celebration

_____ **20.** Strokes can result in paralysis which, in turn, can cause the unused muscles to *atrophy.*

When a broken arm or leg is placed in a cast, the muscles begin to *atrophy* from lack of movement.

atrophy

a. to grow stronger

b. to shrink

c. to stretch

d. to disappear

VOCABULARY PRACTICE: WORD-STRUCTURE CLUE EXERCISES

Directions: For each item, there is a sentence that contains an *italicized* word whose word parts give a clue to its meaning. Use the word part that is in boldface to give you a clue to the word's meaning. (See lists on pages 58–62.) Some words contain more than one word part; this will give you additional help in determining the meaning. (When necessary, use context clues to confirm your answer choice.)

_____ **1.** Harold is an **at**ypical student because he started college when he was 16.

    a. typical

    b. not typical

    c. normal

    d. ordinary

_____ **2.** It is easy to understand her on the telephone because of her **dic**tion.

    a. pleasant way of saying things

    b. clear, distinct pronunciation

    c. use of complex words

    d. use of the dictionary

_____ **3.** The serial killer known as Jack the Ripper was a notorious *misogyn*ist who slashed many women to death in London in the late nineteenth century.

    a. someone who fails at marriage

    b. someone who hates marriage

    c. someone who hates women

    d. someone who hates adolescents

_____ **4.** The **biblio**phile owned more than a thousand volumes and was proud of his extensive book collection.

    a. book lover

    b. librarian

    c. bookseller

    d. rare book dealer

_____ **5.** The Vietnam Memorial in Washington, D.C., is a black marble monument that is permanently *inscrib*ed with the names of all persons in the U.S. armed services who died in the Vietnam War.

    a. illustrated

    b. engraved

    c. painted

    d. decorated

_____ **6.** Teenagers who drive recklessly must think they are **im**mortal.

    a. not able to die

    b. above the law

    c. impressive

    d. susceptible to injury

_____ **7.** Lisa tried to *convert* other members of her family to vegetarianism, but they refused to give up meat.

    a. dissuade

    b. discourage

    c. turn aside

    d. turn others to one's way of thinking or behaving

_____ **8.** The lifeguard quickly pulled the child from the bottom of the swimming pool and *reviv*ed him with CPR.

    a. brought back to life or consciousness

    b. expelled water from the lungs

    c. made strong again

    d. rescued

_____ **9.** The historian ***chron**icled* the events leading up to the Persian Gulf War.

    a. disproved

    b. discussed

    c. presented in order

    d. disapproved of

_____ **10.** *Polygamy* is illegal in the United States.

    a. being married to two or more people at the same time

    b. being married to two women at the same time

    c. being married to two men at the same time

    d. being married to two or more people one at a time

_____ **11.** My father has four sisters, and of all my ***paternal*** aunts, I like Aunt Jane best.

    a. pertaining to the father

    b. pertaining to the mother

    c. pertaining to relatives

    d. pertaining to brothers

_____ **12.** Adriana is a ***versatile*** artist who works in clay, stone, and metal.

    a. able to do many different things

    b. hardworking

    c. beginning

    d. outdoor

_____ **13.** We refused to open the front door until the police officer showed us his ***credentials***.

    a. weapon

    b. police car

    c. subpoena

    d. identification or other evidence of authority

_____ **14.** Professor Bowman chose an office on the first floor because she has ***acrophobia***.

    a. a fear of earthquakes

    b. a fear of heights

    c. a fear of work

    d. a fear of thunderstorms

_____ **15.** I tell my sister Mary everything; she has been my best friend and *confidant* all my life.

   a. person you trust will keep your secrets

   b. relative who is close in age

   c. enjoyable companion

   d. person who belongs to a religious order

_____ **16.** The surgeon took a **biopsy** from the tumor and sent it to the laboratory for analysis.

   a. sample of living tissue

   b. fluid

   c. x-ray

   d. report

_____ **17.** The body of the homeless person was sent to the city **morgue** until an identification could be made.

   a. place where dead bodies are kept temporarily

   b. place where bodies are cremated

   c. place where bodies are prepared for burial

   d. place where bodies are maintained in crypts

_____ **18.** Because certain collectors have such **sophisticated** taste in art, their paintings are often featured in art magazines.

   a. too expensive for the average collector

   b. unusual

   c. knowledgeable and informed

   d. modern or contemporary

_____ **19.** Although spanking used to be a common way to handle disciplinary problems, most school districts now prohibit **corporal** punishment.

   a. pertaining to the body

   b. pertaining to the military

   c. pertaining to schools

   d. pertaining to young children

_____ **20.** The young millionaire was a generous **philanthropist** who paid for the new wing of the children's hospital.

   a. one who does things for love of humankind

   b. one who has limited financial resources

   c. one who has great interest in medical research

   d. one who has had a serious illness

VOCABULARY PRACTICE: FIGURATIVE LANGUAGE EXERCISES

Directions:

- Each sentence below from a college textbook contains a *figure of speech (italicized, like this).* Read each sentence. Answer the questions that follow each sentence.
- Remember that to answer the last question for each item correctly, you must *interpret* the meaning of the figurative language.

When I saw the truck coming toward me in my lane, I felt fear wash over me *like a tidal wave.*

_____ **1.** What two things are being compared?

   a.   a truck and a tidal wave

   b.   a truck and fear

   c.   the person and a truck

   d.   fear and a tidal wave

_____ **2.** How are they alike?

   a.   Both are unusual.

   b.   Both are overwhelming.

   c.   Both are temporary.

   d.   Both pertain to water.

_____ **3.** How should this simile be interpreted?

   a.   The driver felt terrified.

   b.   The driver felt irritated.

   c.   The driver felt relieved.

   d.   The driver felt wet.

My supervisor refused to let me have Saturday off to go to my family reunion. Her *heart is a stone!*

_____ **4.** What two things are being compared?

   a.   a family reunion and the supervisor's heart

   b.   the supervisor's heart and a stone

   c.   a stone and a supervisor

   d.   the supervisor and the family

_____ **5.** How are they alike?

   a.   Both are hard and unyielding.

   b.   Both are alive.

   c.   Both are broken.

   d.   Both are attending a reunion.

_____ **6.** How should this metaphor be interpreted?
- *a.* The supervisor is hard-hearted.
- *b.* The family reunion is Saturday.
- *c.* The supervisor dislikes family reunions.
- *d.* The speaker is hard-hearted.

If I lived in Hawaii, I'd go to the beach and *spend 24 hours a day on my surfboard!*

_____ **7.** What is the hyperbole (exaggeration)?
- *a.* living in Hawaii
- *b.* spending 24 hours a day on a surfboard
- *c.* going to the beach
- *d.* knowing how to surf

_____ **8.** How should this hyperbole be interpreted?
- *a.* The person loves to surf.
- *b.* The person wants to live in Hawaii.
- *c.* The person has a lot of free time.
- *d.* The person wants to learn to surf.

The fax machine *went crazy and spit* paper all over the floor.

_____ **9.** What is being given human traits?
- *a.* fax machine
- *b.* paper
- *c.* floor
- *d.* all of the above

_____ **10.** How should this personification be interpreted?
- *a.* The fax machine made strange noises.
- *b.* The floor was covered with paper.
- *c.* The fax machine stopped.
- *d.* The fax machine malfunctioned.

Pat's cousin is *as tall as a telephone pole.*

_____ **11.** What two things are being compared?
- *a.* Pat and her cousin
- *b.* Pat's cousin and a telephone pole
- *c.* Pat and a telephone pole
- *d.* all of the above

12. How are they alike?

  a. Both are tall.

  b. Both have excellent posture.

  c. Both like to talk on the telephone.

  d. Both work for the phone company.

13. How should this simile be interpreted?

  a. Pat is very tall.

  b. Pat's cousin is very tall.

  c. A telephone pole is very tall.

  d. A telephone pole is very straight.

The twin sisters are *as alike* as *mirror images.*

14. What is being compared?

  a. twin sisters

  b. a set of twin sisters and mirror images

  c. twins and sisters

  d. mirror images

15. How are they alike?

  a. They have similar personalities.

  b. They are identical in appearance.

  c. They often behave in the same manner.

  d. They have similar beliefs.

16. How should this metaphor be interpreted?

  a. The twins are identical twins.

  b. The sisters are looking in the mirror.

  c. The sisters are twins.

  d. Mirror images are identical.

After I received an "A" on my history test, I picked up my books and *danced all the way home!*

17. What is the hyperbole (exaggeration)?

  a. receiving an "A" on my history test

  b. picking up my books

  c. dancing all the way home

  d. all of the above

_____ **18.** How should this hyperbole be interpreted?

 a. The person is an excellent student.

 b. The person likes history.

 c. The person was very excited about the history test grade.

 d. The person loves to dance.

Opportunity knocks on everyone's door at least once.

_____ **19.** What is being given human traits?

 a. opportunity

 b. the door

 c. everyone

 d. all of the above

_____ **20.** How should this personification be interpreted?

 a. Some people never have a good opportunity in life.

 b. There are only a few opportunities in each person's life.

 c. No one deserves more than one opportunity in his or her lifetime.

 d. Everybody receives at least one good opportunity during his or her life.

SHOULD TEENAGERS WORK PART-TIME?

From *Human Development*
By Diane E. Papalia and Sally Olds

Did you have a part-time job when you were in high school? If so, you are very typical: eight out of every ten American teenagers have jobs at some point during their school years. Did you work because of necessity or simply to have some spending money? Was the work itself a valuable experience?

According to a report from the National Research Council and the Institute of Medicine, teens who work more than 20 hours per week after school are less likely to finish high school and more likely to use drugs. This was true, regardless of the teens' economic background. The report also noted that young people are injured at work at twice the rate of adults: Approximately 100,000 teens wind up in hospital emergency rooms each year with job-related injuries. Other experts point out, however, that having a job teaches punctuality, money management, and how to work effectively with others. Obviously, there is more than one side to this issue. The selection below, from a human development textbook, presents both positive and negative effects of part-time work on teenage students.

---

1   Many teenage students today hold part-time jobs. This trend conforms to the American belief of the moral benefits derived from working. However, some research challenges the value of part-time work for teenage students who do not have to work to help support their families. Let's look at both sides of the issue.

2   On the *positive* side, paid work is generally believed to teach young people to handle money responsibly. It helps them develop good work habits, such as promptness, reliability, and efficient management of time

3   A good part-time job helps a teenager assume responsibility and work with people of different ages and backgrounds. It enables an adolescent to learn workplace skills, such as how to find a job and how to get along with employers, co-workers, and sometimes the public. By helping a young person learn more about a particular field of work, it may guide her or him in choosing a career. Furthermore, by showing adolescents how demanding and difficult the world of work is and how unprepared they are for it, part-time jobs, especially menial ones, sometimes motivate young people to continue their education.

4   On the *negative* side, research has questioned the benefits of part-time work and has identified serious costs. Most high school students who work part-time have low-level, repetitive jobs in which they do not learn skills useful later in life. Teenagers who work are no more independent in making financial decisions and are not likely to earn any more money as adults than those who do not hold jobs during high school.

| **Prediction Exercises** |

Directions: Use the skill of predicting to anticipate what the upcoming paragraphs will be about.

| **Prediction Exercise** |

What do you *predict* the next few paragraphs will be about?

_____

_____

5   Outside work seems to undermine performance in school, especially for teenagers who work more than 15 to 20 hours per week. Grades, involvement in school, and attendance decline. Students who work more than 15 hours a week are more likely to drop out of school and thus to be less prepared for careers and for life.

6   There are several drawbacks to working while you are a student. Young people who work long hours are less likely to eat breakfast, exercise, get enough sleep, or have enough leisure time. They spend less time with their families and may feel less close to them. They have little contact with adults on the job, and their jobs usually reinforce gender stereotypes. Some teenagers spend their earnings on alcohol or drugs, develop cynical attitudes toward work, and cheat or steal from their employers.

7   However, some of these undesirable effects may result, not from working itself, but from the factors that motivate some teenagers to take jobs. Some may want to work because they are already uninterested in school or feel alienated from their families or because they want money to buy whatever they want. Jobs may actually help keep such young people out of trouble by providing legal ways for them to earn money.

Prediction Exercise

What do you *predict* the next few paragraphs will be about?

_____

_____

Source: Adapted from Diane E. Papalia and Sally Olds, *Human Development,* 7th ed., p. 360. Copyright © 1998 McGraw-Hill. Reprinted by permission of The McGraw-Hill Companies.

HUMAN
DEVELOPMENT

Comprehension and Vocabulary Quiz

This quiz has four parts. Your instructor may assign some or all of them.

Comprehension

Directions: Items 1–5 test your comprehension (understanding) of the material in this selection. These questions are much like those that a content area instructor (such as a psychology professor) would expect you to know after studying this selection. For each comprehension question below, use information from the selection to determine the correct answer. Refer to the selection as you answer the questions. Write your answer in the space provided.

_____ **1.** A good part-time job helps a teenager
    a. become independent from his or her parents.
    b. spend more time with his or her family.
    c. learn workplace skills such as how to get along with employers and co-workers.
    d. decide whether or not to continue his or her education.

_____ **2.** A negative aspect of teenagers working part-time is that it
    a. interferes with their social life.
    b. seems to hurt their academic performance.
    c. causes them to sleep too much on weekends.
    d. prohibits any participation in athletic events.

_____ **3.** Which of the following is a benefit of teenagers working?
    a. may teach them how to handle money responsibly
    b. encourages the development of good work habits
    c. allows them to assume responsibility
    d. all of the above

_____ **4.** Based on information in this selection we can conclude that
    a. teenagers should not work part-time.
    b. teenagers should work part-time.
    c. a teenager's parents should decide whether their child should work part-time.
    d. whether teenagers should work part-time when they don't have to is a complex issue.

_____ **5.** Teenagers who work more than 15 hours per week
    a. are more likely to drop out of school.
    b. cause more discipline problems at school.
    c. are more likely to save money for their college education.
    d. tend to cheat their employers or steal from them.

Vocabulary in Context

Directions: Items 6–10 test your ability to determine the meaning of a word by using context clues. *Context clues* are words in a sentence that allow the reader to deduce (reason out) the meaning of an unfamiliar word in that sentence. Context clues also enable the reader to determine which meaning the author intends when a word has more than one meaning. For each vocabulary item below, a sentence from the selection containing an important word (*italicized, like this*) is quoted first. Next, there is an additional sentence using the word in the same sense and providing another context clue. Use the context clues from *both* sentences to deduce the meaning of the italicized word. *Be sure the answer you choose makes sense in both sentences.* If you discover that you need to use a dictionary to confirm an answer choice, remember that the meaning you select must still fit the context of *both* sentences. Write your answer in the space provided.

Pronunciation Key: ă pat   ā pay   âr care   ä father   ĕ pet   ē be   ĭ pit
ī tie   îr **pier**   ŏ pot   ō toe   ô paw   oi noise   ou **out**   ŏŏ took   ōō boot
ŭ cut   yōō abuse   ûr **urge**   th thin   *th* **this**   hw **which**   zh vision
ə **about**   Stress mark: ′

_____   **6.** This trend *conforms* to the American belief of the moral benefits derived from working.

Nicole *conforms* to her school's dress code, but she complains constantly about the uniform they must wear.

conforms (kən fôrmz′)

　　a.　complies with
　　b.　resents strongly
　　c.　dislikes intensely
　　d.　enjoys

_____   **7.** This trend conforms to the American belief of the moral benefits *derived* from working.

Residents at the nursing home *derived* great pleasure from visits by college-age volunteers.

derived (dĭ rīvd′)

　　a.　prevented
　　b.　suffered
　　c.　obtained
　　d.　avoided

_____   **8.** Furthermore, by showing adolescents how demanding and difficult the world of work is and how unprepared they are for it, part-time jobs, especially *menial* ones, sometimes motivate young people to continue their education.

Because Marcos was hired as a waiter, he resented having to do *menial* tasks such as sweeping the floor and refilling salt and pepper shakers.

menial (mē′ nē əl)

a. time-consuming

b. suitable for a servant

c. feminine

d. challenging

_____   **9.** Outside work seems to *undermine* performance in school, especially for teenagers who work more than 15 to 20 hours per week.

Not scheduling sufficient study time will *undermine* a college student's chance of success.

undermine (ŭn′ dər mīn)

a. weaken

b. ruin

c. defeat

d. enhance

_____   **10.** Some teenagers spend their earnings on alcohol or drugs, develop *cynical* attitudes toward work, and cheat or steal from their employers.

Adolescents whose parents have divorced sometimes become *cynical* about marriage.

cynical (sĭn′ ĭ kəl)

a. elated

b. curious

c. eager

d. scornful

Word Structure

Directions: Items 11–15 test your ability to use word-structure clues to help determine a word's meaning. *Word-structure clues* consist of roots, prefixes, and suffixes. In these exercises, you will learn the meaning of a word part (root) and use it to determine the meaning of the several other words that have the same word part. If you discover that you need to use a dictionary to confirm an answer choice, do so. Write your answer in the space provided.

In paragraph 7 of the selection you encountered the word *factors.* This word contains the Latin root *fac,* which means "make" or "do." In this selection, *factor* means something that "*makes* an active contribution to an accomplishment, result, or process." Use the meaning of *fac* and the list of prefixes on pages 60–61 to help you determine the meaning of each of the following words that contain this same root.

_____ **11.** A **factory** is a place where things are

     a. bought.

     b. sold.

     c. traded.

     d. made.

_____ **12.** To feel **satisfaction** means to feel

     a. content.

     b. angry.

     c. silly.

     d. ill.

_____ **13.** To **manufacture** items is to

     a. produce them.

     b. recycle them.

     c. collect them.

     d. donate them.

_____ **14.** In comic books and cartoons, **malefactors** are characters who

     a. are superheroes.

     b. do criminal or evil things.

     c. are able to change form.

     d. are disguised as animals.

_____ **15.** A **benefactor** is a person who

     a. inherits money.

     b. reads widely.

     c. does good by giving money.

     d. grows abundant crops.

Reading Skills Application

Directions: Items 16–20 test your ability to apply certain reading skills to the material in this selection. These are the types of questions that might appear on standardized reading tests and state-mandated basic skills tests. Write your answer in the space provided.

_____ **16.** Which of the following statements best expresses the main idea of the paragraph 6?

a. There are several drawbacks to working while you are a student.

b. Young people who work long hours are less likely to eat breakfast, exercise, get enough sleep, or have enough leisure time.

c. They spend less time with their families and may feel less close to them.

d. They have little contact with adults on the job, and their jobs usually reinforce gender stereotypes.

_____ **17.** The author has used which of these patterns to organize the information in the selection?

a. a contrast between the advantages and disadvantages of teenagers working part-time

b. the causes of teenagers working part-time

c. a sequence of reactions of teenagers to working part-time

d. a list of the ways teenagers benefit from working part-time

_____ **18.** Which of the following is not mentioned as a drawback to teenagers who work part-time?

a. spending less time with their families and feeling less close to them

b. being less likely to get enough sleep

c. developing cynical attitudes toward work

d. not being able to meet and make new friends

_____ **19.** Which of the following statements represents an accurate assessment of the author's objectivity?

a. The author is biased in favor of teenagers working part-time.

b. The author is biased against teenagers working part-time.

c. The author presents both sides of the issue objectively.

d. It is not possible to evaluate the author's objectivity.

_____ **20.** What is the meaning of *demanding* as it is used in paragraph 3 of the selection?

a. requiring much effort

b. highly interesting

c. frustrating

d. exhausting

Writing and Collaborating to Enhance Your Understanding

Option for collaboration: Your instructor may direct you to work with other students or, in other words, to work *collaboratively.* In that case, you should form groups of three or four students as directed by your instructor and work together to complete the exercises. After your group discusses each item and agrees on the answer, have a group member record it. Every member of your group should be able to explain all of your group's answers.

1. **Reacting to What You Have Read:** In this selection the authors look at both sides of the issue of students working part-time when it is not a financial necessity. Which side of the issue do you support? Give the reasons you think high school students should or should not work part-time.

    _____

    _____

    _____

    _____

2. **Comprehending the Selection Further:** Many college students work part-time (or even full-time!), but how much is *too* much? What, in your opinion, is the maximum number of hours per week a full-time college student should attempt to work? In your opinion, what are the worst kinds of jobs for college students? What are the best kinds of jobs for them? (Be sure to answer all of these questions.)

    _____

    _____

    _____

    _____

3. **Overall Main Idea of the Selection:** In one sentence tell what the authors want readers to understand about teenagers working part-time. (Be sure to include the words "teenagers working part-time" in your overall main idea sentence.)

    _____

    _____

    _____

    _____

Read More about It on the World Wide Web

To learn more about the topic of this selection, visit these websites or use your favorite search engine (such as Yahoo®) to discover more about these authors and this topic on your own. Whenever you go to *any* website, it is a good idea to evaluate it critically. Are you getting good information—that is, information that is accurate, complete, and up-to-date? Who sponsors the website? How easy is it to use the features of the website?

http://www.todaysteensinc.com/about_us.htm

http://netec.wustl.edu/WoPEc/data/Papers/dgrkubcen199643.html

SELECTION **2-2**
BUSINESS

MCDONALDIZATION: THE SUN NEVER SETS ON THE GOLDEN ARCHES

From *Understanding Business*

By William G. Nickels, James M. McHugh, and Susan M. McHugh

Nearly everyone in America—certainly every child—recognizes McDonald's "golden arches." This business textbook selection explains why McDonald's is the premier example of a global franchiser: McDonald's has been supremely successful in tailoring its outlets to the values of the countries in which its franchised restaurants are located. (A franchiser is a company that sells people the right to offer its products or services in a given territory.) Also, it will help you to know that the word "abroad" means "in a foreign country" or "not of one's own country."

About the title: There was once a famous saying, "The sun never sets on the British Empire." The British Empire began in the 16th century, and at the height of its glory (around 1900), it included Australia, Canada, India, New Zealand, extensive portions of Africa, and many smaller territories throughout the world. In other words, the British Empire was so vast and extended to so many parts of the globe that it was always daytime somewhere in the empire. The authors of this selection have entitled it, "The Sun Never Sets on the Golden Arches" to suggest the global vastness of McDonald's "empire." They have 30,000 restaurants in 121 countries.

1   The tremendous expansion of franchising, led by the U.S. companies, has changed the landscape of the global market. Today small, midsize, and large franchises cover the globe, offering business opportunities in areas from exercise to education. Still, when the word *franchise* comes to mind, one name dominates all others: "McDonaldization" symbolizes the spread of franchising and the weaving of American pop culture into the world fabric. Whether in South Africa, Mexico, Germany, or Hong Kong, no one adapts better and blends the franchise values into the local culture better than McDonald's.

2   For example, after setting up its first franchises in Hong Kong in 1975, McDonald's altered the breakfast menu after realizing that customers there liked burgers for breakfast, then preferred chicken or fish for the rest of the day. The company also found that it was advisable to keep napkin dispensers away from the customers. It seems that older people in Hong Kong who went through hard times after World War II took huge wads of napkins from the holders and stuffed them in their pockets. Now it's one napkin per customer. McDonald's even spruced up the notoriously dirty toilet facilities that were a negative trademark of Hong Kong restaurants.

3   In Hong Kong, as in all markets in which it operates, the company continuously listens to customers and adapts to their preferences. For example, McDonald's quickly responded to Hong Kong customers' anxious appetite for promotions. Recently, to the delight of Hong

Prediction Exercises

Directions: Use the skill of predicting to anticipate what the upcoming paragraphs will be about.

Prediction Exercise

What do you *predict* the next paragraph will be about?

_____

_____

_____

_____

Competition today is global. That means that companies from all over the world can compete in the United States, just as U.S. firms seek new markets beyond our borders. This McDonald's restaurant, for example, is in Moscow. McDonald's actually sells more hamburgers and fries in other countries than it does in the United States, and their expansion internationally is also faster. *(Les Stone/ CORBIS SYGMA)*

Kong customers, McDonald's offered popular Japanese cat figures called Hello Kitty dolls as a follow-up to a very popular Snoopy doll promotion. Even executives at high-tech companies and leading financiers gladly waited in line for the Hello Kitty dolls coveted by their children. Hong Kong children also cannot wait to visit "Suk-Suk" McDonald (Uncle Ronald McDonald) on their birthdays, since the company began to tout such events on local television. The company also encourages college students in Hong Kong to use the local McDonald's as a place to socialize and study.

4   By using adaptive strategies in global markets, McDonald's reaps a large payoff. The company today derives more than half of its $72 billion in sales from abroad. Hong Kong actually boasts two of the world's busiest McDonald's, and about half of the city's 6.8 million people eat at a McDonald's restaurant every week. James L. Watson, a Harvard University anthropologist, perhaps said it best: "McDonald's has become a very important part of global culture. The company's efforts involving hygiene in its restrooms is just one example. Their efforts caused other restaurants to follow the lead. That's not bad diplomacy."

Prediction Exercise

What do you *predict* the next paragraph will be about?

_____

_____

_____

_____

Source: Adapted from William G. Nickels, James M. McHugh, and Susan M. McHugh, *Understanding Business,* 6th ed., p. 69. Copyright © 2002 McGraw-Hill. Reprinted by permission of The McGraw-Hill Companies.

BUSINESS

Comprehension and Vocabulary Quiz

This quiz has four parts. Your instructor may assign some or all of them.

Comprehension

Directions: Items 1–5 test your comprehension (understanding) of the material in this selection. These questions are much like those that a content area instructor (such as a business professor) would expect you to know after studying this selection. For each comprehension question below, use information from the selection to determine the correct answer. Refer to the selection as you answer the questions. Write your answer in the space provided.

_____ 1. In 1975 McDonald's franchises in Hong Kong changed their breakfast menu because
   a. they discovered customers preferred chicken and fish instead of burgers.
   b. they realized customers liked burgers for breakfast.
   c. their prices were too high.
   d. French fries and milkshakes did not fit the local culture.

_____ 2. A large part of McDonald's success as a global franchiser results from
   a. the appeal of low-priced fast food.
   b. improving the hygiene in its restrooms.
   c. the popularity of "McDonaldization."
   d. adapting to customer preferences.

_____ 3. How much of McDonald's total sales come from abroad?
   a. $72 billion
   b. $6.8 million
   c. more than half of its total sales
   d. a relatively small portion of its total sales

_____ 4. McDonald's has become a tremendous success in Hong Kong because
   a. it has responded to Hong Kong customers' love of promotions like the Hello Kitty dolls and the Snoopy doll.
   b. it knows how to blend American pop culture with the local culture.
   c. It encourages college students to use the restaurants as a place to socialize and study.
   d. all of the above

_____ 5. Today, McDonald's
   a. is expanding internationally faster than it is expanding in the United States.
   b. has restaurants in virtually every country in the world.
   c. changes its menus often in order to spread American pop culture.
   d. is a leader in international diplomacy.

Vocabulary in Context

Directions: Items 6–10 test your ability to determine the meaning of a word by using context clues. *Context clues* are words in a sentence that allow the reader to deduce (reason out) the meaning of an unfamiliar word in that sentence. Context clues also enable the reader to determine which meaning the author intends when a word has more than one meaning. For each vocabulary item below, a sentence from the selection containing an important word (*italicized, like this*) is quoted first. Next, there is an additional sentence using the word in the same sense and providing another context clue. Use the context clues from *both* sentences to deduce the meaning of the italicized word. *Be sure the answer you choose makes sense in both sentences.* If you discover that you need to use a dictionary to confirm an answer choice, remember that the meaning you select must still fit the context of *both* sentences. Write your answer in the space provided.

Pronunciation Key: ă pat   ā pay   âr care   ä father   ĕ pet   ē be   ĭ pit
ī tie   îr **pier**   ŏ pot   ō toe   ô paw   oi noise   ou **out**   ŏŏ took   ōō boot
ŭ cut   yōō abuse   ûr **urge**   th **thin**   *th* **this**   hw **which**   zh vision
ə **about**   Stress mark: ´

6. Whether in South Africa, Mexico, Germany, or Hong Kong, no one *adapts* better and blends the franchise values into the local culture better than McDonald's.

Philip is a popular speaker because he always *adapts* his presentation to the particular audience to whom he is speaking.

adapts (ə dăpts´)

a. reveals

b. stumbles through

c. explains carefully

d. adjusts according to circumstances

7. Hong Kong children also cannot wait to visit "Suk-Suk" McDonald (Uncle Ronald McDonald) on their birthdays, since the company began to *tout* such events on local television.

The movie studio has planned a multimillion dollar advertising campaign to *tout* its new science fiction thriller.

tout (tout)

a. to cancel without prior notice

b. to publicize loudly or extravagantly

c. to sponsor

d. to recall

_____ **8.** By using such adaptive strategies in global markets, McDonald's *reaps* a large payoff.

A person who lies invariably *reaps* the consequences.

reaps (rēps)

  a. to avoid by using deception
  b. to misunderstand
  c. to obtain in return
  d. to suffer

_____ **9.** The company today *derives* more than half of its $72 billion in sales from abroad.

A typical volunteer *derives* great satisfaction from doing charitable work.

derives (dĭ rīvs′)

  a. to spend
  b. to receive
  c. to give up
  d. to save

_____ **10.** James L. Watson, a Harvard University *anthropologist,* perhaps said it best: "McDonald's has become a very important part of global culture."

Because of her interests in various cultures of the world, Marie decided to become an anthropologist.

anthropologist (ăn thrə pŏl′ ə jĭst)

  a. one who studies the development and behavior of humans and their cultures
  b. one who studies the development of towns and cities
  c. one who studies ancient manuscripts
  d. one who studies the behavior of bees and ants

Word Structure

Directions: Items 11–15 test your ability to use word-structure clues to help determine a word's meaning. *Word-structure clues* consist of roots, prefixes, and suffixes. In these exercises, you will learn the meaning of a word part (root) and use it to determine the meaning of the several other words that have the same word part. If you discover that you need to use a dictionary to confirm an answer choice, do so. Write your answer in the space provided.

In paragraph 3 of the selection you encountered the word **promotions.** This word contains the Latin root **mot,** which means "to move" or "motion." The word *promotions* refers to methods of "moving" merchandise (increasing sales of merchandise) through advertising, publicity, or discounting. Use the meaning of ***mot*** and the list of prefixes on pages 60–61 to help you determine the meaning of each of the following words that contain this same root.

_____ **11.** If a person in the military is **demoted,** he or she
    a.   stays at the same rank for an unusually long period of time.
    b.   is moved to a lower rank.
    c.   is moved to a higher rank.
    d.   is forced to withdraw completely from the military.

_____ **12.** A **remote** control allows you to change TV channels
    a.   by pressing buttons on the TV set.
    b.   through preprogramming the VCR.
    c.   without having to get up and move to the TV set itself.
    d.   after consulting the TV schedule.

_____ **13.** If there is a **commotion,** there is
    a.   an all-night party going on.
    b.   agitated movement or a disturbance of some sort.
    c.   a loud, noisy celebration.
    d.   a bus or a train going by.

_____ **14.** **Emotion** refers to
    a.   the moving or stirring up of feelings.
    b.   feelings that are dormant.
    c.   feelings that are not apparent or obvious.
    d.   the suppression or control of feelings.

_____ **15.** A **motive**
    a.   prevents an action from occurring.
    b.   causes an action to stop.
    c.   slows down a process.
    d.   moves a person to do something.

Reading Skills Application

Directions: Items 16–20 test your ability to apply certain reading skills to the material in this selection. These are the types of questions that might appear on standardized reading tests and state-mandated basic skills tests. Write your answer in the space provided.

_____ **16.** In paragraph 2 of the selection, *spruced up* means
    a.   to neaten in appearance.
    b.   to decorate with trees.
    c.   to enlarge or expand.
    d.   to seal up or close.

_____ **17.** Based on the material presented in the selection, which of the following is a logical conclusion?

    a. McDonald's is the most successful company in the world.

    b. McDonald's franchises were more difficult to establish in Hong Kong than in other foreign cities.

    c. Toy giveaways and other similar promotions are the key to McDonald's worldwide success.

    d. Other companies who want to offer international franchises could benefit from emulating McDonald's adaptability.

_____ **18.** What pattern is used to organize the information in paragraph 4 of the selection?

    a. comparison and contrast

    b. cause and effect

    c. sequence

    d. list

_____ **19.** Which of the following statements best expresses the main idea of paragraph 4?

    a. By using adaptive strategies in global markets, McDonald's reaps a large payoff.

    b. Hong Kong actually boasts two of the world's busiest McDonald's, and about half of the city's 6.8 million people eat at a McDonald's restaurant every week.

    c. James L. Watson, a Harvard University anthropologist, perhaps said it best: "McDonalds's has become a very important part of global culture."

    d. The company's efforts involving hygiene in its restrooms is just one example.

_____ **20.** Which of the following statements represents an opinion rather than a fact?

    a. The company today derives more than half of its $72 billion in sales from abroad.

    b. Hong Kong actually boasts two of the world's busiest McDonald's, and about half of the city's 6.8 million people eat at a McDonald's restaurant every week.

    c. "Their efforts caused other restaurants to follow the lead."

    d. "That's not bad diplomacy."

Writing and Collaborating to Enhance Your Understanding

Option for collaboration: Your instructor may direct you to work with other students or, in other words, to work *collaboratively.* In that case, you should form groups of three or four students as directed by your instructor and work together to complete the exercises. After your group discusses each item and agrees on the answer, have a group member record it. Every member of your group should be able to explain all of your group's answers.

1. **Reacting to What You Have Read:** Have you ever visited a McDonald's restaurant in some other city, state, or country? If so, there were probably some differences between that franchise and the one you frequent near your home or school. Describe some of the ways you observed that McDonald's franchisers adapted their menus and their restaurants to the local culture. If you have not visited McDonald's in other locations, describe the general types of adaptations you *think* franchisers could make.

   _____

   _____

   _____

   _____

   _____

   _____

   _____

2. **Comprehending the Selection Further:** List some of the "lessons" McDonald's franchisers learned about attracting customers in Hong Kong.

   _____

   _____

   _____

   _____

   _____

   _____

   _____

   _____

3. **Overall Main Idea of the Selection:** In one sentence tell what the author wants readers to understand about the success of McDonald's international franchises. (Be sure to include the phrase "the success of McDonald's international franchises" in your overall main idea sentence.)

_____

_____

_____

_____

_____

Read More about It on the World Wide Web

To learn more about the topic of this selection, visit these websites or use your favorite search engine (such as Yahoo®) to discover more about these authors and this topic on your own. Whenever you go to _any_ website, it is a good idea to evaluate it critically. Are you getting good information—that is, information that is accurate, complete, and up-to-date? Who sponsors the website? How easy is it to use the features of the website?

http://www.mcdonalds.com
http://www.franchiserestaurant.com
http://www.globalhawaii.org

SELECTION **2-3**

HEALTH

RAGE ON THE ROAD: THE DANGER OF AGGRESSIVE DRIVING

From *Understanding Your Health*

By Wayne Payne and Dale Hahn

Nationwide today, men spend an average of 84 minutes per day behind the wheel and women spend an average of 64 minutes. That much time on the road can lead to some frustrating moments.

Have you ever been the victim of an aggressive driver? If so, that person may have been expressing "road rage." And if you got angry in return, you may also have felt road rage. This selection from a health textbook addresses the increase in aggressive driving. It also explains what you can do to avoid feeling road rage yourself and provoking aggressive behavior in other drivers.

1   Motorists are aware of an increasing sense of aggression on America's congested highways. An unthinking act or no provocation at all can result in a deadly face-off with a complete stranger. Over the last six years, aggressive drivers have killed 218 people and injured another 12,610, at a frequency that increases about 7 percent each year. This is just the tip of the iceberg. For every incident serious enough to result in a police report or newspaper story, hundreds or thousands of other incidents take place that are never reported. The problem has become so bad that, according to a National Highway Safety Administration report, the public is more concerned about aggressive drivers (40%) than drunk drivers (33%).

Characteristics of Aggressive Drivers

2   Although there is no profile *per se* of the typical aggressive driver, most aggressive drivers are men between the ages of 18 and 26. Many of these men are poorly educated, and some have criminal records or histories of violence and substance abuse, but hundreds of others are successful men and women, of all ages, with no such history.

3   Between the sexes, men are angered most by police presence and slow driving, whereas illegal behavior and traffic obstructions tend to frustrate women. When all factors are added in, though, men and women do not differ in total driving anger scores. Increasingly, women are acting on their anger. Only 4 percent of recorded aggressive driving incidents involved women drivers, but during the last 15 years the number of fatal accidents involving women drivers has increased dramatically while men's risks have dropped. Most of the increase for women has occurred because more women are on the road at riskier times, but women are also increasingly displaying the more aggressive driving tactics common among men.

Prediction Exercises

Directions: Use the skill of predicting to anticipate what the three subsections of this selection will be about. Use the subheadings to help you.

Prediction Exercise

You have read the first paragraph. What do you predict the next section will be about?

_____

_____

The stress of home, work, and commuting; the anonymity of driving; and other factors can add up to rage on the road. (*FPG International*)

4   Individually, people generally think of themselves as better-than-average drivers. This holds true even among younger people, who consider themselves to be good drivers but their peers to be the worst drivers of any age group. But perceptions and reality are not always identical. While some people are aware of their aggressive tendencies on the road, other people see themselves as innocent and the issue of aggressive driving as everyone else's problem. The truth is we're all human and can let our emotions run away from us.

Causes of Aggressive Driving

5   Violent traffic disputes result not from single incidents but from personal attitudes and accumulated stress in motorists' lives. Specifically, drug use; domestic arguments or violence; racism; the desire to evade or attack police; and the everyday stresses of home, work, and commuting can lead to aggressive driving. For the general population, the anonymity and physical excitement of driving, combined with a feeling of control and power and the ability to drive away, sow the seeds of aggression. Some people drive to "win" rather than to arrive safely at their destination. Adding to this climate are overpowered cars, driver's licenses that are easy to qualify for, and sporadically lax enforcement of traffic laws.

Ways to Avoid Provoking Aggressive Drivers

6   The best way to stay out of driving conflicts is not to be an aggressive driver yourself. You can do a number of things to reduce your stress and thus reduce the ten-

Prediction Exercise

What do you predict this subsection will be about?

_____

_____

_____

Prediction Exercise

What do you predict this subsection will be about?

_____

_____

dency toward aggression. First, allow plenty of time for your trip. We tend to overschedule our days and not allow enough time to get from one place to the next. Sure, under perfect conditions you could cover X number of miles in X amount of time, but weather, traffic, and road construction are facts of life. Not building extra travel time into our schedules causes us to run late when we encounter these variables and then get angry and possibly aggressive. Other ways to reduce stress are to listen to soothing music, improve the comfort of your vehicle, and probably, most of all, understand that you can't control the traffic—only your reaction to it.

7   Practice driving courtesy and keep the following points in mind:

- Do not make obscene gestures.
- Use your horn sparingly.
- Do not block the passing lane.
- Do not switch lanes without signaling.
- Do not block the right-hand turn lane.
- Do not take more than one parking space.
- If you are not disabled, do not park in a space reserved for disabled people.
- Do not allow your door to hit the car parked next to you.
- Do not tailgate.
- If you travel slowly, pull over and allow traffic to pass.
- Avoid unnecessary use of high-beam headlights.
- Do not let the car phone distract you.
- Do not stop in the road to talk to a pedestrian or another driver.
- Do not inflict loud music on neighboring cars.

8   Avoid engaging other drivers by following the limousine drivers' rule: Duty bound to protect their passengers, they do not make eye contact with other drivers. If another driver is following you, don't drive home. Instead, drive to a public place, ideally a police station. This or using your cell phone to call for help is usually enough to scare off the offending driver.

9   Of course, it's hard not to respond when challenged. It may help to look at the other driver's mistakes and actions objectively and not take them personally. Leave their poor behavior as their problem; don't make it yours. Remember how dangerous the situation can become.

10   It's not one driver's job to teach other drivers proper manners. In all certainty, you won't be successful. Instead, try being extra nice to a fellow driver. Courtesy can be as contagious as aggression.

Source: Wayne Payne and Dale Hahn, *Understanding Your Health,* 5th ed., pp. 604–607. Copyright © 1998 McGraw-Hill. Reprinted by permission of The McGraw-Hill Companies.

Comprehension and Vocabulary Quiz

This quiz has four parts. Your instructor may assign some or all of them.

Comprehension

Directions: Items 1–5 test your comprehension (understanding) of the material in this selection. These questions are much like those that a content area instructor (such as a psychology professor) would expect you to know after studying this selection. For each comprehension question below, use information from the selection to determine the correct answer. Refer to the selection as you answer the questions. Write your answer in the space provided.

1. Statistics show that aggressive driving is common, but the problem may be worse than we think because
   a. young drivers have less experience than in the past.
   b. many aggressive driving incidents are never reported.
   c. many drivers are killed every year.
   d. aggressive drivers often go unnoticed.

2. The typical aggressive driver is a
   a. man with a criminal record.
   b. young man or woman between the ages of 16 and 18.
   c. man between the ages of 18 and 26.
   d. young man who is frustrated.

3. Aggressive women drivers tend to become frustrated by
   a. slow driving and the presence of police.
   b. illegal behavior and traffic obstructions.
   c. speed limits and traffic rules.
   d. the presence of children in the car.

4. The best way to avoid driving conflicts is to
   a. observe all traffic rules and speed limits.
   b. not be an aggressive driver yourself.
   c. avoid tailgating and travel slowly and cautiously.
   d. not inflict loud music on neighboring cars.

5. One way to reduce your own chances of becoming an aggressive driver is to
   a. allow plenty of time for your trips.
   b. maintain eye contact with other drivers.
   c. report drivers who disregard traffic rules.
   d. travel slowly and stay in the right-hand lane.

2

A New World of Understanding

Using Core Comprehension Skills When You Read College Textbooks

CHAPTERS IN PART TWO

(© Malcolm Donbar/Hulton Archive/Getty Images)

CHAPTER 3

Determining the Topic

In this chapter you will learn:

- What the topic of a paragraph is and why it is important to understand it.

- What the four clues are for determining the topic of a paragraph.

CONTENTS

What Is the Topic of a Paragraph, and Why Is It Important to Determine and Understand It?

What Are the Clues for Determining the Topic of a Paragraph?

- Clue 1: Look for a Heading or Title That Indicates the Topic

- Clue 2: Look for a Word, Name, or Phrase in the Paragraph That Appears in Special Print

- Clue 3: Look for a Word, Name, or Phrase That Is Repeated throughout the Paragraph

- Clue 4: Look for a Word, Name, or Phrase Referred to throughout the Paragraph by Pronouns or Other Words

Other Things to Keep in Mind When Determining the Topic

- You should use a name, word, or phrase, but never a sentence, to express the topic.

- You must know the difference between "general" and "specific."

- A longer passage has an overall topic.

Developing Chapter Review Cards

Comprehension Practice: Determining the Topic Exercises (1)

Comprehension Practice: Determining the Topic Exercises (2)

Selection 3-1 *(Newspaper Article)*
"Too Many Students Cheat on Sleep"
by Nanci Hellmich

Selection 3-2 *(Human Development)*
"Is There a Better Way to Parent? A Look at Three Parenting Styles"
by Diane E. Papalia and Sally Olds

Selection 3-3 *(Speech Communication)*
"Giving a Speech? If You're Nervous, You're Normal!"
by Hamilton Gregory

WHAT IS THE TOPIC OF A PARAGRAPH, AND WHY IS IT IMPORTANT TO DETERMINE AND UNDERSTAND IT?

KEY TERM

topic

Word, name, or phrase that tells who or what the author is writing about.

The topic is also known as the *subject* or the *subject matter.*

Comprehension Monitoring Question for Topic

"Who or what is this paragraph about?"

Every paragraph is written about something. Whenever you write a paragraph, you have to decide who or what you want to write about. In other words, you have to select a topic. Every paragraph has a topic. The **topic** of a paragraph is a word, name, or phrase that tells who or what the author is writing about. All of the sentences in a paragraph relate in some way to the topic. The topic may be a name (such as *Oprah Winfrey* or *New York City* or *Napoleon*), a word (for instance, *cloning*), or a phrase (such as *good study habits* or *advantages of attending college*). In a writing course or an English course, your instructor may call the topic the *subject* or the *subject matter.*

Why is it important to determine the topic of a paragraph? It is important because determining the topic is the first step in comprehending a paragraph. (This will become clearer to you as you learn about main ideas in Chapters 4 and 5 of this book.) Determining the topic also helps you focus your attention on what you are reading.

After you have read a paragraph, determine its topic by asking yourself this comprehension-monitoring question "Who or what is this paragraph about?" If you answer the question correctly, you will have determined the topic. (Of course, you must understand the meaning of the word or phrase that tells the topic.)

WHAT ARE THE CLUES FOR DETERMINING THE TOPIC OF A PARAGRAPH?

Fortunately, college textbook paragraphs typically contain many clues to help you determine the topic. You can determine the topic of a textbook paragraph by taking advantage of one or more of these clues:

- The topic appears as a *heading,* or *title.*
- The topic appears in *special type* such as **bold print,** *italics,* or **color.**
- The topic *is repeated* throughout the paragraph.
- The topic appears once at the beginning and is then referred to throughout the paragraph by *pronouns* (or other words). (Pronouns are words such as *he, she, it, they,* etc.)

Typically, a paragraph does not have all of these clues, but all paragraphs have at least one of them. The following four examples are paragraphs from college textbooks. Each illustrates and explains one of the four clues that can help you determine the topic of a paragraph.

Clue 1: Look for a Heading or Title That Indicates the Topic

Pay attention to titles and headings because textbook authors often give the topic in the title or heading. Here is an excerpt from a human development textbook. It illustrates this clue (as well as some others). Read this paragraph and notice that its heading indicates its topic.

Marriage

Marriage customs differ widely, but the universality of some form of marriage throughout history and around the world shows that it meets a variety of fundamental needs. Marriage is usually considered the best way to ensure the orderly raising of children. One of its most important economic benefits is the provision for a division of labor within a consuming and working unit. Ideally, it offers intimacy, friendship, affection, sexual fulfillment, companionship, and an opportunity for emotional growth. The high divorce rates show how hard it is to attain these ideals, but the high remarriage rates show that people keep trying.

Source: From Diane Papalia and Sally Olds, *Human Development,* 6th ed. Copyright © 1995 McGraw-Hill. Reprinted by permission of The McGraw-Hill Companies.

Stop and Annotate

Go back to the textbook excerpt above. Underline or highlight the heading, which indicates the topic.

Notice how the heading of this paragraph tells its topic: *marriage.* The term *marriage* indicates the "what" that is discussed in the paragraph. The topic, marriage, is what all the sentences in this paragraph have in common. (Also notice that the word *marriage* is repeated three times in the paragraph and the word *remarriage* is also used.)

Although the heading of a textbook paragraph typically gives the topic, you should always read the entire paragraph carefully to be sure that the heading gives the topic completely and accurately. For example, by itself, a general heading such as *The Crisis* is not complete enough to indicate what a paragraph is about. The paragraph could be about an earthquake, a stock market crash, a political scandal, or some other type of "crisis." When the heading is inadequate, you must read the paragraph to determine the precise topic.

Clue 2: Look for a Word, Name, or Phrase in the Paragraph That Appears in Special Print

A second clue to the topic of a paragraph is the author's use of *italic* or **bold** print or **color** to emphasize a word, name, or phrase. The paragraph below is from a textbook on public speaking. Read this paragraph and notice that the word in italics indicates its topic.

The explosive growth of the World Wide Web is due largely to the development of graphical *browsers,* software that allows you to move easily among the millions of websites. By far the most popular browser is Netscape, which is used at most colleges and universities, though it is facing a stiff challenge from Microsoft's Internet Explorer. Commercial online services such as America Online and Juno offer their own browsers.

Source: Adapted from Stephen Lucas, *The Art of Public Speaking,* 6th ed., pp. 140–141. Copyright © 1998 McGraw-Hill. Reprinted by permission of The McGraw-Hill Companies.

Notice how the word in italics indicates the topic: *browsers.* (Notice also that the word *browsers* appears two more times in the paragraph.) The entire paragraph discusses *browsers,* software that makes it possible to move easily among millions of websites. Keep in mind that a topic can also appear in bold print, and that in many college textbooks such key words are printed in color.

Keep in mind, too, that the topic of a paragraph sometimes consists of a combination of words, or a combination of names, or even phrases. Your task is to identify these "pieces" and put them together to form the complete topic. For example, a paragraph from a health textbook might have the words *bulimia* and *anorexia* in special print. Both of them together would comprise the topic: *bulimia and anorexia.* Or a paragraph might repeatedly mention the names of two U.S. presidents, Bill Clinton and George W. Bush. The complete topic would be *Bill Clinton and George W. Bush.*

Also, be aware that while italics often signal the topic of a paragraph, they are also used by authors merely to show emphasis. For example, an author may put the word "except" or "not" in italics, such as in this sentence: "In general, it is *not* a good idea for college students to work more than 20 hours a week."

Clue 3: Look for a Word, Name, or Phrase That Is Repeated throughout the Paragraph

A third clue to the topic is the repetition of a word, name, or phrase in a paragraph. This clue is helpful when there is no heading and the paragraph does not contain any words in special print. (Even though the previous two examples illustrate other clues, they also illustrate this clue.) Read the paragraph below from a business management textbook. Notice the repeated words that indicate the topic.

> Reference checks are attempts to obtain job-related information about job applicants from individuals who are knowledgeable about the applicants' qualifications. Reference checks can be obtained by mail, by telephone, and in person. Such checks are conducted to verify information on application blanks and résumés and, sometimes, to collect additional data that will facilitate the selection decision. One reason for the widespread use of reference checks is that, according to one estimate, *between 20 and 25 percent* of all candidate application blanks and résumés contain at least one major fabrication.

Source: From Kathryn Bartol and David Martin, *Management,* 2nd ed. Copyright © 1994 McGraw-Hill. Reprinted by permission of The McGraw-Hill Companies.

Notice that the term *reference checks* appears three times in this paragraph, indicating that this is the topic of the paragraph. In addition, when the authors mention "such checks" in the third sentence, they are still referring to *reference checks.* (Notice also that there are words in the last sentence of the paragraph that appear in italics. In this case, though, the authors have not used italics to indicate the topic. Rather, they have used italics to emphasize the large percentage of job candidates who lie on job applications and résumés.)

Keep in mind that it is possible to express the same topic more than one way. For example, the topic of a paragraph on *reference checks* could also be expressed as *checking on references,* or *checking a job applicant's references.*

Clue 4: Look for a Word, Name, or Phrase Referred to throughout the Paragraph by Pronouns or Other Words

A fourth clue to the topic of a paragraph is a word, name, or phrase that usually appears at or near the beginning of the paragraph and is then referred to throughout the paragraph by a pronoun (such as *he, she, it, they, his, her, its,* etc.) or by other words (the topic *smoking* might also be referred to later in the paragraph as *this habit* or *this addiction*). Read this paragraph from a computer science textbook and notice how pronouns are used to refer to the topic.

Bill Gates taught himself programming at age 13. As a Seattle teenager, he and his friends would ride their bicycles to a local computer company to help them look for programming errors. In 1962 he took a leave from high school when TRW offered him a job at $20,000. In 1975 he formed Microsoft Corporation, which wrote system programs for Altair and Apple microcomputers and expanded BASIC for other computers. IBM asked him to write an operating system for its new PC machine. The result was MS-DOS, one of the widest-selling operating systems in the world. This creative genius also directed software development for the MacIntosh and Radio Shack Model 100 microcomputers. Microsoft kept producing winning software such as *Word, Works,* and *Flight Simulator.* In 1987 IBM chose Microsoft's *Windows* for the PS/2 computer. *Windows* has since become a new standard. It is no surprise that this gifted entrepreneur is the richest man in the world.

Source: Adapted from Timothy N. Trainor and Diane Krasnewich, *Computers,* 5th ed. Copyright © 1996 McGraw-Hill. Reprinted by permission of The McGraw-Hill Companies.

Stop and Annotate

Go back to the textbook excerpt above. Underline or highlight the topic, the pronouns, and other words that refer to the topic.

Notice that the name Bill Gates appears only in the first sentence, but it is obvious from the pronouns *he, his,* and *him* that the rest of the paragraph continues to discuss Bill Gates. Notice that when the authors say, "this creative genius" and "this gifted entrepreneur," they are still referring to Bill Gates. Therefore, *Bill Gates* is the topic of this paragraph.

One or more of the four clues described above will always help you determine the topic of a paragraph. However, if the topic is still not clear to you, you may find it helpful to reread the paragraph to determine what all the sentences pertain to.

Determining the topic is the starting point in comprehending as you read. It is also a key to locating the stated main idea sentence of a paragraph, as you will see in Chapter 4.

OTHER THINGS TO KEEP IN MIND WHEN DETERMINING THE TOPIC

There are three helpful things that you should know about determining the topic:

1. You should use a *name, word,* or *phrase,* but never a sentence, to express the topic. This means you must know the difference between a phrase and a sentence.

As you know, the topic of a paragraph not only can be expressed as a word or a name, it can be expressed as a *phrase*. A phrase is a group of words (even a long group of words) that does *not* express a complete thought. A sentence, on the other hand, has a subject and a verb and *always* expresses a complete thought. Phrases can be used to express the topic, but sentences should *never* be used to express a topic.

The left column (below) gives examples of phrases, which could be used as topics. The right column contains sentences that include the topic. The items in the right column could not be used as topics because they are complete sentences.

Could Be Used as a Topic (because it is a phrase)	Could *Not* Be Used as a Topic (because it is a complete sentence)
traveling by plane	Traveling by plane is the fastest way to travel long distances to foreign countries.
fatality rates for passengers traveling by plane	Fatality rates of passengers traveling by plane are significantly lower than fatality rates for passengers traveling by car.
why traveling by plane is the best way to go	There are several reasons why traveling by plane is the best way to go.
how to overcome fear of traveling by plane	Psychologists have several methods to teach people how to overcome fear of traveling by plane.
the truck	The truck ran the stop sign.
the red truck	The red truck ran the stop sign.
the red truck with a broken headlight	The red truck with a broken headlight ran the stop sign.
the red truck with a broken headlight and a noisy muffler	The red truck with a broken headlight and a noisy muffler ran the stop sign.

Practice: Could This Be a Topic?

The topic is a *word, name,* or *phrase* that tells who or what a paragraph is about. Here are some examples of things that could—or could not—be topics:

- Going to college for the first time (*Yes; this could be a topic because it's a phrase.*)
- George W. Bush (*Yes; it's a name.*)
- Happy (*No; this is an adjective, a word that describes, so it could not be a topic.*)
- Happiness (*Yes; this is a noun that tells what a passage is about, so it could be a topic.*)
- Why soccer is popular (*Yes; this is a phrase.*)
- Soccer is popular because it is a fast-moving game. (*No; this is a complete sentence.*)

Directions: Decide whether each item below could be used as a topic that describes who or what a paragraph is about. Write Y for *Yes.* If it does not, write N for *No.* (There are periods after all of them, although not all of them are sentences.)

_____ **1.** Changes in the new tax law.

_____ **2.** The Mississippi River.

_____ **3.** How to change a flat tire.

_____ **4.** Benjamin Franklin.

_____ **5.** The reign of Queen Elizabeth II.

_____ **6.** Silly.

_____ **7.** Why computers are a good choice as a major.

_____ **8.** Washing your hands often can prevent colds.

_____ **9.** Depression.

_____ **10.** The effects of sleep deprivation on college students.

_____ **11.** Why reading skills are a key to success in college.

_____ **12.** Ten tips for passing objective tests.

_____ **13.** Safety measures for airline passengers.

_____ **14.** Yoga is a way to reduce stress.

_____ **15.** Starting a new job.

2. You must know the difference between "general" and "specific."

It is important to be precise when you determine the topic. If you choose a word or phrase that is too general or too specific, you will not be expressing the topic accurately. A topic that is *too general* goes beyond what is discussed in the paragraph. In other words, it is too broad. On the other hand, a topic is *too specific* if it fails to describe all of the things discussed in the paragraph. In other words, it is too narrow.

Suppose, for instance, that the topic of a paragraph is *causes of voter apathy.* As the following chart shows, the words *voter* or *apathy* or even the phrase *voter apathy,* would be too general to express this topic precisely. The phrase *lack of interest in candidates as a cause of voter apathy* would be too specific, even though "lack of interest in candidates" might be mentioned in the paragraph as one cause of voter apathy.

Too General (Too Broad)	Accurate Topic	Too Specific (Too Narrow)
voters	causes of voter apathy	voter apathy due to lack of interest in the candidates
apathy		voter apathy due to lack of interest in the issues
voter apathy		voter apathy because one candidate has an overwhelming likelihood of winning

3. A longer passage has an overall topic.

Just as every paragraph has a topic, longer selections (ones that consist of many paragraphs) have topics, too. In a writing course or an English course, your instructor may call the overall topic the *subject*.

How can you determine the overall topic of a longer selection you read? First, ask yourself the question, "Who or what is this entire selection about?" Then use some of the clues presented in this chapter:

- Look at the title or heading for the entire selection or section.
- Look for a word, name, or phrase that appears in special print.
- Look for a word, name, or phrase that is repeated throughout.

Once you have finished reading an entire selection or section of a textbook, it is a good idea to reflect on the topics of the paragraphs themselves to see who or what they all pertain to. This will also lead you to the overall topic. For example, five paragraphs of a section in a history book might have these topics: Thomas Jefferson's birth, Jefferson's boyhood, his education, his role in writing the Declaration of Independence, and his presidency. The overall topic of the selection would be: *Thomas Jefferson's life*. This overall topic is a general topic that sums up the topics of the five individual paragraphs that comprise the selection.

DEVELOPING CHAPTER REVIEW CARDS

Chapter review cards are a way to select, organize, and review the important information in a textbook chapter. Preparing chapter review cards helps you organize the information so that you can learn and memorize it more easily. In other words, chapter review cards are an effective study tool.

Preparing chapter review cards for each chapter of this book will give you practice in creating these valuable study tools. Once you have learned how to make chapter review cards, you can use actual index cards to create them for textbook material in any of your courses and use them when you study for tests.

Now, complete the chapter review cards for this chapter by answering the questions or following the directions on each "card" below. (The boxes below represent index cards.) The page numbers indicate the place in the chapter the information can be found.

Determining the Topic

1. What is the definition of the *topic* of a paragraph? (See page 121.)

_____

_____

2. List two reasons it is important to determine the topic of a paragraph. (See page 121.)

_____

_____

_____

3. What comprehension monitoring question should you ask yourself in order to determine the topic of a paragraph? (Be sure you write a *question*.) (See page 121.)

_____

_____

Card 1   Chapter 3: Determining the Topic

Clues to Determining the Topic

List four clues textbook authors use to indicate the topic of a paragraph. (See pages 122–124.)

1. _____

_____

2. _____

_____

3. _____

_____

4. _____

_____

Card 2   Chapter 3: Determining the Topic

When Determining the Topic, Keep in Mind . . .

What are the three other things you should keep in mind when you are determining the topic? (See pages 125–127)

1. _____

_____

_____

2. _____

_____

3. _____

_____

_____

Card 3   Chapter 3: Determining the Topic

COMPREHENSION PRACTICE: DETERMINING THE TOPIC EXERCISES (1)

Study the example in the box below to see how the information you learned in this chapter can be used to determine the topic of a paragraph. When you are sure you understand the example, complete the five exercises that follow.

EXAMPLE

This paragraph comes from a speech textbook.

Ethnocentrism is the belief that our own group or culture—whatever it may be—is superior to all other groups or cultures. Because of ethnocentrism, we identify with our group or culture and see its values, beliefs, and customs as "right" or "natural." Moreover, we tend to think of the values, beliefs, and customs of other groups or cultures as "wrong" or "unnatural."

Source: Adapted from Stephen Lucas, *The Art of Public Speaking,* 6th ed., p. 25. Copyright © 1998 McGraw-Hill. Reprinted by permission of The McGraw-Hill Companies.

_____*c*_____ What is the topic of this paragraph?

  a. customs

  b. groups or cultures

  c. ethnocentrism

  d. values, beliefs, and customs

The correct answer is c. There are several clues that suggest *ethnocentrism* is the topic: The word *ethnocentrism* appears in bold print in the first sentence. The word also appears in the second sentence. And all three sentences in the paragraph pertain to the topic *ethnocentrism.* (Topics are important. Be sure you understand the *meaning* of the topic.)

Directions:

- First, read the paragraph carefully.
- Next, determine the topic of the paragraph by using the clues presented in this chapter.
- Then, select the answer choice that gives the topic and write the letter in the space provided. (*Suggestion:* You may find it helpful to mark any clues to the topic.)

1. This paragraph comes from a human development textbook.

In 1990, two psychologists, Peter Salovey and John Mayer, coined the term ***emotional intelligence*** (sometimes called EQ). It refers to the ability to understand and regulate emotions: to recognize and deal with one's own feelings and the feelings of others. Daniel Goleman, the psychologist and science writer who popularized the term, speculates that emotional intelligence may be largely set by mid-adolescence, when the parts of the brain that control how people act on their emotions mature.

Source: Diane E. Papalia and Sally Olds, *Human Development,* 7th ed., p. 417. Copyright © 1998 McGraw-Hill. Reprinted by permission of The McGraw-Hill Companies.

What is the topic of this paragraph?
a. psychologists
b. emotional intelligence
c. understanding and regulating emotions
d. Daniel Goleman

2. This paragraph comes from a psychology textbook.

Daydreams

Many features of directed and flowing consciousness and dreams are combined in the state of waking consciousness called daydreams. They are a period of thinking and feeling that is not bound by what is logical or likely to happen. Daydreams are not a sometime thing; most of us daydream many times each day.

Source: Benjamin B. Lahey, *Psychology,* 6th ed., p. 139. Copyright © 1998 McGraw-Hill. Reprinted by permission of The McGraw-Hill Companies.

What is the topic of this paragraph?
a. flowing consciousness and dreams
b. waking consciousness
c. daydreams
d. a period of thinking and feeling

3. This paragraph comes from a psychology textbook.

The hypothalamus is a small, but vitally important part of the brain. It lies underneath the thalamus, just in front of the midbrain. It is intimately involved in our motives and emotions: eating, drinking, sexual motivation, pleasure, anger, and fear. It also plays a key role in regulating body temperature, sleep, endocrine gland activity, and resistance to disease; controlling glandular secretions of the stomach and intestines; and maintaining the normal pace and rhythm of such body functions as blood pressure and heartbeat. It is the brain center most directly linked to the functions of the autonomic nervous system.

Source: From Benjamin B. Lahey, *Essentials of Psychology,* p. 45. Copyright © 2002 McGraw-Hill. Reprinted by permission of The McGraw-Hill Companies.

What is the topic of this paragraph?
a. a small, but vitally important part of the brain
b. midbrain
c. the brain center
d. the hypothalamus

4. This paragraph comes from a human development textbook.

As teenagers begin to separate from their families and spend more time with peers, they have less time and less need for the emotional gratification they used to get from the sibling bond. Changes in sibling relationships may well precede similar changes in the relationship between adolescents and parents: more independence on the part of the younger person and less authority exerted by the older person over the younger. As children reach high school, their relationships with their siblings become progressively more equal and more distant. Adolescents still show intimacy, affection, and admiration for their brothers and sisters, but they spend less time with them, and their relationships are less intense. Older siblings exercise less power over younger ones, fight with them less, are not as close to them, and are less likely to look to them for companionship.

Source: From Diane E. Papalia and Sally Olds, *Human Development,* 6th ed. Copyright © 1999 McGraw-Hill. Reprinted by permission of The McGraw-Hill Companies.

————— What is the topic of this paragraph?
a. changes in sibling relationships among teenagers

b. teenagers

c. lack of companionship among siblings

d. older siblings

5. This paragraph comes from a management textbook.

Distinguishing between Change and Innovation

In considering more closely the concepts of change and innovation, it is useful to distinguish between the two terms. **Change** is any alteration of the status quo, whereas innovation is a more specialized kind of change. **Innovation** is a new idea applied to initiating or improving a process, product, or service. As long as an idea for bringing about an improvement is perceived as new by the individuals involved, it is generally considered to be an innovation even though outside observers may view it as an imitation of something already existing elsewhere. All innovations imply change; but not all changes are innovations, since changes may not involve new ideas or lead to significant improvements.

Source: From Kathryn M. Bartol and David C. Martin, *Management,* 2nd ed. Copyright © 1994 McGraw-Hill. Reprinted by permission of The McGraw-Hill Companies.

————— What is the topic of this paragraph?
a. change

b. innovation

c. change and innovation

d. the status quo

COMPREHENSION PRACTICE: DETERMINING THE TOPIC EXERCISES (2)

Study the example in the box below to see how the information you learned in this chapter can be used to determine the topic of a paragraph. When you are sure you understand the example, complete the five exercises that follow.

EXAMPLE

This paragraph comes from a psychology textbook.

Pressure

Does the pressure of working for good grades ever get to you? If you have been employed, was it a high-pressure job? The term **pressure** is used to describe the stress that arises from threats of negative events. In school, there is always the possibility that you will not perform well and you will fail. Some jobs are loaded with possibilities for making a mess of things and getting fired. Some unhappy marriages are sources of pressure because one spouse always seems to displease the other, no matter how hard he or she tries to avoid it.

Source: Benjamin B. Lahey, *Psychology,* 6th ed., p. 437. Copyright © 1998 McGraw-Hill. Reprinted by permission of The McGraw-Hill Companies.

Write the topic: *pressure*

Clue(s): *The word pressure appears in the heading and in bold print*

in the paragraph. It also appears several times in the paragraph.

Directions:

- First, read the paragraph carefully.
- Next, determine the topic of the paragraph by using the clues presented in this chapter: *heading, special print, repetition,* and *mentioned at beginning and referred to throughout by pronouns or other words.*
- In the space provided beneath the paragraph, write a word or phrase that tells the topic.
- Then, list the type or types of clues that helped you determine the topic.

1.   This paragraph comes from a computer science textbook.

Facsimile Machines

For many organizations the *facsimile machine,* or fax, has become an increasingly popular way to transmit ideas and important information. Just as a telephone transmits voice messages, a fax machine transmits images of printed material. The data can be a drawing, a photo, a handwritten document, or even your take-out lunch order.

Source: From Timothy N. Trainor and Diane Krasnewich, *Computers!,* 5th ed. Copyright © 1996 McGraw-Hill. Reprinted by permission of The McGraw-Hill Companies.

Write a word, name, or phrase that tells the topic: _____

_____

Clue(s) _____

_____

2. This paragraph comes from a human development textbook.

    Grandparents and great-grandparents are important to their families. They are sources of wisdom, companions in play, links to the past, and symbols of the continuity of family life. They are engaged in the ultimate generative function: expressing the human longing to transcend mortality by investing themselves in the lives of future generations.

    Source: From Diana E. Papalia and Sally Olds, *Human Development,* 6th ed. Copyright © 1999 McGraw-Hill. Reprinted by permission of The McGraw-Hill Companies.

    Write a word, name, or phrase that tells the topic: _____

    _____

    Clue(s) _____

    _____

3. This paragraph comes from a psychology textbook.

    Who are the characters in your dreams? Are they your friends and family? Are there strangers in your dreams? Are you a character in your own dreams? Because we are always the "author" of our dreams, it is not surprising that we often play a leading role. The dreamer has an active role in nearly three-fourths of dreams, and we are absent from our own dreams only 10 percent of the time. About half of the other characters in our dreams are friends, acquaintances, or family members, but the other half are people we do not know or cannot recognize or are animals 4 percent of the time. The characters in dreams are about an even mixture of men and women, with men being slightly more likely to dream about men than women are.

    Source: Adapted from Benjamin B. Lahey, *Psychology,* 6th ed., p. 145. Copyright © 1998 McGraw-Hill. Reprinted by permission of The McGraw-Hill Companies.

    Write a word, name, or phrase that tells the topic: _____

    _____

    Clue(s) _____

    _____

4.   This paragraph comes from a government textbook.

African-Americans have made progress since the 1960s in winning election to public office. Although the percentage of black elected officials is still far below the proportion of African-Americans in the population, it has risen sharply over recent decades. As of 1997, there were more than 30 black members of Congress and 200 black mayors—including the mayors some of the largest cities, such as Atlanta and Detroit.

Source: Thomas E. Patterson, *We the People,* 2nd ed., p. 140. Copyright © 1998 McGraw-Hill. Reprinted by permission of the The McGraw-Hill Companies.

Write a word, name, or phrase that tells the topic: _____

_____

Clue(s) _____

_____

5.   This paragraph comes from a human development textbook.

Sisters are especially vital in maintaining family relationships. Also, older people who are close to their sisters feel better about life and worry less about aging than those without sisters or without close ties to them. Another effect of being close to a sister is that it lifts the morale of older widows. Among a national sample of bereaved adults in the Netherlands, those coping with the death of a sister experienced more difficulty than those who had lost a spouse or a parent.

Source: From Diana E. Papalia and Sally Olds, *Human Development,* 6th ed. Copyright © 1999 McGraw-Hill. Reprinted by permission of The McGraw-Hill Companies.

Write a word, name, or phrase that tells the topic: _____

_____

_____

Clue(s) _____

_____

SELECTION 3-1 · TOO MANY STUDENTS CHEAT ON SLEEP

NEWSPAPER ARTICLE

USA Today
By Nanci Hellmich

Wouldn't it be great if people, like whales, could sleep with half of their brains at a time? Unfortunately, we can't. Being exhausted has become part of our culture—we are truly the nation of the "walking weary." In a national survey conducted in 2001, almost half of the respondents reported that they slept six hours or less each night. Professor James Maas, the author of the The Power of Sleep *whose research is described in this article, believes that anyone who gets less than six to seven hours of sleep per night (more than a third of the U.S. population) is getting inadequate rest.*

Do you get enough sleep? If you are like most college students, the answer is very likely no. Adolescents and parents of newborns are among the most sleep deprived. Dr. Maas's research indicates that to be fully alert all day, adolescents need nearly 10 hours of sleep at night. He has also found that parents of newborns lose 450–700 hours of sleep the first year of their baby's life.

Without enough sleep, a person's attention wanders; organization, new learning, and memory are impaired. In fact, even minimal sleep loss can have highly detrimental effects on cognition, mood, performance, productivity, and communication. Moreover, researchers are now investigating possible links between sleep deprivation and obesity, diabetes, hypertension, and a weakened immune system.

Why is it so easy to fall behind on sleep? Can a person catch up on sleep by sleeping more on the weekends? This article presents Professor Maas's answers to these questions. In addition, he describes what is required for a "good night's sleep."

---

1   Sleep-deprived college kids are often walking zombies, and James Maas, a psychology professor at Cornell University in Ithaca, N.Y., is doing something about it. He's helping the university design sleep-friendly rooms in new dormitories.

2   Maas recently surveyed 1,500 college students about how much they sleep. He found that they are getting only 6.1 hours of sleep a night, when they need 9 to 9½ hours to be fully alert all day.

3   "Kids just think they are invincible. They take No Doz and drink coffee, coffee, and coffee," he says.

4   In his survey, he also found other information about students' sleep habits:

- 81% take at least one nap a week during the school week; 17% nap every day.

- Students vary the time they go to bed by 90 minutes during the week, which violates an important rule of sleep—to keep a regular schedule for going to bed and getting up.

- Their bedtime is usually two hours later on weekends than during the week.

5   Students often discuss their wacky sleeping schedules with Maas. One young woman told him that she went

Annotation Practice Exercises

Directions: For each exercise below, write the *topic* of the paragraph on the lines beside the paragraph.

Annotation Exercise

Topic of paragraph 2:

_____

_____

_____

Annotation Exercise

Topic of paragraph 4:

_____

_____

137

for two weeks in a row with one or two hours of sleep a night. Then she crashed—sleeping 11 to 14 hours a day, snoozing through phone calls and her alarm clock.

6   When students try to catch up on sleep on the weekends, it often backfires, Maas says. They might sleep until noon on Sunday, throwing off their bedtime that night.

7   If they go to bed late, then have to go to an 8 A.M. class Monday, "they put themselves into virtual jet lag without ever getting on a plane," says Maas, author of *The Power of Sleep.*

8   For a good night's sleep, it's important to have a quiet, dark, and cool bedroom, and dormitories are generally not quiet or dark, Maas says. The university is preparing to build a series of dorms, and Maas is consulting with the architects. He has recommended that they put in high-quality mattresses and draperies that really make the room dark.

9   He also has designed special lighting. Maas suggests having two lights above the headboard of the dorm bed. One would be a reading light that is narrowly focused. At the press of a button, the light would slowly dim 15 minutes before the student wanted to go to sleep, making the student increasingly tired, he says. The second light would be part of the morning wake-up system. It would come on 15 minutes before the student's alarm went off. "It would be a daylight spectrum lamp of high intensity that would wake them up before the raucous alarm and help reset their biological clocks."

Annotation Exercise

Topic of paragraph 6:

_____

_____

Annotation Exercise

Topic of paragraph 9:

_____

_____

Source: Adapted from Nanci Hellmich, *USA Today,* Wednesday, March 24, 1999. Life Section, p. 1. Copyright © 1999 USA Today. Reprinted by permission of USA Today.

Comprehension and Vocabulary Quiz

This quiz has four parts. Your instructor may assign some or all of them.

Comprehension

Directions: Items 1–5 test your comprehension (understanding) of the material in this selection. These questions are much like those that a content area instructor (such as a psychology professor) would expect you to know after reading this selection. For each comprehension question below, use information from the selection to determine the correct answer. Refer to the selection as you answer the questions. Write your answer in the space provided.

_____ **1.** In order to be fully alert all day, how many hours of sleep do college students need each night?
  a. 6 to 6½ hours
  b. 7 to 7½ hours
  c. 8 to 8½ hours
  d. 9 to 9½ hours

_____ **2.** College students often violate an important "rule of sleep" because they
  a. get less than 6.1 hours of sleep a night.
  b. take NoDoz and drink coffee.
  c. vary the time they go to bed by 90 minutes during the week.
  d. go to bed earlier on weekends.

_____ **3.** According to Professor Maas, it is difficult to get a good night's sleep if
  a. your bedroom isn't dark enough.
  b. you are a busy college student.
  c. your bedroom is cool.
  d. you are sleep-deprived.

_____ **4.** Professor Maas claims that college students often "put themselves into virtual jet lag without ever getting on a plane" by
  a. sleeping 11 to 14 hours a day.
  b. taking frequent naps and drinking coffee in order to wake up.
  c. failing to get enough sleep after a weekend trip.
  d. failing to get enough sleep during the weekends and throwing off their bedtime on Sunday night.

_____ **5.** Professor Maas believes that
  a. college students must reset their biological clocks on the weekends.
  b. it is possible for college students to get the rest they need.
  c. too many college students have unusual work schedules that cause them to cheat on sleep.
  d. college students should use their weekends to catch up on sleep.

Vocabulary in Context

Directions: Items 6–10 test your ability to determine the meaning of a word by using context clues. *Context clues* are words in a sentence that allow the reader to deduce (reason out) the meaning of an unfamiliar word in that sentence. Context clues also enable the reader to determine which meaning the author intends when a word has more than one meaning. For each vocabulary item below, a sentence from the selection containing an important word (*italicized, like this*) is quoted first. Next, there is an additional sentence using the word in the same sense and providing another context clue. Use the context clues from *both* sentences to deduce the meaning of the italicized word. *Be sure the answer you choose makes sense in both sentences.* If you discover that you need to use a dictionary to confirm an answer choice, remember that the meaning you select must still fit the context of *both* sentences. Write your answer in the space provided.

Pronunciation Key: ă pat   ā pay   âr care   ä father   ĕ pet   ē be   ĭ pit
ī tie   îr **pier**   ŏ pot   ō toe   ô paw   oi noise   ou **out**   ŏŏ **took**   ōō boot
ŭ **cut**   yōō abuse   ûr **urge**   th **thin**   *th* **this**   hw **which**   zh vision
ə **about**   Stress mark: ′

---

6. Sleep-deprived college kids are often walking *zombies,* and James Maas, a psychology professor at Cornell University in Ithaca, N.Y., is doing something about it.

   After watching TV until 3 A.M., we felt like *zombies* the next day.

   zombies (zŏm′ bēz)

   a. idiots
   b. authorities on late-night TV
   c. close friends
   d. mechanical devices that only look human

7. Kids just think they are *invincible.*

   No invading army was ever able to capture the massive, stone fortress; it was *invincible.*

   invincible (ĭn vĭn′ sə bəl)

   a. unconquerable
   b. made of stone
   c. solid; impenetrable
   d. protected by luck

_____ 8. When students try to catch up on shut-eye on the weekends, it often *backfires*.

When I take a shortcut, it often *backfires,* and I end up getting completely lost.

backfires (băk′ fīrz)

a. blows up; explodes

b. causes conflict with other people

c. produces an unexpected, undesirable effect

d. increases in length or duration

_____ 9. They might sleep until noon on Sunday, *throwing off* their bedtime that night.

Throwing off a baby's feeding and sleep schedule can make the baby irritable and fussy.

throwing off (thrō′ ĭng ôf)

a. following closely

b. changing; disrupting

c. making very slight changes in

d. getting rid of

_____ 10. It would be a daylight spectrum lamp of high intensity that would wake them up before the *raucous* alarm and help reset their biological clocks.

At the zoo the high-pitched, *raucous* chatter of the monkeys set our nerves on edge.

raucous (rô′ kəs)

a. soothing and calming

b. going on and off; intermittent

c. pleasing; pleasant

d. harsh and rough-sounding

Word Structure

Directions: Items 11–15 test your ability to use word-structure clues to help determine a word's meaning. *Word-structure clues* consist of roots, prefixes, and suffixes. In these exercises, you will learn the meaning of a word part (root) and use it to determine the meaning of the several other words that have the same word part. If you discover that you need to use a dictionary to confirm an answer choice, do so. Write your answer in the space provided.

In paragraph 9 of the selection you encountered the word *spectrum.* This word contains the Latin root *spec,* which means "to look" or "to see." The word *spectrum* has many meanings, but in this passage, the word *spectrum* refers to *seeing* the energy (light) from a radiant source (here, a light bulb) distributed and arranged in order of the wavelengths. ("Daylight spectrum" light is full-spectrum light that looks like natural daylight.) Use the meaning of *spec* and the list of prefixes on pages 60–61 to help you determine the meaning of each of the following words that contain this same root.

_____ 11. If you make a **spectacle** of yourself at a party, other people are likely to
   a.   stop and watch you.
   b.   applaud you.
   c.   wish they were you.
   d.   report you to the police.

_____ 12. If a person wishes in **retrospect** that he or she had finished college, the person wishes this
   a.   in vain.
   b.   as a joke.
   c.   while looking back at the past.
   d.   in great frustration and regret.

_____ 13. A **spectator** at a baseball game is a person who
   a.   plays in the game.
   b.   umpires the game.
   c.   sells food in the stands.
   d.   watches the game.

_____ 14. A **prospector** is a person who
   a.   wants free land.
   b.   looks for mineral deposits or oil.
   c.   seeks adventure.
   d.   leads people to new territories.

_____ 15. A **specimen** is a sample of tissue or other material that a doctor or scientist
   a.   looks at in order to study it.
   b.   preserves in chemicals.
   c.   stores in a laboratory.
   d.   obtains from another researcher.

Reading Skills Application

Directions: Items 16–20 test your ability to apply certain reading skills to the material in this selection. These are the types of questions that might appear on standardized reading tests and state-mandated basic skills tests. Write your answer in the space provided.

_____ **16.** In paragraph 1 of the selection, when the author compares sleep-deprived college students with "walking zombies," he means that those students

    a.   have had a spell placed on them.

    b.   are unhealthy and need medical attention.

    c.   are functioning like nonthinking robots.

    d.   are wearing attention-getting clothes.

_____ **17.** According to information in the selection, most college students

    a.   generally get an adequate amount of sleep each night.

    b.   get only enough sleep on weekends.

    c.   get an average of 11 to 14 hours of sleep each day.

    d.   usually get approximately three hours less sleep each night than they need.

_____ **18.** From information given in the selection, it can be concluded that college students would be better rested if they

    a.   kept a regular schedule for going to bed and getting up.

    b.   took short naps more frequently during the school week.

    c.   slept until noon on Sunday if they did not get enough sleep during the week.

    d.   reduced their use of coffee and No Doz.

_____ **19.** Which of the following patterns is used to organize the information in paragraphs 6–7 of the selection?

    a.   list

    b.   sequence

    c.   comparison and contrast

    d.   cause and effect

_____ **20.** Which of the following statements best represents the main idea of paragraph 2?

    a.   College students average 6.1 hours per night, according to a survey.

    b.   A recent survey revealed that college students typically do not get the sleep they need.

    c.   Most college students need 9 to 9½ hours to be fully alert the next day.

    d.   Professor Maas recently conducted a survey of 1,500 college students.

Writing and Collaborating to Enhance Your Understanding

Option for collaboration: Your instructor may direct you to work with other students or, in other words, to work *collaboratively.* In that case, you should form groups of three or four students as directed by your instructor and work together to complete the exercises. After your group discusses each item and agrees on the answer, have a group member record it. Every member of your group should be able to explain all of your group's answers.

1. **Reacting to What You Have Read:** On average, how many hours of sleep do you get on weeknights? How many hours of sleep per night do you think you need in order to be completely rested and fully alert all day? If you are not currently getting enough sleep, what changes could you make that would allow you to get enough sleep? (Be sure to answer all three questions.)

    _____

    _____

    _____

    _____

    _____

2. **Comprehending the Selection Further:** Why will the special dormitory lighting system Professor Maas designed be effective? (The system is described in paragraph 9.)

    _____

    _____

    _____

    _____

    _____

    _____

3. **Overall Main Idea of the Selection:** In one sentence tell what the author wants readers to understand about college students getting enough sleep. (Be sure to use the words "college students" and "sleep" in your overall main idea sentence.)

_____

_____

_____

_____

_____

_____

Read More about It on the World Wide Web

To learn more about the topic of this selection, visit these websites or use your favorite search engine (such as Yahoo®) to discover more about this author and this topic on your own. Whenever you go to *any* website, it is a good idea to evaluate it critically. Are you getting good information—that is, information that is accurate, complete, and up-to-date? Who sponsors the website? How easy is it to use the features of the website?

http://www.onbusiness.net/expertpages/expertpages,m/jamesmaasclients.html

http://www.sleepmedservices.com/abs337755761.html

http://www.sleepfoundation.org/about.html#sleep

SELECTION 3-2

HUMAN DEVELOPMENT

IS THERE A BETTER WAY TO PARENT? A LOOK AT THREE PARENTING STYLES

From *Human Development*

By Diane E. Papalia and Sally Olds

What kind of parents did you have? What kind of a parent are you, or what kind of parent will you be? Psychologist Diana Baumrind has studied three different styles of parenting and found that one style of parenting enhances children's competence more than the others.

Baumrind: Three Parenting Styles

1   Why does Stacy hit and bite the nearest person when she cannot finish a jigsaw puzzle? What makes David sit and sulk when he cannot finish the puzzle, even though his teacher offers to help him? Why does Consuelo work on the puzzle for 20 minutes and then shrug and try another? Why are children so different in their responses to the same situation? Temperament is a major factor, of course; but some research suggests that *styles of parenting* may affect children's competence in dealing with their world.

2   In her pioneering research, Diana Baumrind studied 103 preschool children from 95 families. Through interviews, testing, and home studies, she measured how children were functioning, identified three parenting styles, and described typical behavior patterns of children raised according to each.

3   *Authoritarian parents* value control and unquestioning obedience. They try to make children conform to a set standard of conduct and punish them arbitrarily and forcefully for violating it. They are more detached and less warm than other parents. Their children tend to be more discontented, withdrawn, and distrustful.

4   *Permissive parents* value self-expression and self-regulation. They consider themselves resources, not models. They make few demands and allow children to monitor their own activities as much as possible. When they do have to make rules, they explain the reasons for them. They consult with children about policy decisions and rarely punish. They are warm, noncontrolling, and undemanding. Their preschool children tend to be immature—the least self-controlled and the least exploratory.

5   *Authoritative parents* respect a child's individuality but also stress social values. They have confidence in their ability to guide children, but they also respect children's independent decisions, interests, opinions, and personalities. They are loving, consistent, demanding,

---

Annotation Practice Exercises

Directions: For each exercise below, write the topic of the paragraph on the lines beside the paragraph.

Annotation Exercise

Topic of paragraph 2:

_____

_____

_____

Annotation Exercise

Topic of paragraph 3:

_____

_____

Annotation Exercise

Topic of paragraph 4:

_____

_____

firm in maintaining standards, and willing to impose limited, judicious, punishment—even occasional, mild spanking when necessary, within the context of a warm, supportive relationship. They explain the reasoning behind their stands and encourage verbal given-and-take. Their children apparently feel secure in knowing both that they are loved and what is expected of them. These preschoolers tend to be the most self-reliant, self-controlled, self-assertive, exploratory, and content.

6   Why does authoritative parenting seem to enhance children's competence? It may well be because authoritative parents set reasonable expectations and realistic standards. In authoritarian homes, children are so strictly controlled that often they cannot make independent choices about their own behavior. In permissive homes, children receive so *little* guidance that they may become uncertain and anxious about whether they are doing the right thing. In authoritative homes, children know when they are meeting expectations and can decide whether it is worth risking parental displeasure or other unpleasant consequences to pursue a goal. These children are expected to perform well, fulfill commitments, and participate actively in family duties as well as family fun. They know the satisfaction of meeting responsibilities and achieving success.

Annotation Exercise

Topic of paragraph 5:

_____

_____

Annotation Exercise

Topic of paragraph 6:

_____

_____

_____

_____

Comprehension and Vocabulary Quiz

This quiz has four parts. Your instructor may assign some or all of them.

Comprehension

Directions: For each comprehension question below, use information from the selection to determine the correct answer. Refer to the selection as you answer the questions. Write your answer in the space provided.

_____ 1. Baumrind's research suggests that, in addition to temperament, children's competence in dealing with the world may be influenced by
    a. the general level of the children's intelligence.
    b. the parenting style of their parents.
    c. the experiences that children have in school.
    d. the socio-economic level of their family.

_____ 2. Parents who value unquestioning obedience and control are referred to as
    a. authoritative parents.
    b. permissive parents.
    c. authoritarian parents.
    d. noncontrolling parents.

_____ 3. Compared with children who experience authoritarian or authoritative parenting styles, preschool children of permissive parents tend to be
    a. more discontented, withdrawn, and distrustful.
    b. immature, less self-controlled, and less exploratory.
    c. more self-reliant and self-controlled.
    d. more content and secure.

_____ 4. With regard to punishing their children, authoritative parents tend
    a. never to spank their children.
    b. to spank their children often and forcefully.
    c. to use occasional, mild spanking when necessary.
    d. to use force to make children conform to strict standards.

_____ 5. Authoritative parenting seems to enhance a child's competence because authoritative parents
    a. allow children to express their unique personalities.
    b. make children conform to a set standard of conduct.
    c. allow children to monitor their own activities as much as possible.
    d. set reasonable expectations and realistic standards for their children.

Vocabulary in Context

Directions: Use the context clues from *both* sentences to deduce the meaning of the italicized word. *Be sure the answer you choose makes sense in both sentences.* If you discover that you need to use a dictionary to confirm an answer choice, remember that the meaning you select must still fit the context of *both* sentences. Write your answer in the space provided.

Pronunciation Key: ă pat ā pay âr **care** ä father ĕ pet ē be ĭ pit
ī tie îr **pier** ŏ pot ō toe ô **paw** oi **noise** ou **out** ŏŏ **took** ōō **boot**
ŭ **cut** yōō abuse ûr **urge** th **thin** *th* **this** hw **which** zh **vision**
ə **about**   Stress mark: ′

6. *Temperament* is a major factor, of course; but some research suggests that styles of parenting may affect children's competence in dealing with their world.

   Some breeds of dogs, such as cocker spaniels and labrador retrievers, make good family pets because of their gentle, calm *temperament.*

   temperament (tĕm′ prə mənt)

   a. typical manner of reacting
   b. hostility; anger
   c. inability to get along with other people
   d. impulsiveness

7. *Authoritarian* parents value control and unquestioning obedience.

   Nobody likes the new soccer coach because he is as *authoritarian* as a dictator.

   authoritarian (ə thôr ĭ târ′ ē ən)

   a. expecting others to obey without question
   b. skilled in leadership
   c. pertaining to an author
   d. demanding an unreasonable amount of hard work

8. *Permissive* parents value self-expression and self-regulation.

   The substitute teacher was so *permissive* that she allowed the children to do whatever they wanted.

   permissive (pər mĭs′ ĭv)

   a. asking permission; seeking approval
   b. gloomy; expecting the worst
   c. lenient; likely to give permission
   d. lazy; unmotivated

_____ **9.** *Authoritative* parents respect a child's individuality but also stress social values.

Because the principal was so *authoritative,* the students did not hesitate to follow her instructions during the fire drill.

authoritative (ə thôr ′ĭ tā tĭv)

  a. proud

  b. hysterical

  c. deserving scorn or ridicule

  d. arising from proper authority

_____ **10.** Temperament is a major factor, of course; but some research suggests that styles of parenting may affect children's *competence* in dealing with their world.

Because of our tour guide's extraordinary *competence,* we thoroughly enjoyed our sightseeing in Paris.

competence (kom′ pĭ təns)

  a. ability; skill

  b. improvement; progress

  c. inadequacy; ineptitude

  d. inability to achieve or produce

Word Structure

Directions: In paragraph 5 of the selection you encountered the word *impose.* This word contains the Latin root *pos,* which means to "put" or "place." The word *impose* means to *place* or *put* one's own values, beliefs, etc., on another person. Use the meaning of *pos* and the list of prefixes on pages 60–61 to help you determine the meaning of each of the following words that contain this same root. Write your answer in the space provided.

_____ **11.** If you take a picture off the wall and **reposition** it, you

  a. rehang it in a different place.

  b. store it away.

  c. put it in a closet.

  d. clean it.

_____ **12.** If you accidentally **transpose** the letters in a word when you are typing, you

  a. delete the letters.

  b. put the letters in the wrong order.

  c. capitalize the letters.

  d. add extra letters.

13. To **compose** a tune means to
    a.   place notes in an order that makes a melody.
    b.   alter the sequence of notes in an existing melody.
    c.   plagiarize someone else's melody.
    d.   record the tune you create.

14. If a business person **proposes** that his or her company develop a new product, the person
    a.   builds a model of the product.
    b.   suggests or puts forth the idea for the product.
    c.   hires someone to design the product.
    d.   researches the potential market for the product.

15. Bank vaults and safety deposit boxes are *repositories* for extremely important or valuable items. A **repository** is a place in which items are
    a.   stored until they can be sold.
    b.   left indefinitely.
    c.   auctioned off.
    d.   put for safekeeping.

Reading Skills Application

Directions: Apply your reading skills to answer the questions below. Write your answer in the space provided.

16. The authors' primary purpose for writing this selection is to
    a.   describe three styles of parenting and their effects on children.
    b.   persuade parents to adopt an authoritarian parenting style.
    c.   explain how parents develop parenting styles.
    d.   instruct parents how to change their parenting style.

17. Which of the following is the meaning of *conform* as it is used in the third paragraph?
    a.   cherish
    b.   create
    c.   obey
    d.   ignore

_____ **18.** Based on information in the selection, which of the following represents a logical conclusion about the effect of parenting style on children's competence?

    a. An authoritarian parenting style is the best style.

    b. A permissive parenting style is the best style.

    c. An authoritative parenting style is the best style.

    d. There is no one best parenting style.

_____ **19.** Which of the following statements is the main idea of paragraph 6?

    a. Children know the satisfaction of meeting responsibilities and achieving success.

    b. Authoritative parenting seems to enhance children's competence because authoritative parents set reasonable limits and realistic expectations.

    c. In authoritarian homes, children are so strictly controlled that they cannot make independent choices about their own behavior.

    d. In permissive homes, children receive so little guidance that they may become uncertain and anxious about whether they are doing the right thing.

_____ **20.** Which of the following best describes the authors' tone?

    a. impassioned

    b. humorous

    c. sarcastic

    d. factual

HUMAN
DEVELOPMENT

Collaboration Option

Writing and Collaborating to Enhance Your Understanding

Option for collaboration: Work together in groups to complete the exercises below. Have one group member record your answers, but make sure that every member of your group can explain all of your group's answers.

1. **Reacting to What You Have Read:** Was the parenting style of your parents (or the person or persons who reared you) authoritarian, permissive, or authoritative? Describe some of their actions as parents and their attitudes towards children that cause you to view them this way.

_____

_____

_____

_____

_____

_____

SELECTION **3-3**

SPEECH
COMMUNICATION

GIVING A SPEECH? IF YOU'RE NERVOUS, YOU'RE NORMAL!

From *Public Speaking for College and Career*
By Hamilton Gregory

It has been said that dying is the only thing Americans fear more than having to give a speech! To rank the fear of these two things so closely together indicates the extent to which many adults dread public speaking. Not surprisingly, many college students feel a bit panicky at the thought of having to give an oral report or make a presentation in class (Some find it difficult even to make a comment or to ask a question in class.) In this selection from a public speaking textbook, the author describes four causes of this nervousness and reassures readers that it is an entirely normal feeling.

If public speaking makes you unusually nervous, consider enrolling in a speech course or joining a group such as Toastmasters. You will be with a supportive group of people who share the same anxiety. You will gain valuable instruction, practice and—most importantly—confidence. Being able to speak well in public is an asset that will serve you well in college, in organizations to which you belong, and in your career.

1   If you want to know what extreme pressure is, consider the plight of Mookie Wilson of the New York Mets. In game 6 of the 1986 World Series, Wilson walked to the plate in the bottom of the 10th inning with the weight of the world on his shoulders. His team was one out away from losing the Series to the Boston Red Sox.

2   First pitch, a strike. Second pitch, a strike. Now the Mets were one strike away from defeat. Then, despite the almost unbearable tension, Wilson hit a grounder into right field that won the game for the Mets and sent the Series to game 7, which the Mets won two nights later, 8–5. Without Wilson's grace under pressure, the Mets would not have become the world champions.

3   Six years later, Wilson faced another great challenge: stage fright. By now he had retired as a player and had become a coach for the Mets and a public speaker for the club's community outreach program. In his first speeches, Wilson says, he did not speak well because of his shakiness: "Speaking to 50 people was harder than playing in front of 50,000." But he learned how to control his stage fright, and he developed into an "exceptionally skilled public speaker," according to the *New York Times.*

4   How did Wilson learn to control his nerves? "Number one, I spent more time preparing. Number two, I stopped thinking about myself and poured my heart and soul into reaching the audience."

5   His techniques must have worked beautifully because today he is one of the most sought-after speakers in the New York area. His audiences—at schools, hospitals, and youth groups—consider him a dynamic speaker, a man of "character, charisma, and class."

Annotation Practice Exercises

Directions: For each exercise below, write the *topic* of the paragraph on the lines beside the paragraph.

Annotation Exercise

Topic of paragraph 3:

_____

_____

_____

157

6   If you experience nervousness as a public speaker, you are not alone. Most people—even heroes like Wilson—suffer from stage fright when called upon to speak in public. In fact, when researchers ask Americans to name their greatest fears, the fear of speaking to a group of strangers is listed more often than fear of snakes, insects, lightning, deep water, heights, or flying in airplanes. With training and practice, you will be able to control your nervousness and—like Mookie—become a confident speaker.

Reasons for Nervousness

7   Is it foolish to be afraid to give a speech? Is this fear as groundless as a child's fear of monsters? I used to think so, back when I first began making speeches. I was a nervous wreck, and I would often chide myself by saying, "Come on, relax; it's just a little speech. There's no good reason to be scared." But I was wrong. There *is* good reason to be scared. In fact, there are *four* good reasons for nervousness when giving a speech.

8   **Fear of Being Stared At.**   In the animal world, a stare is a hostile act. Dogs, baboons, and other animals sometimes defend their territory by staring. Their hostile gaze alone is enough to turn away an intruder. We human beings have similar reactions; it is a part of our biological makeup to be upset by stares. Imagine that you are riding in a crowded elevator with a group of strangers. Suddenly you realize that the other people are staring directly at you. Not just glancing. *Staring.* You probably would be unnerved and frightened because a stare can be as threatening as a clenched fist—especially if it comes from people you don't know. That is why public speaking can be so frightening. You have a pack of total strangers "attacking" you with unrelenting stares, while you are obliged to stand alone, exposed and vulnerable—a goldfish in a bowl, subject to a constant scrutiny.

9   **Fear of Failure.**   "We're all afraid of looking stupid," says Jim Seymour, a columnist for *PC* magazine. "I give about 40 speeches a year. . . . Yet every single time I get ready to walk out in front of an audience, I get that old, scary feeling: *What if I make a fool of myself?* That's as deeply embedded in our psyches as our DNA chains are embedded in our cells, I suspect; I don't know anyone who doesn't get the sweats at the prospect of looking dumb to someone else."

Topic of paragraph 7:

_____

_____

_____

Baseball hero Mookie Wilson kept his nerves under control during a tense moment in a famous World Series game, and later he learned how to control his nerves in another situation: public speaking. (*Mark S. Levine, New York Mets*)

10   **Fear of Rejection.**   What if we do our best, what if we deliver a polished speech, but the audience still does not like us? It would be quite a blow to our ego because we want to be liked and, yes, even loved. We want people to admire us, to consider us wise and intelligent, and to accept our ideas and opinions. We don't want people to dislike us or reject us.

11   **Fear of the Unknown.**   Throughout our lives we are apprehensive about doing new things, such as going to school for the first time, riding a bus without our parents, or going out on our first date. We cannot put a finger on exactly what we are afraid of, because our fear is vague and diffused. What we really fear is the unknown; we worry that some unpredictable disaster will occur. When we stand up to give a speech, we are sometimes assailed by this same fear of the unknown because we cannot predict the outcome of our speech. Fortunately, this fear usually disappears, as we become experienced in giving speeches. We develop enough confidence to know that nothing terrible will befall us, just as our childhood fear of riding in a bus by ourselves vanished after two or three trips.

12   All four of these fears are as understandable as the fear of lightning. There is no reason to be ashamed of having them.

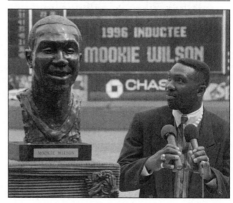

(*AP Photo/Chris Kasson*)

Source: Adapted from Hamilton Gregory, *Public Speaking for College and Career*, 6th ed., pp. 28–30. Copyright © 2002 McGraw-Hill. Reprinted by permission of The McGraw-Hill Companies.

Comprehension and Vocabulary Quiz

This quiz has four parts. Your instructor may assign some or all of them.

Comprehension

Directions: For each comprehension question below, use information from the selection to determine the correct answer. Refer to the selection as you answer the questions. Write your answer in the space provided.

_____ 1. The first thing baseball hero Mookie Wilson did in order to learn to control his nerves when giving a speech was
 a. to pour his heart and soul into reaching his audiences.
 b. to spend more time preparing for the speech.
 c. to learn to relax.
 d. to get to know his audiences better.

_____ 2. Feeling nervous before giving a speech is
 a. caused by strangers in the audience "attacking" you with unrelenting stares.
 b. less common than fear of snakes, insects, and lightning.
 c. normal.
 d. a blow to our ego.

_____ 3. When speaking to a group, our fear of the unknown usually lessens as we
 a. learn to look directly at people in the audience.
 b. learn to control our egos.
 c. become less afraid of "looking stupid."
 d. become more experienced in giving speeches.

_____ 4. The fear of rejection contributes to our nervousness when speaking to a group because
 a. we have a strong need for people to admire us and accept our ideas and opinions.
 b. we want to reject the idea of giving a speech.
 c. we do not know who will reject us.
 d. all of the above.

_____ 5. All of the following are good reasons to be nervous about speaking to a group of strangers *except*
 a. we are apprehensive about doing something new.
 b. we are afraid of looking foolish.
 c. we fear that we have not prepared and rehearsed our speech adequately.
 d. we fear that people in the audience won't like us or accept our ideas.

Vocabulary in Context

Directions: Use the context clues from *both* sentences to deduce the meaning of the italicized word. *Be sure the answer you choose makes sense in both sentences.* If you discover that you need to use a dictionary to confirm an answer choice, remember that the meaning you select must still fit the context of *both* sentences. Write your answer in the space provided.

Pronunciation Key: ă pat   ā pay   âr care   ä father   ĕ pet   ē be   ĭ pit
ī tie   îr **pier**   ŏ pot   ō toe   ô paw   oi **noise**   ou **out**   ŏŏ **took**   ōō boot
ŭ cut   yōō abuse   ûr **ur**ge   th **thin**   *th* **this**   hw **which**   zh **vision**
ə **about**   Stress mark: ´

---

6. If you want to know what extreme pressure is, consider the *plight* of Mookie Wilson of the New York Mets.

Having your luggage stolen while you are traveling can leave you in a *plight.*

plight (plīt)

  a.   difficult situation

  b.   dangerous situation

  c.   exhausting situation

  d.   amusing situation

7. Is this fear as *groundless* as a child's fear of the bogeyman?

The judge ruled that the charges against the defendant were *groundless* and dismissed the case.

groundless (ground´ lĭs)

  a.   severe

  b.   able to be disputed

  c.   without basis

  d.   upsetting

8. You have a pack of total strangers "attacking" you with *unrelenting* stares, while you are obliged to stand alone, exposed and vulnerable—a goldfish in a bowl, subject to a constant scrutiny.

Once we entered the grocery store, my children were so *unrelenting* in their demands for candy that I finally gave in and bought them some.

unrelenting (ŭn rĭ lĕn´ tĭng)

  a.   loud; vocal

  b.   constant; persistent

       c.   unreasonable

       d.   hostile; hateful

_____   **9.** We cannot put a finger on exactly what we are afraid of, because our fear is vague and *diffused.*

The patient's anxiety was so *diffused* that the psychiatrist was unable to identify the specific source of it.

diffused (dĭ fyōōzd′)

       a.   intense; focused

       b.   overwhelming to the point of incapacitating

       c.   distinct; clear

       d.   not concentrated on any one thing

_____   **10.** When we stand up to give a speech, we are sometimes *assailed* by this same fear of the unknown because we cannot predict the outcome of our speech.

After the tornado struck the state, the governor was *assailed* with criticism for not responding quickly enough to help its victims.

assailed (ə sāld′)

       a.   attacked

       b.   frightened

       c.   praised

       d.   ignored

Word Structure

Directions: In paragraph 10 of the selection you encountered the word *rejection.* This word contains the Latin root **ject,** which means "to throw." The word *rejection* literally means that someone or something is "*tossed* back" (not accepted). Use the meaning of *ject* and the list of prefixes on pages 60–61 to help you determine the meaning of each of the following words that contain this same root. Write your answer in the space provided.

_____   **11.** If a referee or umpire **ejects** players from a game, he or she

       a.   throws them out.

       b.   cautions them against making future violations.

       c.   calls a penalty on them.

       d.   signals to them.

_____   **12.** If you are **dejected,** you are feeling

       a.   angry.

       b.   cheerful.

       c.   optimistic.

       d.   downcast.

_____ **13.** If you **interject** your opinion into a conversation your friends are having, you

    a. keep your opinion to yourself.

    b. interrupt them by tossing in your opinion.

    c. ask them if they would like to know your opinion.

    d. decide your opinion is worthless.

_____ **14.** A film **projector** is designed to

    a. throw images on a screen.

    b. block images from the screen.

    c. blur images.

    d. capture images on film.

_____ **15.** If you receive an **injection,** the substance is

    a. given as a pill.

    b. dispensed as a cream.

    c. pushed beneath the skin.

    d. placed in an inhaler.

Reading Skills Application

Directions: Apply your reading skills to answer the questions below. Write your answer in the space provided.

_____ **16.** The information in paragraphs 7–12 of the selection is organized according to which of the following patterns?

    a. comparison-contrast

    b. problem-solution

    c. sequence

    d. cause-effect

_____ **17.** The author's primary purpose for writing this selection is to

    a. persuade readers to become more like Mookie Wilson.

    b. instruct readers how to overcome their nervousness.

    c. persuade readers to get more practice making speeches.

    d. inform readers as to why giving a speech can make a person nervous.

_____ **18.** Which of the following statements best expresses the main idea of paragraph 7?

    a. There are four good reasons to be scared when you give a speech.

    b. It is foolish to be afraid to give a speech.

    c. The fear of giving a speech is groundless.

    d. You can calm yourself by saying, "Relax, it's just a little speech."

_____ **19.** In paragraph 1 the phrase *with the weight of the world on his shoulders* means

    a. feeling pain in the back.

    b. feeling angry.

    c. feeling great pressure.

    d. feeling challenged.

_____ **20.** Based upon information in the selection, it can be inferred that

    a. the fear of rejection is stronger in people than the fear of failure.

    b. throughout our lives we are apprehensive about doing new things.

    c. it is reassuring to know that it is normal to feel nervous about speaking in public.

    d. most people eventually adjust to being stared at.

SELECTION 3-3

SPEECH
COMMUNICATION

Collaboration Option

Writing and Collaborating to Enhance Your Understanding

Option for collaboration: Work together in groups to complete the exercises below. Have one group member record your answers, but make sure that every member of your group can explain all of your group's answers.

1. Reacting to What You Have Read: Have you ever been a victim of "mike fright"? Freezing up when a microphone or camcorder is thrust in one's face is a common experience. Describe a situation when your nervousness or fear interfered with your speaking in the classroom or some other public setting.

_____

_____

_____

_____

_____

_____

_____

_____

2. **Comprehending the Selection Further:** List and explain the four common reasons for nervousness when we are giving a speech.

3. **Overall Main Idea of the Selection:** In one sentence tell what the author wants readers to understand about being nervous when giving a speech. (Be sure to use the words "nervous" and "giving a speech" in your overall main idea sentence.)

Read More about It on the World Wide Web

To learn more about the topic of this selection, visit these websites or use your favorite search engine (such as Yahoo®) to discover more about this author and this topic on your own. Whenever you go to *any* website, it is a good idea to evaluate it critically. Are you getting good information—that is, information that is accurate, complete, and up-to-date? Who sponsors the website? How easy is it to use the features of the website?

http://www.toastmasters.org
http://fripp.com/art.helpishere.html
http://fripp.com/art.10tips.html
http://www.ag.iastate.edu/aginfo/speechindex.html

(© Comstock Images)

C H A P T E R 4

Locating the Stated Main Idea

CHAPTER OBJECTIVES

In this chapter you will learn:

- What a stated main idea sentence is and why it is important to locate and understand it.

- The method for identifying the stated main idea sentence.

- Which sentence can be the stated main idea sentence in a paragraph.

WHAT YOU NEED TO LEARN

What Is a Stated Main Idea Sentence, and Why Is It Important to Locate and Understand It?

What Is the Method for Identifying the Stated Main Idea Sentence?

Which Sentence in a Paragraph Can Be the Stated Main Idea Sentence?

- First Sentence of the Paragraph

- Last Sentence of the Paragraph

- A Sentence within the Paragraph

Other Things to Keep in Mind When Locating the Stated Main Idea Sentences:

- All stated main idea sentences have certain characteristics in common.

- Avoid these three common mistakes when locating the stated main idea.

- Signal words or phrases can give you a clue to locating a stated main idea or to locating a stated main idea that is presented as a conclusion.

- A longer passage often has an overall main idea sentence that is stated.

CREATING YOUR SUMMARY

Developing Chapter Review Cards

Comprehension Practice: Locating the Stated Main Idea Exercises (1)

Comprehension Practice: Locating the Stated Main Idea Exercises (2)

READINGS

Selection 4-1 *(Business)*
"Good Boss? Bad Boss? Three Leadership Styles"
by William G. Nickels, James M. McHugh, and Susan M. McHugh

Selection 4-2 *(Marketing)*
"Need a Job? Identifying Your Job
Opportunities"
by Eric N. Berkowitz, et al.

Selection 4-3 *(Human Development)*
"Engagement and Marriage: The Same—Yet
Different—Worldwide"
by Diane Papalia, Sally Olds, and Ruth Feldman

WHAT YOU NEED TO LEARN

WHAT IS A STATED MAIN IDEA SENTENCE, AND WHY IS IT IMPORTANT TO LOCATE AND UNDERSTAND IT?

You already know that every paragraph has a topic. In addition, every paragraph has a main idea. It is the one idea about the topic the author considers most important for the reader to understand. Frequently, an author states the main idea directly as one of the sentences in the paragraph. When the author presents the main idea by stating it as one of the sentences in a paragraph, it is called a *stated* main idea. A **stated main idea sentence** is the sentence in a paragraph that contains both the topic and the author's single most important point about this topic. For this reason, of course, a paragraph can have only one main idea.

In a writing or English course, your instructor may call the stated main idea sentence of a paragraph the *topic sentence.* Think about the name "topic sentence." It tells you a lot about a main idea: It must contain the *topic.* And, it tells you that the main idea must be a *sentence.* Remember that the sentence must also tell the author's most important point about the topic. Be sure you understand that you are looking for the *author's* most important point, not what you think is most important or simply find interesting. (Sometimes the main idea is *not* directly stated by the author as one of the sentences in the paragraph. This is called an *implied* main idea, and you will learn about it in Chapter 5.)

Here are some examples of topics and main idea sentences an author might create. In a paragraph whose topic is *Benjamin Franklin,* the author might write this sentence as a stated main idea: *A Founding Father of the United States, Benjamin Franklin was a genius who achieved remarkable success in a wide range of fields.* Or in a paragraph whose topic is *injuries caused by airbags,* the author might state his main idea this way: *To avoid injuries caused by airbags, children under the age of 12 should be buckled in the back seat of a car.* Notice that the topic must always appear in the main idea sentence.

Because stated main ideas are so important, authors sometimes draw attention to them by using certain phrases. Watch for phrases such as these since they often appear in the main idea sentence and signal it: *The point is; it is obvious that; it is important to understand that; in short; therefore;* and *in conclusion.* These phrases often appear at the beginning of the main idea sentence, but they can appear within the sentence. For example, either of these two sentences could be the stated main idea of a paragraph: *Therefore, no person can serve more than two terms as president of the United States* or *No person, therefore, can serve more than two terms as president of the United States.*

Why is it important to locate and understand stated main idea sentences? It is important because the stated main idea sentence is the sentence the author includes for the purpose of stating the single most important point he or she wants the reader to understand. Therefore, understanding main ideas is a key to identifying and learning the important material (in other words, material you will see on tests). There are several ways that understanding the main idea can help you when you are studying. Understanding main ideas will enable you to

- Comprehend more accurately and completely the material you are reading.
- Underline or highlight the most important material in your textbooks.
- Take better notes.
- Organize information into outlines and summaries.
- Locate and memorize more easily the important material for tests.
- Make higher test grades.

WHAT IS THE METHOD FOR IDENTIFYING THE STATED MAIN IDEA SENTENCE?

The way to identify the stated main idea sentence is to look for a sentence that has the two necessary "ingredients": the *topic* and the author's *most important point* about the topic. Here is a simple formula that shows the two essential elements of all main idea sentences:

| The *topic* | + | author's *most important point* about the topic | = | Main idea sentence |

Comprehension Monitoring Question for Stated Main Idea

"What is the single most important point the author wants me to understand about the topic of this paragraph?"

You must begin, of course, by reading the paragraph and determining its topic. Then, locate the main idea by finding the sentence that answers the comprehension monitoring question, "What is the single most important point the author wants me to understand about the topic of this paragraph?" When you find a sentence that contains the topic *and* answers this question (tells the author's most important point about the topic), you have found the stated main idea sentence.

Next, make sure that the sentence you are considering as the main idea makes complete sense *by itself.* A stated main idea sentence must always make complete sense by itself. (If the topic is missing, the sentence will not make sense by itself.) In other words, the sentence would make sense even if, for some reason, you were not allowed to see the other sentences of the paragraph. For example, the following sentence could be a stated main idea because it makes sense by itself: *Franklin Roosevelt is considered one of the greatest U.S. presidents of the 20th century.* The following sentence, however, could not be a stated main idea sentence because it does not make complete sense by itself: *He is considered one the greatest U.S. presidents of the 20th century.* This sentence does not make complete sense by itself because we do not know who *he* is. The sentence does not include the topic, a president's name. Without the topic, the reader does not know which president the author is referring to. Remember, a stated main idea sentence must contain the actual word, name, or phrase that is the topic *as well as* tell the author's single most important point about the topic.

Then, be sure the sentence you have chosen is a general sentence. The main idea sentence is often the most general sentence in a paragraph, that is, one that "sums up" the details but does not include them. For example, the main idea of a business textbook paragraph might be this general statement: *There are many important decisions to make when starting a computer software company.* The words *many important decisions* are very general; the rest of the information in the paragraph (the supporting details given in the other sentences) would explain specifically what the "important decisions" are. (In Chapter 6 you will learn about identifying supporting details.)

Finally, see if the other sentences in the paragraph explain or tell more about the sentence you have chosen. That is, see if the other sentences in the paragraph tell more about the sentence you are considering for the main idea sentence. If you have located the correct sentence, the other sentences in the paragraph will be supporting details that explain, illustrate, or prove the general point expressed by the main idea sentence. For example, a main idea might be, *sexually transmitted diseases present a particular threat to young adults.* The supporting details in this paragraph might give examples of specific diseases, such as HIV, hepatitis B, genital herpes, and gonorrhea, along with the threats posed by each.

Now let's see how the information above can be applied to a paragraph from a college textbook. Reread the paragraph below. (It is from a psychology textbook, and you read it earlier in the Chapter 3 practice exercises.) The topic of the paragraph is the *hypothalamus.*

> The hypothalamus is a small, but vitally important part of the brain. It lies underneath the thalamus, just in front of the midbrain. It is intimately involved in our motives and emotions: eating, drinking, sexual motivation, pleasure, anger, and fear. It also plays a key role in regulating body temperature, sleep, endocrine gland activity, and resistance to disease. It controls glandular secretions of the stomach and intestines and it maintains the normal pace and rhythm of such body functions as blood pressure and heartbeat. It is the brain center most directly linked to the functions of the autonomic nervous system.

Source: From Benjamin B. Lahey, *Essentials of Psychology,* p. 45. Copyright © 2002 McGraw-Hill. Reprinted by permission of The McGraw-Hill Companies.

To begin with, we can see that the first sentence contains the topic *(hypothalamus)* and that it tells the author's most important point about the hypothalamus *(that it is a small, but vitally important part of the brain).* Did you notice, in fact, that the first sentence is the *only* sentence that contains the topic? The first sentence also makes complete sense by itself. It is also a very general sentence. Finally, we can see that this general statement is explained by the details in the other sentences of the paragraph. (The supporting details describe the various functions the hypothalamus performs for the body. It is obvious that these functions are "vitally important.") Therefore, it is clear that the first sentence is the stated main idea sentence.

WHICH SENTENCE IN A PARAGRAPH CAN BE THE STATED MAIN IDEA SENTENCE?

As you probably already know, a stated main idea sentence often occurs at the very beginning of a paragraph. The next most likely place is at the end of a paragraph. But stated main idea sentences sometimes appear within a paragraph. A stated main idea sentence can be highlighted or underlined because it always appears as a sentence in the paragraph. Let's look at three textbook excerpts that illustrate these three placements of a stated main idea sentence.

First Sentence of the Paragraph

The first sentence of a paragraph is often the stated main idea sentence. Authors frequently begin a paragraph with a stated main idea sentence. They do this because they know that putting a main idea sentence first can make the paragraph clearer and easier to understand. Also, by giving the main point first, authors know that readers usually find it easier to locate the main idea. Furthermore, authors know that it will be easier for readers to identify the supporting details when they already know the main idea.

The following excerpt from a biology textbook shows such a paragraph. The topic of this paragraph is *cells*. Read the paragraph and ask yourself, "What is the most important point the author wants me to understand about *cells?*" (The sentence that answers this question, the first sentence, is the stated main idea sentence.)

Cells are quite small. A frog's egg, at about one millimeter in diameter, is large enough to be seen by the human eye. Most cells are far smaller than one millimeter; some are even as small as one micrometer—one thousandth of a millimeter. Interior parts of cells (inclusions and macromolecules) are even smaller still than a micrometer and are measured in terms of manometers.

Source: Adapted from Sylvia S. Mader, *Biology*, 6th ed., p. 59. Copyright © 1998 McGraw-Hill. Reprinted by permission of The McGraw-Hill Companies.

Stop and Annotate

Go back to the textbook excerpt above. Underline or highlight the stated main idea sentence, the first sentence of the paragraph.

In this excerpt, the first sentence is a general one that tells the most important point the author wants you to know: *Cells are quite small.* The other sentences in the paragraph support the main idea sentence by illustrating and explaining how tiny cells and their parts are. In this paragraph, then, the first sentence states the main idea, and the rest of the sentences are supporting details that tell more about it.

Last Sentence of the Paragraph

The stated main idea sentence is sometimes the last sentence of the paragraph. Authors sometimes prefer to make the last sentence of a paragraph the stated main idea. The reason is that in some cases they know it helps the reader if they conclude (end) the paragraph with the most important point they want to make. This is especially true when the author knows an explanation is required before the reader can understand the main idea, or the author may wish to lead up to an important general conclusion (the main idea). Putting the main idea sentence last is also a way authors can emphasize it or draw attention to it.

Read the excerpt below, from a health textbook. As the title suggests, the topic of this paragraph is *bulimia and anorexia.* As you read the paragraph, ask yourself, "What is the most important point the authors want me to understand about *bulimia and anorexia?*" (The sentence that answers this question, the last sentence, is the stated main idea sentence.)

Bulimia and Anorexia

Bulimia, a disorder characterized by eating followed by vomiting, may occur with anorexia nervosa or as a separate illness with different psychological roots. According to the U.S. Food and Drug Administration, the symptoms of bulimia are found in 40 to 50 percent of people with anorexia nervosa. As with anorexia, the majority of bulimia victims are women, typically in their early twenties, college-educated, single, and white. Unlike those with anorexia, the victims of bulimia tend to be of nearly normal weight and have healthy, outgoing personalities. The greatest difference is that a person with anorexia turns away from food while a person with bulimia is obsessively drawn to it. It is obvious that there are important similarities and differences between the eating disorders bulimia and anorexia.

Source: Adapted from Marvin Levy, Mark Dignan, and Janet Shirreffs, *Targeting Wellness: The Core,* pp. 76–77. Copyright © 1992 McGraw-Hill. Reprinted by permission of The McGraw-Hill Companies.

Stop and Annotate

Go back to the textbook excerpt above. Underline or highlight the stated main idea sentence, the last sentence of the paragraph.

In this paragraph, the first sentence defines bulimia and how it is related to anorexia nervosa (another eating disorder). The second sentence explains the percentage of bulimic people who also have anorexia. The third sentence describes similarities among those who have these eating disorders. The next two sentences describe differences in the people who have these disorders and the major difference between the two disorders. Notice that the last sentence, the stated main idea, contains the topic and that it is a general statement that tells the authors' most important point about bulimia and anorexia. To draw attention to this important sentence, the authors begin it with *It is obvious.*

A Sentence within the Paragraph

The stated main idea sentence may appear within the paragraph. Sometimes the stated main idea sentence is not the first *or* the last sentence of a paragraph. Instead, it is one of the other sentences in the paragraph.

At times, authors prefer *not* to begin a paragraph with the stated main idea. Authors sometimes prefer to begin a paragraph with an important question instead, and then use the second sentence—the main idea sentence—to answer it. (The main idea can never *be* a question, however.) Or authors may choose to begin a paragraph with an introductory statement or with familiar or interesting examples. At other times, authors begin by stating a widely held misconception they wish to refute. Or they may prefer to begin by presenting a surprising or controversial statement designed simply to get the reader's attention. Once they have the reader's attention, they present their main idea sentence.

Here is a paragraph from a human development textbook in which the second sentence is the main idea sentence. The topic is *parents' influence on children's choice of peers.* (In this paragraph *peers* means friends.) As you read this paragraph, ask yourself, "What is the most important point the author wants me to understand about parents' influence on children's choice of peers?"

> Can parents really influence who their children choose as friends? Actually, parents have considerable indirect influence on their children's choice of peers. This influence is indirect because parents help shape prosocial or antisocial behavior, which leads children to gravitate toward particular crowds. In a study of 3,781 high school students, the extent to which parents monitored adolescents' behavior and schoolwork, encouraged achievement, and allowed joint decision making were related to academic achievement, drug use, and self-reliance. These behaviors, in turn, were linked with membership in such peer groups as "populars, jocks, brains, normals, druggies, and outcasts."

Source: From Diane E. Papalia and Sally Olds, *Human Development,* 6th ed. Copyright © 1999 McGraw-Hill. Reprinted by permission of The McGraw-Hill Companies.

Stop and Annotate

Go back to the textbook excerpt above. Underline or highlight the stated main idea sentence, the second sentence of the paragraph.

The second sentence contains the topic and tells the authors' most important point about this topic: *Actually, parents have considerable indirect influence on their children's choice of peers.* Notice that the paragraph opens with a question. The authors have included the question to lead the reader to their most important point, the *answer* to this question. In this paragraph, it is the second sentence that answers this question. (You may have been tempted to select the question as the main idea. Remember that a stated main idea *never* appears in the form of a question.) The third sentence explains why the parents' influence on their children's choice of friends is indirect. The last two sentences describe a research study that indicates that parents do, in fact, influence their children's choice of peers.

OTHER THINGS TO KEEP IN MIND WHEN LOCATING THE STATED MAIN IDEA SENTENCE

Here are four helpful things that you should remember about locating stated main idea sentences.

---

1. All stated main idea sentences have certain characteristics in common.

- The main idea sentence must contain the topic of the paragraph.
- The main idea sentence must tell the author's single most important point about that topic.
- The main idea sentence makes complete sense by itself.
- The main idea sentence is a general one that sums up the details in the paragraph.
- The rest of the sentences in the paragraph explain or tell more about the main idea sentence.

2. Avoid these three common mistakes when locating the stated main idea.

- It is a mistake to think you can take a shortcut and determine the main idea by looking only at the first and last sentences of a paragraph. Unless you read the whole paragraph, you may miss a stated main idea sentence that appears somewhere in the middle. Be sure to read the entire paragraph *before* you try to determine the stated main idea sentence.
- Avoid choosing a sentence as the main idea merely because it contains familiar or interesting information.
- Do not select a question from a paragraph as the main idea because the stated main idea is always written as a statement (a sentence). The stated main idea is *never* written in the form of a question. The stated main idea sentence, however, will often be the *answer* to a question the author presents at the beginning of a paragraph.

3. Signal words or phrases can give you a clue to locating a stated main idea and to locating a stated main idea that is presented as a *conclusion*.

Authors sometimes include a signal word or a phrase in a paragraph in order to make a stated main idea obvious to the reader. These clues may appear in stated main ideas that are located at the beginning, middle, or end of a paragraph. These are words and phrases that often introduce a main idea sentence or appear in it:

Obviously . . .	Generally speaking . . .
Overall . . .	The fact is . . .
To sum up . . .	The truth is . . .
The point is . . .	In reality . . .

Sometimes an author will want to emphasize a stated main idea in a paragraph by presenting it as a *conclusion*. A stated conclusion is simply a main idea that the author expresses as the final point in the paragraph. When an author states a conclusion, he or she typically places it at the end of a paragraph. And often this paragraph is at the end of an entire selection. Authors use signal words or phrases such as these in order to indicate that the conclusion is their main idea:

In conclusion . . .	As a result . . .
It is clear, then, . . .	As one can see . . .
Consequently . . .	So . . .
Therefore . . .	For these reasons . . .
Finally . . .	The point is this . . .
Thus . . .	Obviously, then, . . .

4. A longer passage often has an overall main idea that is stated.

Authors sometimes include an *overall* stated main idea to present the general point of an entire selection. (A longer passage might consist of a section of a textbook chapter, a short reading selection, or an essay.) Often, the introductory or concluding sentence of a longer selection expresses the most important point or the overall message of the entire passage. In other words, an overall main idea sums up the main ideas of the individual paragraphs in the selection, just as the main idea of a paragraph sums up the individual details in the paragraph. Assume, for example, that a passage consists of five paragraphs and begins with this overall main idea stated in an introductory paragraph: *There are several things students can do to make the most of their study time.* The main ideas of the other four paragraphs might be: (1) making a study schedule can help students manage their time; (2) studying at the same time every day is also helpful; (3) using small amounts of free time to study is a useful technique; and (4) studying in the same place each day can also make study time more productive. As you can see, the overall main idea of this passage, *There are several things students can do to make the most of their study time,* is a general statement that sums up the four main ideas of the entire selection.

In a writing course or an English course, you may hear your instructor refer to the overall stated main idea of a selection as the *thesis sentence.* The thesis sentence usually appears at the beginning of a selection.

CREATING YOUR SUMMARY

DEVELOPING CHAPTER REVIEW CARDS

Chapter review cards are a way to select, organize, and review the important information in a textbook chapter. Preparing chapter review cards helps you organize the information so that you can learn and memorize it more easily. In other words, chapter review cards are an effective study tool.

Preparing chapter review cards for each chapter of this book gives you practice in creating these valuable study tools. Once you have learned how to make chapter review cards, you can use actual index cards to create them for textbook material in any of your courses and use them when you study for tests.

Now, complete the chapter review cards for this chapter by answering the questions or following the directions on each "card" below. (The boxes below represent index cards.) The page numbers indicate the place in the chapter the information can be found.

Stated Main Idea Sentences

1. What is the definition of the *stated main idea* of a paragraph? (See page 169.)

   _____

   _____

2. Why is it important to locate and understand the stated main idea of a paragraph? (See page 170.)

   _____

   _____

3. What question should you ask yourself in order to locate the stated main idea of a paragraph? Be sure you write a *question*. (See page 170.)

   _____

   _____

Card 1   Chapter 4: Locating the Stated Main Idea

The Importance of Understanding Main Ideas

List six ways understanding main ideas can help you when you are studying. (See page 170.) Understanding main ideas will enable you to:

1. _____

_____

2. _____

_____

3. _____

4. _____

5. _____

_____

6. _____

Card 2   Chapter 4: Locating the Stated Main Idea

How to Locate the Stated Main Idea Sentence of a Paragraph

Write the formula that shows the two essential elements of a main idea sentence. (See page 170.)

List three places where the stated main idea sentence may occur in a paragraph. (See pages 172–174.)

1. _____

2. _____

3. _____

Card 3   Chapter 4: Locating the Stated Main Idea

When Locating the Stated Main Idea, Keep in Mind . . .

The five characteristics of a stated main idea sentence are: (See page 175.)

1. _____
2. _____
   _____
3. _____
4. _____
5. _____

List three common mistakes students make when locating the stated main idea sentence. (See page 175.)

1. _____
   _____
2. _____
3. _____

Card 4   Chapter 4: Locating the Stated Main Idea

When Locating the Stated Main Idea, Keep in Mind . . .

1. List the signal words or phrases that can give you a clue to locating a stated main idea. (See page 175.)

   _____
   _____
   _____

2. List the signal words or phases that can give you a clue to locating a stated main idea that is presented as a *conclusion*. (See page 176.)

   _____
   _____
   _____
   _____

Card 5   Chapter 4: Locating the Stated Main Idea

COMPREHENSION PRACTICE: LOCATING THE STATED MAIN IDEA EXERCISES (1)

Study the example in the box below to see how information you learned in this chapter can be used to locate the stated main idea of a paragraph. When you are sure you understand the example, complete the five exercises that follow.

EXAMPLE

This excerpt comes from a speech textbook. It was used in Chapter 3 to illustrate strategies for determining the topic of a paragraph. As you can see, its topic is *ethnocentrism*. Reread the paragraph and ask yourself, "What is the single most important point the author wants me to understand about ethnocentrism?"

Ethnocentrism is the belief that our own group or culture—whatever it may be—is superior to all other groups or cultures. Because of ethnocentrism, we identify with our group or culture and see its values, beliefs, and customs as "right" or "natural." Moreover, we tend to think of the values, beliefs, and customs of other groups or cultures as "wrong" or "unnatural."

Source: Adapted from Stephen Lucas, *The Art of Public Speaking*, 6th ed., p. 25. Copyright © 1998 McGraw-Hill. Reprinted by permission of The McGraw-Hill Companies.

The topic of this paragraph is *ethnocentrism*.

_____*a*_____ What is the stated main idea of this paragraph?

 a. Ethnocentrism is the belief that our own group or culture—whatever it may be—is superior to all other groups or cultures.

 b. Because of ethnocentrism, we identify with our group or culture and see its values, beliefs, and customs as "right" or "natural."

 c. Moreover, we tend to think of the values, beliefs, and customs of other groups or cultures as "wrong" or "unnatural."

The correct answer is a. The first sentence is the stated main idea sentence because it tells the single most important point the author wants you to know about ethnocentrism: what ethnocentrism is. The other two sentences in the paragraph explain more about ethnocentrism by describing its effect on people.

Directions:

- First, read the paragraph carefully. Notice that you are given the topic of each paragraph.
- Then locate the stated main idea sentence by asking yourself, "What is the single most important point the author wants me to understand about the topic?"
- Select the answer choice that expresses the main idea of the paragraph and write the letter in the space provided.

1. This paragraph comes from a human development textbook.

Exercise

Adults who exercise regularly obtain many benefits. Physical activity helps them maintain desirable body weight and builds muscles. Exercise also strengthens the heart and lungs. It lowers blood pressure, protects against heart attacks, stroke, diabetes, cancer, and osteoporosis (a thinning of the bones that tends to affect middle-aged and older women and causes fractures). It also relieves anxiety and depression and lengthens life.

Source: From Diane E. Papalia and Sally Olds, *Human Development,* 6th ed. Copyright © 1999 McGraw-Hill. Reprinted by permission of The McGraw-Hill Companies.

The topic of this paragraph is *exercise,* or *exercising regularly.*

What is the stated main idea of this paragraph?

a. Adults who exercise regularly obtain many benefits.

b. Physical activity helps them maintain desirable body weight and builds muscles.

c. Exercise also strengthens heart and lungs.

d. It also relieves anxiety and depression, and lengthens life.

2. This paragraph comes from a sociology textbook.

Health practitioners are still studying the various methods of transmitting the HIV virus. The reason for this is that there is still no vaccine or cure for AIDS (acquired immunodeficiency syndrome). While there are encouraging new therapies to treat people with HIV and AIDS, there is currently no way to eradicate AIDS medically. The point is, since there is no cure for AIDS, it is essential that people protect themselves by reducing the transmission of the HIV virus.

Source: From Richard T. Schaefer and Robert Lamm, *Sociology,* 6th ed. Copyright © 1997 McGraw-Hill. Reprinted by permission of The McGraw-Hill Companies.

The topic of this paragraph is *transmission of the HIV virus.*

What is the stated main idea of this paragraph?

a. Health practitioners are still studying the various methods of transmitting the HIV virus.

b. The reason for this is that there is still no vaccine or cure for AIDS (acquired immunodeficiency syndrome).

c. While there are encouraging new therapies to treat people with HIV and AIDS, there is currently no way to eradicate AIDS medically.

d. The point is, since there is no cure for AIDS, it is essential that people protect themselves by reducing the transmission of the HIV virus.

3. This paragraph comes from a government textbook.

Members of Congress, once elected, are likely to be reelected. Members of Congress can use their office to publicize themselves. They pursue a "service strategy" of responding to the needs of individual constituents and secure pork barrel projects for their state or district. House members gain a greater advantage from these activities than do senators, whose larger constituencies make it harder for them to build close personal relations with voters and whose office is more likely to attract a strong challenger.

Source: From Thomas E. Patterson, *We the People,* 2nd ed. Copyright © 1999 McGraw-Hill. Reprinted by permission of The McGraw-Hill Companies.

The topic of this paragraph is *members of Congress.*

What is the stated main idea of this paragraph?
a. Members of Congress, once elected, are likely to be reelected.
b. Members of Congress can use their office to publicize themselves.
c. They pursue a "service strategy" of responding to the needs of individual constituents and secure pork barrel projects for their state or district.
d. House members gain a greater advantage from these activities than do senators, whose larger constituencies make it harder for them to build close personal relations with voters and whose office is more likely to attract a strong challenger.

4. This paragraph comes from a biology textbook.

Human beings have always polluted their surroundings, but in the past it was easier for them to move on and live somewhere else. They knew that, given time, the environment would take care of pollution they left behind and they relied on the "out of sight, out of mind" philosophy. Today, an increasing human population, which uses an increasing amount of energy sources, no longer has the luxury to ignore pollution. The human population is approximately 7 billion. Our overall energy consumption has gone up by a hundredfold from 2,000 kcal/person/day to 230,000 kcal/person/day in modern industrial nations like the United States. This high energy consumption allows us to mass produce many useful and economically affordable organic products that pollute the atmosphere and groundwater, damage forests and lakes, cause global warming, and even deplete the ozone layer.

Source: Adapted from Sylvia S. Mader, *Biology,* 6th ed., p. 45. Copyright © 1998 McGraw-Hill. Reprinted by permission of The McGraw-Hill Companies.

The topic of this paragraph is *human population and pollution.*

What is the stated main idea of this paragraph?
a. Human beings have always polluted their surroundings, but in the past it was easier for them to move on and live somewhere else.
b. Today, an increasing human population, which uses an increasing amount of energy sources, no longer has the luxury to ignore pollution.
c. The human population is approximately 7 billion.
d. This high energy consumption allows us to mass produce many useful and economically affordable organic products that pollute the atmosphere and groundwater, damage forests and lakes, cause global warming, and even deplete the ozone layer.

5.   This paragraph comes from a health textbook.

Volunteering

All major religions teach that it is more blessed to give than to receive. Of course, service benefits those in need, but volunteering is also good for the volunteer. It provides companionship, friendship, and fellowship in working toward a common goal. In our mobile society, volunteering allows us to meet people and thereby feel less isolated. Volunteering allows us to use skills and talents that we normally don't use at our daily jobs. In this way, volunteering encourages us to branch out, to learn new things, and become more well rounded.

Source: From Wayne Payne and Dale Hahn, *Understanding Your Health,* 5th ed. Copyright © 1995 McGraw-Hill. Reprinted by permission of The McGraw-Hill Companies.

The topic of this paragraph is *volunteering.*

What is the stated main idea of this paragraph?

a.   All major religions teach that it is more blessed to give than to receive.

b.   Of course, service benefits those in need, but volunteering is also good for the volunteer.

c.   Volunteering allows us to use skills and talents that we normally don't use at our daily jobs.

d.   In this way, volunteering encourages us to branch out, to learn new things, and become more well rounded.

COMPREHENSION PRACTICE: LOCATING THE STATED MAIN IDEA EXERCISES (2)

Study the example in the box below to see how the information you learned in this chapter can be used to locate the stated main idea of a paragraph. When you are sure you understand the example, complete the five exercises that follow.

EXAMPLE

This paragraph comes from a psychology textbook. It was used in Chapter 2 to illustrate strategies for determining the topic of a paragraph. As you can see, the topic is *pressure.* Reread the paragraph and ask yourself, "What is the single most important point the author wants me to understand about pressure?"

Pressure

Does the pressure of working for good grades ever get to you? If you have been employed, was it a high-pressure job? The term **pressure** is used to describe the stress that arises from threats of negative events. In school, there is always the possibility that you will not perform well and you will fail. Some jobs are loaded with possibilities for making a mess of things and getting fired. Some unhappy marriages are sources of pressure because one spouse always seems to displease the other, no matter how hard he or she tries to avoid it.

Source: Adapted from Benjamin B. Lahey, *Psychology,* 6th ed., p. 437. Copyright © 1998 McGraw-Hill. Reprinted by permission of The McGraw-Hill Companies.

Write the topic: _pressure_

Underline or highlight the main idea sentence in the paragraph.

Explanation: The topic of this paragraph, *pressure,* appears in the heading and in bold print. The word *pressure* also appears several times in the paragraph. The third sentence has been underlined because it is the main idea sentence. It tells the author's most important point: the definition of *pressure* as it is used in psychology. The remaining sentences give examples of sources of pressure.

Directions:

- First, read the paragraph carefully.
- Next, determine the topic of the paragraph, since it will help you locate the stated main idea sentence. Write it in the space provided beneath the exercise. Remember that the topic is expressed as a word, a name, or a phrase. Do not write a sentence for the topic.
- Then, locate the stated main idea sentence by asking yourself, "What is the single most important point the author wants me to understand about the topic?"
- Finally, underline or highlight the *entire* stated main idea sentence.

1. This paragraph comes from a health and wellness textbook.

> Perhaps you have heard of liposuction. In this procedure unwanted fat is sucked through a hollow tube after a surgical incision has been made. It was introduced in the United States several years ago. Now, about 100,000 Americans undergo liposuction every year. Not everyone agrees on its value: While liposuction may remove some unwanted fat, it does not cure obesity or deal with the underlying causes of weight problems. Liposuction has become one of the most popular and controversial forms of cosmetic surgery.

Source: Adapted from Marvin Levy, Mark Dignan, and Janet Shirreffs, *Targeting Wellness: The Core,* p. 68. Copyright © 1992 McGraw-Hill. Reprinted by permission of The McGraw-Hill Companies.

Write *one word* that tells the topic: _____

Now *underline or highlight the* **stated main idea sentence** in the paragraph.

2. This paragraph comes from a government textbook.

Political Apathy

> Just as some people who did not grow up watching football would not attend the Super Bowl even if it were free and being played across the street, some people would not bother to vote even if a ballot were delivered to their door. A sense of political apathy—a general lack of interest in or concern with politics—is often the consequence of childhood socialization. This can occur when parents do not value

voting and other forms of political participation. As a result, their children are likely to display a similar attitude when they reach voting age.

Source: From Thomas E. Patterson, *We the People,* 2nd ed. Copyright © 1999 McGraw-Hill. Reprinted by permission of The McGraw-Hill Companies.

Write a *two-word phrase* that tells the topic: _____

_____

Now *underline or highlight the* **stated main idea sentence** in the paragraph.

3. This paragraph comes from a biology textbook.

Beneficial Insects

Insects are necessary for the cross-fertilization of many crops. Bees pollinate almost $10 billion worth of food crops per year in the United States alone, and this value does not include pollination of forage crops for livestock or pollination by other insects. In addition, some insects produce useful materials: honey and beeswax from bees, silk from silk-worms, and shellac from a wax secreted by the lac insects. Although most of us think of insects primarily as pests, humanity would have great difficulty in surviving if all of these beneficial insects were suddenly to disappear.

Source: Adapted from Cleveland P. Hickman, Jr., Larry S. Roberts, and Allan Larson, *Biology of Animals,* 7th ed. (Boston: WCB/McGraw-Hill, 1998), p. 520.

Write a *two-word phrase* that tells the topic: _____

_____

Now *underline or highlight the* **stated main idea sentence** in the paragraph.

4. This paragraph comes from a child development textbook.

Even children without histories of highly aggressive behavior can become more aggressive after watching television violence. This was dramatically demonstrated by research that compared children's behavior before and after TV was introduced in some isolated Canadian towns. Watching TV violence in childhood has been linked to aggressive behavior at age 18 and serious criminal behavior at age 30.

Source: From Laura Steinberg and Roberta Meyer, *Childhood.* Copyright © 1995 McGraw-Hill. Reprinted by permission of The McGraw-Hill Companies.

Write a *phrase* that tells the topic: _____

_____

Now *underline or highlight the* **stated main idea sentence** in the paragraph.

5. This paragraph comes from a sociology textbook.

Xenocentrism is the belief that the products, styles, or ideas of one's society are inferior to those that originate elsewhere. In a sense, it is reverse ethnocentrism. For example, people in the United States often assume that French fashions or Japanese electronic devices are superior to our own. Are they, or are people unduly charmed by the lure of goods from exotic places? Such fascination with British china or Danish glassware can be damaging to competitors in the United States. Some companies have responded by creating products that *sound* European, such as Häagen-Dazs ice cream (made in New Jersey) or Nike shoes (produced in Oregon).

Source: From Richard T. Schaefer and Robert P. Lamm, *Sociology,* 6th ed. Copyright © 1997 McGraw-Hill. Reprinted by permission of The McGraw-Hill Companies.

Write *one word* that tells the topic: _____

_____

Now *underline or highlight the* **stated main idea sentence** in the paragraph.

SELECTION 4-1

BUSINESS

GOOD BOSS? BAD BOSS? THREE LEADERSHIP STYLES

From *Understanding Business*

By William G. Nickels, James M. McHugh, and Susan M. McHugh

How would you describe your leadership style? Is there one "best" style of leadership? This selection from a business text addresses that question.

1   Nothing has challenged researchers in the area of management more than the search for the "best" leadership traits, behaviors, or styles. Thousands of studies have been made just to find leadership traits, that is, characteristics that make leaders different from other people. Intuitively, you would conclude about the same thing that researchers have found: leadership traits are hard to pin down. In fact, results of most studies on leadership have been neither statistically significant nor reliable. Some leaders are well groomed and tactful, while others are unkempt and abrasive—yet the latter may be just as effective as the former.

2   Just as there is no one set of traits that can describe a leader, there's also no one style of leadership that works best in all situations. Even so, we can look at a few of the most commonly recognized leadership styles and see how they may be effective.

3   **Autocratic leadership** involves making managerial decisions without consulting others. Such a style is effective in emergencies and when absolute followership is needed—for example, when fighting fires. Autocratic leadership is also effective sometimes with new, relatively unskilled workers who need clear direction and guidance.

4   Coach Phil Jackson used an autocratic leadership style to take the Los Angeles Lakers to a National Basketball Association championship in 2000. By following his leadership, a group of highly skilled *individuals* became a winning *team.*

5   **Participative (democratic) leadership** consists of managers and employees working together to make decisions. Research has found that employee participation in decisions may not always increase effectiveness, but it usually increases job satisfaction. Many new, progressive organizations are highly successful at using a democratic style of leadership that values traits such as flexibility, good listening skills, and empathy. John Chambers, CEO of Cisco Systems, is an example of a participative leader.

6   Organizations that have successfully used this style include Wal-Mart, FedEx, IBM, Xerox, AT&T, and most

Annotation Practice Exercises

Directions: For each exercise below, write the topic of the paragraph on the lines beside the paragraph. Then, locate the stated main idea of the paragraph and underline or highlight it.

Annotation Exercise

Topic of paragraph 3:

_____

_____

Determine the *stated main idea* and underline or highlight it.

Annotation Exercise

Topic of paragraph 5:

_____

_____

Determine the *stated main idea* and underline or highlight it.

smaller firms. At meetings in such firms, employees discuss management issues and resolve those issues together in a democratic manner. That is, everyone has an equal say. Many firms have placed meeting rooms throughout the company and allow all employees the right to request a meeting.

7   **Laissez-faire (free rein) leadership** involves managers setting objectives and employees being relatively free to do whatever it takes to accomplish those objectives. In certain organizations, where managers deal with doctors, engineers, or other professionals, often the most successful leadership style is laissez-faire. The traits needed by managers in such organizations include warmth, friendliness, and understanding. More and more firms are adopting this style of leadership with at least some of their employees.

8   Individual leaders rarely fit neatly into just one of these categories. Researchers illustrate leadership as a continuum with varying amounts of employee participation, ranging from purely boss-centered leadership to subordinate-centered leadership (see Figure 1).

9   Which leadership style is best? Research tells us that successful leadership depends largely on who's being led and in what situations. It also supports the notion that any leadership style, ranging from autocratic to laissez-faire, may be successful depending on the people and the situation. A manager may be autocratic but friendly with a new trainee; democratic with an experienced employee who has many good ideas that can only be fostered by a flexible manager who's a good listener; and laissez-faire with a trusted, long-term supervisor who probably knows more about operations than the manager does.

10   There's no such thing as a leadership trait that is effective in all situations, or a leadership style that always works best. A truly successful leader has the ability to use the leadership style most appropriate to the situation and the employees involved.

One of the more successful autocratic leaders in business today is Tom Siebel, founder and head of Siebel Systems. He is described as very demanding and someone who is unwilling to take "No" for an answer. As you might expect, he is not the most beloved manager, but few executives are as effective when measured by company performance. (*Barbel Schmidt*)

Annotation Exercise

Topic of paragraph 7:

_____

_____

Determine the *stated main idea* and underline or highlight it.

Source: Adapted from William G. Nickels, James M. McHugh, and Susan McHugh, *Understanding Business,* 6th ed., pp. 216–219. Copyright © 2002 McGraw-Hill. Reprinted by permission of The McGraw-Hill Companies.

FIGURE 1: VARIOUS LEADERSHIP STYLES

Boss-centered ◄ · Subordinate-centered
leadership · ► leadership

Use of authority by manager

Area of freedom for
subordinates

Manager makes decision and announces it	Manager "sells" decision	Manager presents ideas and invites questions	Manager presents tentative decision subject to change	Manager presents problem, gets suggestions, makes decision	Manager defines limits, asks group to make decision	Manager permits subordinates to function within limits defined by superior

Autocratic　　　　　　　　　　　　　Participative/democratic　　　　　　Laissez-faire/
free rein

Source: Reprinted by permission of the *Harvard Business Review.* An exhibit from "How to Choose a Leadership Pattern" by Robert Tannenbaum and Warren Schmidt (May/June 1973). Copyright © 1973 by the Harvard Business Review School Publishing Corporation. All Rights Reserved.

BUSINESS

Comprehension and Vocabulary Quiz

This quiz has four parts. Your instructor may assign some or all of them.

Comprehension

Directions: Items 1–5 test your comprehension (understanding) of the material in this selection. These questions are much like those that a content area instructor (such as a business professor) would expect you to know after studying this selection. For each comprehension question below, use information from the selection to determine the correct answer. Refer to the selection as you answer the questions. Write your answer in the space provided.

_____   **1.** A style of leadership that involves managers and employees working together to make decisions is called
   a. laissez-faire leadership.
   b. autocratic leadership.
   c. free-rein leadership.
   d. democratic or participative leadership.

_____   **2.** Managers who wish to adopt a laissez-faire leadership style need traits such as
   a. empathy, flexibility, and good listening skills.
   b. devotion and dedication.
   c. understanding, friendliness, and warmth.
   d. firmness and directness.

_____   **3.** Autocratic leadership can be most effective
   a. when employee participation is desired.
   b. in emergencies and when absolute followership is needed.
   c. for managers who deal with doctors, engineers, and other professionals.
   d. when the manager is a good listener.

_____   **4.** Research has shown that when managers and employees work together to make decisions
   a. it implies power over others.
   b. motivation to do a good job declines.
   c. it usually improves the way employees feel about their jobs.
   d. they both feel relatively free to do whatever it takes to get the job done.

———————— **5.** A manager should

    a. always set objectives and leave employees free to do whatever it takes to accomplish them.

    b. use the leadership style most appropriate to the situation and the employees involved.

    c. use a variety of leadership styles so employees will know that the manager is friendly and caring.

    d. select a leadership style that is comfortable and use it consistently.

Vocabulary in Context

Directions: Items 6–10 test your ability to determine the meaning of a word by using context clues. *Context clues* are words in a sentence that allow the reader to deduce (reason out) the meaning of an unfamiliar word in that sentence. Context clues also enable the reader to determine which meaning the author intends when a word has more than one meaning. For each vocabulary item below, a sentence from the selection containing an important word (*italicized, like this*) is quoted first. Next, there is an additional sentence using the word in the same sense and providing another context clue. Use the context clues from *both* sentences to deduce the meaning of the italicized word. *Be sure the answer you choose makes sense in both sentences.* If you discover that you need to use a dictionary to confirm an answer choice, remember that the meaning you select must still fit the context of *both* sentences. Write your answer in the space provided.

Pronunciation Key: ă **pat** ā **pay** âr **care** ä **father** ĕ **pet** ē **be** ĭ **pit**
ī **tie** îr **pier** ŏ **pot** ō **toe** ô **paw** oi **noise** ou **out** ŏŏ **took** ōō **boot**
ŭ **cut** yōō **abuse** ûr **urge** th **thin** *th* **this** hw **which** zh **vision**
ə **about** Stress mark: ´

———————— **6.** Many new, *progressive* organizations are highly successful at using a democratic style of leadership that values traits such as flexibility, good listening skills, and empathy.

    The college's foreign language department received national recognition because its *progressive* teaching methods enable students to speak a foreign language reasonably well after only two semesters of instruction.

    progressive (prə grĕs´ ĭv)

    a. increasing in severity

    b. characterized by new ideas or progress

    c.   increasing steadily in difficulty

    d.   characterized by innovative teaching methods

7. Many new, progressive organizations are highly successful at using a democratic style of leadership that values traits such as flexibility, good listening skills, and *empathy.*

My aunt has so much *empathy* that she laughs when the main character in a movie laughs and cries when the person cries.

empathy (ĕm′ pə thē)

    a.   feeling sympathy for someone

    b.   feeling hostile towards someone

    c.   feeling whatever another person is feeling

    d.   feeling sorry for someone

8. At meetings in such firms, employees discuss management issues and *resolve* those issues together in a democratic manner.

Husbands and wives who are unable to *resolve* their marital problems often benefit from counseling or mediation.

resolve (rĭ zŏlv′)

    a.   deal with successfully; clear up

    b.   dissolve; melt

    c.   break into smaller components or parts

    d.   define; put into words

9. More and more firms are *adopting* this style of leadership with at least some of their employees.

Our college's student organizations are formally *adopting* new guidelines that make membership open to everyone.

adopting (ə dŏpt′ ĭng)

    a.   agreeing to take and follow

    b.   assuming the role of parents

    c.   discontinuing

    d.   disregarding

10. A manager may be autocratic but friendly with a new trainee; democratic with an experienced employee who has many good ideas that can only be *fostered* by a flexible manager who's a good listener; and laissez-faire with a trusted, long-term supervisor who probably knows more about operations than the manager does.

The research study confirmed that participating in organized sports *fostered* teamwork and cooperation in elementary school age children.

fostered (fô′ stərd)

a. hindered the development of
b. changed the level of
c. ruined the possibility of
d. promoted the development of

Word Structure

Directions: Items 11–15 test your ability to use word-structure clues to help determine a word's meaning. *Word-structure clues* consist of roots, prefixes, and suffixes. In these exercises, you will learn the meaning of a word part (root) and use it to determine the meaning of the several other words that have the same word part. If you discover that you need to use a dictionary to confirm an answer choice, do so. Write your answer in the space provided.

In paragraph 3 of the selection you encountered the word *autocratic.* This word contains the Greek root *auto,* which means "self." In this passage, the word *autocratic* describes a person who has all of the power to him*self* or her*self* (such as a dictator or a very controlling boss). Use the meaning of *auto* and the list of prefixes on pages 60–61 to help you determine the meaning of each of the following words that contain this same root.

_____ **11.** If a hot iron shuts off **automatically** after 15 minutes of non-use, the iron shuts off
   a. when the person picks it up again.
   b. by itself.
   c. only if it is set on a low temperature.
   d. when the person using it turns it off.

_____ **12.** If an airplane is flying on **autopilot,** it is flying
   a. in circles.
   b. in the wrong direction.
   c. without the pilot controlling it directly.
   d. at a high altitude.

_____ **13.** Most teenagers like to think that they are **autonomous.** In other words, they like to think that they are
   a. independent and self-governing.
   b. selfish and self-centered.

    c.   extremely mature.

    d.   smarter than their parents.

_____ **14.** "Didactics" is the art of teaching or instruction. An **autodidact** is someone who is

    a.   currently enrolled in school.

    b.   receiving tutoring.

    c.   uninterested in learning.

    d.   self-taught.

_____ **15.** If you write an **autobiography** some day, you will be writing

    a.   an adventure story.

    b.   a mystery.

    c.   the story of your life.

    d.   the story of someone else's life.

Reading Skills Application

Directions: Items 16–20 test your ability to apply certain reading skills to the material in this selection. These are the types of questions that might appear on standardized reading tests and state-mandated basic skills tests. Write your answer in the space provided.

_____ **16.** Which of the following best describes the authors' tone in this selection?

    a.   emotional

    b.   humorous

    c.   factual

    d.   sentimental

_____ **17.** The main idea of paragraph 3 is which of the following statements?

    a.   Autocratic leadership involves making managerial decisions without consulting others.

    b.   Motivation comes from threats, punishment, and intimidation of all kinds.

    c.   Such a style is effective in emergencies and when absolute followership is needed.

    d.   Some football, basketball, and soccer coaches have used this style.

_____ **18.** The pattern of organization used in paragraph 9 of the selection is

    a.   a list.

    b.   cause and effect.

    c.   a sequence.

    d.   a series.

_____ **19.** The authors' purpose in writing this selection is to

    a. present the reasons people develop one of three leadership styles.

    b. describe three leadership styles and explain when each is appropriate, and with whom.

    c. explain why some leadership styles are more effective than others.

    d. persuade managers to adopt a laissez-faire leadership style.

_____ **20.** As used in paragraph 8 of the selection, the phrase *subordinate-centered leadership* refers to a leadership style in which

    a. employees below the top ranks are empowered.

    b. all employees share the power equally.

    c. the boss has all of the power.

    d. the power shifts from group to group depending on the situation.

BUSINESS

Collaboration Option

Writing and Collaborating to Enhance Your Understanding

Option for collaboration: Your instructor may direct you to work with other students or, in other words, to work *collaboratively.* In that case, you should form groups of three or four students as directed by your instructor and work together to complete the exercises. After your group discusses each item and agrees on the answer, have a group member record it. Every member of your group should be able to explain all of your group's answers.

1. Reacting to What You Have Read: Think of a boss or coach or teacher you have had. What leadership style did that person have? Did you like or dislike his or her style? Explain why.

_____

_____

_____

_____

_____

_____

_____

2. **Comprehending the Selection Further:** Using the leadership terminology in this selection, describe your primary leadership style. Explain circumstances in which you have had a leadership role (at your job, in an organization you belong to, as a member of a team, etc.). Explain the behaviors you use that are characteristic of your primary style.

_____

_____

_____

_____

_____

_____

_____

_____

3. **Overall Main Idea of the Selection:** In one sentence tell what the authors want readers to understand about leadership styles. (Be sure to include the words "leadership styles" in your overall main idea sentence.)

_____

_____

_____

_____

_____

Read More about It on the World Wide Web

To learn more about the topic of this selection, visit these websites or use your favorite search engine (such as Yahoo®) to discover more about this author and this topic on your own. Whenever you go to _any_ website, it is a good idea to evaluate it critically. Are you getting good information—that is, information that is accurate, complete, and up-to-date? Who sponsors the website? How easy is it to use the features of the website?

http://www.luc.edu/orgs/gannon/

http://wlo.org/

http://www.motivation-tools.com/workplace/index.htm

NEED A JOB? IDENTIFYING YOUR JOB OPPORTUNITIES

From *Marketing*
By Eric N. Berkowitz, et al.

Today, many college students work while they are attending college and, certainly, they seek jobs when they leave college. This selection from a marketing textbook explains some of the many resources that are available to help students find jobs. Before utilizing these resources, of course, students should analyze their aptitudes and interests to identify the types of jobs that would be most suitable and enjoyable for them.

A study conducted in 2001 found that information technology is still the best field in which to look for a job, since virtually every industry today depends on computers. Health care is also a growing industry.

---

1   To identify and analyze the job market, you must conduct some research to determine what industries and companies offer promising job opportunities. Several sources that can help in your search are discussed below.

College Placement Office

2   Your college placement office is an excellent source of job information. Personnel in that office can (1) inform you about which companies will be recruiting on campus, (2) alert you to unexpected job openings, (3) advise you about short-term and long-term career prospects, (4) offer advice on résumé construction, (5) assess your interviewing strengths and weaknesses, and (6) help you evaluate a job offer. In addition, the office usually contains a variety of written materials focusing on different industries and companies and tips on job hunting.

Online Career and Employment Services

3   Many companies no longer make frequent on-campus visits. Instead, they may use the many online services available to advertise an employment opportunity or to search for candidate information. The National Association of Colleges and Employers, for example, maintains a site on the World Wide Web called JobWeb (http://www.jobweb.org). Similarly, the Online Career Center (http://www.occ.com) is a database of employment ads, candidate résumés, and other career-related information. Some of the information resources include career guidance, a cover letter library, occupational profiles, and résumé templates. Employers may contact students directly when the candidate's qualifications meet their specific job requirements. The advantage of this

Directions: For each exercise below, write the topic of the paragraph on the lines beside the paragraph. Then, locate the stated main idea of the paragraph and underline or highlight it.

Topic of paragraph 2:

_____

_____

Determine the *stated main idea* and underline or highlight it.

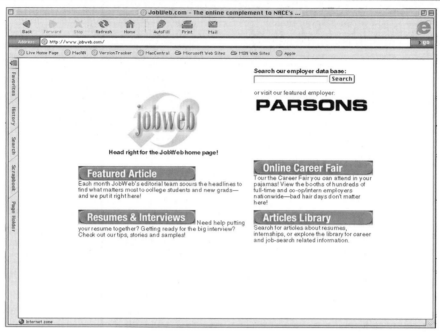

Source: Reprinted from JobWeb (www.jobweb.com) with permission of the National Association of Colleges and Employers, copyright holder. Reprinted by permission from Microsoft Corporation.

system for students is that, regardless of the size or location of the campus they are attending, many companies have access to their résumé. Your school's career center may also have a "home page" that offers online job search information and links to other World Wide Web sites.

Library

4   The public or college library can provide you with reference material that, among other things, describes successful firms and their operations, defines the content of various jobs, and forecasts job opportunities. For example, *Fortune* publishes lists of the 1,000 largest U.S. and global companies and their respective sales and profits; Dun & Bradstreet publishes directories of all companies in the United States with a net worth of at least $500,000. A librarian can indicate reference materials that will be most pertinent to *your* job search.

Advertisements

5   Help-wanted advertisements provide an overview of what is happening in the job market. Local (particularly Sunday editions) and college newspapers, trade press

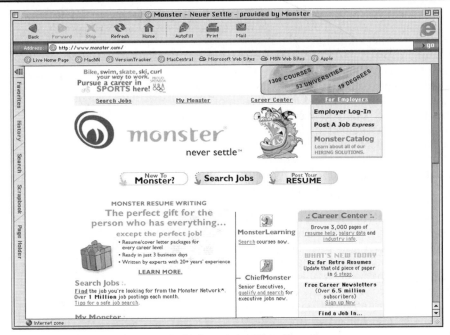

Source: Reprinted by permission of Monster.com. Reprinted by permission of Microsoft Corporation.

(such as *Marketing News* or *Advertising Age*), and business magazines (such as *Sales and Marketing Management*) contain classified advertisement sections that generally have job-opening announcements, often for entry-level positions. Reviewing the want ads can help you identify what kinds of positions are available and their requirements and job titles, which firms offer certain kinds of jobs, and levels of compensation.

Employment Agencies

6   An employment agency can make you aware of several job opportunities very quickly because of its large number of job listings available through computer databases. Many agencies specialize in a particular field (such as sales and marketing). The advantages of using an agency include that it (1) reduces the cost of a job search by bringing applicants and employers together, (2) often has exclusive job listings available only by working through the agency, (3) performs much of the job search for you, and (4) tries to find a job that is compatible with your qualifications and interests. Employment agencies are much maligned because some engage in questionable business practices, so check with the Better Business Bureau or your business contacts to determine the quality of the various agencies.

Personal Contacts

7   An important source of job information that students often overlook is their personal contacts. People you know often may know of job opportunities, so you should advise them that you're looking for a job. Relatives and friends might aid your job search. Instructors you know well and business contacts can provide a wealth of information about potential jobs and even help arrange an interview with a prospective employer. They may also help arrange "informational interviews" with employers who do not have immediate openings. These interviews allow you to collect information about an industry or an employer and give you an advantage if a position does become available. It is a good idea to leave your résumé with all your personal contacts so they can pass it along to those who might be in need of your services. Student organizations (such as the student chapter of the American Marketing Association and Pi Sigma Epsilon, the professional sales fraternity) may be sources of job opportunities, particularly if they are involved with the business community. Local chapters of professional business organizations (such as the American Marketing Association and Sales and Marketing Executives International) also can provide job information; contacting their chapter president is a first step in seeking assistance from these organizations. In the past decade, small employers have provided the greatest growth in employment, and their most common source of new employees is through personal referrals.

State Employment Office

8   State employment offices have listings of job opportunities in their state and counselors to help arrange a job interview for you. Although state employment offices perform functions similar to employment agencies, they differ in listing only job opportunities in their state and providing their services free.

Direct Contact

9   Another means of obtaining job information is direct contact—personally communicating to prospective employers (either by mail or in person) that you would be interested in pursuing job opportunities with them. Often you may not even know whether jobs are available in these firms. If you correspond with the companies in writing, a letter of introduction and an attached résumé should serve as your initial form of communication. Your major goal in direct contact is ultimately to arrange a job interview.

Annotation Exercise

Topic of paragraph 7:

_____

_____

Determine the *stated main idea* and underline or highlight it.

Comprehension and Vocabulary Quiz

This quiz has four parts. Your instructor may assign some or all of them.

Comprehension

Directions: For each comprehension question below, use information from the selection to determine the correct answer. Refer to the selection as you answer the questions. Write your answer in the space provided.

1. To learn which companies may be recruiting on your campus, you should
   a. ask other students.
   b. contact your state employment office.
   c. visit your college's placement office.
   d. interview several professors who may have business contacts in your major field of study.

2. Reviewing help-wanted ads can enable you to
   a. learn about successful firms and their operations.
   b. get an overview of the kinds of positions that are available and their job requirements.
   c. make personal contacts.
   d. determine which companies provide outstanding entry-level salaries.

3. An important source of job information that students often overlook is
   a. their college placement office.
   b. help-wanted advertisements.
   c. their personal contacts.
   d. flyers posted on campus.

4. One advantage of using an employment agency is that
   a. one will often be available to you on campus.
   b. it will provide career counseling and job training.
   c. it will often have job listings that are available only by working through the agency.
   d. it will guarantee you a good position with a reputable firm.

5. Small employers usually find new employees through
   a. help-wanted advertisements in college newspapers.
   b. online services, such as a site on the World Wide Web.
   c. personal contacts.
   d. college professors' referrals.

Vocabulary in Context

> *Directions:* Use the context clues from *both* sentences to deduce the meaning of the italicized word. *Be sure the answer you choose makes sense in both sentences.* If you discover that you need to use a dictionary to confirm an answer choice, remember that the meaning you select must still fit the context of *both* sentences. Write your answer in the space provided.

Pronunciation Key: ă **pat** ā **pay** âr **care** ä **father** ĕ **pet** ē **be** ĭ **pit**
ī **tie** îr **pier** ŏ **pot** ō **toe** ô **paw** oi **noise** ou **out** ŏŏ **took** ōō **boot**
ŭ **cut** yōō **abuse** ûr **urge** th **thin** *th* **this** hw **which** zh **vision**
ə **about**   Stress mark: ′

---

6. To identify and analyze the job market, you must *conduct* some marketing research to determine what industries and companies offer promising job opportunities.

Both candidates decided to *conduct* pubic opinion surveys to determine which issues concerned voters most.

conduct (kən dŭkt′)

a. to reduce

b. to direct

c. to ignore

d. to avoid

7. To identify and analyze the job market, you must conduct some marketing research to determine what industries and companies offer *promising* job opportunities.

The doctor was not sure if the patient would recover completely, but he said that the prognosis looked *promising.*

promising (prŏm′ ĭ sĭng)

a. likely to develop in a desirable manner

b. guaranteed or certain

c. filled with hope

d. unpredictable; uncertain

8. One advantage of an employment agency is that it tries to find a job that is *compatible* with your qualifications and interests.

It is helpful to students to enroll in classes in which the instruction is *compatible* with their learning style.

compatible (kəm păt′ ə bəl)

> *a.* working in agreeable combination with
> *b.* beneath; at a level below
> *c.* mismatched; incongruent
> *d.* inappropriate for

_____ **9.** Employment agencies are much *maligned* because some engage in questionable business practices, so check with the Better Business Bureau or your business contacts to determine the quality of the various agencies.

The senator said that his opponent had *maligned* him and that he intended to file a lawsuit against him for slander.

maligned (mə līnd′)

> *a.* unfairly accused
> *b.* made harmful statements about
> *c.* honored; held in high esteem
> *d.* dealt with in a joking manner

_____ **10.** Employment agencies are much maligned because some engage in *questionable* business practices, so check with the Better Business Bureau or your business contacts to determine the quality of the various agencies.

It is good advice to avoid any behavior that makes you appear to be of *questionable* character.

questionable (kwĕs′ chə nə bəl)

> *a.* pertaining to conducting an investigation
> *b.* of doubtful morality or respectability
> *c.* leaving no room for doubt
> *d.* providing answers to questions

Word Structure

Directions: In paragraph 1 of the selection you encountered the word ***conduct.*** This word contains the Latin root ***duct,*** which means "lead." In this passage, the word *conduct* means to *lead* (direct) the course of something (in this case, to direct research about job opportunities). Use the meaning of ***duct*** and the list of prefixes on pages 60–61 to help you determine the meaning of each of the following words that contain this same root. Write your answer in the space provided.

_____ **11.** If kidnappers **abduct** a child, they
> *a.* take the child away by using force.
> *b.* use persuasion to entice the child.
> *c.* return the child in exchange for money.
> *d.* pay others to take the child.

_____ **12.** If you go through a club's ceremony to **induct** you, you are
   a.   denied membership.
   b.   declared the president.
   c.   admitted as a member.
   d.   forced to resign as a member.

_____ **13.** The **conductor** of an orchestra
   a.   compliments the orchestra.
   b.   plays in the orchestra.
   c.   leads the orchestra.
   d.   arranges the music for the orchestra.

_____ **14.** The **introduction** of a textbook is designed to
   a.   guide students as to how to use the book.
   b.   provide the answers to exercises in the book.
   c.   tell about the authors.
   d.   advertise other books by the same author.

_____ **15.** In the reasoning process known as **induction,** a set of specific details or facts
   a.   produces conflicting results.
   b.   leads to a general conclusion.
   c.   cancels each other out.
   d.   can be disproved.

Reading Skills Application

Directions: Apply your reading skills to answer the questions below. Write your answer in the space provided.

_____ **16.** Which of the following represents the main idea of the selection?
   a.   Your college placement office is the best source of job information.
   b.   Employment agencies, advertisements, and personal contacts are key ways to identify job opportunities.
   c.   To identify and analyze the job market, you must conduct some marketing research to determine what industries and companies offer promising opportunities that relate to the results of your self-analysis.
   d.   There are many sources that can help you in your search.

_____ **17.** The information in this selection is organized according to which of the following patterns?
   a.   contrast
   b.   list
   c.   comparison
   d.   sequence

_____ **18.** Which of the following is the meaning of *compensation* as it is used in paragraph 5?

    a. pay

    b. importance

    c. interest

    d. enjoyment

_____ **19.** Based on information in the selection, which of the following is a logical inference?

    a. The more sources one uses to identify job opportunities, the greater the likelihood of finding a suitable job.

    b. Online career and employment services are the most efficient way to locate job opportunities.

    c. Finding a job is easy if you know how to use certain resources.

    d. Luck plays an important part in finding a job.

_____ **20.** The authors' primary purpose in writing this selection is to

    a. persuade readers to seek jobs.

    b. inform readers how to conduct a job search.

    c. entertain readers who are seeking jobs.

    d. instruct readers about successful job interviews.

SELECTION 4-2

MARKETING

Collaboration Option

Writing and Collaborating to Enhance Your Understanding

Option for collaboration: Work together in groups to complete the exercises below. Have one group member record your answers, but make sure every member of your group can explain all of your group's answers.

1. **Reacting to What You Have Read:** Which of the resources mentioned in the selection have you used to find a job? How effective were they?

_____

_____

_____

_____

_____

_____

2. **Comprehending the Selection Further:** Which of the resources mentioned in the selection do you think might be most helpful to college students who are seeking permanent employment? Which of these resources were new to you?

_____

_____

_____

_____

_____

_____

_____

3. **Overall Main Idea of the Selection:** In one sentence tell what the authors want readers to understand about identifying job opportunities. (Be sure to include the words "job opportunities" in your overall main idea sentence.)

_____

_____

_____

_____

_____

Read More about It on the World Wide Web

To learn more about the topic of this selection, visit these websites or use your favorite search engine (such as Yahoo®) to discover more about this author and this topic on your own. Whenever you go to _any_ website, it is a good idea to evaluate it critically. Are you getting good information—that is, information that is accurate, complete, and up-to-date? Who sponsors the website? How easy is it to use the features of the website?

http://www.jobweb.com

http://www.monster.com

http://www.careerbuilder.com

SELECTION 4-3
HUMAN DEVELOPMENT

ENGAGEMENT AND MARRIAGE: THE SAME—YET DIFFERENT—WORLDWIDE

From *Human Development*

By Diane E. Papalia, Sally Olds, and Ruth Feldman

You have certain concepts that come to mind when you hear the words "becoming engaged" and "being married." Perhaps "becoming engaged" conjures up images of a man—possibly on bended knee—asking the woman he loves to marry him and giving her a diamond engagement ring. "Being married" might bring to mind images of a couple living together in a place of their own, having and raising children, growing old together, and eventually becoming grandparents.

Virtually every culture includes customary ways couples become engaged, as well as views as to what constitutes "marriage." However, these vary considerably, and many are quite different from what the typical American thinks of. In this human development textbook selection, you will learn just how different these concepts can be for people who live in other countries and in other cultures.

Marriage

1   In Tibet, a man and his father have the same wife. In Zaire, it's just the opposite: a woman shares her husband with her mother. In many African societies, a woman—often one who is married to a man but is infertile—may take a "wife" to bear and care for her children. *Polygyny*—man's marriage to more than one woman at a time—is common in Islamic countries, African societies, and parts of Asia. In *polyandrous* societies, where women generally wield more economic power, a woman may take several husbands—in some Himalayan regions, a set of brothers. Marriage customs vary widely, but the universality of some form of marriage throughout history and around the world shows that it meets fundamental needs.

2   In most societies, marriage is considered the best way to ensure orderly raising of children. It allows for a division of labor within a consuming and working unit. Ideally, it offers intimacy, friendship, affection, sexual fulfillment, companionship, and an opportunity for emotional growth. In certain Eastern philosophical traditions, the harmonious union of a male and female is considered essential to spiritual fulfillment and the survival of the species. Clearly, society views marriage as providing many types of benefits.

3   Today some benefits of marriage, such as sex, intimacy, and economic security, are not confined to wedlock. Still, among a national sample of more than 2,000 adults ages 18 to 90, married people tended to be happier than unmarried people. Contrary to earlier studies, men and women were found to benefit equally from a

Annotation Practice Exercises

Directions: For each exercise below, write the topic of the paragraph on the lines beside the paragraph. Then, locate the stated main idea of the paragraph and underline or highlight it.

Annotation Exercise

Topic of paragraph 1:

_____

_____

Determine the *stated main idea* and underline or highlight it.

Annotation Exercise

Topic of paragraph 2:

_____

_____

Determine the *stated main idea* and underline or highlight it.

marital attachment, but in different ways—women from economic support and men from emotional support.

Entering Matrimony

4   Historically and across cultures, the most common way of selecting a mate has been through arrangement, either by the parents or by professional matchmakers. Among the chief considerations in arranged marriages are the wealth and social status of the families to be joined by the marriage. Sometimes betrothal takes place in childhood. The bride and groom may not even meet until their wedding day. Since the Renaissance, with the evolution of the nuclear family, free choice of mates on the basis of love has become the norm in the western world, but in Japan, 25 to 30 percent of marriages still are arranged.

5   The typical "marrying age" varies across cultures. In Eastern Europe, people tend to marry in or before their early 20s, as Ingrid Bergman did. But industrialized nations such as her native Sweden are seeing a trend toward later marriage as young adults take time to pursue educational and career goals or to explore relationships. In Canada, the average age of first marriage has risen from about 23 to 27 since 1961. In the United States, the median age of the first-time bridegrooms is nearly 27, and of first-time brides, 25—a rise of more than three years since 1975.

6   The transition of married life brings major changes in sexual functioning, living arrangements, rights and responsibilities, attachments, and loyalties. Among other things, marriage partners need to redefine the connection with their original families, balance intimacy with autonomy, and establish a fulfilling sexual relationship. To help newlyweds adjust, some traditional societies give them extra privacy; in other societies, their sexual and other activities are subject to prescribed rules and supervision. In some cultures, newlyweds set up their own household; in other cultures, they live with parents, temporarily or permanently. In some societies, such as the Rajputs of Khalapur, India, husband and wife live, eat, and sleep apart. In contrast to Anglo-American cultures, where the chief purpose of marriage is seen as love and companionship, the sole purpose of marriage in Rajput society is reproduction; emotional and social support come from same-sex relatives and friends.

Marriage is universal, though dress, celebratory customs, and even the number of partners, vary. This Indian couple in Durban, South Africa, may have been introduced by a matchmaker—worldwide, the most common way of selecting a mate. (*Andy Bernhauf, Photo Researchers*)

Annotation Exercise

Topic of paragraph 5:

_____

_____

Determine the *stated main idea* and underline or highlight it.

Source: Adapted from Diane Papalia, Sally Olds, and Ruth Feldman, *Human Development,* 8th ed., pp. 539–540. Copyright © 2001 McGraw-Hill. Reprinted by permission of The McGraw-Hill Companies.

SELECTION 4-3
HUMAN
DEVELOPMENT

Comprehension and Vocabulary Quiz

This quiz has four parts. Your instructor may assign some or all of them.

Comprehension

Directions: For each comprehension question below, use information from the selection to determine the correct answer. Refer to the selection as you answer the questions. Write your answer in the space provided.

_____ **1.** Most married people today
  a. tend to be happier than unmarried people.
  b. are better off financially than unmarried people.
  c. waited until they were in their 30s before deciding to get married.
  d. require extra privacy and emotional support.

_____ **2.** In Anglo-American cultures, the chief purpose of marriage seems to be
  a. sexual fulfillment.
  b. love and companionship.
  c. reproduction.
  d. setting up a household and redefining a connection to their original families.

_____ **3.** When a man is married to more than one woman at a time it is called
  a. monogamy.
  b. polyandry.
  c. polygyny.
  d. an arranged marriage.

_____ **4.** In *polyandrous* societies
  a. a man may take several wives.
  b. the majority of marriages are arranged.
  c. wives have more household duties and a greater responsibility for caring for children.
  d. women generally wield more economic power.

_____ **5.** Today, most first-time brides and bridegrooms in the United States
  a. tend to marry soon after high school.
  b. live with parents temporarily or permanently.
  c. are following the trend toward later marriage.
  d. find marriage overwhelming and stressful.

Vocabulary in Context

Directions: Use the context clues from *both* sentences to deduce the meaning of the italicized word. *Be sure the answer you choose makes sense in both sentences.* If you discover that you need to use a dictionary to confirm an answer choice, remember that the meaning you select must still fit the context of *both* sentences. Write your answer in the space provided.

Pronunciation Key: ă pat   ā pay   âr care   ä father   ĕ pet   ē be   ĭ pit
ī tie   îr pier   ŏ pot   ō toe   ô paw   oi noise   ou out   ŏŏ took   ōō boot
ŭ cut   yōō abuse   ûr urge   th thin   *th* this   hw which   zh vision
ə about   Stress mark: ′

---

6. In certain *Eastern* philosophical traditions, the harmonious union of a male and female is considered essential to spiritual fulfillment and the survival of the species.

Because my niece had traveled to several Asian countries and found them fascinating, she majored in *Eastern* religions in college.

Eastern (ē′ stərn)

a. pertaining to the eastern part of the earth, especially Asia and its neighboring islands

b. pertaining to island countries located in the southeastern part of the world

c. located on the east coast of countries

d. pertaining to ancient countries

7. Still, among a national sample of more than 2,000 adults ages 18 to 90, married people *tended* to be happier than unmarried people.

In the 18th and 19th centuries, American families *tended* to be larger than families in the 20th century.

tended (tĕn′ dəd)

a. were inclined or likely

b. were opposed

c. were unable

d. were forced

8. Historically and across cultures, the most common way of selecting a mate has been through arrangement, either by the parents or by professional *matchmakers.*

My immigrant grandparents told me that their marriage was arranged by a *matchmaker* and that this was a common practice in the old country.

matchmaker (măch′ mā kər)

 a. person who manufactures safety matches

 b. an older relative who chooses the husband or wife for a younger relative

 c. person who is paid a fee by parents to locate a suitable marriage partner for their son or daughter

 d. computer website on which people seeking spouses can register

_____   **9.** Sometimes *betrothal* takes place in childhood.

Yesterday's newspaper featured a lengthy article about the *betrothal* of the socially prominent bachelor and his aristocratic fiancée and announced their wedding next June.

betrothal (bĭ trō′ thəl)

 a. wedding ceremony

 b. premarital counseling entered into voluntarily

 c. mutual promise for a future marriage

 d. prenuptial agreement

_____   **10.** Since the Renaissance, with the evolution of *nuclear family,* free choice of mates on the basis of love has become the norm in the western world, but in Japan, 25 to 30 percent of marriages still are arranged.

In the United States, the *nuclear family* is the norm, but in many countries a much larger group of relatives live together as a family.

nuclear family (no͞o′ klē ə r făm′ ə lē)

 a. a family group consisting of all living relatives

 b. a family group that consists only of father, mother, and children

 c. a family group that consists of parents, children, and maternal relatives

 d. a family group that consists of parents, children, and all in-laws

Word Structure

Directions: In paragraph 6 of the selection you encountered the word **pre-scribed.** This word contains the Latin root **scrib,** which means "to write" or "to record." The word *prescribed* literally means "put in *writing* before" (something else can occur). In the selection, the phrase "prescribed rules and supervision" means that the rules have been set down (*written*) by some authority (and, thus, must be obeyed). Use the meaning of **scrib** and the list of prefixes on pages 60–61 to help you determine the meaning of each of the following words that contain this same root. Write your answer in the space provided.

_____ **11.** If a court reporter **transcribes** the proceedings recorded during a trial, the court reporter

    a. stores information on a computer disk.

    b. writes out the information in complete form.

    c. alters the information by shortening it.

    d. checks the notes for errors in spelling and punctuation.

_____ **12.** When you **subscribe** to a magazine, you

    a. sign an agreement to pay for a specific number of issues.

    b. read it every month.

    c. recycle the issue after you have read it.

    d. remove your name from the mailing list.

_____ **13.** In the Middle Ages, a **scribe's** job was to

    a. read documents and manuscripts to illiterate peasants.

    b. translate documents written in other languages.

    c. record information and make copies of documents and manuscripts.

    d. memorize and recite important documents.

_____ **14.** When children **scribble,** they

    a. draw pictures.

    b. paint with finger paints.

    c. cut out shapes from colored paper.

    d. make meaningless marks or lines.

_____ **15.** If the names of military heroes are **inscribed** on a marble monument, their names are

    a. printed in block letters.

    b. written in gold.

    c. chiseled in the stone.

    d. crossed out.

Reading Skills Application

Directions: Apply your reading skills to answer the questions below. Write your answer in the space provided.

_____ **16.** Which pattern is used to organize the information in paragraph 3?

    a. list

    b. sequence

    c. cause-effect

    d. comparison-contrast

_____ **17.** Based on information presented in the selection, parents in which country would be more likely to seek an arranged marriage for their children?

    a. America

    b. Zaire

    c. Japan

    d. Canada

_____ **18.** In paragraph 1, *universality* is used to mean which of the following?

    a. success

    b. adoption

    c. retreat from

    d. condition of occurring everywhere

_____ **19.** The authors of the selection present which of the following types of support?

    a. case studies

    b. expert testimony

    c. research studies

    d. personal experience

_____ **20.** Based upon information in the selection, which of the following represents a logical conclusion?

    a. Marriages based on love are more successful than arranged marriages.

    b. Marriages of many types can be successful.

    c. Marriages between Rajputs are empty and unfulfilling.

    d. Throughout the world, various societies' concepts of marriage are becoming more similar.

Collaboration Option

Writing and Collaborating to Enhance Your Understanding

Option for collaboration: Work together in groups to complete the exercises below. Have one group member record your answers, but make sure every member of your group can explain all of your group's answers.

1. **Reacting to What You Have Read:** What do you view as the primary purpose of marriage? What, in your opinion, is necessary for a marriage to be a successful marriage?

    _____

    _____

    _____

    _____

    _____

    _____

    _____

    _____

2. **Comprehending the Selection Further:** How do you think a person's age at the time of marriage is likely to affect the success of the marriage? In your opinion, what do you think is the minimum age a man should be before he marries? A woman? Explain your answer.

    _____

    _____

    _____

    _____

    _____

    _____

    _____

    _____

    _____

3. **Overall Main Idea of the Selection:** In one sentence tell what the author wants readers to understand about engagement and marriage. (Be sure to include the phrase "engagement and marriage" in your overall main idea sentence.)

_____

_____

_____

_____

_____

Read More about It on the World Wide Web

To learn more about the topic of this selection, visit these websites or use your favorite search engine (such as Yahoo®) to discover more about this author and this topic on your own. Whenever you go to *any* website, it is a good idea to evaluate it critically. Are you getting good information—that is, information that is accurate, complete, and up-to-date? Who sponsors the website? How easy is it to use the features of the website?

http://www.themuslimwoman.com/marriage/

http://uwselc.uws.edu.au/Kuwait_Wedding.htm

http://www.hawaii.edu/oceanic/rotuma/os/ceremonies/marriagemod.htm

(© PhotoDisc)

C H A P T E R **5**

Formulating an Implied Main Idea

CHAPTER OBJECTIVES

In this chapter you will learn:

- What an implied main idea sentence is and why it is important to be able to formulate one.

- Three methods of formulating an implied main idea sentence.

Selection 5-1 *(Art Appreciation)*
"Two Artistic Tributes: The Vietnam Memorial
and the AIDS Quilt"
by Rita Gilbert

Selection 5-2 *(Biology)*
"Causes of Cancer"
by Sylvia Mader

Selection 5-3 *(Psychology)*
"Why Relationships Develop and What Makes
Them Last"
by Benjamin Lahey

WHAT YOU NEED TO LEARN

WHAT IS AN IMPLIED MAIN IDEA SENTENCE, AND WHY IS IT IMPORTANT TO BE ABLE TO FORMULATE ONE?

KEY TERM
implied main idea
sentence

A sentence formulated by the
reader that expresses the
author's main point about
the topic.

An implied main idea is also
known as an *unstated main*
idea, an *indirectly stated main*
idea, and *a formulated main*
idea.

You already know that every paragraph has a main idea. But did you know that there are paragraphs that do not have *stated* main idea sentences? In such paragraphs, authors *suggest* the most important point, even though they do not state it directly in a single sentence. In other words, the author *implies* the main point.

When authors do not state the main idea directly in one sentence it is the reader's job to infer (reason out) the main point and write a sentence that expresses it. An **implied main idea sentence** is a sentence formulated by the reader that expresses an author's main point about the topic. In other words, when authors give the reader all the information needed to understand the main point, but do not state that point directly in one sentence, the reader must formulate that sentence. (In this book the terms *implied main idea sentence* and *formulated main idea sentence* are used interchangeably since they refer to the same thing.)

Why is it important for you to formulate an implied main idea sentence whenever the author does not state the main idea? There are several reasons: First, you limit your comprehension unless you are able to formulate main ideas that are implied. Also, when you formulate main ideas, it helps you remember material better. Finally, college instructors assume that students will read carefully enough to understand both stated and implied main ideas. Test items are just as likely to be based on implied main ideas as on stated main ideas.

To repeat, when an author implies the main idea, *you,* the reader, must reason out the author's main idea and formulate a sentence that expresses it. It will be reassuring to you to know that all the elements you need in order to formulate the main idea are already in the paragraph.

In this chapter, you will learn three "formulas" that you can use to "formulate" an implied main idea. The particular formula you use will depend on the type of information the author gives you in the paragraph. As you will learn, sometimes the only thing you need to do is add an essential word or a phrase to a sentence in the paragraph. In other cases, all you need to do is combine two or more sentences in the paragraph into one sentence. In still other cases, you will have to summarize ideas from several sentences or make a general inference based on the details. When a paragraph consists only of facts, descriptions, explanations, or examples that merely suggest the author's main point, it will be up to you to infer and then formulate a general main idea sentence. Remember, the main idea sentence you formulate must always be *based on* what is presented in the paragraph.

To be an effective reader, then, you must be able to formulate the main idea sentence when the author implies it, just as you must be able to locate the main idea when the author states it directly.

WHAT ARE THREE METHODS FOR FORMULATING AN IMPLIED MAIN IDEA SENTENCE?

Comprehension Monitoring Question for Implied Main Idea

"What is the single most important point the author wants me to *infer* about the topic of this paragraph?"

As always, you must begin by reading the paragraph and determining its topic. If you cannot locate a stated main idea sentence, ask yourself this comprehension monitoring question, "What is the single most important point the author wants me to *infer* about the topic of this paragraph?" Then use one of the three "formulas" explained below to help you create the "formulated" main idea sentence. How can you determine which formula to use? The formula you need to use will depend on what the author gives you to start with in the paragraph.

Here is an explanation of each formula, along with a simple example and an example from a college textbook.

Formula 1: Add an Essential Word or Phrase to a Sentence in the Paragraph That Almost States the Main Idea

Sometimes, an author expresses *most* of the main idea in one sentence of the paragraph, yet that sentence lacks an essential piece of information. You must add that essential information to make the sentence express the *complete* main idea. Quite often, a sentence may need to have the topic (a word, name, or phrase) inserted to make it express the main idea completely.

When you read a paragraph that has a sentence that almost states the main idea yet lacks essential information, use **Formula 1** to create the complete main idea sentence:

| Sentence that *almost* states the main idea | + | Essential word or phrase that needs to be added (usually the topic) | = | Formulated main idea sentence |

Here is a very simple paragraph that has been created to show how this formula can be applied. Read the paragraph and determine the topic by asking yourself "Who or what is this about?" Notice that there is a sentence that *almost* states the main idea, yet lacks an essential piece of information. Find that sentence.

Bob is excellent with customers. He is knowledgeable about our company's products. Moreover, he is a hard worker who always exceeds the sales goals. He is the best salesperson at our company.

Here is Formula 1 with the appropriate information from the paragraph:

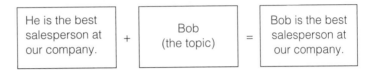

| He is the best salesperson at our company. | + | Bob (the topic) | = | Bob is the best salesperson at our company. |

The last sentence is the one that almost states the main idea ("He is the best salesperson at our company"), but it lacks the topic (Bob). When that essential information is added, you have the complete formulated main idea sentence: *Bob is the best salesperson at our company.*

When a paragraph contains a sentence that almost states the main idea, yet needs essential information added, it is the type of paragraph to which Formula 1 should be applied.

Here is a paragraph from a marketing textbook that has an implied main idea that can be formulated using Formula 1. The topic of this paragraph is *McDonald's spectacular success.* The second sentence *almost* states the authors' most important point, but it lacks an essential piece of information: the topic. A complete main idea sentence for this paragraph can be formulated by adding the topic, *McDonald's spectacular success,* to the second sentence of the paragraph. This formulated main idea sentence will express the most important point the authors want you to understand in this paragraph.

What explains McDonald's spectacular success? One major reason for it is the extent to which the company maintains strong controls over most aspects of its operations. These controls have helped McDonald's develop a competitive edge in the form of high product and service consistency. A Big Mac is likely to taste pretty much the same whether we are eating it in Boston or Bangkok. As noted economist Robert J. Samuelson reported in praising McDonald's, his Big Mac ordered at an outlet in Tokyo did not "merely taste like an American Big Mac"; it tasted "exactly the same."

Formulated Main Idea Sentence

_____

_____

_____

_____

_____

_____

_____

_____

Source: Adapted from Kathryn M. Bartol and David C. Martin, *Management,* 2nd ed. Copyright © 1994 McGraw-Hill. Reprinted by permission of The McGraw-Hill Companies.

Stop and Annotate

Go back to the textbook excerpt above. Write the formulated main idea sentence in
the space provided by adding
essential information to the
sentence that almost states
the main idea.

The second sentence becomes a complete formulated main idea sentence when the essential phrase *McDonald's spectacular success* is added to it: *One major reason for McDonald's spectacular success is the extent to which the company maintains strong controls over most aspects of its operations.*

Formula 2: Combine Two Sentences That Each Tell Part of the Main Idea

Sometimes a paragraph contains two sentences that each give *part* of the main idea. Each sentence contains important information, yet neither sentence by itself expresses the complete main idea. Therefore, since the author has not stated the main idea as a single sentence, you must *combine* these two sentences into *one* sentence that expresses the complete main idea. (You already know that any main idea must be written as a single sentence.) Often you will be able to use words such as *and, but,* or *however* to join the two sentences. The two sentences you combine may follow one another in the paragraph (for example, the first two sentences of the paragraph). Or they may be separated (for example, the first sentence of the paragraph and the last sentence of the paragraph).

When you realize that two sentences in a paragraph each state *part* of the main idea, use **Formula 2** to create a complete main idea that is a single sentence:

Sentence that expresses *part* of the main idea	+	Sentence that expresses *rest* of the main idea	=	Formulated main idea sentence

Here is another simple paragraph that has been created to show how this formula can be applied. Read the paragraph and notice that there are two sentences that each give part of the main idea but that must be combined into a single sentence to formulate the complete main idea.

Maria is taking a full academic load this semester. She is taking history, psychology, computer science, math, and a writing course. She has classes five days a week. But she still finds time to do volunteer work. On Saturday mornings she is a volunteer at the library. On Sunday afternoons she does volunteer work at the hospital.

Here is Formula 2 with the appropriate information from the paragraph:

Maria is taking a full academic load this semester.	+	But she still finds time to do volunteer work.	=	Maria is taking a full academic load this semester, but she still finds time to do volunteer work.

The first sentence and the fourth sentence express the important information, so they must be combined into a single sentence. Therefore, the formulated main idea sentence would be: *Maria is taking a full academic load this semester, but she still finds time to do volunteer work.*

Here is a paragraph from a psychology textbook that has an implied main idea that can be formulated using Formula 2. As the heading indicates, the topic of this paragraph is *the origins of sexual orientation.* Since the first two sentences each tell half of the main idea, a main idea sentence for this paragraph can be formulated by combining them into a single sentence.

Origins of Sexual Orientation

It is not known why any person develops a particular sexual orientation. However, a good guess is that it develops through a complex interaction of biological and sociocultural factors. John Money has proposed a specific theory of sexual orientation that balances the roles of biological and sociocultural influences. He states that all sexual orientation has its origins in the womb when the nervous system is still developing. Money believes that the brain is shaped during fetal development by a complex interplay of genetics and hormones. The factors organize the brain in a way that predisposes the person toward either heterosexuality or homosexuality. Later, during sensitive periods of development in childhood or adolescence, sexual orientation is shaped by social and interpersonal experiences, but persons are more likely to develop a sexual orientation that is consistent with their biological predisposition.

Formulated Main Idea Sentence

_____

_____

_____

_____

_____

_____

_____

_____

_____

Source: From Benjamin B. Lahey, *Psychology,* 6th ed. Copyright © 1997 McGraw-Hill. Reprinted by permission of The McGraw-Hill Companies.

Stop and Annotate

Go back to the textbook excerpt above. Write the formulated main idea sentence in the space provided by combining the two sentences in the paragraph that together express the complete main idea.

The first two sentences are both more important than the other sentences in the paragraph, but neither sentence by itself expresses the complete main idea. The first sentence explains that we are not exactly certain why a person develops a particular sexual orientation; the second sentence explains the probable reason a particular sexual orientation develops. These two sentences should be combined to formulate a complete main idea sentence: *It is not known why a person develops a particular sexual orientation; however, a good guess, is that it develops through a complex interaction of biological and sociocultural factors.*

Remember that there is more than one correct way to express an implied main idea when you are combining two sentences. What is important is that the main idea is correct and complete. For example, the main idea of the excerpt on page 225 could also be expressed: *It is not known why a person develops a particular sexual orientation, but a good guess is that it develops through a complex interaction of biological and sociocultural factors.* Or *People seem to develop sexual orientation through a complex interaction of biological and sociocultural factors, although the specific reason is not known.*

Formula 3: Summarize Important Ideas into One Sentence or Write One Sentence That Gives a General Inference Based on the Details

With some paragraphs that have implied main ideas, you will either have to formulate a main idea sentence that *summarizes* the important information in the paragraph or else formulate a sentence that gives a *general inference* based on the details. Which of these you do will depend upon the type of information you are given in the paragraph. When you create this kind of formulated main idea sentence, you will often have to use some of your own words along with certain important words from the paragraph.

When a paragraph has important ideas included in several sentences or the paragraph consists only of details, **Formula 3** should be used to formulate the main idea.

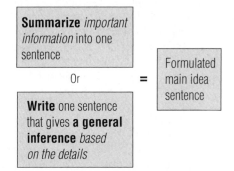

Here is a simple paragraph created to show how you can summarize important ideas to create the formulated main idea. Read the paragraph and notice which ideas have been summarized to create the formulated main idea.

John doesn't trust strangers. He does not trust his neighbors, nor does he trust his co-workers. He does, however, trust members of his family. And he trusts his best friend, Ramon.

Here is Formula 3 with the appropriate information from the paragraph.

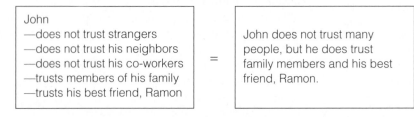

A formulated main idea sentence that summarizes the important information into one sentence is *John does not trust many people but he does trust family members and his best friend, Ramon.* (Of course, the main idea could also be expressed in shorter ways, *John trusts only family members and his best friend,* or *Family members and his best friend are the only people John trusts.*)

A word of caution: Do not create one long sentence in which you merely restate all of the information, such as *John doesn't trust strangers and he does not trust his neighbors and he does not trust his co-workers, but he does, however, trust members of his family and his best friend, Ramon.*

Now consider another type of paragraph, one that consists only of details. When a paragraph consists of details only, you must infer the general point the author is trying to make. Then, formulate one sentence, a main idea sentence, that expresses that point. Although none of the actual details appear in this kind of main idea sentence, the main idea is *based* on those details. For example,

Lynn likes to swim and water ski. She also enjoys snow skiing and ice skating. She has loved basketball since elementary school. She is captain of the tennis team this year. And she is very excited about her upcoming soccer season.

Here is Formula 3 with the appropriate information from the paragraph:

Lynn likes —swimming and water skiing —snow skiing and ice skating —basketball —tennis —soccer	=	Lynn likes many sports.

Here is a formulated main idea sentence that gives a general inference *based* on the details: *Lynn likes many sports.*

Notice that although the word *sports* does not appear in the paragraph, it can be used as a general term to describe the activities mentioned in the details. (Of course, the main idea sentence could also be expressed in any of these ways: *Lynn loves several sports; Lynn enjoys many sports;* or even *Lynn participates in a variety of sports.*)

Here is paragraph from a study skills textbook that has an implied main idea that can be formulated using Formula 3. The topic of the paragraph is *being more successful on future tests.* The implied main idea can be formulated by writing a sentence that summarizes the important information into one sentence.

When you do poorly on a test, don't blame the teacher. Nor should you blame the textbook, or say that a job kept you from studying. Analyze the situation. Identify things you could change to be more successful in the future.

Formulated Main Idea Sentence

_____

_____

_____

_____

Source: Adapted from Robert S. Feldman, *P.O.W.E.R. Learning,* p. 13. Copyright © 2000 McGraw-Hill. Reprinted by permission of The McGraw-Hill Companies.

Stop and Annotate

Go back to the textbook excerpt above. Formulate a sentence that *summarizes* the important information from several sentences into a single sentence and write in the space provided.

To create a main idea for this paragraph, you must examine the details, think about them, and ask yourself, "What is the important point the author wants me to *infer* about being more successful on future tests?" The formulated main idea is *When you do poorly on a test, rather than placing blame, analyze and identify changes you could make to be more successful in the future.*

Here is another paragraph from the same study skills textbook that also has an implied main idea that can be formulated using Formula 3. The topic of the paragraph is *strategies for answering specific kinds of test questions.* The implied main idea can be formulated by writing a sentence that gives a general inference based on the details.

Are there specific strategies for answering various kinds of test questions? For essay questions, be sure to understand each question and each of its parts, interpret action words correctly, write concisely, organize the essay logically, and include examples. For multiple-choice questions, read the questions very carefully and then read all response choices. Educated guessing based on eliminating incorrect response choices is usually a reasonable strategy. For true-false and matching questions, quickly answer all the items that you are sure of and then go back to the remaining items. The best strategy for short-answer and fill-in questions is to be very sure what is being asked. Keep answers complete but brief.

Formulated Main Idea Sentence

_____

_____

_____

_____

_____

Source: Adapted from Robert S. Feldman. *P.O.W.E.R. Learning,* p. 162. Copyright © 2000 McGraw-Hill. Reprinted by permission of The McGraw-Hill Companies.

Stop and Annotate

Go back to the textbook excerpt above. Formulate a sentence that gives a *general inference* based on the details and write it in the space provided.

To create a main idea for this paragraph, you must examine the details, think about them, and ask yourself, "What is the single most general point the author wants me to *infer* about strategies for answering specific kinds of test questions?" A logical formulated main idea is *There are specific strategies for answering various kinds of test questions.*

When you read a paragraph that does not have a stated main idea, use one of the formulas to create a sentence that tells the author's implied main idea. The chart below summarizes the three ways to formulate implied main idea sentences. Once you have read a paragraph and determined what the author gives you to start with (column 1), look beside it (column 2) to see the correct formula to use and how to apply the formula.

THREE WAYS TO FORMULATE IMPLIED MAIN IDEA SENTENCES

What the Author Gives You to Start with in the Paragraph	What You Must Do with the Information in Order to Formulate the Implied Main Idea
A sentence that *almost* states the main idea, but lacks some essential piece of information (usually the topic)	*Use Formula 1.* *Add* the essential piece of information that is missing to that sentence. *How to apply the formula:* You can use the sentence from the paragraph and simply add or insert the information. *or* You can write the main idea in your own words as long as the meaning is the same.
Two sentences in the paragraph that each present *part* of the main idea	*Use Formula 2.* *Combine* them into one sentence (since the main idea must always be written as a single sentence). *How to apply the formula:* You will probably have to add a word or two in order to connect the two sentences (usually words such as *and, but, although,* etc.). *or* You can write the main idea in your own words, as long as the meaning is the same.
Important information in several sentences	*Use Formula 3.* Summarize important information into one sentence.
Details only	*Use Formula 3.* *Write* a *general sentence* that "sums up" the details or expresses the overall point the author is making. *How to apply the formula:* The sentence you write will consist mostly of your own words.

OTHER THINGS TO KEEP IN MIND WHEN FORMULATING AN IMPLIED MAIN IDEA SENTENCE

Here are three helpful things you should know about when formulating main idea sentences that have been implied:

1. You must always use a sentence—not just a phrase—to express a formulated main idea. This means you must know the difference between a sentence and a phrase.

As you know, the main idea of a paragraph must be expressed as a complete sentence. A sentence has a subject and a verb and always expresses a complete thought. A phrase, on the other hand, is a group of words (even a long group of words) that does not express a complete thought. Sentences must be used to express main ideas, but phrases must *never* be used to express a main idea.

The left column (below) gives examples of phrases that could be used as topics. None of the items in this column could be used as main ideas because they are not complete sentences. The right column contains sentences that could be used to express main ideas because they are complete sentences. (Notice that in each case, the topic is part of the complete sentence.)

Could *Not* Be Used as a Formulated Main Idea (because it is a phrase)	Could Be Used as a Formulated Main Idea (because it is a complete sentence)
traveling by plane	Traveling by plane is the fastest way to travel long distances to foreign countries.
fatality rates for passengers traveling by plane	Fatality rates for passengers traveling by plane are lower than fatality rates for passengers traveling by car.
why traveling by plane is the best way to go	There are several reasons why traveling by plane is the best way to go.
how to overcome fear of traveling by plane	Psychologists have several methods to teach people how to overcome fear of traveling by plane.
the truck	The truck ran the stop sign.
the red truck	The red truck ran the stop sign.
the red truck with a broken headlight	The red truck with a broken headlight ran the stop sign.
the red truck with a broken headlight and a noisy muffler	The red truck with a broken headlight and a noisy muffler ran the stop sign.

2. All formulated (implied) main idea sentences must have certain characteristics. A formulated main idea must:

- Be a *complete sentence* that includes the *topic* of the paragraph.
- Express the *author's most important general point about the topic.* (In other words, if the formulated main idea sentence were placed at the beginning of the paragraph, the other sentences would explain, prove, or tell more about it.)
- *Make complete sense by itself* without the reader having to read the rest of the paragraph.

Here is an example of a sentence that would not be meaningful by itself since the reader would not know who "her" refers to: *Most historians consistently rank her among the most effective leaders of the 20th century.* Therefore, this sentence could not be a correctly formulated main idea sentence. On the other hand, this sentence could be a main idea sentence, since it makes sense by itself: *Most historians consistently rank former British Prime Minister Margaret Thatcher among the most effective leaders of the 20th century.*

Remember also that an implied main idea sentence can be worded in various ways, as long as it meets the three requirements.

3. A longer passage often has an implied overall main idea that you must formulate.

Sometimes the reader must formulate an *overall* implied main idea that gives the general point of an entire selection. (A longer passage might consist of a section of a textbook chapter, a short reading selection, or an essay, for example.) The overall formulated main idea is a general statement or inference that is *based on* the main ideas of the selection. That is, the formulated overall main idea sentence summarizes or sums up the main ideas of the individual paragraphs in the selection, just as the main idea of each paragraph sums up the individual details in the paragraph. To be correct, a formulated overall main idea sentence must meet the same requirements as the formulated main idea of a paragraph.

PRACTICE: COULD THIS BE A FORMULATED MAIN IDEA SENTENCE?

The main idea must always be a *sentence;* it must also contain a *topic* and must make *complete sense* by itself. For example,

- There is no greater influence on children than their parents. *(Yes, this could be a stated main idea because the sentence makes complete sense by itself.)*

- There is no greater influence on children. *(No, this could not be a stated main idea sentence because we don't know what the influence is. The sentence does not make complete sense by itself.)*

- The greatest influence on children. *(No; this could not be a stated main idea because it isn't even a sentence.)*

Directions: For the items below, decide whether each could be a formulated main idea sentence. (All of them end with periods, although not all of them are sentences.) If an item contains a topic and makes complete sense by itself, write Y for Yes. If it does not, write N for No.

_____ **1.** The benefits of a healthy diet.

_____ **2.** There are several reasons HIV has not yet been eradicated.

_____ **3.** It was the biggest scare New York City ever experienced.

_____ **4.** The importance of art and music in children's lives.

_____ **5.** It is the best treatment available for preventing a heart attack.

_____ **6.** There are three major types.

_____ **7.** Cell phones can be dangerous if people use them while driving.

_____ **8.** They can be dangerous if people use them while driving.

_____ **9.** Most of them are sleep deprived.

_____ **10.** It was a crowning moment in Olympic history.

_____ **11.** Whether the new plan will work.

_____ **12.** Using a study schedule has several benefits.

_____ **13.** The government should not adopt this policy.

_____ **14.** How working too many hours affects college students' academic success.

_____ **15.** Working too many hours affects college students' academic success.

_____ **16.** He fled from Mecca to Medina.

_____ **17.** Muhammad fled from Mecca to Medina.

_____ **18.** It was the turning point of his life.

_____ **19.** It was the turning point of Muhammad's life.

_____ **20.** Muhammad's flight from Mecca to Medina was the turning point of his life.

DEVELOPING CHAPTER REVIEW CARDS

Chapter review cards are a way to select, organize, and review the important information in a textbook chapter. Preparing chapter review cards helps you organize the information so that you can learn and memorize it more easily. In other words, chapter review cards are an effective study tool.

Preparing chapter review cards for each chapter of this book will give you practice in creating these valuable study tools. Once you have learned how to make chapter review cards, you can use actual index cards to create them for textbook material in any of your courses and use them when you study for tests.

Now, complete the chapter review cards for this chapter by answering the questions or following the directions on each "card" below. (The boxes below represent index cards.) The page numbers indicate the place in the chapter the information can be found.

Implied Main Idea Sentences

1. What is the definition of an *implied main idea sentence?* (See page 221.)

_____

_____

2. List three reasons it is important to understand and formulate the implied main idea of a paragraph. (See page 221.)

_____

_____

_____

_____

3. What question should you ask yourself in order to formulate the implied main idea of a paragraph? Be sure you write a *question.* (See page 222.)

_____

_____

Card 1   Chapter 5: Formulating an Implied Main Idea

Three Ways to Formulate an Implied Main Idea Sentence

Write the three formulas for creating implied main idea sentences. (See pages 222–225.)

Formula 1:

Formula 2:

Formula 3:

What determines which formula you will use? (See page 222.)

_____

_____

Card 2   Chapter 5: Formulating an Implied Main Idea

When Formulating the Implied Main Idea, Keep in Mind . . .

The three characteristics of a correctly formulated implied main idea sentence are: (See page 231.)

1. _____

_____

2. _____

_____

3. _____

_____

Card 3   Chapter 5: Formulating an Implied Main Idea

COMPREHENSION PRACTICE: FORMULATING IMPLIED MAIN IDEA EXERCISES (1)

Study the example below to see how information you learned in this chapter can be used to formulate the implied main idea of a paragraph. When you are sure you understand the example, complete the exercises that follow.

EXAMPLE

This excerpt comes from a health textbook. Its topic is *single parents and child care.* To determine the implied main idea, read the paragraph and ask yourself, "What is the single most important point the author wants me to *infer* about single parents and child care?"

Child Care and Parenting

If single parents can find child care, it is often too costly. The expense of child care can consume 25 percent to 60 percent of the family income. If the parent moves into his or her parents' house to cut costs and have grandparental child care readily available, there may be child-rearing conflicts, with the parent and grandparents setting different rules, which leaves the children confused. Parental authority is weakened if the parent is viewed as a child again.

Source: From Wayne Payne and Dale Hahn, *Understanding Your Health,* 5th ed. Copyright © 1995 McGraw-Hill. Reprinted by permission of The McGraw-Hill Companies.

The topic of this paragraph is *single parents and child care.*

_____ *b* _____ What is the implied main idea of this paragraph?

    a. If single parents can find child care, it is often too costly.

    b. Child care can present several difficulties for single parents.

    c. If the parent moves into his or her parents' house, there may be child-rearing conflicts.

    d. Parental authority is weakened if the parent is viewed as a child again.

The correct answer is b. This formulated main idea is a general sentence that expresses the most important point the author wants you to know about single parents and child care, that it can present several difficulties. Since it was necessary to write a sentence that gives a general inference based on the details in the paragraph, Formula 3 was applied. Choices a, c, and d are not correct because they express difficulties: the cost of child care, the possibility of child-rearing conflicts, and weakened parental authority. Also, choices a and d are stated in the paragraph, so neither can be the implied main idea.

Directions:

- First, read the paragraph carefully. Notice that you are given the topic of each paragraph.
- Then select the answer choice that expresses the implied (formulated) main idea of the paragraph and write the letter in the space provided. Be sure the sentence you select has the characteristics of a main idea sentence that are described on pages 230–231.

1.   This paragraph comes from a biology textbook.

Fossils Tell a Story

Fossils are at least 10,000 years old. They include such items as pieces of bone and impressions of plants pressed into shale. Fossils also include insects trapped in tree resin (amber). They give a record of the history of life as recorded by remains from the past, and, over the last two centuries, paleontologists have studied them and have pieced together the story of past life.

Source: Sylvia S. Mader, *Biology,* 6th ed., p. 296. Copyright © 1998 McGraw-Hill. Reprinted by permission of The McGraw-Hill Companies.

The topic of this paragraph is *fossils.*

————   What is the implied main idea of this paragraph?

a.   Fossils are at least 10,000 years old.

b.   Fossils include such items as pieces of bone, impressions of plants pressed into shale, and insects trapped in tree resin.

c.   Fossils give a record of the history of life as recorded by remains from the past, and, over the last two centuries, paleontologists have studied them and have pieced together the story of past life.

d.   Fossils are at least 10,000 years old and they include insects trapped in tree resin (amber).

2.   This paragraph comes from an information technology textbook.

The World Wide Web, or just the Web, is only a few years old, but is growing at an astounding rate. Tens of thousands of computers are now connected so you can use your computer mouse to point and click your way around the world. On a trip through the Web, you can visit colleges, companies, museums, government departments, and other individuals like yourself. As you move through the Web, you can read data on almost every imaginable topic. You can visit stores to buy things or transfer movies, pictures, games, and other software to your computer, much of it free.

Source: From Dennis P. Curtin et al., *Information Technology.* Copyright © 1996 McGraw-Hill. Reprinted by permission of The McGraw-Hill Companies.

The topic of this paragraph is *the World Wide Web.*

————   What is the implied main idea of this paragraph?

a.   The fast-growing World Wide Web can be used for a wide variety of purposes.

b.   The World Wide Web, or just the Web, is only a few years old, but is growing at an astounding rate.

c.   You can use it to buy things and to transfer movies, pictures, games, and other software to your computer, much of it free.

d.   Tens of thousands of computers allow you to access data on almost every imaginable topic.

3. This paragraph comes from a communications textbook.

Receiving criticism can be tougher than giving it. When people are faced with criticism, the two most common responses are "fight" and "flight." Fighters react by counterattacking. "It's not my fault," they might protest. Another fighting response is to blame the others: "I'm not the only one who's at fault here." Those who prefer flight often avoid those who have criticized them by steering clear of them or not returning their phone calls. However, neither fighting nor fleeing is a very satisfactory way of dealing with the problem.

Source: From Ronald Adler and Jeanne Elmhorst, *Communicating at Work,* 5th ed. Copyright © 1996 McGraw-Hill. Reprinted by permission of The McGraw-Hill Companies.

The topic of this paragraph is *criticism.*

_____ What is the implied main idea of this paragraph?

a. Fighters react to criticism by blaming others and avoiding those who have criticized them.

b. When people are faced with criticism, the two most common responses are "fight" and "flight"; however, neither fighting nor fleeing is a very satisfactory way of dealing with the problem.

c. Receiving criticism can be tougher than giving it.

d. No one likes to receive criticism.

4. This paragraph comes from a computer science textbook.

Modems

Compatibility between the digital signals of computers and the analog signals used by telephones requires special devices for encoding and decoding data. These devices are known as *modems* (from the terms *mod*ulation and *dem*odulation). When two computers exchange data by modems, the sending modem modulates digital data into analog form for transmission over standard telephone lines. The modem at the receiving end demodulates the analog signals back into digital form for input to the receiving computer.

Source: From Timothy N. Trainor and Diane Krasnewich, *Computers!,* 5th ed. Copyright © 1996. McGraw-Hill. Reprinted by permission of The McGraw-Hill Companies.

The topic of this paragraph is *modems.*

_____ What is the implied main idea of this paragraph?

a. Compatibility between the digital signals of computers and the analog signals used by telephones requires modems, special devices for encoding and decoding data.

b. When two computers exchange data, there must be a modem to modulate digital data.

c. The modem at the receiving end demodulates the signals and sends them to the receiving computer.

d. All computers use modems.

5.   This paragraph comes from a human development textbook.

Culture and Children's Prosocial Behavior

Why are children in some cultures more prosocial than others? It may be because they experience more love and less rejection. For example, among the Papago Indians in Arizona, parents are warm, supportive, and nurturing. In contrast, Alores parents in Java are hostile and neglectful. This, among other differences, may account for the cooperative, peaceful personality typical of Papago children, as compared with the hostile, distrustful, and aggressive behavior of Alores children.

Source: Adapted from Diane E. Papalia and Sally Olds, *Human Development,* 6th ed. Copyright © 1999 McGraw-Hill. Reprinted by permission of The McGraw-Hill Companies.

The topic of this paragraph is *culture and children's prosocial behavior.*

—————   What is the implied main idea of this paragraph?

a.   Why are children in some cultures more prosocial than others?

b.   Papago children are cooperative and have peaceful personalities as compared with the hostile, distrustful, and aggressive behavior of Alores children.

c.   There are many differences between Papago children and Alores children.

d.   The reason children in some cultures are more prosocial than others may be because they experience more love and less rejection.

Study the example in the box below to see how information you learned in this chapter can be used to formulate the implied main idea of a paragraph. When you are sure you understand the example, complete the five exercises that follow.

EXAMPLE

This excerpt comes from a communications textbook. As you will see, its topic is *the meaning of a word*. To determine the implied main idea, read the paragraph and ask yourself, "What is the single most important point the author wants me to *infer* about the meaning of a word?"

A common problem encountered in our use of language involves the belief that every word has only one meaning. This, of course, is not true. Surprisingly, the two thousand most frequently used words have approximately fourteen thousand meanings. In your vocabulary, you have these and probably countless words with multiple meanings and uses. The word *cat*, for example, can refer to a domestic animal, a type of tractor, a type of fish, a type of boat, a jazz musician, or a whip. In a similar fashion, the word *lap* can represent the distance around a track, a portion of one's anatomy, the drinking method of a cat or dog, or the sound of water washing gently against the side of a boat.

Source: Larry Samovar and Jack Mills, *Oral Communication: Speaking across Cultures*, 10th ed., p. 256. Copyright ©1998 McGraw-Hill. Reprinted by permission of The McGraw-Hill Companies.

Write the topic: <u>the meaning of a word</u>

Formulate a main idea sentence: <u>A common problem encountered in our use of language involves the belief that every word has only one meaning, but this, of course, is not true.</u>

Explanation: The topic, *the meaning of a word,* appears in the first sentence. In the first sentence, the authors explain a common belief that many people have. In the second sentence they state that this belief is not true. The main idea of this paragraph can be formulated by using Formula 2 and combining these two sentences into a single sentence.

Directions:

- First, read the paragraph carefully.
- Then determine the word, name or phrase that tells the topic, and write it in the space provided.
- Formulate your implied main idea sentence and write it in the space provided. Your formulated main idea sentence must have the characteristics listed on pages 230–231. (Remember that all of these paragraphs have *implied* main ideas. In other words, you cannot underline or use a sentence in the paragraph as your answer for the main idea.)

1. This paragraph comes from a health textbook.

   Bias and Hate Crimes

   One sad aspect of any society is how some segments of the majority treat certain people in the minority. Nowhere is this more violently pronounced than in bias and hate crimes. These crimes are directed at individuals or groups of people solely because of a racial, ethnic, religious, or other difference attributed to the victims. Victims are often verbally and physically attacked, their houses are spray painted with slurs, and many are forced to move from one neighborhood or community to another.

   Source: From Wayne Payne and Dale Hahn, *Understanding Your Health,* 5th ed. Copyright © 1995 McGraw-Hill. Reprinted by permission of The McGraw-Hill Companies.

   Write the topic: _____

   Formulate a main idea sentence: _____

   _____

   _____

   _____

2. This paragraph comes from a communications textbook.

   How can you deal constructively with criticism? There are at least two constructive ways. One way is to seek more information. This shows that you are taking the criticism seriously, but, at the same time, you are not accepting blame for the problem. (Example: "You've said that I'm not demonstrating a good attitude. Can you describe exactly what I'm doing?") A second way is to agree with the facts of the criticism if they are accurate ("You're right. I've been late three times this week.") or to agree with the person's perception ("I can understand why it might seem as if I didn't care about finishing this project on time. I did promise you that it would be done by Friday afternoon, and I missed the deadline. I'd be mad too if I were you.").

   Source: From Ronald Adler and Jeanne Elmhorst, *Communicating at Work,* 5th ed. Copyright © 1996 McGraw-Hill. Reprinted by permission of The McGraw-Hill Companies.

   Write the topic: _____

   Formulate a main idea sentence: _____

   _____

   _____

   _____

3. This paragraph comes from a geography textbook.

A category 1 hurricane has winds of 74–95 mph (miles per hour). Category 2 hurricane winds increase to 96–110 mph. At the category 3 level, the winds reach 111–130 mph. The next higher category hurricanes attain wind speeds of 131–155 mph. Finally, the strongest hurricanes, those in category 5, have wind speeds above 155 mph.

Source: Adapted from Arthur Getis, Judith Getis, and Jerome D. Fellmann, *Introduction to Geography,* 6th ed., p. 117. Copyright © 1998 McGraw-Hill. Reprinted by permission of The McGraw-Hill Companies.

Write the topic: _____

Formulate a main idea sentence: _____

_____

_____

_____

_____

4. This paragraph comes from a psychology textbook.

Narcolepsy

Narcolepsy is a rare sleep disorder, occurring in less than one-half of 1 percent of the general population. However, its impact can be quite serious. The narcoleptic often falls unexpectedly into a deep slumber in the middle of work or even conversations with others, especially when upset or stressed. Often the individual experiences loss of muscle tone and shows a lack of body movement as if she or he has suddenly fallen into dream sleep, but laboratory studies show that narcoleptic sleep is not REM sleep. Often these sudden bouts of sleep cause serious difficulties with the use of dangerous machines and other job-related activities.

Source: From Benjamin B. Lahey, *Psychology: An Introduction,* 6th ed. Copyright © 1997 McGraw-Hill. Reprinted by permission of The McGraw-Hill Companies.

Write the topic: _____

Formulate a main idea sentence: _____

_____

_____

_____

5.   This paragraph comes from a psychology textbook.

Myths about Gays and Lesbians

It is a commonly believed myth that homosexual persons take on the gender roles of the other sex. That is, that gay men act feminine and lesbian women are masculine. In fact, homosexual persons, like heterosexuals, exhibit a wide range of gender roles. Another myth is that gays and lesbians try to seduce heterosexuals into becoming homosexual. Again, no evidence supports this belief.

Source: From Benjamin B. Lahey, *Psychology: An Introduction,* 6th ed. Copyright © 1997 McGraw-Hill. Reprinted by permission of The McGraw-Hill Companies.

Write the topic: _____

Formulate a main idea sentence: _____

_____

_____

_____

SELECTION 5-1

ART APPRECIATION

TWO ARTISTIC TRIBUTES: THE VIETNAM MEMORIAL AND THE AIDS QUILT

From *Living with Art*

By Rita Gilbert

This selection from an art appreciation textbook explains why the Vietnam Memorial and the AIDS Quilt, despite their obvious differences, are two works of art that share a great deal in common. The AIDS Quilt was first displayed in Washington, D.C., in 1987 and then displayed there again in 1992. Because of its ever-increasing size, the last full display of the quilt was in Washington, D.C., in 1996. Since then, sections of it continue to be loaned to schools, libraries, and museums throughout the world to raise public awareness of AIDS and its impact on millions of lives.

1   There are two particular works of art that have much in common. Both commemorate death on a hideously large scale. Both are memorials to *unexpected* death—not the anticipated rest after a long life, but death coming prematurely, striking mostly the young. And both are meant to personalize each death among the many, to celebrate the individual life that was amid a mass tragedy.

2   The Vietnam Memorial in Washington, D.C., is the most-visited spot in the nation's capital. Completed in 1982, the memorial was designed by Maya Ying Lin, who was just twenty-two years old when her entry was selected from more than 1,400 submitted for this government commission.

3   When it was first unveiled to the public, its design was highly controversial. It is, after all, nothing more than two long walls of polished black granite, set into the earth so as to form a V. Many viewers felt "the Wall," as it has come to be called, flouted tradition, that it was not sufficiently respectful of those who fought the bloody Vietnam war. Many thought a statue of a heroic soldier marching off to battle would be more appropriate.

4   But public opinion changes. In time the American public came to accept this memorial—with its 58,000 names carved into the stark granite walls—as the most fitting tribute to those who died. Visitors who had no connection with the war, even young people who cannot remember the war, stand quietly before the roster of names—names on a mass tombstone. Many come to find a particular name, the name of a dead relative chiseled forever into the rock and not to be forgotten. They leave flowers and poems, teddy bears and ribbons, photographs and letters, reminders of the past. Mostly the relatives touch the Wall, running fingers over the carved letters as though to touch once again the life that is gone.

Annotation Practice Exercises

Directions: For each exercise below, write the topic of the paragraph on the lines beside the paragraph. Then formulate a main idea sentence for the paragraph and write it on the lines provided. (Remember that you cannot use any sentence that appears in the paragraph just as it is: the annotation exercise paragraphs do not have stated main ideas.)

Annotation Exercise

Topic of paragraph 3:

_____

_____

Formulate the implied main idea of this paragraph and write your sentence here:

_____

_____

_____

_____

_____

_____

_____

Maya Ying Lin, Vietnam Memorial, Washington, D.C. 1982. Black granite, length 492′. *(Mark Segal/Panoramic Stock Images)*

5   The Vietnam War is long over; no more names will be added to the Wall. But another wave of unexpected death has swept the nation and the world, also striking primarily the young, and it will not pass soon. In the United States, San Francisco has been especially hard-hit by the epidemic, and it was there that the Names Project began. The purpose of the Names Project is simple: to memorialize as *individuals* those who have died from AIDS, to remember that each was a unique human being, though all are bound together by a common death. No better means could have been chosen than the AIDS Quilt.

6   The AIDS Quilt consists of hand-sewn panels. Each commemorates one person who has died from AIDS. Some of the 3 by 6 feet panels have a name and a photograph, others just initials or forms symbolizing that person's interests, abilities, and achievements. Each panel tells a story, a story ended too soon, therefore all the more precious in the telling.

7   The choice of a quilt format is especially meaningful. Historically, quilts have often told lifetime stories, incorporating bits of fabric from important life events. Quilts make us think of warmth and protection and nurturing. And quilting has traditionally been a community activity, so it is natural that a community should form among those grieving death from common illness.

8   Unlike the Vietnam Memorial, the AIDS Quilt cannot possibly remember all who have died. Only those whose friends or families chose to be involved in the Names Project are represented. Tragically, that number has already created work of horrific scope. The illustration here shows

Annotation Exercise

Topic of paragraph 6:

_____

_____

Formulate the implied main idea of this paragraph and write your sentence here:

_____

_____

_____

_____

_____

The NAMES Project, Atlanta. *AIDS Memorial Quilt.* Displayed on the Mall; Washington, D.C., October 1996.
(Paul Margolies, © 1996 NAMES Project Foundation)

the quilt spread out in Washington, D.C., in October of 1996. By that time the quilt had grown to more than 37,000 panels and spread out on the Mall for nearly a mile from the U.S. Capitol to the Washington Monument.

9   As a work of art, the AIDS Quilt presents many contradictions. Few of its panels, individually, might be considered great art, yet the whole makes a powerful artistic statement. In its entirety, as we watch it grow, the work is incomparably sad, yet each panel is the celebration of a single life. Inevitably, the quilt is a work on progress; it cannot be finished until the plague has been stopped. It is art for the dead—trying to make life bearable for the living.

Source: Adapted from Rita Gilbert, *Living with Art,* 5th ed., pp. 79–81. Copyright © 1998 McGraw-Hill. Reprinted by permission of The McGraw-Hill Companies.

Comprehension and Vocabulary Quiz

This quiz has four parts. Your instructor may assign some or all of them.

Comprehension

Directions: Items 1–5 test your comprehension (understanding) of the material in this selection. These questions are much like those that a content area instructor (such as a art appreciation professor) would expect you to know after studying this selection. For each comprehension question below, use information from the selection to determine the correct answer. Refer to the selection as you answer the questions. Write your answer in the space provided.

_____ 1. The most significant difference between the Vietnam Memorial and the AIDS Quilt is that
  a. one is stationary and the other can be moved.
  b. one memorial is complete and the other is not.
  c. one is black and the other is in color.
  d. an individual person designed one memorial and thousands of people designed the other.

_____ 2. The Vietnam Memorial was
  a. completed in 1982 and has 1,400 names carved into its walls.
  b. originally a statue of a heroic soldier marching off to battle.
  c. completed in 1982 and has 58,000 names carved on its granite walls.
  d. constructed in 1996 and includes 37,000 panels.

_____ 3. Each panel of the AIDS Quilt
  a. represents one person who has died from AIDS.
  b. contains a name and a photograph.
  c. gives the initials and achievements of a person who died from AIDS.
  d. can be considered great art.

_____ 4. The choice of a quilt format for the Names Project is especially meaningful because quilts
  a. remind us of death.
  b. are like the stark granite walls of a memorial.
  c. make us think of warmth, protection, and nurturing.
  d. are powerful artistic statements that make life bearable.

_____ 5. Both the AIDS Quilt and the Vietnam Memorial are meant to
  a. memorialize the lives of individuals.
  b. record the names of everyone who died in the Vietnam war or who died from AIDS.
  c. grow as the names of those who have died are added.
  d. memorialize a tragic war and a terrible disease.

Vocabulary in Context

Directions: Items 6–10 test your ability to determine the meaning of a word by using context clues. *Context clues* are words in a sentence that allow the reader to deduce (reason out) the meaning of an unfamiliar word in that sentence. Context clues also enable the reader to determine which meaning the author intends when a word has more than one meaning. For each vocabulary item below, a sentence from the selection containing an important word (*italicized, like this*) is quoted first. Next, there is an additional sentence using the word in the same sense and providing another context clue. Use the context clues from *both* sentences to deduce the meaning of the italicized word. *Be sure the answer you choose makes sense in both sentences.* If you discover that you need to use a dictionary to confirm an answer choice, remember that the meaning you select must still fit the context of *both* sentences. Write your answer in the space provided.

Pronunciation Key: ă **pat** ā **pay** âr **care** ä **father** ĕ **pet** ē **be** ĭ **pit**
ī **tie** îr **pier** ŏ **pot** ō **toe** ô **paw** oi **noise** ou **out** ŏŏ **took** ōō **boot**
ŭ **cut** yōō **abuse** ûr **urge** th **thin** *th* **this** hw **which** zh **vision**
ə **about**   Stress mark: ′

_____ 6. Both works of art *commemorate* death on a hideously large scale.

On Veterans Day, our city holds a ceremony to *commemorate* the sacrifices of those in the armed services who gave their lives for their country.

commemorate (kə mĕm′ ə rāt)

   a. to serve as a remembrance of
   b. to celebrate the victory of
   c. to comment negatively upon
   d. to announce prematurely

_____ 7. Many viewers felt "the Wall," as it has come to be called, *flouted* tradition, that it was not sufficiently respectful of those who fought the bloody Vietnam War.

The man refused to put out his cigarette and was asked to leave because he *flouted* the restaurant's no-smoking rule.

flouted (flou′ təd)

   a. established; created
   b. showed disrespect; had contempt for
   c. improved upon; made better
   d. followed; abided by

_____ **8.** In time the American public came to accept this memorial—with its 58,000 names carved into the *stark* granite walls—as the most fitting tribute to those who had died.

The prison cell was *stark* and uncomfortable; the only furniture in it was a metal cot.

stark (stärk)

a. elaborate; ornate

b. colorful; cheerful

c. bare; plain

d. lonely

_____ **9.** In time the American public came to accept this memorial—with its 58,000 names carved into the stark granite walls—as the most *fitting* tribute to those who had died.

It is only *fitting* that those who work the hardest receive the greatest rewards.

fitting (fĭt′ ĭng)

a. proper; right

b. adjusted correctly

c. logical; reasonable

d. pertaining to luck

_____ **10.** In its entirety, as we watch it grow, the work is *incomparably* sad, yet each panel of the AIDS Quilt is the celebration of a single life.

Monet produced *incomparably* beautiful impressionistic paintings; no other painter can equal his handling of light.

incomparably (ĭn kŏm′ pər ə blē)

a. confusingly

b. incompletely

c. immeasurably

d. slightly

Word Structure

Directions: Items 11–15 test your ability to use word-structure clues to help determine a word's meaning. *Word-structure clues* consist of roots, prefixes, and suffixes. In these exercises, you will learn the meaning of a word part (root) and use it to determine the meaning of the several other words that have the same word part. If you discover that you need to use a dictionary to confirm an answer choice, do so.

In this selection, you encountered the words ***commemorate, memorial,*** and ***memorialize.*** These words all contain the Latin root ***mem,*** meaning "memory." In paragraph 1 *commemorate* means "to honor the memory (of someone or something)." In paragraph 4 *memorial* refers to "a monument that honors the memory of a person or an event." *Memorialize,* in paragraph 5, means "to provide a memorial for" or "to commemorate." Use the meaning of ***mem*** and the list of prefixes on pages 60–61 to help you determine the meaning of each of the following words that contain this same root. Write your answer in the space provided.

_____ **11.** Which of these would be a likely **remembrance** of a date you had with someone special?

    a. a shoe

    b. an embrace

    c. a concert ticket stub

    d. a book

_____ **12.** To **memorize** a poem means

    a. to commit it to memory.

    b. to write it several times.

    c. to say it aloud.

    d. to interpret it correctly.

_____ **13.** If your boss sends you a **memorandum,** he or she sends you

    a. a certificate of achievement.

    b. a financial report.

    c. a written reminder.

    d. computer software.

_____ **14.** If a former U.S. president writes his **memoirs,** he writes

    a. a set of recommendations for the current president.

    b. the history of the country.

    c. an article on his political views.

    d. recollections of his personal experiences.

_____ **15.** If your trip to Paris was **memorable,** it was

    a. taken within the last five years; recent

    b. highly unpleasant in some significant way.

    c. won as a prize in a contest.

    d. worth being remembered; remarkable.

Reading Skills Application

Directions: Items 16–20 test your ability to apply certain reading skills to the material in this selection. These are the types of questions that might appear on standardized reading tests and state-mandated basic skills tests. Write your answer in the space provided.

_____ **16.** According to information in the selection, "the Wall"
- *a.* will have no more names added to it.
- *b.* is a memorial to a single life.
- *c.* includes both names and photographs.
- *d.* cannot be touched by visitors.

_____ **17.** The organization of the overall selection is a
- *a.* list.
- *b.* cause-effect.
- *c.* sequence.
- *d.* comparison-contrast.

_____ **18.** Which of the following represents an opinion rather than a fact?
- *a.* The AIDS Quilt consists of hand-sewn panels.
- *b.* Each panel commemorates one person who has died from AIDS.
- *c.* Some of the 3 by 6 feet panels have a name and a photograph, others just initials or forms symbolizing that person's interests, abilities, and achievements.
- *d.* Each panel tells a story, a story of a life ended too soon, and therefore all the more precious in the telling.

_____ **19.** What is the meaning of *bound* as it is used in paragraph 5?
- *a.* tied with a rope
- *b.* linked
- *c.* stitched together
- *d.* forced

_____ **20.** Which of the following is the main idea of paragraph 7?
- *a.* The choice of a quilt format is especially meaningful.
- *b.* Historically, quilts have often told lifetime stories, incorporating bits of fabric from lifetime events.
- *c.* Quilts make us think of warmth and protection and nurturing.
- *d.* And quilting has traditionally been a community activity, so it is natural that a community should form among those grieving death from common illness.

Collaboration Option

Writing and Collaborating to Enhance Your Understanding

Option for collaboration: Your instructor may direct you to work with other students or, in other words, to work *collaboratively.* In that case, you should form groups of three or four students as directed by your instructor and work together to complete the exercises. After your group discusses each item and agrees on the answer, have a group member record it. Every member of your group should be able to explain all of your group's answers.

1. **Reacting to What You Have Read:** Have you or someone you know ever visited the Vietnam Memorial or seen panels of the AIDS Quilt displayed? Perhaps you have seen one or both on TV. Describe your reactions or those of the person you know who has seen either of these memorials. If you have not seen either in person, what is your reaction to the photos of them in the selection?

    _____

    _____

    _____

    _____

    _____

    _____

2. **Comprehending the Selection Further:** Of the two memorials you read about, which of them produces a stronger emotional response in you? Explain why.

    _____

    _____

    _____

    _____

    _____

    _____

    _____

    _____

    _____

    _____

    _____

3.   **Overall Main Idea of the Selection:** In one sentence tell what the author wants readers to understand about the Vietnam Memorial and the AIDS Quilt. (Be sure to include the words "Vietnam Memorial" and "the AIDS Quilt" in your overall main idea sentence.)

_____

_____

_____

_____

_____

_____

Read More about It on the World Wide Web

To learn more about the topic of this selection, visit these websites or use your favorite search engine (such as Yahoo®) to discover more about this author and this topic on your own. Whenever you go to *any* website, it is a good idea to evaluate it critically. Are you getting good information—that is, information that is accurate, complete, and up-to-date? Who sponsors the website? How easy is it to use the features of the website?

http://thevirtualwall.org/

http://thewall-usa.com

http://www.aidsquilt.org/

http://www.aidsquilt-nyc.org/

CAUSES OF CANCER
From *Human Biology*
By Sylvia Mader

There is hardly anyone whose life hasn't been touched either directly or indirectly by cancer. Cancer is a genetic disease that causes cells to undergo a series of changes or mutations. Ultimately a malignant tumor develops. Unless stopped, the cells grow uncontrollably, spread, and invade tissue in other parts of the body. Tumor cells have certain characteristics in common, but each type of cancer has its own unique series of mutations that leads to the uncontrolled growth. The development of cancer is a gradual process, and it may take decades before a person notices any sign or symptom of a tumor. Cancer takes many different forms, which makes it complex to treat. Cancer is definitely survivable, but the likelihood of survival depends largely on early identification, an accurate diagnosis, and appropriate treatment.

In this biology textbook selection, you will learn about hereditary and environmental causes of cancer. Hereditary means that the tendency to develop a certain type of cancer is passed on to the subsequent generation via the genes. In the selection you will encounter the word allele. *An allele is an alternate form of a gene that affects the same trait as the gene—people who inherit a dominant allele for a certain type of cancer, for example, will develop that type of cancer.*

1   What causes cancer? It seems that cancer is caused by heredity plus environmental effects.

Heredity

2   Already we know that particular types of cancer seem to run in families. For instance, the risk of developing breast, lung, and colon cancers increases two-to-threefold when first-degree relatives have had these cancers. We now know that the mutated tumor-suppressor gene *BRCA1* (breast cancer gene #1) runs in certain families and can be used to predict which members will develop breast cancer.

3   Certain childhood cancers seem to be due to the inheritance of a dominant gene. Retinoblastoma is an eye tumor that usually develops by age three; Wilms tumor is characterized by numerous tumors in both kidneys. In adults, several family syndromes (e.g., Li-Fraumeni cancer family syndrome, Lynch cancer family syndrome, and Warthin cancer family syndrome) are known. Those who inherit a dominant allele develop tumors in various parts of the body.

4   Now that the human genome has been sequenced, it may soon be possible to determine which genetic profiles make a person susceptible to cancer when exposed to particular environmental carcinogens.

Annotation Practice Exercises

Directions: For each exercise below, write the topic of the paragraph on the lines beside the paragraph. Then, formulate a main idea sentence for the paragraph and write it on the lines provided.

Annotation Exercise

Topic of paragraph 3:

_____

_____

Formulate the implied main idea of this paragraph and write your sentence here:

_____

_____

_____

_____

_____

_____

Environmental Carcinogens

5　A **mutagen** is an agent that increases the chances of a mutation, while a **carcinogen** is an environmental agent that can contribute to the development of cancer. Carcinogens are often mutagenic. Among the best-known mutagenic carcinogens are radiation, organic chemicals, and viruses.

Radiation

6　Ultraviolet radiation in sunlight and tanning lamps is most likely responsible for the dramatic increases seen in skin cancer the past several years. Today there are at least six cases of skin cancer for every one case of lung cancer. Nonmelanoma skin cancers are usually curable through surgery, but melanoma skin cancer tends to metastasize and is responsible for 1–2% of total cancer deaths in the United States.

7　Another natural source of radiation is radon gas. In the very rare house with an extremely high level exposure, the risk of developing lung cancer is thought to be equivalent to smoking a pack of cigarettes a day. Therefore, the combination of radon gas and smoking cigarettes can be particularly dangerous. Radon levels can be lowered by improving the ventilation of a building.

8　Most of us have heard about the damaging effects of the nuclear bomb explosions or accidental emissions from nuclear power plants. For example, more cancer deaths are expected in the vicinity of the Chernobyl Power Station (in the former U.S.S.R.), which suffered a terrible accident in 1986. Usually, however, diagnostic X-rays account for most of our exposure to artificial sources of radiation. The benefits of these procedures can far outweigh the possible risk, but it is still wise to avoid any X-ray procedures that are not medically warranted.

9　Despite much publicity, scientists have not been able to show a clear relationship between cancer and radiation from electric power lines, household appliances, and cellular telephones.

Organic Chemicals

10　Tobacco smoke, foods, certain hormones, and pollutants all contain organic chemicals that can be carcinogenic.

11　**Tobacco Smoke**　Tobacco smoke contains a number of organic chemicals that are known carcinogens. It appears that smoking is implicated in the development of cancers of the mouth, larynx, bladder, kidney, and pancreas. The greater the number of cigarettes smoked per day, the earlier the habit starts, and the higher the tar

Industrial chemicals.
Organic chemicals in air and particularly in drinking water are associated with a higher incidence of cancer. *(Bruce Roberts/Photo Researchers, Inc.)*

Annotation Exercise

Topic of paragraph 11:

_____

_____

Formulate the implied main idea of this paragraph and write your sentence here:

_____

_____

_____

_____

_____

_____

_____

_____

_____

_____

content, the more likely it is that cancer will develop. When smoking is combined with drinking alcohol, the risk of these cancers increases even more.

12   Passive smoking, or inhalation of someone else's tobacco smoke, is also dangerous and probably causes a few thousand deaths each year.

13   **Foods and Hormones** Animal testing of certain food additives, such as red dye #2, has shown that some additives are cancer-causing in very high doses. In humans, salty foods and fats appear to make a significant contribution to the development of cancer.

14   Increasingly, studies suggest that hormone replacement therapy can contribute to the development of uterine and breast cancer in women who have taken these hormones for five to ten years.

15   **Pollutants** Industrial chemicals, such as benzene and carbon tetrachloride, and industrial materials, such as vinyl chloride and asbestos fibers, are also associated with the development of cancer. Pesticides and herbicides are dangerous not only to pets and plants but also to our own health because they contain organic chemicals that can cause mutations. It is now generally accepted that dioxin, a contaminant of herbicides, can cause cancers of lymphoid tissues, muscular tissues, and certain connective tissues. The development of cancer is associated with these forms of organic chemicals.

Viruses

16   At least three DNA viruses—hepatitis B virus, Epstein-Barr virus, and human papillomavirus—have been linked to human cancers.

17   In China, almost all persons have been infected with the hepatitis B virus, and this correlates with the high incidence of liver cancer in that country. For a long time, circumstances suggested that cervical cancer was a sexually transmitted disease, and now human papillomaviruses are routinely isolated from cervical cancers. Burkitt lymphoma occurs frequently in Africa, where virtually all children are infected with the Epstein-Barr virus. In China, the Epstein-Barr virus is isolated in nearly all nasopharyngeal cancer specimens.

18   RNA-containing retroviruses, in particular, are known to cause cancers in animals. In humans, the retrovirus HTLV-1 (human T-cell lymphotropic virus, type 1) has been shown to cause adult T-cell leukemia. This disease occurs frequently in parts of Japan, the Caribbean, and Africa, particularly in regions where people are known to be infected with the virus.

Annotation Exercise

Topic of paragraph 15:

_____

_____

Formulate the implied main idea of this paragraph and write your sentence here:

_____

_____

_____

_____

_____

_____

Source: Adapted from Sylvia Mader, *Human Biology,* 7th ed., pp. 448–49. Copyright © 2002 McGraw-Hill. Reprinted by permission of The McGraw-Hill Companies.

Comprehension and Vocabulary Quiz

This quiz has four parts. Your instructor may assign some or all of them.

Comprehension

Directions: For each comprehension question below, use information from the selection to determine the correct answer. Refer to the selection as you answer the questions. Write your answer in the space provided.

_____   **1.** The risk of developing several common types of cancers increases two-to-threefold when
    a. infants are born prematurely.
    b. first-degree relatives have had these cancers.
    c. people are exposed to any environmental carcinogens.
    d. all of the above.

_____   **2.** An example of an environmental carcinogen is
    a. the retrovirus HTLV-1.
    b. some pesticides and herbicides.
    c. X-rays.
    d. all of the above.

_____   **3.** A type of cancer that is caused by ultraviolet radiation that is responsible for 1 to 2 percent of total cancer deaths in the United States is
    a. retinoblastoma.
    b. Lynch cancer.
    c. liver cancer.
    d. melanoma.

_____   **4.** Inhalation of someone else's tobacco smoke, or passive smoking,
    a. can be prevented by improving the ventilation of a building.
    b. increases a person's risk of developing a retrovirus.
    c. may be the cause of a few thousand deaths each year.
    d. all of the above.

_____   **5.** Development of cancer in humans is determined by exposure to environmental carcinogens plus
    a. heredity.
    b. a person's lifestyle.
    c. nutrition and exercise.
    d. viruses and pollutants.

Vocabulary in Context

Directions: Use the context clues from *both* sentences to deduce the meaning of the italicized word. *Be sure the answer you choose makes sense in both sentences.* If you discover that you need to use a dictionary to confirm an answer choice, remember that the meaning you select must still fit the context of *both* sentences. Write your answer in the space provided.

Pronunciation Key: ă pat ā pay âr care ä father ĕ pet ē be ĭ pit
ī tie îr pier ŏ pot ō toe ô paw oi noise ou out ŏŏ took ōō boot
ŭ cut yōō abuse ûr urge th thin *th* this hw which zh vision
ə about Stress mark: ʹ

---

6. We now know that the *mutated* tumor-suppressor gene *BRCA1* (breast cancer gene #1) runs in certain families and can be used to predict which members will develop breast cancer.

The *mutated* variety of corn had kernels of several different colors.

mutated (myōōʹ tā təd)

  a. poisonous; toxic
  b. fundamentally altered
  c. colorful
  d. highly pleasing

7. Now that the human *genome* has been sequenced, it may soon be possible to determine which genetic profiles make a person susceptible to cancer when exposed to particular environmental carcinogens.

Researchers have been able to locate the genes in the human *genome* that are responsible for certain diseases.

genome (jēʹ nōm)

  a. disease prevention
  b. the genetic material of an organism
  c. heredity
  d. family syndrome

8. Nonmelanoma skin cancers are usually curable through surgery, but melanoma skin cancer tends to *metastasize* and is responsible for 1–2 percent of total cancer deaths in the United States.

Because the veterinarian used aggressive chemotherapy, the cancer in the dog's leg did not *metastasize* and the dog recovered.

metastasize (mə tăs′ tə sīz)

  a.   spread to other parts of the body

  b.   respond to radiation treatment

  c.   become stable, but permanent

  d.   shrink and then spontaneously disappear

———   **9.** Radon levels can be lowered by improving the ventilation of a building.

To dispel the strong, unpleasant paint fumes, we increased the *ventilation* by opening the windows and turning on a fan.

ventilation (věn tĭ lā′ shən)

  a.   temperature

  b.   safety

  c.   level of comfort

  d.   circulation of air

———   **10.** Tobacco smoke contains a number of organic chemicals that are known carcinogens, and it is estimated that smoking is also *implicated* in the development of cancers of the mouth, larynx, bladder, kidney, and pancreas.

The accused man said that he did not act alone; in fact, he *implicated* his own brother in the crime.

implicated (ĭm′ plĭ cā təd)

  a.   cleared from suspicion

  b.   proved essential or necessary

  c.   indicated the involvement of

  d.   ruled out

Word Structure

Directions: In paragraph 15 of the selection you encountered the words **pesticides** and **herbicides.** These words contain the Latin root **cide,** which means "to kill" or "killer." A *pesticide* refers to any substance that "kills pests." A *herbicide* is a substance that kills plants or inhibits their growth. Use the meaning of **cide** and the list of roots on pages 60–61 to help you determine the meaning of each of the following words that contain this same root. Write your answer in the space provided.

———   **11.** A person who commits **suicide** kills

  a.   himself or herself.

  b.   a brother.

  c.   a sister.

  d.   a neighbor.

_____ 12. **Parricide** is the killing of

   a. paramours.

   b. parrots.

   c. parents.

   d. paratroopers.

_____ 13. **Patricide** is the killing of

   a. one's own father.

   b. a member of royalty.

   c. a person named Pat.

   d. one's patron.

_____ 14. **Fratricide** is the killing of one's own

   a. brother or sister.

   b. aunt or uncle.

   c. grandmother or grandfather.

   d. niece or nephew.

_____ 15. **Infanticide** is the killing of

   a. an insect.

   b. a spy.

   c. an enemy.

   d. a baby.

Reading Skills Application

Directions: Apply your reading skills to answer the questions below. Write your answer in the space provided.

_____ 16. In paragraph 3, the author uses retinoblastoma, Wilms tumor, and several cancer family syndromes to

   a. illustrate that certain cancers develop because people inherit the dominant genes for them.

   b. prove that specific environmental carcinogens are responsible for cancer.

   c. suggest that it will soon be possible to prevent cancer by altering the genes a person inherits.

   d. indicate that first-degree relatives develop cancer in greater numbers than more distantly related family members.

_____ 17. The material in paragraph 3 of the selection is organized using which of the following patterns?

   a. comparison-contrast

   b. list

   c. sequence

   d. cause-effect

———   **18.** According to information in the selection, three categories of environmental carcinogens are

    a.   radiation, organic chemicals, and viruses.

    b.   tobacco smoke, hormones, and pollutants.

    c.   hepatitis B virus, Epstein-Barr virus, and human papillomavirus.

    d.   ultraviolet radiation, radon gas, and artificial sources of radiation, such as X-ray.

———   **19.** Based upon information in the selection, which of the following represents a logical inference?

    a.   Cancer from organic chemical exposure is inescapable for human beings.

    b.   Exposure to pollutants will steadily decrease as a cause of cancer in humans.

    c.   Exposure to carcinogenic organic chemicals can be reduced.

    d.   Passive smoking is the greatest threat of exposure to the carcinogen in tobacco smoke.

———   **20.** Which of the following statements from the selection represent an opinion rather than a fact?

    a.   Ultraviolet radiation in sunlight and tanning lamps is most likely responsible for the dramatic increases seen in skin cancer the past several years.

    b.   Today there are at least six cases of skin cancer for every one case of lung cancer.

    c.   In China, almost all persons have been infected with the hepatitis B virus, and this correlates with the high incidence of liver cancer in that country.

    d.   Burkitt lymphoma occurs frequently in Africa, where virtually all children are infected with the Epstein-Barr virus.

Collaboration Option

Writing and Collaborating to Enhance Your Understanding

Option for collaboration: Work together in groups to complete the exercises below. Have one group member record your answers, but make sure every member of your group can explain all of your group's answers.

1. **Reacting to What You Have Read:** Perhaps you, someone you know, or some famous person you have read about has confronted cancer. What form of cancer was it? Do you think the cause was primarily due to the person's heredity or due to environmental causes? Explain your answer.

_____

_____

_____

_____

_____

_____

_____

2. **Comprehending the Selection Further:** What precautions or changes could you make to minimize your chances of developing cancer?

_____

_____

_____

_____

_____

_____

_____

_____

3. **Overall Main Idea of the Selection:** In one sentence tell what the author wants readers to understand about the causes of cancer. (Be sure to include the words "cancer" and "caused" in your overall main idea sentence.)

_____

_____

_____

_____

_____

Read More about It on the World Wide Web

To learn more about the topic of this selection, visit these websites or use your favorite search engine (such as Yahoo®) to discover more about this author and this topic on your own. Whenever you go to *any* website, it is a good idea to evaluate it critically. Are you getting good information—that is, information that is accurate, complete, and up-to-date? Who sponsors the website? How easy is it to use the features of the website?

http://www.oncologychannel.com/endometrialcancer/

http://www.cancer.org/

http://class.fst.ohio-state.edu/FST201/lectures/IFTCa.html

http://www.enn.com/news/enn-stories/2001/05/05152001/nitrates_43528.asp

SELECTION 5-3

PSYCHOLOGY

WHY RELATIONSHIPS DEVELOP AND WHAT MAKES THEM LAST

From *Essentials of Psychology*
By Benjamin Lahey

What attracts people to each other? Are men and women attracted by the same things? What is involved in maintaining relationships? Why do people stay in them? Why do people break them off? In this psychology textbook selection, you will learn the answers to these questions.

Interpersonal Attraction

1   Throughout the complicated process of person perception (the process of forming perceptions of others), a unique impression of each person is formed. But, although person perception is a highly personal process, some *general* factors influence whether one person will be attracted to another. These include proximity, similar and complementary characteristics, competence, physical attractiveness, and mutual liking.

Proximity

2   An important, but not very romantic, cause of attraction is proximity, or geographical closeness. It's difficult to fall in love with someone you hardly ever spend time with. Physical closeness and the resulting interpersonal contact are essential to the development of attraction. You are more friendly with people who live next door to you than with people who live farther away. Why does this happen? Physical proximity increases interactions, and repeated exposure to people tends to increase liking. Perhaps you can remember a song you didn't like at first but learned to like after hearing it played on the radio many times—it's the same with people.

Similar and Complementary Characteristics

3   In terms of interpersonal attraction, do "birds of a feather flock together" or do "opposites attract"? Are you more likely to be attracted to someone as a friend or lover who is similar to you in many ways or quite different from you? The answer is *both,* in different ways.

4   It's enjoyable to have a friend who jogs with you, who pats you on the back for the healthy way you eat, and who shares long, delicious philosophical discussions with you. In general, similarity is highly important in attractiveness. We tend to be most attracted to those people who have similar values, interests, and attitudes.

5   Opposites can also attract, however. Sometimes the attractiveness of persons unlike us is purely erotic. But opposites also attract when the opposite characteristic

Annotation Practice Exercises

Directions: For each exercise below, write the topic of the paragraph on the lines beside the paragraph. Then, formulate a main idea sentence for the paragraph and write it on the lines provided. (Remember that you cannot use a sentence just as it is in the paragraph as your main idea sentence.)

complements, or advantageously "fits" with, one of our own characteristics. A woman might also be attracted to the fellow at the party tonight in part because he has an outgoing personality, whereas she is more reserved. She may feel that she is a good listener who gets along better with talkative people than with those who are quiet like herself. And she may feel that, when she is with an outgoing person at social gatherings, he makes it easier for her to interact with other couples than a quiet man does. Similarly, a dominant person might prefer a submissive person, and a person who likes to "take care of" others might prefer someone who likes to be taken care of.

6   Opposites can attract when people who are different from each other *like* each other. It's often more flattering and attractive to be liked by someone who holds opposite values and opinions than by someone who holds similar ones. But opposites usually do not attract; instead, opposites usually repel in personal relationships. A person who intensely advocates liberal causes probably would not like a person who vocally supports conservative causes. And a highly religious person probably would not find a disdain for religion attractive in another person.

Competence

7   We tend to be more attracted to competent than to incompetent people. Intelligence, strength, social skill, education, and athletic prowess are generally thought of as attractive qualities. But people who are seen as *too* competent may suffer a loss in attractiveness, perhaps because it makes us uncomfortable to compare ourselves unfavorably with them.

Physical Attractiveness

8   Other things equal, people tend to be more attracted to physically beautiful people. In the absence of other information, we tend to like beautiful people more and think of them as nicer, better adjusted, more sexual, and more intelligent. Not only is physical attractiveness important, but it also seems to be the *most* important factor in early stages of attraction.

9   But don't despair; there is hope for the rest of us! We might all prefer to be dating someone who looks like a movie star. People actually tend to choose dates and mates who closely match themselves in degree of physical attractiveness. What is more, physical beauty is a highly subjective quality. Thus, even if you do not think your next-door neighbor is just much to look at, chances are that someone else will come along who thinks he or she is just beautiful.

Annotation Exercise

Topic of paragraph 6:

_____

_____

Formulate the implied main idea of this paragraph and write your sentence here:

_____

_____

_____

_____

_____

_____

_____

_____

_____

_____

_____

_____

Annotation Exercise

Topic of paragraph 9:

_____

_____

Formulate the implied main idea of this paragraph and write your sentence here:

_____

_____

_____

_____

_____

_____

10   Perhaps the nicest thing about physical attractiveness and liking, though, is that the relationship goes both ways. Not only is it true that we tend to like people better when we think they are beautiful, but, as we get to like people better, we begin to think they are more beautiful. Thus, to a certain extent, love *is* blind and beauty *is* in the eye of the beholder—and nothing could be nicer.

Mutual Liking

11   Let's end this discussion of factors involved in interpersonal attractiveness on an upbeat note. Liking often leads to liking in return. If Vicky likes Neal, she has made herself more attractive to Neal simply by liking him. Neal, if he is like almost everyone else, will be more attracted to people who like him than to people who do not like him. Liking someone will not turn you into an irresistible beauty, but it will help.

Physical attractiveness seems to be the most important factor in the early stages of attraction between people. *(Esbin/Anderson/Omni Photo)*

12   One reason this seems to be so is that liking someone actually makes you seem more *physically* attractive, especially if a little lust is thrown in. You have heard people say that a person is more beautiful when in love, and it's true. Your eyes are more attractive when you are in love. Your pupils tend to be more dilated (opened) when you look at someone you find sexually attractive, and others find large pupils more attractive sexually. And your posture and movements are often more attractive and seductive. In subtle ways, you are most physically alluring when you are attracted to another person.

13   Another reason that liking tends to lead to liking is that you are nicer to the people whom you like, and being nicer makes you more attractive to them. A number of studies show, for example, that we tend to like people more when they praise us or when they have done favors for us. Favors and praise feel nice, and we like the giver better for having given them to us. Thus, send him flowers or give her a compact disc—it might just tip the balance of love in your favor. As you might expect, there are limits on the impact of praise and favors. If they are excessive, and especially if the other person thinks you are insincere and have selfish motives for giving them, praise and gifts will not lead to increased liking and may even lessen the liking.

Gender Differences in Interpersonal Attraction

14   It's a commonly held belief in our culture that men are not very interested in romantic love but, rather, enter into long-term relationships for the sex and the domestic help (cooking, cleaning, and mending). Women, in contrast, are viewed in our society as approaching relationships in a more emotional, romantic way. The results of

surveys conducted during the 1960s, however, suggested that this popular stereotype not only was incorrect but had reality reversed. Men rated falling in love as being a more important reason for beginning a relationship than did women. Women saw other qualities of the relationship, such as respect and support, as being more important. In one survey, two-thirds of male unmarried college students said they would not marry unless they felt romantic love for their prospective wife, whereas less than one-fourth of college women felt that romantic love was a prerequisite for marriage.

15   However, more recent surveys suggest that things have changed in the United States concerning gender differences in valuing romantic love. Today, the great majority of both women and men feel that being in love is necessary for marriage. Perhaps, as women have come to feel less dependent on marriage for financial support, they have felt able to enter into marriage only when they are in love with their future partner.

16   This does not mean that men and women fall in love for all the same reasons, however. The evidence is clear that women place more emphasis on their romantic partner's intelligence, character, education, occupational stages, ambition, and income than do men. These qualities are not unimportant to men, but they are comparatively more important to women. In contrast, there are no gender differences in how much sense of humor and a pleasant personality are valued in romantic relationships, but men place greater emphasis on physical attractiveness than do women. Again, it is not that physical attractiveness does not play a role in romantic attraction for women (it does), but women place considerably less emphasis on physical attractiveness than do men. Interestingly, these same results have been found in different generations in the United States and across a number of cultures.

17   It is important to keep in mind, however, that there are large differences among the members of both genders. Perhaps the most striking thing about the cognitive algebra of person perception is that different people often seem to be using different equations! Whether a characteristic is considered positive or negative and how much weight it will carry in person perception differ markedly from individual to individual. Because different people evaluate the same characteristics in different ways, some people are going to love you, some are going to dislike you, and the rest will find you so-so.

Maintaining Relationships

18   We have talked about some of the factors that determine whether you will be attracted to another person. But

how about the factors that are involved in maintaining relationships? Assuming that one of the people whom you are attracted to becomes your friend, lover, or spouse, what things determine whether you and your partner will stay in the relationship? So many relationships that begin in joy end in a long cry. Why? Two of the major factors are (1) the difference between what you expect to find in a relationship and what you actually find and (2) the degree to which the relationship is fairly balanced or equitable.

Expectations versus Reality in Relationships

19   When you begin a relationship with someone you do not know very well, part of what you fall in love with is what you *expect* the person to be like. Some expectations may be based on good evidence. One of his friends has told you that he is an especially nice and fair person, so it's reasonable to expect him to be fair and nice to you. You know that he is in the same profession as you, so you can expect to be able to share your workday experiences easily with him. Other expectations are based on less evidence. He has behaved in a strong, self-assured way so far, so you assume that he will always be this way, even though the biggest challenge you have seen him handle is the waiter's mistake of bringing tomato soup instead of minestrone. You *know* that he is a wonderful lover, even though he has only just kissed you goodnight once. He dressed like an outdoorsman, so you expect him to love backpacking as much as you do. And he is well educated, so you feel sure he will share your love of serious literature.

20   The point is that, even when your expectations are fairly well grounded, some of them will turn out to be incorrect. He will not be exactly as you expect him to be before the relationship begins. This is one primary reason relationships end. If the other person turns out to be significantly different from the person you expected, you may be unwilling to stay in the relationship. This disappointment may not lead directly to an end of the relationship; it may affect the relationship indirectly. Disappointment can lead you to be an unenthusiastic or irritable partner, which can lead to discord and unhappy ending of the relationship.

21   Even when you know a person well before beginning a serious relationship, differences between expectations and reality can be a problem. One common source of unfulfilled expectations is the predictable shift from **passionate love** to greater **companionate love.** When two people fall in love, they often feel intense passions that are a heady and magnificent mixture of romantic, sexual, and other feelings. Even in the most healthy and enduring relationships, however, passionate love gradually becomes companionate love—a less intense but wonderful

blend of friendship, intimacy, commitment, and security. Although romantic and sexual emotions often continue to be an important part of companionate love, these feelings almost inevitably become less intense over time.

22   If one or both partners does not expect passionate love to change, or if the change takes place before expected, the reality of passionate love's blending into companionate love can be difficult. On the other hand, if both partners truly want a long-term relationship (many people stay in relationships only as long as the passionate love remains, then leave feeling unfulfilled or hurt), and if the disappointment that often surrounds the lessening of romantic love is handled with compassion on both sides, the transition usually can be managed.

23   Finally, expectations about a love relationship can fail to match its reality because partners change over time. Sometimes, the outdoor person becomes a happy couch potato, and the party animal becomes a health-conscious, jogging vegetarian. If children arrive, and if promotions are received (or not received), these and other changes can alter the reality of the relationship as well. If these changes in one's partner are not welcome, the reality of the changed relationship can be upsetting. Sometimes, however, a change in a partner can make a good relationship even better.

Equity in Relationships

24   What do we know about whether relationships will last? They are more likely to endure when there is equity. In other words, they tend to last when the good things that we give to our partner are about equal to what our partner gives us. These good "things" that partners give to one another are many and varied. They include compliments, back rubs, help with homework, a day off without the kids, flowers, jokes, love making, a willingness to listen about a bad day, interesting meals, kisses, and interesting conversations. They also include things like physical attractiveness (a nice-looking person is enjoyable to look at), honesty, faithfulness, and integrity.

25   If either member of a relationship perceives the relationship to be inequitable, that partner will either take steps to restore equity or will leave the relationship. Interestingly, we become uncomfortable in relationships either when we feel that we receive too little compared with what we give or when we receive too much compared with what we give. In either case, we will be motivated to restore equity by giving more or less or by asking (or in some other way inducing) the other person to give more or less.

Annotation Exercise

Topic of paragraph 24:

_____

_____

Formulate the implied main idea of this paragraph and write your sentence here:

_____

_____

_____

_____

_____

_____

_____

Source: Adapted from Benjamin Lahey, *Essentials of Psychology,* pp. 462–466. Copyright © 2002 McGraw-Hill. Reprinted by permission of The McGraw-Hill Companies.

SELECTION **5-3**
PSYCHOLOGY

Comprehension and Vocabulary Quiz

This quiz has four parts. Your instructor may assign some or all of them.

Comprehension

Directions: For each comprehension question below, use information from the selection to determine the correct answer. Refer to the selection as you answer the questions. Write your answer in the space provided.

1. In relationships, opposites can attract when
   a. an opposite characteristic of a person complements one of our own characteristics.
   b. someone who is different from you *likes* you.
   c. the attractiveness of persons unlike us is purely erotic.
   d. all of the above.

2. One reason a relationship might develop is
   a. expectations versus reality.
   b. competition.
   c. proximity.
   d. all of the above.

3. If either member of a relationship perceives the relationship to be inequitable,
   a. the partner or person who is giving less should give more.
   b. the partner who is giving more should give less.
   c. that partner will either leave the relationship or take steps to restore equity.
   d. both partners should give more.

4. Expectations about a love relationship can fail to match its reality because
   a. partners change over time.
   b. there is often a shift from a passionate love to greater companionate love.
   c. at least some of our expectations will turn out to be incorrect.
   d. all of the above.

5. The most important factor in the early stages of attraction seems to be
   a. physical attractiveness.
   b. equity.
   c. competence.
   d. complementary characteristics.

Vocabulary in Context

Directions: Use the context clues from *both* sentences to deduce the meaning of the italicized word. *Be sure the answer you choose makes sense in both sentences.* If you discover that you need to use a dictionary to confirm an answer choice, remember that the meaning you select must still fit the context of *both* sentences. Write your answer in the space provided.

Pronunciation Key: ă pat   ā pay   âr care   ä father   ĕ pet   ē be   ĭ pit
ī tie   îr **pier**   ŏ pot   ō toe   ô **paw**   oi **noise**   ou **out**   oŏ **took**   ōō boot
ŭ **cut**   yōō abuse   ûr **urge**   th **thin**   *th* **this**   hw **which**   zh vision
ə **about**   Stress mark: ´

6. Sometimes the attractiveness of persons unlike us is purely *erotic.*

   The movie was deemed unsuitable for children under the age of 18 because of the *erotic* scenes between the lovers.

   erotic (ĭ rŏt´ ĭc)

   a.   pertaining to sexual love or desire
   b.   pertaining to physical violence
   c.   characterized by vulgar or offensive language
   d.   dramatically untrue

7. A woman might also be attracted to the fellow at the party tonight in part because he has an outgoing personality, whereas she is more *reserved.*

   My sister is normally very quiet and *reserved,* so her classmates were surprised graduation night when she jumped up on the stage and started to sing with the band.

   reserved (rĭ zûrvd´)

   a.   lacking in feeling
   b.   showing contempt for others
   c.   restrained in words and actions
   d.   vain; arrogant

8. But take note that opposites usually do not attract; instead, opposites usually *repel* in person relationships.

   I won't go to horror shows or war movies because gory scenes *repel* me.

   repel (rĭ pĕl´)

   a.   inspire to imitation
   b.   disgust; cause to avoid
   c.   attract; draw
   d.   influence positively

_____ 9. And a highly religious person probably would not find a *disdain* for religion attractive in another person.

Society has *disdain* for those who neglect or abuse children.

disdain (dĭs dān′)

a. compassion
b. contempt
c. tolerance
d. lack of understanding

_____ 10. Intelligence, strength, social skill, education, and athletic *prowess* are generally thought of as attractive qualities.

The physical *prowess* of Olympic athletes far exceeds that of the general population.

prowess (prou′ ĭs)

a. awards and medals
b. challenges
c. training
d. extraordinary ability

Word Structure

Directions: In paragraph 6 of the selection you encountered the word ***repel.*** This word contains the Latin root ***pel,*** which means "to drive," "to push," or "to thrust." *Repel* literally means "to drive (away) someone or something." Use the meaning of ***pel*** and the list of prefixes on pages 60–61 to help you determine the meaning of each of the following words that contain this same root. Write your answer in the space provided.

_____ 11. A **propeller** is a device that
a. thrusts a vehicle backwards.
b. thrusts airplanes and boats forward.
c. brings an airplane or boat to a gradual halt.
d. pushes a vehicle faster and faster.

_____ 12. If the wind **dispels** the clouds, it
a. drives them away.
b. causes them to form unusual shapes.
c. makes them look fluffy.
d. gives them a pink tinge.

_____ **13.** If you are **compelled** to seek shelter from a hailstorm, you are
    a. too late to seek shelter.
    b. reluctant to seek shelter.
    c. considering seeking shelter.
    d. forced to seek shelter.

_____ **14.** If a student is **expelled** from school, he or she is
    a. asked to wait outside.
    b. driven out or forced to leave.
    c. give a serious warning.
    d. recognized for excellence.

_____ **15.** If your conscience **impels** you to tell the truth, it
    a. prevents you from being truthful.
    b. makes you unable to distinguish the truth.
    c. blurs the truth.
    d. drives you to tell the truth.

Reading Skills Application

Directions: Apply your reading skills to answer the questions below. Write your answer in the space provided.

_____ **16.** Which of the following statements from the selection represents an opinion rather than a fact?
    a. Other things equal, people tend to be more attracted to physically beautiful people.
    b. In the absence of other information, we tend to like beautiful people more and think of them as nicer, better adjusted, more sexual, and more intelligent.
    c. Not only is it true that we tend to like people better when we think they are beautiful, but, as we get to like people better, we begin to think they are more beautiful.
    d. Thus, to a certain extent, love is blind and beauty is in the eye of the beholder—and nothing could be nicer.

_____ **17.** Which of the following best describes the author's tone in paragraph 9?
    a. hostile
    b. sentimental
    c. reassuring
    d. nostalgic

_____ **18.** The pattern that is used to organize the information in paragraph 14 is

    a. comparison-contrast.

    b. problem-solution.

    c. a list.

    d. a sequence.

_____ **19.** Which of the following best describes the author's primary purpose for writing this selection?

    a. to explain why some long-term relationships ultimately fail

    b. to explain factors that attract people to each other and that influence whether they stay in a relationship

    c. to explain how to maintain a relationship

    d. to explain gender differences in attraction and in the maintenance of relationships

_____ **20.** Which of the following represents the main idea of paragraph 24?

    a. Relationships tend to last when the good things that we give to our partner are about equal to what our partner gives us.

    b. These good "things" that partners give to one another are many and varied.

    c. They include compliments, back rubs, help with homework, a day off without the kids, flowers, jokes, love making, a willingness to listen about a bad day, interesting meals, kisses, and interesting conversations.

    d. They also include things like physical attractiveness (a nice-looking person is enjoyable to look at), honesty, faithfulness, and integrity.

SELECTION **5-3**
PSYCHOLOGY

Collaboration Option

Writing and Collaborating to Enhance Your Understanding

Option for collaboration: Work together in groups to complete the exercises below. Have one group member record your answers, but make sure every member of your group can explain all of your group's answers.

1. **Reacting to What You Have Read:** Think of a past or current best friend, boyfriend, girlfriend, or if you are married, your spouse. Describe the role each of these factors played or plays in your attraction to that person:

    proximity _____

    _____

    similar and complementary characteristics _____

    _____

    competence _____

    _____

    physical attractiveness _____

    _____

    mutual liking _____

    _____

2. **Comprehending the Selection Further:** Explain why each of these marriage relationships might or might not be long lasting.

    • A relationship in which both people are deeply committed to each other

    _____

    _____

    • A relationship in which one person cares deeply about the other, but the other does not reciprocate

    _____

    _____

    • A relationship in which neither partner has an especially deep commitment to the other

    _____

    _____

3. **Overall Main Idea of the Selection:** In one sentence tell what the author wants readers to understand about interpersonal attraction and maintaining relationships. (Be sure to mention how one person will be attracted to another and how people maintain a relationship when you formulate your overall main idea sentence.)

_____

_____

_____

_____

_____

Read More about It on the World Wide Web

To learn more about the topic of this selection, visit these websites or use your favorite search engine (such as Yahoo®) to discover more about this author and this topic on your own. Whenever you go to *any* website, it is a good idea to evaluate it critically. Are you getting good information—that is, information that is accurate, complete, and up-to-date? Who sponsors the website? How easy is it to use the features of the website?

http://psychology.about.com/library/weekly/aa021500a.htm/

http://vassun.vassar.edu/~jurubins/love.html

http://www.dushkin.com/connectext/psy/ch10/survey10.mhtml

CHAPTER **6**

Identifying Supporting Details

CHAPTER OBJECTIVES

In this chapter you will learn:

- What supporting details are and why it is important to be able to identify them.

- The method for identifying supporting details.

CONTENTS

WHAT ARE SUPPORTING DETAILS, AND WHY IS IT IMPORTANT TO BE ABLE TO IDENTIFY THEM?

A paragraph consists of more than a topic and a main idea. The topic and the main idea are essential to understanding the paragraph, of course, but it is the *supporting details* that provide the additional information that helps you understand the main idea *completely*.

Do not confuse a paragraph's supporting details with its main idea. Supporting details are *related* to the main idea of a paragraph, but the main idea and supporting details are not the same thing. The supporting details provide *specific* information (such as examples, descriptions, and explanations), while the main idea expresses the most important *general* point the author is making. Types of supporting details are names, dates, places, statistics, results of research studies, and other information that explains the main idea further or illustrates it by giving examples.

As noted above, every detail in a paragraph supports the main idea. However, some details are more important than others. These details are sometimes referred to as "primary details" because they relate *directly* to (support or explain) the main idea. Details that explain other details or that merely give examples are less important. You may hear these less important details referred to as "minor details" or "secondary details." Consider the details in this paragraph whose main idea is the first sentence. The three primary details are italicized. The other details are secondary details that explain these more important details.

Older workers and younger workers tend to have very different attitudes toward their jobs. *Older workers are more committed to their jobs than younger workers.* For example older workers will more often go beyond the job requirements when a situation requires it. They will stay later or carry out extra responsibilities. *Older workers also tend to exhibit less job turnover than younger workers.* It is not unusual to find older workers who have had the same job all of their adult lives. *Finally, older workers report a higher degree of job satisfaction than younger workers.* This may be due to the fact that they are more experienced and, hence, competent; that they have the respect that goes with seniority; and are paid better wages than younger employees who are just starting out.

Why is it important to identify supporting details? There are three reasons. First, the supporting details in a paragraph have an important relationship to the main idea because they explain or tell more about it. With an implied main idea, the supporting details help you formulate the main idea because the main idea is *based on* supporting details.

Second, listing the supporting details after you read a textbook assignment can help you study more efficiently. Consequently, there will be many instances when you will want to list supporting details in order to learn and remember them. This is why you should include important details on the chapter review cards you prepare in your college courses. Instructors often ask test questions based on supporting details—names, dates, places, and other pertinent information. Noting the supporting details that explain, illustrate, or support the main idea of the paragraph will make it easier for you to:

- Mark your textbooks effectively.
- Take notes.
- Remember the material.

And third, identifying the supporting details will help you grasp the pattern of organization of a paragraph. For example, authors may organize supporting details as simple lists, as steps in a process (a sequence), as similarities and differences (comparisons and contrasts), or as reasons and results (causes and effects). (These patterns of organization will be discussed in Chapter 7.)

Along with determining the topic and the main idea, then, identifying supporting details will help you become a more successful reader and student.

WHAT IS THE METHOD FOR IDENTIFYING SUPPORTING DETAILS?

Comprehension Monitoring Question for Identifying Supporting Details

"What additional information does the author provide to help me understand the main idea completely?"

Once you have determined the stated main idea of a paragraph, you have also identified the supporting details: all the rest of the sentences in the paragraph. You can also ask yourself the supporting detail comprehension monitoring question, "What additional information does the author provide to help me understand the main idea completely?" To determine what additional information you need to know, turn the main idea sentence into a question by using the words *who, what, where, when, why,* and *how.* For example, suppose the main idea of a paragraph is: *In any club or organization, the treasurer has several important responsibilities.* You could change this sentence into the question, "*What are* the important responsibilities of the treasurer?" This question would lead you to the details that describe those responsibilities and, therefore, help you understand the main idea completely. (From time to time, you may need to turn a main idea sentence into a two-part question. For example, suppose you read a paragraph with the main idea, "Spreadsheets can serve small business owners many ways." This could be changed into the two-part question: "What are spreadsheets, and how can they serve small business owners?")

As you know, when a paragraph has no stated main idea, you must formulate the main idea. When you read a paragraph of that type, formulate the main idea; then you will be able to identify the supporting details. To confirm that you have correctly identified them, ask yourself, "What additional information does the author provide to help me understand the main idea completely?"

Sometimes when you are reading a paragraph, it will become obvious to you that a list of details is about to be presented. For example, you would know to expect a list of details when an author uses phrases such as *There are many types of* . . . , *There are five reasons that* . . . , *Two kinds of* . . . , *There are several ways* . . . , or *Some symptoms include.* . . .

Often, you will find that supporting details are introduced by signal words such as *for example, first, second, next, and, also, in addition,* and *moreover.* Authors also use other clues such as numbers (1, 2, 3), letters *(a, b, c),* and bullets (• • •) when they present details in the form of a list. (Be aware, however, that in some paragraphs, not every detail will be introduced by a signal word or other clue.)

Here is an excerpt from a health textbook. Its topic is *date rape and post-traumatic stress syndrome.* The first sentence is the main idea: *Nearly all survivors of date rape seem to suffer from the effects of post-traumatic stress syndrome.* This main idea sentence can be turned into the question, "*What* are the effects of post-traumatic stress syndrome that date rape survivors suffer?" Now read the paragraph to identify the details that answer this question.

> Nearly all survivors of date rape seem to suffer from the effects of post-traumatic stress syndrome. They can have anxiety, sleeplessness, eating disorders, and nightmares. Moreover, they can experience guilt concerning their own behavior, poor self-esteem, and the negative judgment of others. In addition, some individuals may require professional counseling.
>
> *Source:* From Wayne Payne and Dale Hahn, *Understanding Your Health,* 5th ed. Copyright © 1995 McGraw-Hill. Reprinted by permission of The McGraw-Hill Companies.

There are eight details that answer the question, "What are the effects of post-traumatic stress syndrome that date-rape survivors suffer?" Notice that the details do, in fact, help you understand more about the main idea by explaining what the effects are. You can also see from examining the second and third sentences that a single sentence can contain more than one supporting detail. Here is a list of the effects of post-traumatic stress syndrome, the eight details in this paragraph:

- anxiety
- sleeplessness
- eating disorders
- nightmares
- guilt
- poor self-esteem
- negative judgment by others
- may require professional counseling

Notice how clearly the details from the paragraph stand out when they are listed on separate lines and identified with bullets. Since you are typically responsible for understanding the supporting details in textbooks, you may find it helpful to list them this way. Of course, including details in your notes and review cards can be especially helpful to you when you study.

Or you may prefer, after you have read a paragraph, to go back and insert a number next to each detail. Numbering the supporting details is helpful for at least three reasons. First, it helps you locate all the details. Second, it helps you

Stop and Annotate

Go back to the textbook excerpt above. Locate the eight supporting details and number them with a small ①, ②, ③, ④, etc.

Underline or highlight the signal words *and, moreover,* and *in addition.*

remember how many details there were in the paragraph. Third, it prevents you from overmarking the paragraph by underlining or highlighting too much.

Here is another example. It is an excerpt from a speech textbook. Its topic is *a person's religion.* The first sentence states the main idea: *A person's religion can influence his or her thinking on a number of matters.* To identify the supporting details that explain the main idea more fully, turn this main idea sentence into the question, *"How* does a person's religion influence his or her thinking on a number of matters?" Now read the paragraph to find the answer to this question.

A person's religion can influence his or her thinking on a number of matters. We are all more than our religion, but, all things considered, you can expect Quakers to oppose all types of violent activity and be in favor of human rights. Someone who is Catholic is likely to oppose abortion and most types of birth control. Jews, for thousands of years, have historically valued education, and are more inclined than others to support a tax increase if the money is earmarked for colleges and universities. Mormons have a strong commitment to self-help and to viewing the church as being part of the family. They believe these two institutions, church and family, not the government, should take care of individuals who have financial problems. Therefore, they are not strong supporters of the current welfare system. And Hindus, with their strong belief in reincarnation, are most likely not to feel rushed in making a decision.

Source: From Larry Samovar and Jack Mills, *Oral Communication: Speaking across Cultures,* 10th ed. Copyright © 1995 McGraw-Hill. Reprinted by permission of The McGraw-Hill Companies.

The supporting details of the paragraph are examples that answer the question, "How does a person's religion influence his or her thinking on a number of matters?" Notice that even though there are five details in this paragraph, only one signal word is used (the word *And* is used to introduce the last example). Here is a list of the five details (the examples) in this paragraph:

- Quakers—oppose all types of violent activity and favor human rights
- Catholics—likely to oppose abortion and most types of birth control
- Jews—value education and are willing to support it with taxes
- Mormons—strong commitment to self-help and to viewing church as part of family
- Hindus—due to their belief in reincarnation, not likely to feel rushed in making a decision

In this list, the supporting details are not written exactly as they appear in the paragraph. When you are listing supporting details, it is not necessary to use the exact words of the paragraph, nor is it necessary to use complete sentences. When you are listing supporting details, you will often want to restate them in your own words in order to keep them brief. Restating someone else's material in your own words is called **paraphrasing.** For example, you could paraphrase the items above in this even briefer way:

- Quakers—against all violence; for human rights
- Catholics—oppose abortion and birth control

Stop and Annotate

Go back to the textbook excerpt above. Locate the five supporting details and number them with a small ①, ②, ③, ④, and ⑤.

Underline or highlight the signal word *And* that helped you identify the last detail.

KEY TERM
paraphrasing

Restating an author's material in your own words.

- Jews—value education and support taxes for it
- Mormons—committed to self-help; church is part of family
- Hindus—because of belief in reincarnation, don't rush to make a decision

There are other ways besides listing to organize supporting details you must learn. Sometimes it is more helpful to organize supporting details as steps in a process (a sequence), in a table or chart that shows similarities and differences (comparisons and contrasts) or reasons and results (causes and effects). These patterns of organization are presented in Chapter 7. Also, you may discover that in some cases, you prefer to include details in your study notes in the form of an outline or a study map. These techniques are presented in Chapter 11.

MAJOR AND MINOR DETAILS AND HOW TO TELL THE DIFFERENCE

KEY TERM
major details

Details that directly support the main idea.

Major details are also known as *primary details.*

All the details in a paragraph ultimately support the main idea by explaining, illustrating, or proving it in some way. In each of the examples presented earlier, all the details *directly* supported (explained) the main idea. Details that directly support the main idea are called **major details** (these are also known as *primary details*). However, there are paragraphs in which some details support or explain *other details*. These are called **minor details** (they are also known as *secondary details*).

The following diagram shows the relationship between the main idea, major details and minor details.

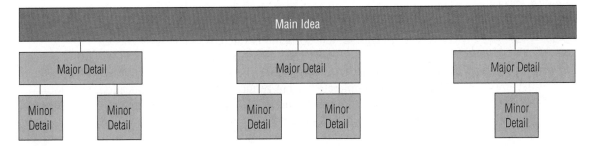

KEY TERM
minor details

Details that support other details.

Minor details are also known as *secondary details.*

Here is a simple paragraph that has been created to illustrate major and minor details. Its topic is *uses of pepper.* Its stated main idea is the first sentence, *Throughout history, pepper has been used many different ways besides as a way to season food.* There are three major details that explain important uses of pepper. The other sentences are minor details that explain the major details.

Throughout history, pepper has had many other uses besides as a way to season food. Pepper was also one of the first ways of preserving meat. During the Crusades pepper was used to preserve sausages. Pepper is still used to preserve meat today. Pepper has also been used as a medicine. In medieval times peppercorns were prescribed to cure aches and pains. Native Americans today use pepper to cure toothaches. Today, pepper is also used to control insects. For example, the French and Dutch use pepper to kill moths and to repel other insects.

The following diagram shows the relationship between the main idea and the major and minor details for this paragraph.

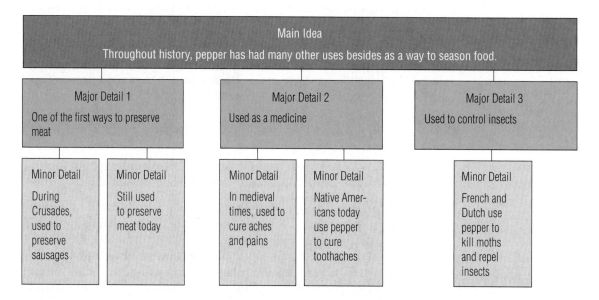

Main Idea
Throughout history, pepper has had many other uses besides as a way to season food.

Major Detail 1	Major Detail 2	Major Detail 3
One of the first ways to preserve meat	Used as a medicine	Used to control insects

Minor Detail	Minor Detail	Minor Detail	Minor Detail	Minor Detail
During Crusades, used to preserve sausages	Still used to preserve meat today	In medieval times, used to cure aches and pains	Native Americans today use pepper to cure toothaches	French and Dutch use pepper to kill moths and repel insects

Stop and Annotate

Go back to the excerpt on page 283. Locate the three major details and number them with a small ①, ②, and ③.

Again, notice that only three details directly answer the main idea question, "How has pepper been used in different ways throughout history besides as a way to season food?" Therefore, these three details are major details. The passage would make sense with only the main idea and those details. However, the author explains even more fully by giving examples of the three ways. Therefore, those details, which explain other details, are minor details.

Remember, to identify the supporting details of a paragraph, ask yourself, "What *additional information* does the author provide to help me understand the main idea completely?" Change the main idea into a question; then look for the major details that answer the question. Be aware that the author might also include minor details to increase your understanding even more. Don't spend too much time worrying about whether a detail is major or minor. The important thing is simply that you distinguish between the main idea and the details.

OTHER THINGS TO KEEP IN MIND WHEN IDENTIFYING SUPPORTING DETAILS

Here are three other helpful things you should know about identifying supporting details:

1. Watch for clues that indicate a list of details.

Watch for:

- Clue phrases such as *There are many types of* . . . , *Five reasons that* . . . , *Two kinds of* . . . , *There are several ways* . . . , or *Some symptoms include* . . . .
- Signal words such as *for example, first, second, next, and, also, in addition,* and *moreover.*
- Items identified with numbers (1, 2, 3) and letters *(a, b, c).*
- Lists with items identified with bullets (• • •).
  Remember, though, that not every detail will be introduced by signal words or other clues.

2. Avoid overmarking your textbook by numbering the supporting details in a paragraph rather than highlighting or underlining them.

When you study, there will be many times when you need to remember information, and numbering the details will make it easier to locate and recall them. Of course, when the details are already presented as bulleted or numbered lists, you may not need to do anything more.

3. Listing the supporting details on separate lines in your study notes can help you learn the information more efficiently.

Writing down the details in your study notes or on notecards is one way to "rehearse" the material and transfer it into your long-term memory. It is especially helpful to write each detail *on a separate line.* That way, each detail stands out, making it easy to see how many there are.

DEVELOPING CHAPTER REVIEW CARDS

Chapter review cards are a way to select, organize, and review the important information in a textbook chapter. Preparing chapter review cards helps you organize the information so that you can learn and memorize it more easily. In other words, chapter review cards are an effective study tool.

Preparing chapter review cards for each chapter of this book will give you practice in creating these valuable study tools. Once you have learned how to make chapter review cards, you can use actual index cards to create them for textbook material in any of your courses and use them when you study for tests.

Now, complete the chapter review cards for this chapter by answering the questions or following the directions on each "card" below. (The boxes below represent index cards.) Beginning with this chapter, the page numbers are omitted on the chapter review cards.

Supporting Details

1. What is the definition of *supporting details?*

_____

_____

2. List three reasons why it is important to identify supporting details.

_____

_____

_____

_____

3. What question should you ask yourself to identify supporting details? Be sure you write a *question.*

_____

_____

Card 1 Chapter 6: Identifying Supporting Details

The Method for Identifying Supporting Details

1. What can be done to a main idea sentence of a paragraph to help you identify details that support it?

_____

_____

_____

2. List some signal words and other clues an author may provide to help you identify a list of supporting details.

_____

_____

_____

_____

_____

Card 2   Chapter 6: Identifying Supporting Details

When Identifying Supporting Details, Keep in Mind . . .

Write the three things you should remember about identifying supporting details.

1. _____

_____

2. _____

_____

3. _____

_____

Card 3   Chapter 6: Identifying Supporting Details

COMPREHENSION PRACTICE: IDENTIFYING SUPPORTING DETAILS EXERCISES (1)

Study the example in the box below to see how information you learned in this chapter can be used to identify the supporting details of a paragraph. When you are sure you understand the example, complete the five exercises that follow.

EXAMPLE

This excerpt comes from a communications textbook. Its topic is *barriers to listening*. Read the paragraph; then determine the main idea by asking yourself, "What is the most important point the authors want me to understand about barriers to listening?" To identify supporting details, ask yourself, "What additional information do the authors provide in order to help me understand more about barriers to listening?"

Mental distractions are perhaps the most common of all the barriers to listening and the most difficult to overcome. Mental distractions occur when we talk silently to our favorite companion—ourselves. It is a very natural tendency to make ourselves the central character in our daydreams and fantasies. However, when we "visit" with ourselves, we often forget about the speaker. How many times a day, when you are supposed to be listening, do you instead find yourself thinking about your next meal, planning tomorrow's activities, or evaluating what you did yesterday?

Source: From Larry Samovar and Jack Mills, *Oral Communication: Speaking across Cultures,* 10th ed. Copyright © 1995 McGraw-Hill. Reprinted by permission of The McGraw-Hill Companies.

The topic of this paragraph is *barriers to listening.*

_____*b*_____ What is the main idea of this paragraph?

    a. How many times a day, when you are supposed to be listening, do you instead find yourself thinking about your next meal, planning tomorrow's activities, or evaluating what you did yesterday?

    b. Mental distractions are perhaps the most common of all the barriers to listening and the most difficult to overcome.

    c. Mental distractions occur when we visit with ourselves.

The correct answer is b. The first sentence of the paragraph is the stated main idea because it tells the single most important point the authors want you to know about mental distractions: they are perhaps the most common of all barriers to listening and are the most difficult to overcome. Answer choice *a* is a question, and the main idea is always a sentence and never a question.

_____*c*_____ Which of the following is a supporting detail?

    a. Mental distractions are barriers to listening.

    b. Mental distractions are perhaps the most common of all the barriers to listening and the most difficult to overcome.

    c. Thinking about your next meal.

The correct answer is c. Thinking about your next meal is an example of a common mental distraction. Answer choice *a* gives the topic of the paragraph. Choice *b* is the stated main idea.

Directions:

- First, read the paragraph carefully. Notice that you are given the topic of each paragraph.
- Then answer the questions about the paragraph's main idea and supporting details. Remember that main ideas are general and details are specific.

1. This paragraph comes from a human development textbook.

There are several drawbacks to working while you are a student. Young people who work long hours are less likely to eat breakfast, exercise, get enough sleep, or have enough leisure time. They spend less time with their families and may feel less close to them. They have little contact with adults on the job, and their jobs usually reinforce gender stereotypes. Some teenagers spend their earnings on alcohol or drugs, develop cynical attitudes toward work, and cheat or steal from their employers.

Source: From Diane E. Papalia and Sally Olds, *Human Development,* 6th ed. Copyright © 1999 McGraw-Hill. Reprinted by permission of The McGraw-Hill Companies.

The topic of this paragraph is *working while you are a student.*

_____   What is the main idea of this paragraph?
  a.   Being a student has several drawbacks.
  b.   Students who work spend less time with their families and feel less close to them.
  c.   There are several drawbacks to working while you are a student.

_____   Which of the following is a supporting detail?
  a.   Students who work are less likely to get enough sleep.
  b.   Working while you are a student can have many negative effects.
  c.   Some teenagers work while they are in school.

2. This paragraph comes from a communication textbook.

Cultures differ in the degree to which they tolerate ambiguity. That is to say, people from cultures such as the Greek, Japanese, French, and Portuguese do not like the unknown. They function much more efficiently when the uncertainties they face are reduced. However, some cultures have a very high tolerance for the ambiguous nature of life. People from the United States, Denmark, Sweden, Ireland, and Great Britain are quite different. They do not suffer great feelings of stress when some issues are left unresolved.

Source: From Larry Samovar and Jack Mills, *Oral Communication: Speaking across Cultures,* 10th ed. Copyright © 1995 McGraw-Hill. Reprinted by permission of The McGraw-Hill Companies.

The topic of this paragraph is *tolerating ambiguity,* or *dealing with the unknown.*

_____   What is the main idea of this paragraph?
  a.   People from cultures such as the Greek, Japanese, French, and Portuguese do not like the unknown.
  b.   Cultures differ in the degree to which they tolerate ambiguity.
  c.   People from the United States suffer great feelings of stress when some issues are left unresolved.

———————   Which of the following is a supporting detail?

a. People from the United States, Denmark, Sweden, Ireland, and Great Britain do not suffer great feelings of stress when some issues are left unresolved.

b. Most people like the unknown.

c. Cultures differ in the degree to which they tolerate ambiguity.

3. This paragraph comes from a management textbook.

> Nonverbal communication is communication by means of elements and behaviors that are not coded into words. Studies estimate that nonverbal aspects account for between 65 and 93 percent of what is communicated. It is quite difficult to engage in verbal communication without some accompanying form of nonverbal communication. Important categories of nonverbal communication include kinesic behavior (body movements), proxemics (the influence of space on communication), paralanguage (vocal aspects of communication), and object language (the communicative use of material things such as clothing or cosmetics).

Source: From Kathryn M. Bartol and David C. Martin, *Management,* 2nd ed. Copyright © 1994 McGraw-Hill. Reprinted by permission of The McGraw-Hill Companies.

The topic of this paragraph is *nonverbal communication.*

———————   What is the main idea of this paragraph?

a. Kinesic behavior is an important category of nonverbal communication.

b. Studies estimate that nonverbal aspects account for between 65 and 93 percent of what is communicated.

c. Nonverbal communication is communication by means of elements and behaviors that are not coded into words, and verbal communication is almost always accompanied by nonverbal communication.

———————   Which of the following is a supporting detail?

a. Nonverbal communication is communication by means of elements and behaviors that are not coded into words.

b. One type of nonverbal communication is kinesic behavior (body movement).

c. Nonverbal communication is effective.

4. This paragraph comes from a health textbook.

A Realistic Perspective on Stress and Life

Although we would like our lives to be stress-free, reality dictates otherwise. Therefore it is desirable that we approach life with a tough-minded optimism that provides a sense of hope and anticipation, as well as an understanding that life will never be without stress. The following suggestions can help you cope with today's fast-paced demanding lifestyle:

- *Do not be surprised by trouble.* Anticipate problems and see yourself as a problem solver.
- *Search for solutions.* Act on a partial solution, even when a complete solution seems distant.
- *Take control of your own future.* Do not view yourself as a victim.

- *Move away from negative thought patterns.* Do not extend or generalize difficulties from one area into another.
- *Rehearse success.* The very act of "imaging," in which a person sees himself or herself performing skillfully, has proven beneficial in a variety of performance-oriented activities.
- *Accept the unchangeable.* Cope as effectively as possible with those events over which you have no direct control; beyond a certain point, however, you must let go of those things over which you have little control.
- *Live each day well.* Combine activity, contemplation, and a sense of cheerfulness with the many things that must be done each day. Remember that our lives are far more heavily influenced by day-to-day events than they are by the occasional milestones in life.
- *Act on your capacity for growth.* Undertake new experiences and then extract from them new information about your own interests and capacities.
- *Allow time for renewal.* Make time for yourself. Foster growth in each of the multiple dimensions of health—physical, emotional, social, intellectual, spiritual, occupational, and environmental.
- *Tolerate mistakes.* Mistakes, carefully evaluated, can serve as the basis for even greater control and more likely success in those activities you have undertaken.

Source: From Wayne Payne and Dale Hahn, *Understanding Your Health,* 5th ed. Copyright © 1995 McGraw-Hill. Reprinted by permission of The McGraw-Hill Companies.

The topic of this paragraph is *coping with stress.*

_____   What is the main idea of this paragraph?

a. To cope with stress, anticipate problems and see yourself as a problem solver.

b. A tough-minded optimism can provide a sense of hope and anticipation.

c. Our lives will never be without stress, but there are things that can help you cope with today's fast-paced lifestyle.

_____   Which of the following is a supporting detail?

a. Although we would like our lives to be stress-free, reality dictates otherwise.

b. There are things you can do to cope with stress.

c. Take control of your own future by not viewing yourself as a victim.

5.   This passage comes from a geography textbook.

The amount of damage an area sustains during an earthquake is governed in part by factors over which people have no control. These include the type of soil and rock underlying the areas that are struck. Also the depth of the quake and the way the seismic waves travel are factors. Finally, the quake's impact on ground movement affects the amount of damage that occurs.

Source: Arthur Getis, Judith Getis, and Jerome D. Fellmann, *Introduction to Geography,* 6th ed., p. 60. Copyright © 1998 McGraw-Hill. Reprinted by permission of The McGraw-Hill Companies.

The topic of this paragraph is *the amount of damage caused by an earthquake.*

What is the main idea of this paragraph?

a. There is usually serious damage caused by earthquakes' seismic waves.

b. The amount of damage an area sustains during an earthquake is governed in part by factors over which people have no control.

c. An earthquake's impact on ground movement affects the amount of damage that occurs.

Which of the following is a supporting detail?

a. People have only slight control over how much damage an area will have during a disaster.

b. The damage from an earthquake depends on the type of soil and rock underlying the areas that are struck.

c. The amount of damage an area sustains during an earthquake is governed in part by factors over which people have no control.

COMPREHENSION PRACTICE: IDENTIFYING SUPPORTING DETAILS EXERCISES (2)

Study the example in the box below to see how information you learned in this chapter can be used to identify the supporting details of a paragraph. When you are sure you understand the example, complete the five exercises that follow.

EXAMPLE

This excerpt comes from a biology textbook. Its topic is *animal research.* Read the paragraph; then determine the main idea by asking yourself, "What is the most important point the authors want me to understand about animal research?" To identify supporting details, ask yourself, "What additional information do the authors provide in order to help me understand more about animal research?"

Medical and veterinary progress depend on animal research. Every drug and every vaccine developed to improve the human condition has first been tested on an animal. Animal research has enabled medical science to eliminate smallpox and polio. It has provided immunization against previously common and often deadly diseases, such as diphtheria, mumps, and rubella. Animal research has helped create treatments for cancer, diabetes, and heart disease. It has also helped in the development of surgical procedures such as heart surgery, blood transfusions, and cataract removal. AIDS research is wholly dependent on animal studies largely because of the similarity of simian AIDS. Recent work indicates that cats, too, may prove to be useful models for the development of an AIDS vaccine.

Source: Adapted from Cleveland P. Hickman, Jr., Larry S. Roberts, and Allan Larson, *Biology of Animals,* 7th ed., p. 14. Copyright © 1998 McGraw-Hill. Reprinted by permission of The McGraw-Hill Companies.

The topic of this paragraph is *animal research*.

Write the main idea sentence *Medical and veterinary progress depend on*

animal research.

List the supporting details:

* *every drug and every vaccine developed to improve the human condition*

    has first been tested on an animal

* *enabled medical science to eliminate smallpox and polio*

* *provided immunization against previously common and deadly diseases*

* *helped in the development of surgical procedures*

* *helped in AIDS research*

Explanation: The main idea of this paragraph is stated (the first sentence). The rest of the paragraph presents details that explain the many ways that animal research has helped medical and veterinary progress.

Directions:

* First, read the paragraph carefully. Notice that you are given the topic of each paragraph.
* Then copy or write the main idea sentence. (Some main ideas are stated; some are implied.)
* Finally, list the supporting details *on separate lines* in the spaces provided. The directions in each exercise indicate the number of details you should list. You may find it helpful to number them first in the paragraph or mark other clues that signal details.

1.   This paragraph comes from a communications textbook.

Types of Interviews

There are several different types of interviews, and each has a particular purpose. (1) *Survey interviews* gather information from a number of people. They are used to provide information from which to draw conclusions, make interpretations, and determine future action. Manufacturers and advertisers use them to assess market needs and learn consumer reactions to new products. Employers use them to gather employees' ideas about how space should be allotted in a new location or how much a new benefits program might be needed. (2) *Diagnostic interviews* allow health care professionals, attorneys, counselors, and other business and professional workers to gather information that helps them to respond to the needs of their clientele. (3) *Research interviews* provide information upon which to base future decisions. An entrepreneur who is thinking about opening a chain of restaurants might interview others with related experience when developing the concept and question people familiar with the target area to collect ideas about locations and clientele. On a more personal level, an employee thinking about a career change might interview several people who work in the field she is considering to seek advice about how to proceed. (4) *Investigative interviews* gather information to determine the causes of an event, usually a problem. Finally, (5) *exit interviews* help to determine why an employee is leaving an organization.

Source: From Ronald Adler and Jeanne Elmhorst, *Communicating at Work,* 5th ed. Copyright © 1996 McGraw-Hill. Reprinted by permission of The McGraw-Hill Companies.

The topic of this paragraph is *types of interviews.*

Write the main idea sentence:

_____

_____

_____

List and number on separate lines the five supporting details, the types of interviews and their description:

_____

_____

_____

_____

_____

_____

_____

_____

_____

2. This selection comes from a communications textbook.

Wearing appropriate clothes when you are interviewed by a potential employer is vitally important. In one survey, recruiters ranked clothing as the leading factor in shaping their initial impressions of applicants (ahead of physical attractiveness and résumé). Furthermore, 79 percent of the recruiters stated that their initial impressions influenced the rest of the interview. While the best attire to wear will depend on the job you are seeking, it is always safest to dress on the conservative side if you have any doubts.

Source: From Ronald Adler and Jeanne Elmhorst, *Communicating at Work,* 5th ed. Copyright © 1996 McGraw-Hill. Reprinted by permission of The McGraw-Hill Companies.

The topic of this paragraph is *wearing appropriate clothes to an interview.*

Write the main idea sentence:

_____

_____

_____

List the three supporting details. Use a bullet for each detail and start each detail on a new line.

_____

_____

_____

_____

_____

_____

_____

3. This selection comes from an oceanography textbook.

Color

Some sea animals, like jellyfish, are transparent and blend with their background. Some fish conceal themselves with bright color bands and blotches. These colors disrupt the outline of the fish and may draw the predator's attention away from a vital area to a less important region. For example, a black stripe may hide the eye while a false eye spot appears on a tail or fin. Color is also used to send a warning. Organisms that sting, taste foul, bear sharp spines, or have poisonous flesh are often striped and splashed with color, for example, sea slugs and some poisonous shellfish. Dark colors on backs and light ones on undersides are also common among fish that swim near the surface in well-lighted water (for example, salmon, rockfish, herring, and tuna). This color pattern allows the fish to blend with the bottom when seen from above and with the surface when seen from below. It is obvious that color plays an important role in protecting fish and sea animals.

Source: Adapted from Alison B. Duxbury and Alyn C. Duxbury, _Fundamentals of Oceanography_ (Boston: WCB/McGraw-Hill, 1996), p. 231.

The topic of this paragraph is _color in fish and sea animals._

Write the main idea sentence:

_____

_____

_____

List the four *major* (primary) supporting details. Use a bullet for each major detail and start each detail on a new line.

_____

_____

_____

_____

_____

_____

_____

4. This selection comes from a communications textbook.

Minority Students

Although enrollment patterns at colleges and universities vary, the overall number of minority students is increasing. Today, according to the most recent figures available, about one in five college students is a minority student. African-Americans, Hispanic-Americans, Asian-Americans, and Native Americans represent the largest groups of minority students.

Source: From *Communicating at Work,* 5th ed., by Ronald Adler and Jeanne Elmhorst. Copyright © 1996 McGraw-Hill. Reprinted by permission of The McGraw-Hill Companies.

The topic of this paragraph is *minority students in colleges and universities.*

Write the main idea sentence:

_____

_____

_____

_____

List the two supporting details. Use a bullet for each detail and start each detail on a new line.

_____

_____

_____

_____

_____

_____

5. This selection comes from a childhood development textbook.

All children of divorce are affected in some way. But younger children show the greatest signs of stress. There are two reasons for this. First, young children have few relationships outside the family to which they can turn for emotional support. Second, grasping the reasons for divorce is particularly hard for young children because they are emotionally and cognitively immature. Since they tend to view the world from their own perspective and are limited in their ability to reason logically, they tend to blame themselves for their parents' breakup.

Source: From Laurence Steinberg and Roberta Meyer, *Childhood.* Copyright © 1995 McGraw-Hill. Reprinted by permission of The McGraw-Hill Companies.

The topic of this paragraph is *the effect of divorce on children.*

Write the main idea sentence:

_____

_____

_____

List the two *major* supporting details. Use a number for each detail and start each detail on a new line.

_____

_____

_____

_____

_____

_____

SELECTION **6-1**

INFORMATION
TECHNOLOGY

WHO NEEDS CASH WHEN YOU'VE GOT A SMART CARD?

From *Information Technology*
By Dennis P. Curtin, et al.

Imagine yourself at a shopping mall where you make several small purchases, use a pay phone, and have lunch—all without using a single credit card, writing a single check, or even using any cash. In the near future, all of us will be able to do this—if we have smart cards. A smart card student ID could replace multiple cards students now carry—ATM cards, prepaid phone cards, and credit cards— as well as contain a transcript, résumé, medical record, and other useful information. This selection from an information technology textbook explains how smart cards will be used in the future.

1   The typical smart card contains a printed image and message, usually an advertisement from the issuer or information about the user, such as a photo and name.

2   Embedded in the smart card is a special type of integrated circuit that stores information in electronic form. It controls who uses this information and how it is used. The smart card chip holds about 16 kilobytes of information and that is expected to increase to 32K within a few years. That's enough to store up to 3,200 words of text or a digital snapshot of your finger print, palm print, or retinal scan.

Applications

3   The most common smart card is the prepaid phone card. In France almost all public telephones accept prepaid smart cards. Over 100 million are used annually. As calls are made, their cost is deducted from the card and a display on the telephone indicates how many units are left on the card. When no units are left, a new card must be procured. It is expected that smart cards will be used for pay phones in over 100 countries by the end of the century with over 1 billion cards used annually. However, smart cards are also used as cash cards, ID cards, medical record storage, and cellular phone activators.

4   In many parts of Europe and Asia, smart phone cards store account and PIN numbers (personal account and ID number) so that the same cellular phone can be used by different people who simply insert or swipe through their smart card to activate the phone. Airlines and hotel chains are using smart cards to store passenger frequent flyer and frequent guest credits. And smart cards are in wide distribution in the trucking industry where they are used as debit cards for tolls and transit fees, and to keep track of records such as weigh station reports, bills of lading, and state registrations. MasterCard International is

---

Annotation Practice Exercises

Directions: For each exercise below, write the topic and the main idea of the paragraph on the lines beside the paragraph. (You may need to formulate the main idea.) Then, identify the supporting details and list them *separately* on the lines provided.

Annotation Exercise

Topic of paragraph 2:

_____

Main idea sentence:

_____
_____
_____
_____

List the supporting details on separate lines:

_____
_____
_____
_____
_____
_____
_____

committed to the use of smart card technology because this innovation will offer enhanced card security and provide you with faster and safer ways to use your MasterCard to make purchases and payments. Smart cards bring banks as close as your computer. Virtual banking can offer many services over the Internet or specially equipped phones.

Adding Money to a Card

5   Some cards are fixed in value. You purchase them from vending machines, banks, or other outlets in amounts of $1 and up. As you use the card to make purchases, the balance falls. When it's zero, you recycle it or even sell it to a collector. (With billions in use, just throwing them away would create a major environmental problem.) Other cards are more like an electronic purse or wallet that you can spend from and add to. You can insert the card into ATM machines, phones, or card readers next to your PC to have them refilled. Basically, you would just have funds transferred to your card from a credit card or bank account.

The Retailer's Machine

6   To make a purchase, you hand the retailer the smart card and he inserts it into a machine, much like credit cards today. The big difference is that the machine doesn't have to dial into a central computer to find account information because it's stored right in the card. The retailer's machine deducts the amount of the purchase from the card right in the store. The retailer then collects from the bank or other organization that sold you the card. You are not involved because you have already paid for it. For security, new smart cards are virtually impossible to steal and use because they require the entry of a PIN (personal ID number). The retailer cannot deduct funds from the card unless you first key in a PIN.

Security

7   Some smart cards are smarter than others. The simplest cards, such as phone cards, are virtually impossible to copy or falsify, but offer no protection in case of loss. If you lose one, anyone can use it. Other smart cards have one password to restrict its use to one person or machine, and the most sophisticated cards manage several passwords and can use authentication and ciphering techniques to combine total freedom with total security.

Examples of smart cards. *(Gemplus)*

Annotation Exercise

Topic of paragraph 7:

_____

_____

Main idea sentence:

_____

_____

_____

_____

_____

List the supporting details on separate lines:

_____

_____

_____

_____

_____

_____

_____

8   The smart card, in association with a well-designed security system, has been demonstrated to be an effective weapon against payment fraud. The electronic purse is also an effective protection against counterfeit coins and bank notes. In France pay phone break-ins fell from 44,000 in 1985, before cards were widely used, to zero in 1994. As card-operated public phones ceased to be a target for theft, they were less often out-of-order. The same benefits can be found in many other applications where coin-operated machines have suffered from low reliability, required regular coin collection, and borne the cost and loss of service caused by vandalism.

Retailer's smart card reader. *(Gemplus)*

Source: Dennis P. Curtin, et al., *Information Technology,* pp. 124–125. Copyright © 1998 McGraw-Hill 1998. Reprinted by permission of The McGraw-Hill Companies.

Comprehension and Vocabulary Quiz

This quiz has four parts. Your instructor may assign some or all of them.

Comprehension

Directions: Items 1–5 test your comprehension (understanding) of the material in this selection. These questions are much like those that a content area instructor (such as an information technology professor) would expect you to know after studying this selection. For each comprehension question below, use information from the selection to determine the correct answer. Refer to the selection as you answer the questions. Write your answer in the space provided.

_____   **1.** A smart card is embedded with
    a. information about your savings and checking accounts.
    b. a record of your purchases.
    c. a special type of integrated circuit that stores information.
    d. up to 32,000 words of text or PIN numbers.

_____   **2.** Currently, the most common type of smart card is the
    a. identification card.
    b. prepaid phone card.
    c. credit card.
    d. debit card.

_____   **3.** Smart card chips hold
    a. about 16 kilobytes of information.
    b. 3,200 kilobytes of information.
    c. 100 million kilobytes of information.
    d. more than 1 billion kilobytes of information.

_____   **4.** When you use a smart card in a store, the retailer's machine automatically
    a. deducts the purchase price directly from your bank account.
    b. dials into a central computer to find your account information.
    c. deducts the purchase price from the balance on your smart card.
    d. records information that describes your purchases.

_____   **5.** In the future, the use of smart cards will be
    a. increasingly common.
    b. restricted to those who already utilize credit cards.
    c. determined by whether card security can be improved.
    d. regulated by the government.

Vocabulary in Context

Directions: Items 6–10 test your ability to determine the meaning of a word by using context clues. *Context clues* are words in a sentence that allow the reader to deduce (reason out) the meaning of an unfamiliar word in that sentence. Context clues also enable the reader to determine which meaning the author intends when a word has more than one meaning. For each vocabulary item below, a sentence from the selection containing an important word (*italicized, like this*) is quoted first. Next, there is an additional sentence using the word in the same sense and providing another context clue. Use the context clues from *both* sentences to deduce the meaning of the italicized word. *Be sure the answer you choose makes sense in both sentences.* If you discover that you need to use a dictionary to confirm an answer choice, remember that the meaning you select must still fit the context of *both* sentences. Write your answer in the space provided.

Pronunciation Key: ă pat   ā pay   âr care   ä father   ĕ pet   ē be   ĭ pit
ī tie   îr pier   ŏ pot   ō toe   ô paw   oi noise   ou out   ŏŏ took   ōō boot
ŭ cut   yōō abuse   ûr urge   th thin   *th* this   hw which   zh vision
ə about   Stress mark: ʹ

_____ 6. *Embedded* in the card is a special type of integrated circuit that stores information in electronic form and controls who uses this information and how it is used.

Scientists estimated that the fossils *embedded* in the rock layer were at least 10,000 years old.

embedded (ĕm bĕdʹ ĭd)

a. found by accident or chance
b. firmly fixed in a surrounding mass
c. discovered
d. placed intentionally

_____ 7. When no units are left, a new card must be *procured*.

After the hurricane, the Buxton family *procured* food and clothing from the Red Cross.

procured (prō kyōōrd)

a. obtained
b. purchased
c. borrowed
d. refused

_____ **8.** For security, new smart cards are *virtually* impossible to steal and use because they require the entry of a PIN (personal ID number).

At our lake house, away from the noises of the city, it is *virtually* silent.

virtually (vûr′ chōō ə lē)

a. enjoyably

b. almost totally

c. never

d. typically

_____ **9.** The smart card, in association with a well-designed security system, has been demonstrated to be an effective weapon against payment *fraud.*

The company that sent out false sweepstakes forms was charged with mail *fraud.*

fraud (frôd)

a. deception designed to obtain unfair or unlawful gain

b. any crime punishable by a prison sentence

c. a scam carried out by two individuals working together

d. a system of giving refunds

_____ **10.** As card-operated public phones *ceased* to be a target for theft, they were less often out-of-order.

Once the rain *ceased,* the soccer tournament resumed.

ceased (sēsd)

a. started

b. began to intensify

c. stopped

d. increased

Word Structure

Directions: Items 11–15 test your ability to use word-structure clues to help determine a word's meaning. *Word-structure clues* consist of roots, prefixes, and suffixes. In these exercises, you will learn the meaning of a word part (root) and use it to determine the meaning of the several other words that have the same word part. If you discover that you need to use a dictionary to confirm an answer choice, do so.

In paragraph 4 of the selection you encountered the word *innovation.* This word contains the Latin root *nov,* which means "new." The word *innovation* literally means "something *new.*" Use the meaning of *nov* and the list of prefixes on pages 60–61 to help you determine the meaning of each of the following words that contain this same root. Write your answer in the space provided.

_____ **11.** If you are a **novice** at skiing, you are

    a. a beginner.

    b. learning very quickly.

    c. not interested in the sport.

    d. looking for an outdoor sport.

_____ **12.** A *nova* is a variable star that suddenly increases to several times its original brightness, but eventually returns to its original appearance. Astronomers call this a **nova** because

    a. it is a phenomenon that does not occur very often.

    b. it temporarily looks like a new or different star.

    c. it breaks into several different stars.

    d. they do not know why this phenomenon happens.

_____ **13.** At the turn of the 20th century, the automobile was still a **novel** invention. In other words, it was still

    a. strikingly new or different.

    b. unsafe to the point of dangerous.

    c. extremely expensive.

    d. inefficient and unreliable.

_____ **14.** If you **renovate** your kitchen, you

    a. make it more efficient.

    b. repaint it.

    c. replace the refrigerator.

    d. make it "like new" again.

_____ **15.** Once the **novelty** of a toy wears off, children tend to

    a. put it in a safe place to save it for later.

    b. play with it often because they have grown very fond of it.

    c. become bored with it because it is no longer new.

    d. break it because they are frustrated with it.

Reading Skills Application

Directions: Items 16–20 test your ability to apply certain reading skills to the material in this selection. These are the types of questions that might appear on standardized reading tests and state-mandated basic skills tests. Write your answer in the space provided.

_____ **16.** Which of the following represents the main idea of the entire selection?

    a. The typical smart card contains a printed image and message, usually an advertisement from the issuer or information about the user, such as a photo and name.

    b. Because smart cards use integrated circuits to store large amounts of information in electric form, they offer both a wide range of applications and virtual security.

    c. With its integrated circuit, the smart card has been demonstrated to be an effective weapon against payment fraud.

    d. Smart cards can be used as phone cards, cash cards, ID cards, for medical record storage, and many other uses.

_____ **17.** In paragraph 5, certain types of smart cards are described as being *like an electronic purse or wallet.* By this, the authors mean that

    a. "money" can be credited or debited from the card just as actual money can be put into or removed from a purse or wallet.

    b. the cards are smaller and more convenient to carry than an actual purse or wallet.

    c. the cards have unique styles and designs, just like purses and wallets.

    d. the cards are less likely to be stolen than a purse or wallet.

_____ **18.** According to information in the selection, smart cards

    a. are used to make 100 million telephones annually.

    b. will eventually be used for pay phones in more than 100 countries.

    c. are currently used by more than 2 billion people.

    d. can hold 3,200 kilobytes of information.

_____ **19.** The primary purpose the authors wrote this selection is to

    a. persuade people to use smart cards.

    b. inform readers of the wide array of present uses of smart cards.

    c. instruct readers how to obtain, use, and "refill" smart cards.

    d. inform readers about smart cards, their use, and the security issues associated with them.

_____ **20.** Which of the following best represents the writers' point of view regarding the value of smart cards?

    a. Well-designed smart cards can offer convenience, security, and even help reduce fraud.

    b. The best use of smart cards is for prepaid phone service.

    c. Smart cards are valuable only if they offer total security.

    d. The people who are most likely to use smart cards are those who have PCs at home because they can refill the cards.

Collaboration Option

Writing and Collaborating to Enhance Your Understanding

Option for collaboration: Your instructor may direct you to work with other students or, in other words, to work *collaboratively.* In that case, you should form groups of three or four students as directed by your instructor and work together to complete the exercises. After your group discusses each item and agrees on the answer, have a group member record it. Every member of your group should be able to explain all of your group's answers.

1. **Reacting to What You Have Read:** Do you think that smart cards will ever completely replace cash? Why or why not?

    _____

    _____

    _____

    _____

    _____

    _____

    _____

2. **Comprehending the Selection Further:** What are some likely future applications of smart cards specifically for college students? On separate lines below, list as many possible applications as you can think of.

    _____

    _____

    _____

    _____

    _____

    _____

    _____

    _____

    _____

    _____

3. **Overall Main Idea of the Selection:** In one sentence tell what the authors want readers to understand about smart cards. (Be sure to include the words "smart cards" in your overall main idea sentence.)

_____

_____

_____

_____

_____

_____

Read More about It on the World Wide Web

To learn more about the topic of this selection, visit these websites or use your favorite search engine (such as Yahoo®) to discover more about this author and this topic on your own. Whenever you go to *any* website, it is a good idea to evaluate it critically. Are you getting good information—that is, information that is accurate, complete, and up-to-date? Who sponsors the website? How easy is it to use the features of the website?

http://www.smart-card.co.uk
http://www.smartcardbasics.com
http://www.smartcardclub.co.uk

SELECTION 6-2
HISTORY

THE LIFE OF BUDDHA: THE PATH TO NIRVANA

From *The 100: A Ranking of the Most Influential Persons in History*
By Michael Hart

Gautama Buddha lived approximately 2,500 years ago (563 to 483 B.C.E.). He founded Buddhism, a worldwide religion that has influenced millions of people. Historian Michael Hart ranks Buddha among the top five most influential persons in the history of the world. In this selection he tells about Buddha's 80-year life and his beliefs, and he explains why he considers Buddha so influential.

Seated Buddha, from Gandhara, India
(now Pakistan). Kushan period, 2nd–3rd
century c.e. Sonte, 36 × 22½ × 8″.
(*The Seattle Art Museum* [*Eugene Fuller Memorial Collection*])

Annotation Practice Exercises

Directions: For each exercise below, write the topic and the main idea of the paragraph on the lines beside the paragraph. Then, identify the supporting details and list them *separately* on the lines provided.

Annotation Exercise

Topic of paragraph 1:

_____

_____

Main idea sentence:

_____

_____

_____

_____

List the supporting details on separate lines:

_____

_____

_____

_____

_____

_____

_____

_____

1   Gautama Buddha, whose original name was Prince Siddhartha, was the founder of Buddhism, one of the world's great religions. Siddhartha was the son of a king ruling in Kapilavastu, a city in northeast India, near the borders of Nepal. Siddhartha himself (of the clan of Gautama and the tribe of Sakya) was purportedly born in 563 B.C., in Lumbini, within the present borders of Nepal. He was married at sixteen to a cousin of the same age. Brought up in the luxurious royal palace, Prince Siddhartha did not want for material comforts.

2   Nevertheless, Siddhartha was profoundly dissatisfied. He observed that most human beings were poor and continually suffered from want. Even those who were wealthy were frequently frustrated and unhappy, and all humans were subject to disease and ultimately succumbed to death. Surely, Siddhartha thought, there must be more to life than transitory pleasures, which were all too soon obliterated by suffering and death.

3   When he was twenty-nine, just after the birth of his first son, Gautama decided that he must abandon the life he was living and devote himself wholeheartedly to the search for truth. He departed from the palace, leaving behind his wife, his infant son, and all his worldly possessions, and became a penniless wanderer. For a while he studied with some of the famed holy men of the day, but after mastering their teachings, he found their solutions to the problems of the human situation unsatisfactory. It was widely believed that extreme asceticism was the pathway to true wisdom. Gautama therefore attempted to become an ascetic by engaging in extreme fasts and self-mortification for several years. Eventually, however, he realized that tormenting his body only clouded his brain, without leading him any closer to true wisdom. He therefore resumed eating normally and abandoned asceticism.

4   In solitude, he grappled with the problems of human existence. Finally, one evening, as he sat beneath a giant fig tree, all the pieces of the puzzle seemed to fall into place. Siddhartha spent the whole night in deep reflection, and when the morning came, he was convinced that he had found the solution and that he was now a Buddha, an "enlightened one."

5   At this time, he was thirty-five years old. For the remaining forty-five years of his life, he traveled throughout northern India, preaching his new philosophy to all who were willing to listen. By the time he died, in 483 B.C., he had made thousands of converts. Though his words had not been written down, his disciples had memorized many of his teachings, and they were passed to succeeding generations by word of mouth.

6   The principal teachings of the Buddha can be summarized in what Buddhists call the "Four Noble Truths." These are: first, that human life is intrinsically unhappy; second, that the cause of this unhappiness is human selfishness and desire; third, that individual selfishness and desire can be brought to an end—the resulting state, when all desire and cravings have been eliminated, is termed *nirvana* (literally "blowing out" or "extinction"); fourth, that the method of escape from selfishness and

Annotation Exercise

Topic of paragraph 6:

_____

_____

Main idea sentence:

_____

_____

_____

_____

_____

List the supporting details on separate lines:

_____

_____

_____

_____

_____

_____

_____

_____

_____

desire is what is called the "Eightfold Path": right views, right thought, right speech, right action, right livelihood, right effort, right mindfulness, and right meditation.

7   Buddha, as the founder of one of the world's major religions, clearly deserves a place among the most influential people in history. Since there are only about 200 million Buddhists in the world, compared with over 800 million Moslems and about one billion Christians, it would seem evident that Buddha has influenced fewer people than either Muhammad or Jesus. However, the difference in numbers can be misleading. One reason that Buddhism died out in India is that Hinduism absorbed many of its ideas and principles. In China, too, large numbers of persons who do not call themselves Buddhists have been strongly influenced by Buddhist philosophy.

8   Buddhism, far more than Christianity or Islam, has a very strong pacifist element. This orientation toward non-violence has played a significant role in the political history of Buddhist countries.

Source: Adapted from Michael Hart, *The 100: A Ranking of the Most Influential Persons in History* (Carol Publishing Group, 1978), pp. 52–55.

Comprehension and Vocabulary Quiz

This quiz has four parts. Your instructor may assign some or all of them.

Comprehension

Directions: For each comprehension question below, use information from the selection to determine the correct answer. Refer to the selection as you answer the questions. Write your answer in the space provided.

_____ **1.** Gautama Buddha spent the first 29 years of his life
     a. as a penniless wanderer.
     b. as a prince in a royal palace.
     c. training to become a holy man.
     d. as an ascetic.

_____ **2.** The term "Buddha" means
     a. enlightened one.
     b. royal prince.
     c. ascetic.
     d. one whose teachings are passed to succeeding generations.

_____ **3.** The teachings of Buddha were memorized by his disciples and then
     a. written down in a holy book called *The Four Noble Truths.*
     b. passed on by word of mouth.
     c. developed into the "Eightfold Path."
     d. adopted by Hinduism and Christianity.

_____ **4.** One of the four principal teachings of the Buddha is that
     a. Buddhism is open to all.
     b. individual selfishness and desire can be brought to an end.
     c. happiness is the natural state of human life.
     d. human life is intrinsically happy.

_____ **5.** Buddhism has a strong orientation toward
     a. peace and nonviolence.
     b. other religions such as Hinduism and Islam.
     c. the teachings of Muhammad and Jesus.
     d. asceticism and self-mortification.

Vocabulary in Context

Directions: Use the context clues from *both* sentences to deduce the meaning of the italicized word. *Be sure the answer you choose makes sense in both sentences.* If you discover that you need to use a dictionary to confirm an answer choice, remember that the meaning you select must still fit the context of *both* sentences. Write your answer in the space provided.

Pronunciation Key: ă pat ā pay âr care ä father ĕ pet ē be ĭ pit
ī tie îr pier ŏ pot ō toe ô paw oi noise ou out ŏŏ took ōō boot
ŭ cut yōō abuse ûr urge th thin *th* this hw which zh vision
ə about   Stress mark: ʹ

_____ **6.** Brought up in the luxurious royal palace, Prince Siddhartha did not want for *material* comforts.

Many people complain that American society places too much emphasis on clothes, cars, electronic devices, and other *material* goods.

material (mə tĭrʹ ē əl)

a. pertaining to cloth
b. pertaining to a humble lifestyle
c. pertaining to physical well-being
d. pertaining to things that are inexpensive

_____ **7.** Gautama therefore attempted to become an *ascetic,* for several years engaging in extreme fasts and self-mortification.

Because Jake is an *ascetic,* he chooses to live alone in a small mountain cabin with no electricity, no running water, and no telephone.

ascetic (ə sĕtʹ ĭk)

a. extremely religious person
b. person who leads a life of self-discipline and without comforts
c. person who plans things in a careful, detailed manner
d. extremely unfriendly

_____ **8.** Siddhartha spent the whole night in deep reflection, and when the morning came, he was convinced that he had found the solution and that he was now a Buddha, an "*enlightened* one."

We all suddenly felt *enlightened* after hearing our math professor explain the difficult concepts in a way we could understand.

enlightened (ĕn līt′ nd)

a. made lighter

b. relieved; free from worry

c. having spiritual or intellectual insight

d. confused and frustrated

_____   **9.** The principal teachings of the Buddha can be summarized in what Buddhists call the "Four Noble Truths": first, that human life is *intrinsically* unhappy.

Because the judge is *intrinsically* fair, she is effective and well highly respected.

intrinsically (ĭn trĭn′ zĭk lē)

a. inherently or naturally

b. from time to time

c. partially or incompletely

d. never

_____   **10.** Buddhism, far more than Christianity or Islam, has a very strong *pacifist* element.

Last week, antiwar demonstrators and other *pacifist* groups held protests in the nation's capital.

pacifist (păs′ ə fĭst)

a. opposed to war or violence as a means of settling disputes

b. from the Pacific coast region

c. well-organized politically

d. pertaining to religion

Word Structure

Directions: In paragraph 3 of the selection you encountered the word *self-mortification.* This word contains the Latin root **mort,** which means "death." The word *mortification* means "to discipline (one's body and physical appetites) by self-denial or self-inflicted privation." You can see the connection with the meaning of the root because if one "disciplined" and "denied" one's body to an extreme, it would result in death. (*Mortify* also has come to mean "to humiliate" and "to feel shame or wounded pride.") Use the meaning of **mort** and the list of prefixes on pages 60–61 to help you determine the meaning of each of the following words that contain this same root. Write your answer in the space provided.

_____ 11. A **mortuary** is a
  a. funeral home.
  b. sacred shrine.
  c. public area.
  d. type of wreath.

_____ 12. An autopsy, or **post mortem** examination, is conducted
  a. on weekdays only.
  b. only after employees complete their routine duties.
  c. on the body after a person has died.
  d. by a person involved in criminal investigation.

_____ 13. A **mortician** is a person who
  a. knows emergency procedures.
  b. counsels families.
  c. presides at a religious service.
  d. is a funeral director or undertaker.

_____ 14. If a hospital patient is **moribund,** the person is
  a. ill.
  b. dying.
  c. in intensive care.
  d. on a heart monitor.

_____ 15. If a solider receives a **mortal** wound, it is
  a. a serious injury.
  b. a head wound.
  c. an injury that causes extensive blood loss.
  d. a fatal wound.

Reading Skills Application

Directions: Apply your reading skills to answer the questions below. Write your answer in the space provided.

_____ 16. Based on information in the selection, which of the following represents a logical inference about Buddha and his "search for truth"?
  a. Buddha regretted his decision to leave his home and family to "search for truth."
  b. If Buddha had grown up in poverty, he might never have begun a "search for truth."
  c. Buddha's family and friends thought his decision to "search for truth" was foolish.
  d. Buddha failed in his "search for truth" and died bitter and frustrated.

_____   **17.** Which of the following represents an opinion about Buddha rather than a fact?
   a.   He was married at 16 to a cousin the same age.
   b.   He therefore resumed eating normally and abandoned asceticism.
   c.   By the time he died, in 483 B.C., he had made thousands of converts.
   d.   Buddha, as the founder of one of the world's majors religions, clearly deserves a place among the most influential people in history.

_____   **18.** Which of the following is the meaning of *clouded* as it is used in paragraph 3?
   a.   refreshed
   b.   strengthened
   c.   confused
   d.   destroyed

_____   **19.** In paragraph 4 the author says, "all the pieces of the puzzle seemed to fall into place" for Siddhartha, to mean that Siddhartha
   a.   finally achieved the insight into human existence that he had sought for so long.
   b.   gave up because none of the solutions he found had worked.
   c.   continued to be puzzled and perplexed about the human condition.
   d.   became puzzled by the challenges that seemed to befall him.

_____   **20.** The pattern of organization in paragraphs 1–6 can best be described as a
   a.   list.
   b.   sequence.
   c.   cause and an effect.
   d.   comparison.

Collaboration Option

Writing and Collaborating to Enhance Your Understanding

Option for collaboration: Work together in groups to complete the exercises below. Have one group member record your answers, but make sure that every member of your group can explain all of your group's answers.

1. **Reacting to What You Have Read:** Many people today buy more things than they can afford and, although they have more possessions, they complain that they are still not truly happy. Why do you think this is so?

_____

_____

_____

_____

_____

_____

_____

2. **Comprehending the Selection Further:** Do you agree with Buddha's first "Noble Truth" that human life is intrinsically unhappy? Explain why you agree or disagree.

_____

_____

_____

_____

_____

_____

_____

_____

3. **Overall Main Idea of the Selection:** In one sentence tell what the author
    wants readers to understand about Buddha. (Be sure to include the name
    "Buddha" in your overall main idea sentence.)

    _____

    _____

    _____

    _____

    _____

    _____

    _____

Read More about It on the World Wide Web

To learn more about the topic of this selection, visit these websites or use
your favorite search engine (such as Yahoo®) to discover more about this author
and this topic on your own. Whenever you go to *any* website, it is a good idea
to evaluate it critically. Are you getting good information—that is, information
that is accurate, complete, and up-to-date? Who sponsors the website? How
easy is it to use the features of the website?

http://www.edepot.com/buddha.shtml
http://www.buddhanet.net/
http://www.fwbo.org/buddhism.html

LEARN TO CONTROL YOUR ASSETS—AND YOU MAY BECOME A MILLIONAIRE

From *Understanding Business*
By William G. Nickels, James M. McHugh, and Susan M. McHugh

Most Americans spend everything they earn, and many spend more each month than they earn. In 1970 Americans rang up approximately $100 billion in credit card expenditures. By the year 2000, it mushroomed to roughly nine times that amount. The average American saves only 1 to 2 percent of each paycheck. (The average Japanese person, in contrast, saves 20%!) Even more frightening, the average American has only $44,000 in his or her retirement plan. This means many of them will face the hard, unpleasant reality of trying to live on an inadequate Social Security check later in their lives.

Are you a college student who feels you never have enough money? Does your money just seem to disappear every month? Does it seem impossible to save up enough money for a big purchase, such as a car? At this point in your life, are you already unable to pay your credit card bill each month? This business textbook selection gives specific strategies for bringing your financial assets under control and putting yourself on the road to financial well-being. (By the way, if you think the only way you could become a millionaire is to win the lottery, you'll make a surprising discovery when you read this selection.)

---

1   The only way to save enough money to do all of the things you want to do later in life is to make more than you spend! We know you may find it hard to save today, but saving money isn't only possible, it's imperative if you want to accumulate enough to be financially secure. The following are six steps you can take today to get control of your finances.

Step 1: Take an Inventory of Your Financial Assets

2   To take inventory of your financial assets, you need to develop a balance sheet for yourself. A balance sheet is a statement that reports your financial condition at a specific time. A balance sheet starts the fundamental accounting equation: Assets = Liabilities + Owner's Equity. You can develop your own balance sheet by listing your assets (e.g., TV, VCR, DVD, computer, bicycle, car, jewelry, and clothes) on one side of the sheet and your debts on the other. Assets include anything you own. For our purpose, evaluate your assets based on their current value, not purchase price as required in formal accounting statements.

3   If the value of your liabilities exceeds the value of your assets, you aren't on the path to financial security. You need some discipline in your life, a small price to pay for never having to face the unpleasant possibility of bankruptcy.

Directions: For each exercise below, write the topic and the main idea of the paragraph on the lines beside the paragraph. Then, identify the supporting details and list them *separately* on the lines provided.

Topic of paragraph 2:

_____

_____

Main idea sentence:

_____

_____

_____

_____

_____

_____

4   Since we're talking about accounting, let's talk about an income statement. An income statement shows your profit after costs, expenses, and taxes; it summarizes all your resources. At the top of the income statement is revenue (everything you take in from your job, investments, etc.). You subtract all your costs and expenses to get net income or profit. Software programs such as Quicken and websites such as www.dinkytown.net have a variety of tools that can easily help you with these calculations.

5   This may also be an excellent time to think about how much money you will need to accomplish all your goals. The more you visualize your goals, the easier it is to begin saving for them.

Step 2: Keep Track of All Your Expenses

6   You may often find yourself running out of cash. This is known as a cash flow problem: too little cash coming in and too much cash going out. In such circumstances, the only way to trace where the money is going is to keep track of every cent you spend. Keeping records of your expenses can be a rather tedious but necessary chore if you want to learn discipline. Actually, it could turn out to be an enjoyable task because it gives you such a feeling of control. Here's what to do: Carry a notepad with you wherever you go and record what you spend as you go through the day. That notepad is your journal. At the end of the week, record your journal entries into a record book or computerized accounting program.

7   Develop certain categories (accounts) to make the task easier and more informative. For example, you can have a category called "food" for all food you bought from the grocery or the convenience store during the week. You might want to have a separate account for meals eaten away from home because you can dramatically cut such costs if you make your lunches at home. Other accounts could include automobile, clothing, utilities, entertainment, donations to charity, and gifts. Most people like to have a category called "miscellaneous" where they put expenditures for things like café latte. You won't believe how much you fritter away on miscellaneous items unless you keep a detailed record for at least a couple of months.

8   You can develop your accounts based on what's most important to you or where you spend the most money. Once you have recorded all of your expenses, it is relatively easy to see where you are spending too much money and what you have to do to save more money.

List the supporting details on separate lines:

_____

_____

_____

_____

_____

_____

_____

Annotation Exercise

Topic of paragraph 6:

_____

_____

Main idea sentence:

_____

_____

_____

_____

_____

List the supporting details on separate lines:

_____

_____

_____

_____

_____

_____

_____

POSSIBLE COST-SAVING CHOICES

Budgeting your money requires making choices. The effect of the choices you make today can have a dramatic impact on your financial future. Compare the differences these few choices you can make now would mean to your future net worth. If you would make the lower-cost choices every month during your four years of college, and invest the savings in a mutual fund earning 12 percent compounded annually, you would have nearly $9,000 when you graduate.

First Choice Cost per Month	Alternate Choice Cost per Month	Savings per Month
Starbucks caffe latte $3.00 for 20 days = $60.00	Quick Trip's Cappuccino $.60 for 20 days = $12.00	$48.00
Fast-food lunch of burger, fries, and soft drink $4.00 for 20 days = $80.00	Lunch brought from home $2 for 20 days = $40.00	40.00
Evian bottled water $1.50 for 20 days = $30.00	Generic bottled water $.50 for 20 days = $10.00	20.00
CD = $15.00	Listen to your old CDs = $0.00	15.00
Banana Republic T-shirt = $34.00	Old Navy T-shirt = $10.00	<u>24.00</u>
	Total savings per month	$147.00
	Total savings through 4 years of college	× 48 months $7,056.00
	12% compounded annually	$8,969.00

Step 3: Prepare a Budget

9   Once you know your financial situation and your sources of revenue and expenses, you're prepared to make a personal budget. Remember, budgets are financial plans. Items that are important in a household budget include mortgage or rent, utilities, food, life insurance, car insurance, and medical care. You'll need to make choices regarding how much to allow for such expenses as eating out, entertainment, and so on. Keep in mind that what you spend now reduces what you can save later. For example, spending $3.50 for a pack of cigarettes a day adds up to about $25 a week, $100 a month, $1,200 a year. If you saved that $1,200 each year instead, at 12 percent compounded annually you would have over $550,000 in 35 years—that's more than half of your million-dollar goal right there. Other cost-saving choices you might consider are listed in the table above.

10   You'll learn that running a household is similar to running a small business. It takes the same careful record keeping, the same budget processes and forecasting, the same control procedures, and often (sadly) the same need to periodically borrow funds. Suddenly, concepts such as credit and interest rates become only too real. This is where knowledge of finance, investments, and budgeting pays off. Thus, the time you spend learning budgeting techniques will benefit you throughout your life.

Step 4: Pay Off Your Debts

11   The first thing to do with the money remaining after you pay your monthly bills is to pay off your debts. Start with the debts that carry the highest interest rates. Credit card debt, for example, may be costing you 16 percent or more a year. Merely paying off such debts will set you on a path toward financial freedom. It's better to pay off a debt that costs 16 percent than to put the money in a bank account that earns, say, only 3 percent.

Step 5: Start a Savings Plan

12   It's important to save each month in a separate account for large purchases you're likely to make (such as a car). Then, when it comes time to make that purchase, you'll have the cash so you won't have to pay finance charges. You should save at least enough for a significant down payment so you can reduce the finance charges. The figure on the right compares the costs of financing versus paying cash for a $15,000 car.

13   The best way to save money is to *pay yourself first.* That is, take your paycheck, take out money for savings, and then plan what to do with the rest. You can arrange with your bank or mutual fund to deduct a certain amount every month. You will be pleasantly surprised when the money starts accumulating and earning interest over time. With some discipline, you can eventually reach your goal of becoming a millionaire. It's not as difficult as you may think. You simply have to save $6 a day and be patient. After 35 years, you'll have accumulated a million dollars. Well, not exactly. You will have saved just $76,440. But if you invest that money each year and make 12 percent compound interest, it would be worth $1 million in 35 years.

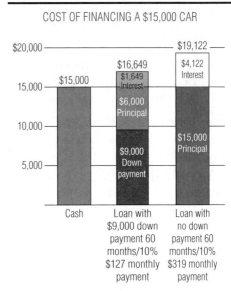

COST OF FINANCING A $15,000 CAR

Financing the purchase of a $15,000 car costs over $4,000, or 27.5 percent, more than paying cash. If you had saved during your college years as illustrated here, you would have $9,000 for a down payment, reducing your finance charges to only $1,649.

Step 6: Borrow Money Only to Buy Assets That Have the Potential to Increase in Value

14   Don't borrow money for ordinary expenses; you'll only get into more debt that way. If you have budgeted for emergencies, such as car repairs and health care costs, you should be able to stay financially secure. Only the most unexpected of expenses should cause you to borrow. It is hard to wait until you have enough money to buy what you want, but learning to wait is a critical part of self-discipline.

15   If you follow all six of these steps, you'll not only have money for investment but you'll have developed most of the financial techniques needed to become a millionaire. At first you may find it hard to live within a budget. Nonetheless, the payoff is well worth the pain.

Annotation Exercise

Topic of paragraph 14:

_____

_____

Main idea sentence:

_____

_____

_____

_____

_____

_____

List the supporting details on separate lines:

_____

_____

_____

_____

_____

_____

_____

_____

_____

_____

Source: Adapted from William G. Nickels, James M. McHugh, and Susan M. McHugh, _Understanding Business,_ 6th ed., pp. 678–681. Copyright © 2002 McGraw-Hill. Reprinted by permission of The McGraw-Hill Companies.

Comprehension and Vocabulary Quiz

This quiz has four parts. Your instructor may assign some or all of them.

Comprehension

Directions: For each comprehension question below, use information from the selection to determine the correct answer. Refer to the selection as you answer the questions. Write your answer in the space provided.

_____ **1.** An example of a financial liability is
    a. your computer, TV, etc.
    b. a mutual fund.
    c. credit card debt.
    d. your assets.

_____ **2.** Recording in a journal every cent you spend will
    a. make it easy to see what you have to do to save more money.
    b. give you a feeling of control.
    c. make it easy to see where you are spending too much money.
    d. all of the above.

_____ **3.** Making a personal budget
    a. helps you identify cost-saving choices you could make to save money.
    b. reduces what you can save later.
    c. helps you evaluate your assets.
    d. all of the above.

_____ **4.** One of the things you should do before you pay off debts and start a savings plan is
    a. to pay yourself first.
    b. to prepare a budget.
    c. to buy only cost-saving assets that will increase in value.
    d. all of the above.

_____ **5.** After paying your monthly bills, the first thing you should do with the remaining money is
    a. invest the money in a mutual fund that earns at least 3 percent.
    b. increase your assets.
    c. pay off debts that carry the highest interest rates.
    d. buy assets that have the potential to increase in value.

Vocabulary in Context

Directions: Use the context clues from *both* sentences to deduce the meaning of the italicized word. *Be sure the answer you choose makes sense in both sentences.* If you discover that you need to use a dictionary to confirm an answer choice, remember that the meaning you select must still fit the context of *both* sentences. Write your answer in the space provided.

Pronunciation Key: ă **pat** ā **pay** âr **care** ä **father** ĕ **pet** ē **be** ĭ **pit**
ī **tie** îr **pier** ŏ **pot** ō **toe** ô **paw** oi **noise** ou **out** oŏ **took** ōō **boot**
ŭ **cut** yōō **abuse** ûr **urge** th **thin** *th* **this** hw **which** zh **vision**
ə **about**   Stress mark: ′

6. We know you may find it hard to save today, but saving money isn't only possible, it's *imperative* if you want to accumulate enough to be financially secure.

To avoid a penalty, it is *imperative* that you pay your income tax by April 15 or file for an extension.

imperative (ĭm pĕr′ ə tĭv)

a. silly; foolish

b. irrelevant; inconsequential

c. necessary; essential

d. preferable; desirable

7. We know you may find it hard to save today, but saving money isn't only possible, it's imperative if you want to accumulate enough to be financially *secure.*

In order for children to feel *secure,* they must be confident that their parents love them and will take care of them.

secure (sĭ kyōōr′)

a. safe; protected

b. cheerful; happy

c. wealthy; affluent

d. adventurous; risk-taking

8. If the value of your *liabilities* exceeds the value of your assets, you aren't on the path to financial security.

The car dealership turned down Tom's application for financing because he had too many *liabilities:* high credit card debt, a student loan, and a short-term bank loan.

liabilities (lī ə bĭl′ ĭ tēs)

a.   credit cards

b.   debts

c.   money orders

d.   bank loans

_____   **9.** Keeping records of your expenses can be a rather *tedious* but necessary chore if you want to learn discipline.

Transferring the company's files to a new set of filing cabinets was a *tedious* chore that we dreaded.

tedious (tē′ dē əs)

a.   unusually difficult

b.   boring; tiresome

c.   unexpected

d.   complicated

_____   **10.** You won't believe how much you *fritter away* on miscellaneous items unless you keep a detailed record for at least a couple of months.

It is easy to *fritter away* time in the student lounge and then not have enough time to study.

fritter away (frĭt′ ər   ə wā′)

a.   set aside

b.   save

c.   take delight in

d.   waste

Word Structure

Directions: In paragraph 3 of the selection you encountered the word ***bankruptcy.*** This word contains the Latin root ***rupt,*** which means "to break," "to tear," or "to burst." *Bankruptcy* literally means "to *break* the bank," or, in colloquial terms, to be "broke." In other words, it means to have no money and, therefore, be unable to pay one's debts. Use the meaning of ***rupt*** and the list of prefixes on pages 60–61 to help you determine the meaning of each of the following words that contain this same root. Write your answer in the space provided.

_____   **11.** If your appendix **ruptures,** it

a.   bursts.

b.   leaks.

c.   curves.

d.   corrodes.

_____   **12.** If the network **interrupts** a television program to broadcast a storm
warning, the network

    a.   cancels the rest of the show that is being televised.

    b.   temporarily loses its picture.

    c.   goes off the air.

    d.   breaks into the regular program.

_____   **13.** If protesters **disrupt** a speech the president is giving, they

    a.   applaud and cheer enthusiastically.

    b.   link arms and sway from side to side.

    c.   turn their backs on him.

    d.   say and do things that cause the president temporarily to stop speaking.

_____   **14.** When a volcano **erupts,** the lava

    a.   bursts forth from the crater.

    b.   solidifies.

    c.   turns into powdery ashes.

    d.   cools and hardens.

_____   **15.** If the chief of police is found to be **corrupt,** it means the person

    a.   has mastered law enforcement policies and procedures.

    b.   violates rules of ethics and breaks laws.

    c.   is mentally ill.

    d.   is determined to be incompetent.

Reading Skills Application

Directions: Apply your reading skills to answer the questions below. Write
your answer in the space provided.

_____   **16.** Which of the following patterns is used to organize the information in the
selection?

    a.   comparison-contrast

    b.   list

    c.   sequence

    d.   cause-effect

_____   **17.** Which of the following statements from the selection best expresses the
main idea of paragraph 9?

    a.   Once you know your financial situation and your sources of revenue
and expenses, you're prepared to make a personal budget.

    b.   Remember, budgets are financial plans.

    c.   You'll need to make choices regarding how much to allow for such
expenses as eating out, entertainment, and so on.

    d.   Keep in mind that what you spend now reduces what you can save later.

_____ **18.** Which of the following best describes the authors' purpose for writing this selection?

    a.   to inform readers about how financial planners can help people learn to manage their money

    b.   to instruct readers how to become financially secure by gaining control of their money

    c.   to persuade readers not to use credit cards or accumulate debt

    d.   to entertain readers with stories of how people who are just like they are have become financial successes

_____ **19.** Which of the following would the authors most likely agree with?

    a.   No one enjoys being on a budget.

    b.   With discipline, anyone can become a millionaire.

    c.   People would make better financial decisions if they understood the importance of it and knew what to do.

    d.   Most college students are extravagant and wasteful with their money.

_____ **20.** According to data from the bar graph in the selection, how much more interest would a person pay by making no down payment on a car than by making a down payment of $9,000?

    a. $4,112

    b. $4,000

    c. $2,473

    d. $1,649

BUSINESS

Collaboration Option

Writing and Collaborating to Enhance Your Understanding

Option for collaboration: Work together in groups to complete the exercise below. Have one group member record your answers, but make sure every member of your group can explain all of your group's answers.

1. **Reacting to What You Have Read:** Which of the six steps presented in this selection do you think might be the most difficult for you to implement? (There may be more than one.) Explain your reasons.

    _____

    _____

    _____

    _____

    _____

    _____

    _____

    _____

2. **Comprehending the Selection Further:** The six steps presented in this selection can help you avoid several common financial problems or bad habits about managing money. List and explain at least three of them.

    _____

    _____

    _____

    _____

    _____

    _____

    _____

    _____

    _____

3. **Overall Main Idea of the Selection:** In one sentence tell what the authors want readers to understand about controlling their assets? (Be sure to include the phrase "control your assets" in your overall main idea sentence.)

_____

_____

_____

_____

_____

Read More about It on the World Wide Web

To learn more about the topic of this selection, visit these websites or use your favorite search engine (such as Yahoo®) to discover more about this author and this topic on your own. Whenever you go to *any* website, it is a good idea to evaluate it critically. Are you getting good information—that is, information that is accurate, complete, and up-to-date? Who sponsors the website? How easy is it to use the features of the website?

http://www.arthritis.org/resources/financial_planning/taking_stock/saving_investing.asp

http://www.the-money-advisor.com/money-article38.php

http://www.dinkytown.net

(© Arthur Thévenart/CORBIS)

CHAPTER 7

Recognizing Authors' Writing Patterns

CHAPTER OBJECTIVES

In this chapter you will learn:

- What authors' writing patterns are and why it is important to be able to recognize them.

- The method for recognizing authors' writing patterns.

WHAT YOU NEED TO LEARN

What Are Authors' Writing Patterns, and Why Is It Important to Be Able to Recognize Them?

What Is the Method for Recognizing Authors' Writing Patterns?

- List Pattern
- Sequence Pattern
- Comparison-Contrast Pattern
- Cause-Effect Pattern

Transition Words

Other Things to Keep in Mind When Recognizing Authors' Writing Patterns

- Lists and sequences differ in an important way.
- Avoid identifying every paragraph as having a list pattern.
- Authors often mix patterns in the same paragraph.
- A longer selection may contain several patterns and have an overall pattern as well.
- Many textbook paragraphs consist of only a definition and explanation of an important term.

CREATING YOUR SUMMARY

Developing Chapter Review Cards

Comprehension Practice: Recognizing Authors' Writing Patterns Exercises (1)

Comprehension Practice: Recognizing Authors' Writing Patterns Exercises (2)

READINGS

Selection 7-1 *(Atlas)*
"Vietnam: A Country in Transition"
Rand McNally Publishing Company

Selection 7-2   *(Health)*
"Achoooo! You've Caught Another Cold!"
by Wayne Payne and Dale Hahn

Selection 7-3   *(Government)*
"The Right to Vote: Valued but Under Utilized"
by Thomas E. Patterson

WHAT ARE AUTHORS' WRITING PATTERNS, AND WHY IS IT IMPORTANT TO BE ABLE TO RECOGNIZE THEM?

KEY TERM
writing patterns

Ways authors organize the information they present.

Writing patterns are also known as *organizational patterns, patterns of development,* and *thinking patterns.*

In this chapter you will learn another skill that can help you improve your reading comprehension: recognizing authors' patterns of writing. **Writing patterns** are simply ways authors organize the information they present. You may hear writing patterns referred to as *patterns of organization, patterns of development,* or *thinking patterns.* These are all names for the same thing.

All of us use certain patterns to organize our thoughts in ways that seem logical to us. When people write, they use these same patterns to organize information. In other words, the patterns authors use are the same thinking patterns that you use every day. If you can identify the pattern a writer is using and "think along" with the author as you read, then you will find it easier to comprehend what he or she is saying. In this chapter you will be introduced to four common writing patterns textbook authors use:

- List pattern
- Sequence pattern
- Comparison-contrast pattern
- Cause-effect pattern

The specific pattern an author uses depends on the important relationship among the ideas he or she presents. That is, the pattern an author chooses depends on the relationship he or she wants to make clear or emphasize. The author chooses the most logical pattern that will accomplish this.

Just as textbook authors use patterns to organize their thoughts, so do you and all college students. Here are some everyday examples of how college students might use these patterns to organize their thoughts. Notice how the content of their comments matches the pattern of organization being used.

"I'm taking four courses this semester: history, psychology, reading, and math." *(list pattern)*

"I have my history class first, then psychology class. On alternate days, I have my reading class first, then my math class." *(sequence pattern)*

333

Stop and Annotate

Go back to the textbook excerpt. Underline or highlight the signal words *five strategies*. Then highlight the numbers that announce each strategy.

aids to help the listeners grasp the more complicated concepts. (3) Use down-to-earth language; avoid technical jargon. If you feel that you must use a specialized word, be sure to explain it. (4) Repeat key ideas, using different language each time. (5) Give vivid examples.

Source: Adapted from Hamilton Gregory, *Public Speaking for College and Career,* 6th ed., p. 82. Copyright © 2002 McGraw-Hill. Reprinted by permission of The McGraw-Hill Companies.

In this paragraph, the author uses the phrase "There are five strategies" to alert readers to expect a list. The order in which the details (the suggestions) are presented is not important. What is important is that there are five suggestions and what each strategy is. This paragraph included numbers, but not every paragraph does.

As you learned in Chapter 6, you should number (rather than underline or highlight) the supporting details when you are marking your textbook. Writing a small number beside each detail helps you avoid overmarking your book. Also, you can see at a glance how many items there are in the list. This is important since every item in a list may not have a signal word or other clue to introduce it. Whenever items in a list are not numbered, you should write in the numbers.

The next excerpt is from a computer science textbook. It illustrates the list pattern in a very obvious way: Each of the items in the list is bulleted. The topic of the paragraph is *the components of a computer system,* and its formulated main idea is, *Five components are integral to every computer system* or *There are five components that are integral to every computer system.* As you read the paragraph, ask yourself, "What are the five components that are integral to every computer system?"

Computers come in many sizes—from computers that occupy entire rooms, to notebook-sized computers, to computers as small as your fingernail. Although computer hardware is the most visible part of a computer, it is merely one part of a *computer system.* (A system is a collection of elements that work together to solve a specific problem.) Regardless of size, every computer needs the other components of the system to produce results. The components of a computer system are:

- People
- Data
- Procedures
- Hardware
- Software

These components are integral to every computer system. Every time you use a computer to generate information, you become one of the five system components.

Source: From Timothy N. Trainor and Diane Krasnewich, *Computers!,* 5th ed. Copyright © 1996 McGraw-Hill. Reprinted by permission of The McGraw-Hill Companies.

Stop and Annotate

Go back to the textbook excerpt. Underline or highlight the phrase *The components of a computer system are* and the colon that signals a list. Then write a small ①, ②, ③, ④, and ⑤ beside the five items on the list.

In this paragraph, the list (of the components in a computer system) is set off from the rest of the paragraph. It is announced by the phrase "The components of a computer system are" and also by a colon (:). Each of the five items on the list is bulleted so that it stands out clearly. Writing small numbers beside each item on the list will help you see (and remember) that there are five components.

Sequence Pattern

In the **sequence pattern** a list of items is presented *in a specific order* because the order is important. The sequence pattern is a type of list, but it differs from a simple list because the order of the items matters. A common type of sequence is a series of events presented in the order in which they happened. For this reason, the sequence pattern is sometimes called *time order, chronological order,* a *process,* or a *series.* Sets of directions (e.g., recipes, instructions for changing a tire or for loading a software program on a computer) are examples of sequences that you encounter daily. Examples of processes include life cycles described in a biology textbook or a description in a government textbook about how legislation is created.

To emphasize or set off separate items in a sequence pattern, authors often use:

- Words such as *first, second, third, then, next, finally.*
- Words and phrases that refer to time, such as dates, days of the week, names of months or phrases such as *during the 20th century* or *in the previous decade.*
- Enumeration (*1, 2, 3,* etc.).
- Letters (*a, b, c,* etc.).
- Signal words such as *steps, stages, phases, progression, process, series,* and even the word *sequence.* (These often occur in the main idea sentence.)

Below is an excerpt from a music appreciation textbook. In this excerpt, the author uses a sequence pattern to show the order in which certain events occurred. The topic of this paragraph is *African-American musicians in the 20th century.* The formulated main idea of this paragraph is, *For many years, African-American musicians were barred as performers and conductors in established opera companies and symphony orchestras, but this began to change by the middle of the 20th century.* Read the paragraph and notice the dates that indicate that the events are being presented in chronological order.

Stop and Annotate

Go back to the textbook excerpt. Underline or highlight the dates and the references to different decades that signal a sequence. Then write a ① beside *baritone Todd Duncan . . . ,* a ② beside *contralto Marian Anderson . . . ,* a ③ beside the phrase *During the 1950s and 1960s . . . ,* and a ④ beside the phrase *starting in the 1970s. . . .*

African-American Musicians in the Twentieth Century

For many years, African-American musicians were admitted as students in music schools but were barred as performers and conductors in established opera companies and symphony orchestras. Color barriers in major American opera companies were not broken until the baritone Todd Duncan performed at the New York City Opera in 1945 and the contralto Marian Anderson sang at the Metropolitan Opera in 1955. During the 1950s and 1960s black conductors like Dean Dixon and Everett Lee had to go to Europe to find permanent positions, but starting in the 1970s, important conducting posts were occupied by such musicians as Henry Lewis, who directed the New Jersey Symphony, and James DePreist, who led the Quebec Symphony.

Source: From Roger Kamien, *Music: An Appreciation,* 3rd brief ed. Copyright © 2000 McGraw-Hill. Reprinted by permission of The McGraw-Hill Companies.

The four supporting details in this sequence are identified by specific dates (1945 and 1955) and references to different decades of the 20th century (the 1950s, the 1960s, and the 1970s). Important events from these different decades are presented in order. In this paragraph, the order of the information is important because the sequence shows the progressive acceptance of African-American musicians.

Comparison-Contrast Pattern

KEY TERM
comparison-contrast pattern

Similarities (comparisons) between two or more things are presented, differences (contrasts) between two or more things are presented, or both similarities and differences are presented.

The comparison-contrast pattern is also known as *ideas in opposition.*

Often writers want to emphasize comparisons and contrasts. A *comparison* shows how two or more things are similar (alike). A *contrast* points out the differences between them. In the **comparison-contrast pattern** similarities (comparisons) between two or more things are presented, differences (contrasts) between two or more things are presented, or both similarities and differences are presented.

To signal comparisons, authors use words such as *similarly, likewise, both, same,* and *also.* To signal contrasts, authors use clues such as *on the other hand, in contrast, however, while, whereas, although, nevertheless, different, unlike,* and *some . . . others.* Contrasts are also signaled by words in a paragraph that have opposite meanings, such as *liberals and conservatives, Internet users and non-Internet users,* and *people who attended college and people who never attended college.*

As the heading suggests, the following excerpt from an art appreciation textbook has as its topic, *the mall,* or more specifically, *how the mall is similar to the old-time village green and the medieval cathedral.* (A *green* was a grassy area in the center of a town that was set aside for use by the community as a whole.) The stated main idea is the first sentence, *The mall has become the equivalent of the old-time village green, a gathering place as comprehensive as the medieval cathedral.* As you read the paragraph, ask yourself, "In what way has the mall become the equivalent of the old-time village green and the medieval cathedral?"

The Mall

The mall has become the equivalent of the old-time village green, a gathering place as comprehensive as the medieval cathedral. In those days, the cathedral played a vital role in people's daily lives. Today, that role has largely been assumed by the mall. Like village greens and cathedrals, malls provide nearly all the social activities one could want. This gathering place provides opportunities for sports and entertainment, music and dramatic performances, socializing with friends, having a meal or a snack, and of course, buying or simply admiring an endless array of consumer goods. The people of medieval Europe walked, so their obvious gathering place was the cathedral in the center of town. However, the people of suburban North America drive cars; their obvious gathering place is the mall.

Source: From Rita Gilbert, *Living with Art,* 5th ed. Copyright © 1996 McGraw-Hill. Reprinted by permission of The McGraw-Hill Companies.

Stop and Annotate

Go back to the textbook excerpt. Underline or highlight the clues that signal a comparison-contrast pattern: *equivalent, old-time* and *today, The people of medieval Europe* and *However, the people of suburban North America.*

The words *old-time* and *today, The people of medieval Europe,* and *However, the people of suburban North America* are also clues or signals that the author is presenting a contrast. The village green, the cathedral, and the mall are being compared since all have served or serve the similar function of being gathering places for people during different periods in history. The word *equivalent* in the main idea sentence signals this comparison.

Cause-Effect Pattern

The **cause-effect pattern** presents reasons (causes) of events or conditions and results (effects) of events or conditions. Authors often use these words to indicate a cause: *because, the reasons, causes, is due to,* and *is caused by.* These words are often used to indicate an effect: *therefore, consequently, thus, as a consequence, led to, the result, as a result, the effect was,* and *this resulted in.*

In reality, causes always precede effects, and authors typically present causes first and then their effects. However, authors sometimes present an effect and *then* state its cause. Read these two sentences: *The extreme changes in the weather are due to El Niño* and *El Niño has caused extreme changes in the weather.* Both sentences have the same message. And, in both cases, *El Niño* is the cause and *the extreme changes in weather* is the effect. The order the cause and effect are presented in does not change which one is the cause and which one is the effect. Do not assume that whatever is mentioned first in a sentence is always the cause! You must determine which event occurred first in reality.

The following excerpt from a business textbook uses the cause-effect pattern. Its topic is *two-income families.* The stated main idea is the first sentence, *Several factors have caused a dramatic growth in two-income families.* As you read the paragraph ask yourself, "What has caused the dramatic growth in two-income families?"

Two-Income Families

Several factors have caused a dramatic growth in two-income families. The high costs of housing and of maintaining a comfortable lifestyle have made it difficult if not impossible for many households to live on just one income. Furthermore, many women today simply want a career outside the home.

Source: From William G. Nickels, James M. McHugh, and Susan M. McHugh, *Understanding Business,* 4th ed. Copyright © 1999 McGraw-Hill. Reprinted by permission of The McGraw-Hill Companies.

In this paragraph, the word *caused* signals a cause-effect pattern. (Notice that it is the only clue word in the paragraph.) The "effect" or result the authors want to present is expressed at the end of the stated main idea: *the dramatic growth in two-income families.* The authors then present two other causes that contribute to the increase in the number of two-income families. The two reasons (causes) are presented in the details: the high costs of housing and of maintaining a comfortable lifestyle, and the fact that many women today want a career outside the home.

SUMMARY OF PARAGRAPH PATTERN SIGNALS AND CLUE WORDS

1. List Pattern

and

also

another

moreover

in addition

first, second, third

finally

1, 2, 3 . . .

a, b, c . . .

bullets (•)

asterisks (*)

words that announce lists

(such as *categories, kinds, types, ways,*
 classes, groups, parts, elements,
 characteristics, features, etc.)

2. Sequence Pattern

first, second third

now, the, next, finally

dates

1, 2, 3 . . .

a, b, c . . .

steps

phases

progression

words that refer to time

series

stages

when

before, during, after

at last

process, spectrum, continuum

hierarchy

instructions and directions

3. Comparison-Contrast Pattern

Comparisons:

similarly

likewise

both

same

also

resembles

parallels

in the same manner

in the same way

words that compare

  (adjectives that describe comparisons,
  such as *safer, slower, lighter,*
   more valuable, less toxic, etc.)

Contrasts:

in contrast

however

on the other hand

whereas

while

although

nevertheless

instead (of)

different

unlike

conversely

rather than

as opposed to

some . . . others

opposite words

4. **Cause-Effect Pattern**

<u>Causes:</u>

The reason(s)

the causes(s)

because

is due to (<u>cause</u>)

was caused by (<u>cause</u>)

(<u>cause</u>) *led to*

resulted from (<u>cause</u>)

since

<u>Effects:</u>

the result(s)

the effect(s)

the outcome

the final product

therefore

thus

consequently

as a consequence

hence

on that account

resulted in, results in (<u>effect</u>)

(<u>effect</u>) *was caused by*

(<u>effect</u>) *is due to*

led to (<u>effect</u>)

(<u>effect</u>) *resulted from*

Both the cause and the effect:

- (effect) *is due to* (<u>cause</u>)
- (effect) *resulted from* (<u>cause</u>)
- (effect) *was caused by* (<u>cause</u>)
- (<u>cause</u>) *led to* (<u>effect</u>)
- (<u>cause</u>) *results in* (<u>effect</u>)

<u>Some questions that indicate cause-effect:</u>

- *What causes* (effect)? (Answer will be the cause.)
- *Why does* (effect) *occur?* (Answer will be the cause.)
- *What is the reason for* (effect)? (Answer will be the cause.)
- *How can* (effect) *be explained?* (Answer will be the cause.)
- *What does* (cause) *lead to?* (Answer will be the effect.)

As you read, be alert for clues to the author's pattern of organization. Use signal words and transitions to help you. Recognizing the pattern or "big picture" is a skill that will make you a more effective, efficient reader.

OTHER THINGS TO KEEP IN MIND WHEN RECOGNIZING AUTHORS' WRITING PATTERNS

Here are five other helpful things you should know about recognizing authors' writing patterns:

1. Lists and sequences differ in an important way.

Items in a list appear in no specific order; however, items in a sequence are presented in a specific order because the order is important. On a shopping list, for example, it makes no difference what order the items are in: "eggs, bread, milk" is the same as "milk, bread, eggs." In a recipe, however, the steps occur in a very specific order because the sequence is important: "Add eggs and milk to the mixture, stir well, and then bake" is obviously not the same as "Bake, stir well, and then add eggs and milk to the mixture."

2. Avoid identifying every paragraph as having a list pattern.

At first, it may seem as if every paragraph uses a list pattern. Whenever you encounter what appears to be a list, be cautious and ask yourself this additional question, "a list of *what?*" Your answer should help you recognize when the author is using one of the other patterns instead. For instance, if your answer is "a list of *events in a particular order,*" then the paragraph has a sequence pattern. If your answer is "a list of *similarities or differences,*" the paragraph has a comparison-contrast pattern. If your answer is "a list of *causes, reasons, or results,*" then the paragraph has a cause-effect pattern. View a paragraph as having a list pattern only when you are certain that no other pattern can be used to describe the way the ideas are organized.

Sometimes the same clue words may be used in more than one pattern. For example, words such as *first, second,* and *third* are used for items in a sequence, but they can also be used to indicate items in a list (even though the order is not important).

3. Authors often mix patterns in the same paragraph.

Each of the textbook excerpts in this chapter was used to illustrate a single pattern. However, authors often use a combination of two or more patterns in the same paragraph. This is called a *mixed pattern.* For example, a paragraph might present a series of events (sequence pattern) that led to a certain result (cause-effect pattern). Or an author could present causes and effects (cause-effect pattern), but describe some effects that were positive and other effects that were negative (comparison-contrast pattern). Remember, authors use the patterns or a combination of patterns that they believe organizes and presents their material in the most logical way.

4. A longer selection may contain several patterns and have an overall pattern as well.

In addition to individual paragraphs, longer selections are often organized by an overall pattern. An entire selection may be organized as a list, a sequence, a comparison-contrast, or a cause-effect pattern. For example, you already know that a biography, the story of a person's life, usually follows a sequence pattern. Science textbooks often present information as steps in a process (sequence) and history textbooks often present information as causes and effects. Other subjects frequently use the comparison-contrast pattern to organize the information being presented.

Remember, a longer textbook selection can consist of paragraphs with different patterns, and have an overall pattern as well. For example, a section in a history textbook might discuss several events (causes) leading up to World War II, yet have a sequence as the overall pattern.

5. Many textbook paragraphs consist of only a definition and explanation of an important term.

College textbooks present many new and important terms and their definitions. Sometimes, instead of presenting information organized according to one of the patterns described in this chapter, a textbook paragraph simply presents the definition and explanation of an important term. The rest of the paragraph generally consists of examples or further explanation.

In a history textbook, for example, you might read the following paragraph:

> The term *genocide* refers to the deliberate destruction of an entire race or nation. For example, the Holocaust was conducted in Germany during World War II. In it, the Nazis attempted to exterminate European Jews and others.

The term *genocide* is defined. Then the author presents an example of genocide.

DEVELOPING CHAPTER REVIEW CARDS

Chapter review cards are a way to select, organize, and review the important information in a textbook chapter. Preparing chapter review cards helps you organize the information so that you can learn and memorize it more easily. In other words, chapter review cards are an effective study tool.

Preparing chapter review cards for each chapter of this book will give you practice in creating these valuable study tools. Once you have learned how to make chapter review cards, you can use actual index cards to create them for textbook material in any of your courses and use them when you study for tests.

Now, complete the chapter review cards for this chapter by answering the questions or following the directions on each "card" below. (The boxes below represent index cards.)

Authors' Writing Patterns

1. What is the definition of a *writing pattern?*

_____

2. What are four common writing patterns textbook authors use?

_____

_____

3. What are four advantages to recognizing authors' writing patterns?

_____

_____

_____

4. What comprehension monitoring question should you ask yourself in order to recognize an author's writing pattern?

_____

Card 1   Chapter 7: Recognizing Authors' Writing Patterns

Authors' Writing Patterns

Define these four writing patterns commonly used by textbook authors.

List: _____

_____

Sequence: _____

_____

Comparison-Contrast: _____

_____

Cause-Effect: _____

_____

Card 2   Chapter 7: Recognizing Authors' Writing Patterns

Signal Words and Other Clues to Authors' Writing Patterns

Write the signal words and other clues that identify each of the four writing patterns.

List:

_____

_____

Sequence:

_____

_____

Comparison-Contrast:

_____

_____

Cause-Effect:

_____

_____

Card 3   Chapter 7: Recognizing Authors' Writing Patterns

As You Recognize Authors' Writing Patterns, Keep in Mind . . .

1. What is the difference between the list pattern and the sequence pattern?

   _____

   _____

2. What additional question should you ask yourself to avoid identifying every paragraph as having a list pattern?

   _____

   _____

3. What is a mixed pattern?

   _____

   _____

4. What is an overall pattern?

   _____

   _____

Card 4   Chapter 7: Recognizing Authors' Writing Patterns

COMPREHENSION PRACTICE: RECOGNIZING AUTHORS' WRITING PATTERNS EXERCISES (1)

Study the example in the box below to see how information you learned in this chapter can be used to recognize an author's writing pattern. When you are sure you understand the example, complete the five exercises that follow.

EXAMPLE

This excerpt comes from a speech textbook. Its topic is *browsers*. Read the paragraph; then determine the main idea by asking yourself, "What is the single most important point the authors want me to understand about browsers?" Then ask yourself, "What pattern did the authors use to organize the supporting details?"

> The explosive growth of the World Wide Web is <u>due</u> largely <u>to</u> the development of graphical *browsers*, software that allows you to move easily among the millions of websites. By far the most popular browser is Netscape, which is employed at most colleges and universities, though it is facing a stiff challenge from Microsoft's Internet Explorer. Commercial online services such as CompuServe, Prodigy, and America Online offer their own browsers.

Source: From Stephen Lucas, *The Art of Public Speaking*, 6th ed. Copyright © 1998 McGraw-Hill. Reprinted by permission of The McGraw-Hill Companies.

The topic of this paragraph is *browsers*.

_____ *b* _____ What is the main idea of this paragraph?

    a. By far the most popular browser is Netscape, which is employed at most colleges and universities, though it is facing a stiff challenge from Microsoft's Internet Explorer.

    b. The explosive growth of the World Wide Web is due largely to the development of graphical *browsers,* software that allows you to move easily among the millions of web sites.

    c. Commercial on-line services such as CompuServe, Prodigy, and America Online offer their own browsers.

The correct answer is b. The first sentence is the stated main idea. The other two sentences are details that explain more about it.

_____ *c* _____ Which writing pattern did the authors use to organize the supporting details?

    a. sequence

    b. comparison-contrast

    c. cause-effect

The correct answer is c. The words *due to* in the stated main idea indicate the cause-effect pattern. The effect is *the explosive growth of the World Wide Web.* The cause is *the development of graphical browsers.*

1.   This paragraph comes from a management textbook.

Hierarchy of Needs Theory

One of the most widely known theories of motivation is the **hierarchy of needs theory,** developed by psychologist Abraham Maslow and popularized during the early 1960s, which argues that individual needs form a five-level hierarchy. According to this hierarchy, our first need is for survival, so we concentrate on the basic **physiological needs,** such as food, water, and shelter, until we feel fairly sure that these needs are covered. Next, we concern ourselves with **safety needs,** which pertain to the desire to feel safe and secure, and free from threats to our existence. Once we feel reasonably safe and secure, we turn our attention to relationships with others to fulfill our **belongingness needs,** which involve the desire to affiliate with and be accepted by others. With support from loved ones, we focus on **esteem needs,** which are related to the two-pronged desire to have a positive self-image and to have our contributions valued and appreciated by others. Finally, we reach the highest level, **self-actualization needs,** which pertain to developing our capabilities and reaching our full potential. At this level, we concern ourselves with such matters as testing our creativity, seeing our innovative ideas translated into reality, pursuing new knowledge, and developing our talents in uncharted directions.

Source: From Kathryn Bartol and David Martin, *Management,* 2nd ed. Copyright © 1994 McGraw-Hill. Reprinted by permission of The McGraw-Hill Companies.

The topic of this paragraph is *Maslow's hierarchy of needs theory.*

What is the main idea of this paragraph?

a.   Maslow's hierarchy of needs theory states that people have five levels of needs that range from basic survival needs to higher-level needs.

b.   The hierarchy of needs theory is one of the most widely known theories of motivation.

c.   Maslow created a widely known theory.

d.   Finally, we reach the highest level, self-actualization needs, which pertain to developing our capabilities and reaching our full potential.

Which writing pattern did the authors use to organize the supporting details?

a.   cause-effect

b.   list

    c.   sequence

    d.   comparison-contrast

2.   This paragraph comes from a government textbook.

       Conservatives are defined as individuals who emphasize the marketplace as the means of distributing economic benefits but look to government to uphold traditional social values. In contrast, **liberals** favor activist government as an instrument of economic redistribution but reject the notion that government should favor a particular set of social values. True liberals and conservatives could be expected to differ, for instance, on the issues of homosexual rights (a social values question) and government-guaranteed health care (an economic distribution question). Liberals would view homosexuality as a private issue and believe that government should see to it that everyone has access to adequate medical care. Conservatives would oppose government-mandated access to health care and favor government policies that discourage homosexual lifestyles.

    Source: From Thomas E. Patterson, *We the People,* 2nd ed. Copyright © 1998 McGraw-Hill. Reprinted by permission of The McGraw-Hill Companies.

    The topic of this paragraph is *conservatives and liberals.*

    What is the main idea of this paragraph?

    a.   Conservatives are defined as individuals who emphasize the marketplace as the means of distributing economic benefits but look to government to uphold traditional social values.

    b.   Conservatives and liberals both believe that government should uphold traditional social values.

    c.   Conservatives and liberals have opposite viewpoints on economic issues and social values.

    d.   Conservatives and liberals each blame the other for the nation's problems.

    Which writing pattern did the author use to organize the supporting details?

    a.   cause-effect

    b.   comparison-contrast

    c.   sequence

    d.   list

3.   This paragraph comes from a business textbook.

The Increase in the Number of Older Americans

       Americans aged 45 to 54 (referred to as "baby-boomers") are currently the richest group in U.S. society. They spend more than others on everything except health care and thus represent a lucrative market for restaurants, transportation, entertainment, education, and so on. What do such demographic changes mean for you and for businesses in the future? Think of the products the middle-aged and elderly will need—medicine, nursing homes, assisted-living facilities, adult day care, home health care, recreation, and the like—and you'll see opportunities for successful businesses of the 21st century. Older citizens with money will demand more and better health care, more recreation and travel, and new and different products and services of all kinds. Consequently, businesses that cater to them will have the opportunity for exceptional growth in the near future.

Source: From William G. Nickels, James M. McHugh, and Susan M. McHugh, *Understanding Business,* 4th ed. Copyright © 1999 McGraw-Hill. Reprinted by permission of The McGraw-Hill Companies.

The topic of this paragraph is *older Americans and their effect on business.*

_____ What is the main idea of this paragraph?

a. Americans aged 45 to 54 (referred to as "baby-boomers") are currently the richest group in the United States.

b. Businesses that cater to older Americans will have exceptional growth opportunities in the future.

c. Those with money will demand more and better health care, more recreation and travel, and new and different products and services of all kinds.

d. Older citizens with money with demand more products and services of all kinds.

_____ Which writing pattern did the authors use to organize the supporting details?

a. cause-effect

b. sequence

c. comparison-contrast

d. list

4. This paragraph comes from a psychology textbook.

Who Is More Likely to Be Acquitted?

Although we would like to believe that all of us would be treated equally in court, it is not always the case. Your chance of being acquitted in a criminal trial in the United States is better if you are physically attractive, wealthy, and white. In contrast, poor people are more likely to be convicted than affluent ones when charged with similar assault and larceny charges. Physically attractive defendants are less likely to be convicted than unattractive ones, unless the attractiveness seemed to play a part in the crime (as in a swindle). And racially prejudiced jury members are more likely to convict African-Americans than whites.

Source: From Benjamin B. Lahey, *Psychology: An Introduction,* 6th ed. Copyright © 1997 McGraw-Hill. Reprinted by permission of The McGraw-Hill Companies.

The topic of this paragraph is *who is more likely to be acquitted.*

_____ What is the main idea of this paragraph?

a. Your chance of being acquitted in a criminal trial in the United States is better if you are physically attractive, wealthy, and white.

b. We should all be treated equally in court.

    c.   When charged with similar assault and larceny charges, poor people are more likely to be convicted than affluent ones.

    d.   Jury members should be screened more carefully.

_____ Which writing pattern did the author use to organize the supporting details?

    a.   list

    b.   comparison-contrast

    c.   sequence

    d.   cause-effect

5. This paragraph comes from a speech communications textbook.

Characteristics of an Emotionally Well Person

The characteristics most people associate with being emotionally well (and very likely psychologically well also) are listed below. Emotionally well people:

- Feel comfortable about themselves.
- Are capable of experiencing the full range of human emotions.
- Are not overwhelmed by their emotions (either positive or negative emotions).
- Accept life's disappointments.
- Feel comfortable with others.
- Receive and give love easily.
- Feel concern for others when appropriate.
- Establish goals, both short term and long term.
- Function autonomously where and when appropriate.
- Generally trust others.

Source: From Ronald Adler and Jeanne Elmhorst, *Communicating at Work,* 5th ed. Copyright © 1996 McGraw-Hill. Reprinted by permission of The McGraw-Hill Companies.

The topic of this paragraph is *the characteristics of an emotionally well person.*

_____ What is the main idea of this paragraph?

    a.   Emotionally well people always feel comfortable about themselves.

    b.   There are certain characteristics that are associated with being an emotionally well person.

    c.   To be an emotionally well person, you must feel comfortable with others and trust them.

    d.   Emotionally well people receive and give love easily.

_____ Which writing pattern did the authors use to organize the supporting details?

    a.   list

    b.   comparison-contrast

    c.   cause-effect

    d.   sequence

COMPREHENSION PRACTICE: RECOGNIZING AUTHORS' WRITING PATTERNS EXERCISES (2)

Study the example in the box below to see how information you learned in this chapter can be used to recognize an author's writing pattern. When you are sure you understand the example, complete the five exercises that follow.

EXAMPLE

This excerpt comes from a government textbook. Its topic is *the death penalty*. Read the paragraph; then determine the main idea by asking yourself, "What is the most important point the author wants me to understand about the death penalty?" Then, ask yourself, "What pattern did the authors use to organize the supporting details?"

The Death Penalty

All but a dozen states permit the death penalty as a punishment for crime, but they <u>vary greatly</u> in its application. About ten states with the death penalty have not executed a single prisoner since 1976, when the Supreme Court reinstated the death penalty as a constitutionally permissible form of punishment. <u>Other</u> states have executed only a few prisoners during this period. <u>On the other hand,</u> a few states, most of which are located in the South, have applied the death penalty frequently. The state of Texas alone accounted for a third of the 257 executions that took place between 1976 and 1994.

Source: From Thomas E. Patterson, *We the People,* 2nd ed. Copyright © 1998 McGraw-Hill. Reprinted by permission of The McGraw-Hill Companies.

The topic of this paragraph is *the death penalty.*

Write the main idea sentence: <u>All but a dozen states permit the death penalty</u>

<u>as a punishment for crime, but they vary greatly in its application.</u>

_____

Which writing pattern did the author use to organize the supporting details?

comparison-contrast

Explanation: The stated main idea is the first sentence of this paragraph. The words *vary greatly* suggest a contrast. Also the supporting details contrast how frequently or infrequently the death penalty is applied from state to state.

Directions:

- First, read the paragraph carefully. Notice that you are given the topic of each paragraph.
- Next, write the main idea sentence. (It may be stated or implied.)
- Then, tell the writing pattern the author used to organize the details in the paragraph.
- Finally, list the clue words or signals that caused you to choose that pattern.

1. This paragraph comes from a speech communications textbook.

The Résumé

Whether you type your résumé yourself or have it done for you, the final product should reflect the professional image you want to create. It should meet these criteria:

- Be neat and error-free.
- Contain plenty of white space to avoid crowding.
- Be printed on heavyweight paper, either white or a light neutral color.
- Be reproduced clearly on a high-quality printer or copy machine.

Source: From Ronald Adler and Jeanne Elmhorst, *Communicating at Work,* 5th ed. Copyright © 1996 McGraw-Hill. Reprinted by permission of The McGraw-Hill Companies.

The topic of this paragraph is *the résumé.*

Write the main idea sentence:

_____

_____

_____

_____

Which writing pattern did the authors use to organize the supporting details?

_____

Write the clue(s) that caused you to choose this pattern.

_____

_____

2. This paragraph comes from an accounting textbook.

Because accounting and bookkeeping both are concerned with financial information and records, some people mistakenly think they are the same thing. In fact, accounting involves much more than bookkeeping. Although bookkeeping is critical to developing useful accounting information, it is only the clerical part of accounting. That is, bookkeeping is the part of accounting that records transactions and other events, either manually or with computers. In contrast, accounting involves analyzing transactions and events, deciding how to report them in financial statements, and interpreting the results. Accounting also involves designing and implementing systems to produce useful reports and to control the operations of the organization. Accounting involves more professional expertise and judgment than bookkeeping because accountants must analyze complex and unusual events.

Source: From Kermit D. Larson and Barbara Chiapetta, *Fundamental Accounting Principles,* 14th ed. Copyright © 1996 McGraw-Hill. Reprinted by permission of The McGraw-Hill Companies.

The topic of this paragraph is *accounting and bookkeeping.*

Write the main idea sentence:

_____

_____

_____

_____

Which writing pattern did the authors use to organize the supporting details?

_____

Write the clue(s) that caused you to choose this pattern.

_____

_____

3. This paragraph comes from a speech communications textbook.

Having a Sense of Humor

Recognizing the humor in daily situations and occasionally being able to laugh at yourself will make you feel better not only about others but also, more importantly, about yourself. Additional benefits are that others will enjoy being associated with you, and your ability to perform physically and to recover from injuries and illnesses will probably be enhanced. For example, any student-athlete who has experienced a career-threatening injury can attest that sense of humor was a key ingredient in relation to the speed and extent of recovery.

Source: Adapted from Ronald Adler and Jeanne Elmhorst, *Communicating at Work,* 5th ed. Copyright © 1996 McGraw-Hill. Reprinted by permission of The McGraw-Hill Companies.

The topic of this paragraph is *having a sense of humor.*

Write the main idea sentence:

_____

_____

_____

_____

Which writing pattern did the authors use to organize the supporting details?

_____

Write the clue(s) that caused you to choose this pattern.

_____

_____

4. This paragraph comes from a health textbook.

Time Management

Although there is no single best approach to managing your time, most experts suggest that it is helpful to follow certain general steps.

• Keep a log of how you use your time for one week. Check about each half hour to see what you are doing at that time.

• Analyze these records, and eliminate those activities that take too much time relative to their importance.

• Once you have made these eliminations, divide your time into blocks so that related activities can be scheduled together. There should be a block for each major area of responsibility. Examples might include academics, employment, recreation, and socializing.

• Finally, schedule specific activities within each block of time. Attempt to complete each activity you start.

Reassess your activities occasionally and make adjustments when necessary.

Source: From Wayne Payne and Dale Hahn, *Understanding Your Health,* 5th ed. Copyright © 1998 McGraw-Hill. Reprinted by permission of The McGraw-Hill Companies.

The topic of this paragraph is *time management.*

Write the main idea sentence:

_____

_____

_____

Which writing pattern did the authors use to organize the supporting details?

_____

Write the clue(s) that caused you to choose this pattern.

_____

_____

5. This paragraph comes from a business textbook.

What's the difference between mergers and acquisitions? A **merger** is the result of two firms forming one company. Sounds like a marriage, doesn't it? An **acquisition** is one company buying the property and obligations of another company. It is more like buying a house than entering a marriage.

Source: From William G. Nickels, James M. McHugh, and Susan M. McHugh, *Understanding Business,* 4th ed. Copyright © 1999 McGraw-Hill. Reprinted by permission of The McGraw-Hill Companies.

The topic of this paragraph is *mergers and acquisitions.*

Write the main idea sentence:

_____

_____

_____

_____

_____

Which writing pattern did the authors use to organize the supporting details?

_____

Write the clue(s) that caused you to choose this pattern.

_____

_____

SELECTION **7-1**
ATLAS

VIETNAM: A COUNTRY IN TRANSITION

From *The World: Afganistan to Zimbabwe*
Rand McNally Publishing Company

Although most college students today are too young to remember the Vietnam War and two-thirds of those living in Vietnam were born after what they call "The American War," the war has had a significant impact on both Vietnam and the United States. The Vietnam War was fought from 1954 to 1975 between North and South Vietnam, two parts of what was once the French colony of Indochina. After French troops were withdrawn, the country divided into the Communist north and a non-Communist south. Although the United States' involvement was controversial and ultimately failed, it fought during the 1960s and 1970s on the side of South Vietnam. The government of South Vietnam fell to the Communists in 1975. Much of the 1980s was spent rebuilding from the decades of turmoil. Recently, Vietnam has rejoined the world stage and has forged a friendship with the same Americans it once fought. Today, there are many Americans of Vietnamese descent.

People and Influences

1   Despite centuries of foreign invasion and domination, the people of Vietnam remain remarkably homogeneous; ethnic Vietnamese compose the majority of the population. Chinese influence, however, is seen in the religion of Taoism. Most people live along two rivers, the Red in the north and the Mekong in the south, separated by mountains. The official language is Vietnamese, but a history of foreign intervention is reflected in the wide use of French, English, Chinese, and Russian.

Economy and Land

2   The Vietnamese economy has struggled to overcome the effects of war and the difficulties inherent in unifying the once-divided country. Vietnam is a fertile land populated with rice farmers. Agriculture, centered in the fertile southern plains, continues to employ nearly 70 percent of the people. The landscape of Vietnam ranges from mountains to plains, and the climate is tropical. In contrast to other Asian countries, Vietnam now has one of the fastest-growing Asian economies, and its economy is one of the most stable.

Annotation Practice Exercises

Directions: For each exercise below, write the topic and the main idea of the paragraph on the lines beside the paragraph. Then identify the writing pattern the authors used to organize the supporting details.

Annotation Exercise

Topic of paragraph 2:

_____

_____

Main idea sentence:

_____

_____

_____

_____

_____

Writing pattern:

_____

_____

History and Politics

3   The first Vietnamese lived in what is now northern Vietnam. After centuries of Chinese rule, Vietnam finally became independent in the 1400s, but civil strife continued for nearly two centuries. French missionary activity began in the early seventeenth century, and by 1883 all of present-day Vietnam, Cambodia, and Laos were under French rule. When Germany occupied France during World War II, control of French Indochina passed to the Japanese until their defeat in 1945. The French presence continued until 1954, when Vietnamese Communists led by Ho Chi Minh gained control of North Vietnam. United States aid to South Vietnam began in 1961 and ended, after years of conflict, with a cease-fire in 1973. Communist victory and unification of the country as the Socialist Republic of Vietnam was achieved in 1975. Vietnamese military policy resulted in fighting with China and the occupation of Cambodia until 1989.

Topic of paragraph 3:

_____

_____

Main idea sentence:

_____

_____

_____

_____

_____

_____

Writing pattern:

_____

_____

The Socialist Republic of Vietnam and neighboring countries

VIETNAM AT A GLANCE

Official name   Socialist Republic of Vietnam

People

Population   73,760,000

Density   579/square mile

Urban   20%

Capital   Hanoi (population 905,939)

Ethnic groups   Kinh 87%, Hao 2%, Tay 2%

Languages   Vietnamese, French, Chinese, English, Khmer, indigenous

Religions   Buddhist, Taoist, Roman Catholic, indigenous, Islamic

Life expectancy   66 female, 62 male

Literacy   88%

Politics

Government   Socialist republic

Parties   Communist

Suffrage   Universal, over 18

Memberships   United Nations

Subdivisions   50 provinces, 3 municipalities

Economy

GNP $72 billion

Per capita income $1,034

Trade partners   Japan, Singapore, Thailand, Eastern European countries

Exports   Rice and other agricultural products, handicrafts, coal, minerals

Imports   Petroleum, steel, railroad equipment, chemicals, pharmaceuticals, cotton

Land

Description   Southeastern Asia

Area   127,428 square miles

Highest point   Phan Si Pang, 10,312 ft.

Lowest point   Sea level

Source: Text and table adapted from *The World: Afghanistan to Zimbabwe,* New York: Rand McNally Publishing, 1996, p. 201. Copyright © 1996 by Rand McNally R.L. 02-S-67. Reprinted with permission.

SELECTION 7-1
ATLAS

Comprehension and Vocabulary Quiz

This quiz has four parts. Your instructor may assign some or all of them.

Comprehension

Directions: Items 1–5 test your comprehension (understanding) of the material in this selection. These questions are much like those that a content area instructor (such as a history professor) would expect you to know after studying this selection. For each comprehension question below, use information from the selection to determine the correct answer. Refer to the selection as you answer the questions. Write your answer in the space provided.

_____   **1.** The official name of Vietnam today is
    a.   Hanoi.
    b.   Vietnam.
    c.   The Vietnamese Communist Republic.
    d.   The Socialist Republic of Vietnam.

_____   **2.** The largest ethnic group in Vietnam is
    a.   Tay.
    b.   Khmer.
    c.   Kinh.
    d.   Hao.

_____   **3.** The economy of Vietnam is likely to improve if
    a.   it can import more rice in order to feed its people.
    b.   the country can resolve its political and social problems.
    c.   it can export more petroleum and cotton.
    d.   the fighting with China ends.

_____   **4.** The Vietnamese Communists led by Ho Chi Minh gained control of North Vietnam in
    a.   1945.
    b.   1954.
    c.   1961.
    d.   1975.

_____   **5.** Following the cease-fire in 1973 and the Communist victory in 1975
    a.   control of French Indochina passed to the Japanese.
    b.   North and South Vietnam were reunified.
    c.   Vietnam's economy made a dramatic recovery.
    d.   the Socialist Republic of Vietnam was defeated.

Vocabulary in Context

Directions: Items 6–10 test your ability to determine the meaning of a word by using context clues. *Context clues* are words in a sentence that allow the reader to deduce (reason out) the meaning of an unfamiliar word in that sentence. Context clues also enable the reader to determine which meaning the author intends when a word has more than one meaning. For each vocabulary item below, a sentence from the selection containing an important word (*italicized, like this*) is quoted first. Next, there is an additional sentence using the word in the same sense and providing another context clue. Use the context clues from *both* sentences to deduce the meaning of the italicized word. *Be sure the answer you choose makes sense in both sentences.* If you discover that you need to use a dictionary to confirm an answer choice, remember that the meaning you select must still fit the context of *both* sentences. Write your answer in the space provided.

Pronunciation Key: ă pat ā pay âr care ä father ĕ pet ē be ĭ pit
ī tie îr pier ŏ pot ō toe ô paw oi noise ou out ŏŏ took ōō boot
ŭ cut yōō abuse ûr urge th thin *th* this hw which zh vision
ə about Stress mark: ´

---

6. The Vietnamese economy has struggled to overcome the effects of war and the difficulties *inherent* in unifying the once-divided country.

Stress is *inherent* in divorce.

inherent (ĭn hîr´ ənt)

   a. existing as an essential element

   b. existing as an unrelated factor

   c. existing as a soothing force

   d. existing as an unknown factor

7. The landscape of Vietnam ranges from mountains to plains, and the climate is *tropical*.

Tropical weather is characteristic of the Caribbean islands.

tropical (trŏp´ ĭ kəl)

   a. variable

   b. cold and wet

   c. extremely dry

   d. hot and humid

3. **Overall Main Idea of the Selection:** In one sentence tell what the authors want readers to understand about Vietnam. (Be sure to include the name "Vietnam" in your overall main idea sentence.)

_____

_____

_____

_____

_____

_____

Read More about It on the World Wide Web

To learn more about the topic of this selection, visit these websites or use your favorite search engine (such as Yahoo®) to discover more about this author and this topic on your own. Whenever you go to *any* website, it is a good idea to evaluate it critically. Are you getting good information—that is, information that is accurate, complete, and up-to-date? Who sponsors the website? How easy is it to use the features of the website?

http://kicon.com/

http://coombs.anu.edu.au/WWWVLPages/VietPages/
WWWVL-Vietnam.html

http://www.cia.gov/cia/publications/factbook/geos/vm.html

SELECTION **7-2**

HEALTH

ACHOOOO! YOU'VE CAUGHT ANOTHER COLD!

From *Understanding Your Health*
By Wayne Payne and Dale Hahn

People often joke (or complain!) that scientists can put an astronaut on the moon but they can't find a cure for the common cold. Although there isn't a cure for this nuisance, there are things that you can do to relieve your symptoms, and even, perhaps, protect yourself from catching a cold in the first place.

1 The common cold, an acute upper-respiratory-tract infection, must reign as humankind's supreme infectious disease. Also known as **acute rhinitis,** this highly contagious viral infection can be caused by any of the nearly 200 known rhinoviruses. Colds are particularly common when people spend time in crowded indoor environments, such as classrooms.

2 The signs and symptoms of a cold are fairly predictable. Runny nose, watery eyes, general aches and pains, a listless feeling, and a slight fever all may accompany a cold in its early stages. Eventually the nasal passages swell, and the inflammation may spread to the throat. Stuffy nose, sore throat, and coughing may follow. The senses of taste and smell are blocked, and appetite declines.

3 When you notice the onset of symptoms, you should begin managing the cold promptly. After a few days, most of the cold's symptoms subside. In the meantime, you should isolate yourself from others, drink plenty of fluids, eat moderately, and rest. Antibiotics are effective only against bacterial infections—not viral infections like colds.

4 Some of the many OTC (over-the-counter or nonprescription) cold remedies can help you manage a cold. These remedies will not cure your cold but may lessen the discomfort associated with it. Nasal decongestants, expectorants, cough syrups, and aspirin or acetaminophen can give some temporary relief. Using some of these products for more than a few days is not recommended, however, because this may produce a rebound effect.

Annotation Practice Exercises

Directions: For each exercise below, write the topic and the main idea of the paragraph on the lines beside the paragraph. Then, identify the writing pattern the authors used to organize the supporting details.

Annotation Exercise

Topic of paragraph 2:

_____

_____

Main idea sentence:

_____

_____

_____

_____

_____

Writing pattern:

_____

_____

5   Sometimes a cold persists. There may be prolonged chills, fever above 103 degrees Fahrenheit, chest heaviness, or aches, shortness of breath, coughing up rust-colored mucus, or persistent sore throat or hoarseness. If this happens, you should contact a physician.

6   Unfortunately, preventing colds appears to be nearly impossible. Because we now consider colds to be transmitted most readily by hand contact, you should wash your hands frequently.

Washing your hands often is the best way to prevent the common cold. *(FPG International)*

Annotation Exercise

Topic of paragraph 5:

_____

_____

Main idea sentence:

_____

_____

_____

_____

_____

Writing pattern:

_____

Annotation Exercise

Topic of paragraph 6:

_____

_____

Main idea sentence:

_____

_____

_____

_____

_____

Writing pattern:

_____

HEALTH

Comprehension and Vocabulary Quiz

This quiz has four parts. Your instructor may assign some or all of them.

Comprehension

Directions: For each comprehension question below, use information from the selection to determine the correct answer. Refer to the selection as you answer the questions. Write your answer in the space provided.

_____ **1.** The common cold, also known as acute rhinitis, is caused by

    a. bacterial infections.

    b. rhinoviruses.

    c. cold, damp weather.

    d. drafts and chills.

_____ **2.** Colds are particularly common among people who

    a. spend time outdoors.

    b. spend time in crowded indoor environments.

    c. have swollen nasal passages.

    d. are overtired and stressed.

_____ **3.** Which of the following will *not* help you manage your cold?

    a. taking antibiotics

    b. drinking plenty of fluids

    c. getting plenty of sleep

    d. eating in moderation

_____ **4.** Decongestants, expectorants, cough syrups, and aspirin

    a. can cause shortness of breath and persistent sore throat.

    b. will cure your cold.

    c. can cause a rebound effect.

    d. will not give you any relief from a cold.

_____ **5.** Colds are easily transmitted by

    a. washing your hands.

    b. shaking hands with someone.

    c. bacteria floating in the air.

    d. talking to someone who has a cold.

_____ 13. If a **temporal** childhood fantasy is to become a superhero, the fantasy
      a. endures into adolescence.
      b. disappears as soon as it occurs.
      c. lasts a lifetime.
      d. lasts for only a limited time.

_____ 14. The *tempo* of life is slower in Latin American countries than in European countries. **Tempo** means
      a. enjoyment or pleasure.
      b. pace.
      c. length or duration.
      d. destruction or extinction.

_____ 15. A museum of **contemporary** art is a museum that
      a. contains primarily art works that have been donated to it.
      b. displays only sculptures and large-scale works of art.
      c. focuses on paintings from other countries.
      d. features modern art or art from the present time.

Reading Skills Application

Directions: Apply your reading skills to answer the questions below. Write your answer in the space provided.

_____ 16. Which of the following is the main idea of the first paragraph?
      a. There are nearly 200 known rhinoviruses that can cause the highly contagious viral infection known as acute rhinitis.
      b. The common cold, known as acute rhinitis, is an upper-respiratory-tract infection that is probably humankind's most infectious disease.
      c. Colds are especially common in classrooms and other crowded indoor environments.
      d. The common cold is also known as acute rhinitis.

_____ 17. What is the meaning of *managing* as it is used in the third paragraph?
      a. enjoying
      b. ignoring
      c. avoiding
      d. treating

_____ 18. According to information in the selection,
      a. OTC cold remedies can cure colds.
      b. OTC cold remedies may lessen the discomfort associated with colds.
      c. Nasal decongestants and cough syrups always produce rebound effects.
      d. OTC cold remedies can be used for as long as cold symptoms last.

_____ **19.** The primary purpose the authors wrote this selection is to

    a. inform readers what colds are, how to treat them, and how to prevent them.

    b. persuade readers to avoid others who have colds.

    c. illustrate the range of symptoms that can accompany these highly contagious upper-respiratory-tract infections.

    d. instruct readers about steps they can take to avoid catching colds.

_____ **20.** The pattern of organization in paragraph 1 is which of the following?

    a. list

    b. definition

    c. sequence

    d. contrast

HEALTH

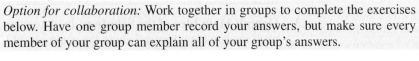

Collaboration Option

Writing and Collaborating to Enhance Your Understanding

Option for collaboration: Work together in groups to complete the exercises below. Have one group member record your answers, but make sure every member of your group can explain all of your group's answers.

1. **Reacting to What You Have Read:** Did your mother, grandmother, or any other member of your family have any special ways to treat a cold? Did they have any special ways to *prevent* a cold? List or describe them. (If they did not have any, describe any folk remedies you have heard about.)

_____

_____

_____

_____

_____

_____

_____

_____

_____

	Essential Obligation	Very Important Obligation	Somewhat Important	Personal Preference
Treating all people equally regardless of race or ethnic background	57%	33%	6%	4%
Voting in elections	53	29	9	9
Working to reduce inequality and injustice	41	42	12	6
Being civil to others with whom we may disagree	35	45	14	6
Keeping fully informed about the news and other public issues	30	42	19	10
Donating blood or organs to help with medical needs	20	37	18	26
Volunteering time to community service	16	42	26	16

TABLE

OPINIONS ON OBLIGATIONS OF CITIZENS

Americans rank voting as one of the essential obligations of citizenship.

Source: From Thomas Patterson, *The American Democracy*, 4th ed. Copyright © 1999 McGraw-Hill. Reprinted by permission of The McGraw-Hill Companies.

have won the right to vote with passage of the Fifteenth Amendment after the Civil War, but they were effectively disenfranchised in the South by a number of electoral tricks, including poll taxes, literacy tests, and whites-only primary elections. The poll tax was a fee of several dollars that had to be paid before one could register to vote. Since most blacks in the South were too poor to pay the poll tax, it barred them from voting. Not until the ratification of the Twenty-fourth Amendment in 1964 was the poll tax outlawed in national elections. Supreme Court decisions and the Voting Rights Act of 1965 swept away other legal barriers to fuller participation of African Americans.

4   In 1971, the Twenty-sixth Amendment extended voting rights to include those eighteen years of age or older. Previously, nearly all states had restricted voting to those twenty-one years of age or older.

5   Today virtually any adult American—rich or poor, man or woman, black or white—who is determined to vote can legally and actually do so. Americans attach great importance to the power of their votes. They claim that voting is important. They view it as the greatest source of influence over political leadership and their strongest protection against an uncaring or corrupt government. They also rank voting as one of the most essential obligations of citizenship (see Table). In view of this

Annotation Exercise

Topic of paragraph 5:

_____

_____

Main idea sentence:

_____

_____

_____

_____

_____

_____

Writing pattern:

_____

_____

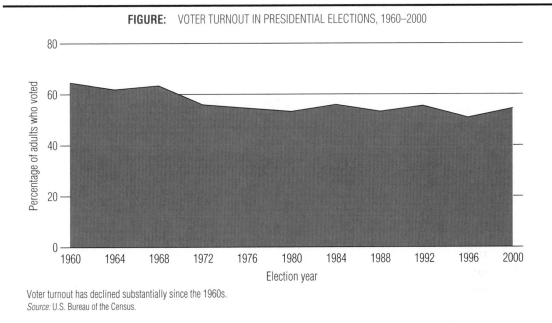

FIGURE: VOTER TURNOUT IN PRESIDENTIAL ELECTIONS, 1960–2000

Voter turnout has declined substantially since the 1960s.
Source: U.S. Bureau of the Census.

attitude and the historical struggle of various groups to gain voting rights, however, the surprising fact is that Americans are not active voters. Millions of them choose not to vote regularly, a tendency that is in sharp contrast with citizens of most other Western democracies.

Factors in Voter Turnout: The United States in Comparative Perspective

6   **Voter turnout** is the proportion of persons of voting age who actually vote in a given election. Since the 1960s the turnout level in presidential elections has not reached 60 percent (see Figure). In 2000, only about half of all adults cast a vote for president.

7   Voter turnout is even lower in the midterm congressional elections that take place between presidential elections. Midterm election turnout has not reached 50 percent since 1920, nor made it past the 40 percent mark since 1970. After a recent midterm election, the cartoonist Rigby showed an election clerk eagerly asking a stray cat that had wandered into a polling place, "Are you registered?"

8   Nonvoting is far more prevalent in the United States than in nearly all other democracies. In recent decades, turnout in major national elections has averaged less than 60 percent in the United States, compared with more 90 percent in Belgium, more than 80 percent in France

Annotation Exercise

Topic of paragraph 7:

_____

_____

Main idea sentence:

_____

_____

_____

_____

_____

_____

Writing pattern:

_____

_____

and Denmark, and more than 70 percent in Great Britain and Germany. The disparity in turnout between the United States and other nations is not so great as these official voting rates indicate, however. Some nations calculate turnout solely on the basis of eligible adults, while the United States bases its figures on all adults, including noncitizens and other ineligible groups (e.g., convicted felons). The United States also ranks high on "spoiled" ballots—ones that are cast but not counted for reasons of human or machine error. Nevertheless, even when such statistical disparities are corrected, turnout in U.S. elections remains low in comparison with that of nearly every other Western democracy.

9   Why don't more Americans vote? Voting does not require vast amounts of time. It takes most people longer to go to a video store and select a movie than it takes them to go to the neighborhood polling place and cast a ballot. Thus the relatively low voter turnout rate of Americans must be attributable to other causes: registration requirements, the frequency of elections, and the lack of clear-cut differences between the political parties.

Annotation Exercise

Topic of paragraph 9:

_____

_____

_____

_____

Main idea sentence:

_____

_____

_____

_____

_____

Writing pattern:

_____

_____

Source: Adapted from Thomas E. Patterson. *We the People: A Concise Introduction to American Politics,* 4th ed., pp. 186–190. Copyright © 2002 McGraw-Hill. Reprinted by permission of The McGraw-Hill Companies.

GOVERNMENT

Comprehension and Vocabulary Quiz

This quiz has four parts. Your instructor may assign some or all of them.

Comprehension

Directions: For each comprehension question below, use information from the selection to determine the correct answer. Refer to the selection as you answer the questions. Write your answer in the space provided.

_____ **1.** Suffrage for women in the United States was attained with the ratification of the
  a. Fifteenth Amendment after the Civil War.
  b. Nineteenth Amendment in 1920.
  c. Twenty-fourth Amendment in 1964.
  d. Twenty-sixth Amendment in 1971.

_____ **2.** Americans tend to rank voting
  a. as only somewhat important.
  b. as one of the most essential obligations of citizenship.
  c. higher than most other Western democracies.
  d. higher during midterm congressional elections.

_____ **3.** During the 2000 presidential election, voter turnout was slightly above
  a. 40 percent.
  b. 50 percent.
  c. 62 percent.
  d. 80 percent.

_____ **4.** The low voter turnout rate of Americans must be attributable to
  a. the lack of clear-cut differences between the political parties.
  b. the frequency of elections.
  c. registration requirements.
  d. all of the above.

_____ **5.** Voting rights were extended to include those 18 years of age or older in
  a. 1920.
  b. 1964.
  c. 1971.
  d. 2000.

Vocabulary in Context

Directions: Use the context clues from *both* sentences to deduce the meaning of the italicized word. *Be sure the answer you choose makes sense in both sentences.* If you discover that you need to use a dictionary to confirm an answer choice, remember that the meaning you select must still fit the context of *both* sentences. Write your answer in the space provided.

Pronunciation Key: ă **pat**   ā **pay**   âr **care**   ä **father**   ĕ **pet**   ē **be**   ĭ **pit**
ī **tie**   îr **pier**   ŏ **pot**   ō **toe**   ô **paw**   oi **noise**   ou **out**   o͝o **took**   o͞o **boot**
ŭ **cut**   yo͞o **abuse**   ûr **urge**   th **thin**   *th* **this**   hw **which**   zh **vision**
ə **about**   Stress mark: ´

_____ 6. Women did not secure the vote until 1920, with the ratification of the Nineteenth Amendment.

Officials from both countries met last week for a ceremony celebrating the *ratification* of their new trade agreement.

ratification (răt ə fĭ cā´ shən)

a. open discussion

b. complete dissolution

c. quick reversal

d. formal approval

_____ 7. They seemed to have won the right to vote with passage of the Fifteenth Amendment after the Civil War, but they were effectively *disenfranchised* in the South by a number of electoral tricks, including poll taxes, literacy tests, and whites-only primary elections.

Many women continue to feel *disenfranchised,* because in certain jobs, they are still not paid the same wages that men are for doing the same work.

disenfranchised (dĭs ĕn frăn´ chīzd)

a. hostile; angry

b. deprived of a legal right

c. offended

d. unwilling to cooperate

_____ 8. Since most blacks in the South were too poor to pay the poll tax, it *barred* them from voting.

In the Olympics, athletes who test positive for steroids or other banned performance-enhancing drugs are *barred* from competition.

barred (bärd)

a. excluded

b. listed

c. encouraged

d. convinced

_____ **9.** Nonvoting is far more *prevalent* in the United States than in nearly all other democracies.

Asthma and other chronic respiratory problems are more *prevalent* in densely populated urban areas than in rural areas.

prevalent (prĕv′ ə lənt)

a. important

b. irritating

c. damaging

d. widespread

_____ **10.** The *disparity* in turnout between the United States and other nations is not so great as these official voting rates indicate, however.

The *disparity* in the two bank tellers' accounts of the missing money made the bank president suspicious.

disparity (dĭ spăr′ ĭ tē)

a. increase

b. change

c. difference

d. decrease

Word Structure

Directions: In paragraph 4 of the selection you encountered the word ***include.*** This word contains the Latin root ***clude,*** which means "to close," or "to shut." *Include* literally means "to close in," or "to contain (something) within as part of the whole." Use the meaning of ***clude*** and the list of prefixes on pages 60–61 to help you determine the meaning of each of the following words that contain this same root. Write your answer in the space provided.

_____ **11.** If a sign at an amusement park says, "Children under age 5 are **excluded** from this ride," it means these children

a. must be accompanied by a parent or adult.

b. are not permitted to ride.

c. are required to have a ticket.

d. are restricted in the number of times they can ride.

_____ **12.** If a person's coronary artery is **occluded,** the artery is

    a. torn through.

    b. blocked.

    c. weak.

    d. punctured.

_____ **13.** If you seek a **secluded** spot for a picnic, you are looking for a place that is

    a. far enough away to shut out other people and noise.

    b. green and grassy.

    c. situated in an open area.

    d. in a field or meadow.

_____ **14.** If a broken arm **precludes** you from participating in a tennis tournament, your broken arm

    a. limits your participation.

    b. increases your participation.

    c. prevents your participation.

    d. delays your participation.

_____ **15.** If diplomats **conclude** negotiations between their countries, they

    a. begin or enter into them.

    b. continue or maintain them.

    c. close out or finish them.

    d. break off or terminate.

Reading Skills Application

Directions: Apply your reading skills to answer the questions below. Write your answer in the space provided.

_____ **16.** Based on information from the selection, it can be inferred that

    a. during the 21st century voter turnout in the United States is likely to exceed that of other countries.

    b. there is virtually no difference between voter turnout in midterm congressional elections and presidential elections.

    c. women did not secure the vote until 1920.

    d. throughout most of this nation's history, there was a general belief that those under the age of 21 could not be intelligent voters.

_____ **17.** According to the selection, which of the following represents the order in which these three groups were able to exercise their right to vote?

    a. African Americans, women, 18-year-olds

    b. women, 18-year-olds, African Americans

    c. women, African Americans, 18-year-olds

    d. 18-year-olds, African Americans, women

_____ **18.** According to the graph in this selection (Figure), voter turnout increased in which of these years?

   a. 1976

   b. 1980

   c. 1984

   d. 1988

_____ **19.** What is the meaning of *secure* in paragraph 2 of the selection?

   a. acquire

   b. fasten

   c. protect

   d. buy

_____ **20.** Which of the following patterns was used to organize the information in paragraph 8 in the selection?

   a. list

   b. comparison-contrast

   c. cause-effect

   d. sequence

SELECTION 7-3

GOVERNMENT

Collaboration Option

Writing and Collaborating to Enhance Your Understanding

Option for collaboration: Work together in groups to complete the exercises below. Have one group member record your answers, but make sure every member of your group can explain all of your group's answers.

1. Reacting to What You Have Read: If you are qualified to vote, do you? Why or why not? If you are not yet qualified to vote, do you think you will exercise this right when you are? Why or why not?

_____

_____

_____

_____

_____

2. **Comprehending the Selection Further:** List at least three reasons
    (according to the selection) that U.S. citizens *do not* vote and three reasons
    why they *should* vote.

    Reasons why U.S. citizens do not vote:

    _____

    _____

    _____

    _____

    _____

    Reasons why U.S. citizens should vote:

    _____

    _____

    _____

    _____

    _____

3. **Overall Main Idea of the Selection:** In one sentence tell what the author
    wants readers to understand about our right to vote.

    _____

    _____

    _____

    _____

Read More about It on the World Wide Web

To learn more about the topic of this selection, visit these websites or use
your favorite search engine (such as Yahoo®) to discover more about this author
and this topic on your own. Whenever you go to *any* website, it is a good idea
to evaluate it critically. Are you getting good information—that is, information
that is accurate, complete, and up-to-date? Who sponsors the website? How
easy is it to use the features of the website?

http://lwv.org/where/democracy/demo_voter.html
http://www.motorvoter.com/motorhome.htm
http://www.usdoj.gov/crt/voting/intro_b.htm

A New World of Reading and Thinking Critically

CHAPTERS IN PART THREE

(© Dennis Marsico/CORBIS)

CHAPTER 8

Reading Critically

CHAPTER OBJECTIVES

In this chapter you will learn:

- What critical reading is and why it is important.

- How to determine an author's point of view.

- How to determine an author's purpose.

- How to determine an author's intended audience.

- How to determine an author's tone.

CONTENTS

What Is Critical Reading, and Why Is It Important?

What Is Meant by Author's Point of View, and How Can You Determine It?

What Is Meant by Author's Purpose, and How Can You Determine It?

What Is Meant by Author's Intended Audience, and How Can You Determine It?

What Is Meant by Author's Tone, and How Can You Determine It?

Other Things to Keep in Mind When Reading Critically:

- You should avoid seeing the purpose of everything you read as to *inform*.

- If the author's purpose is to persuade you to adopt his or her point of view, you should determine which side of an issue he or she favors.

- Understanding the author's tone will enable you to grasp the true or intended meaning, even when the author's words may appear to be saying something different.

- There are two forms of irony: irony in tone and irony in situations.

- Sarcasm and irony are not the same thing.

Developing Chapter Review Cards

Comprehension Practice: Critical Reading Exercises (1)

Comprehension Practice: Critical Reading Exercises (2)

Selection 8-1   *(Economics)*
"Ticket Scalping: A Bum Rap?"
by Campbell McConnell and Stanley Brue

Selection 8-2   *(Nonfiction)*
"Thomas Edison: Man of Inspiration"
by Charles Edison

Selection 8-3   *(Literature)*
"A Day Away"
by Maya Angelou

WHAT YOU NEED TO LEARN

WHAT IS CRITICAL READING, AND WHY IS IT IMPORTANT?

KEY TERM

critical reading

Gaining additional insights and understanding that go beyond comprehending the topic, main idea, and supporting details.

Critical reading is also referred to as *critical reasoning or critical thinking.*

When you read, you should always identify the basic information of topic, main idea, and supporting details. You will also find it helpful to note the author's organizational pattern, especially if you are reading a textbook. However, to gain a greater understanding, you often need to go beyond these basic elements. In other words, you must read critically. **Critical reading** means going *beyond* comprehending the topic, main idea, and supporting details to gain additional insights and understanding.

It is important to be able to read critically so that you can understand an author's message accurately and completely. Your professors expect you to be able to do this for material that you read.

In this chapter, you will be introduced to these critical reading skills:

- Determining an author's point of view (the author's position on an issue).
- Determining an author's purpose (the author's reason for writing).
- Determining an author's intended audience (whom the author had in mind as his or her readers).
- Determining an author's tone (a way the author reveals his or her attitude toward the topic).

Reading critically involves asking certain comprehension monitoring questions after you read a passage. The purpose of asking yourself these questions is to help you think more completely and accurately about what you have read. Once you have asked yourself these questions, you must take time to reread and reconsider the author's message in depth. By doing this, you can make more intelligent judgments about what you are reading. It is in this way that you will gain additional insights and greater understanding when you read.

Let's take a closer look at the four critical reading skills listed above and the comprehension monitoring questions that will guide you toward reading critically.

WHAT IS MEANT BY AUTHOR'S POINT OF VIEW, AND HOW CAN YOU DETERMINE IT?

KEY TERM
point of view

An author's position (opinion) on an issue.

Point of view is also known as the *author's argument* or the *author's bias.*

Comprehension Monitoring Question for Determining an Author's Point of View

"What is the author's position on this issue?"

There is always more than one side to any issue. An author may be in *favor* of an issue (that is, he or she supports it) or he or she may be *opposed* to it (that is, he or she is against it). For example, one author might have this point of view on state lotteries: "State lotteries encourage gambling and should be prohibited." Another author may have the opposite point of view: "State lotteries are harmless entertainment and should be allowed." **Point of view** refers to an author's position on an issue. The author's position, of course, is his or her opinion on an issue. Point of view is also known as the *author's argument* (the overall main idea the author is "arguing" for) and the *author's bias* (the side of an issue the author favors).

It is important that you recognize an author's point of view. If you do not understand the author's point of view, you will not know which side of an issue he or she favors.

To determine the author's point of view, critical readers ask themselves this comprehension monitoring question, "What is the author's position on this issue?" To answer this question, look for words that reveal the author's point of view, that is, his or her support of or opposition to something. Here are some examples of wording that reflects a point of view in favor of having a state lottery:

- *Supporting* state lotteries is *essential* because . . .
- The proposed lottery will *benefit* all the citizens of our state because . . .

Here are examples of wording that reflects a point of view in opposition to the same issue:

- It is *not in the best interest of* the state to have a lottery because . . .
- Voters should *oppose* the creation of a state lottery because . . .
- Concerned citizens should *speak out against* the proposed lottery because . . .

Now read the following excerpt. It is from a health textbook, and its title, *Smoking,* indicates the topic. The stated main idea is, *Since the damage from smoking can be reversed, people who smoke should consider quitting, regardless of how long they have smoked.* Read this passage, and then determine the authors' point of view by asking yourself, "What is the authors' position on the issue of smoking?"

Smoking

For years it was commonly believed that if you had smoked for many years, it was pointless to try to quit; the damage to one's health could never be reversed. However, the American Heart Association now indicates that by quitting smoking, regardless of how long or how much you have smoked, your risk of heart disease declines rapidly. For people who have smoked a pack or less of cigarettes per day, within three years after quitting smoking their heart disease risk is virtually the same as those who never smoked. Since the damage from smoking can be reversed, people who smoke should consider quitting, regardless of how long they have smoked. Of course, if you have just started to smoke, the healthy approach would be to quit now before the nicotine controls your life and damages your heart.

What is the authors' point of view?
_____
_____
_____
_____
_____

Source: From Wayne Payne and Dale Hahn, *Understanding Your Health,* 5th ed. Copyright © 1998 McGraw-Hill. Reprinted by permission of The McGraw-Hill Companies.

Stop and Annotate

Go back to the textbook excerpt. Write the authors' point of view in the space provided.

In this excerpt the authors give their point of view (their position) on smoking: They are opposed to smoking, and they want smokers to quit. They state what they believe smokers should do (stop smoking) and explain why they hold this position (no matter how long a person has smoked, stopping smoking reverses the damage). To convey how strongly they are opposed to smoking, they urge readers, "*quit now* before nicotine *controls* your life and *damages* your heart."

Here is another excerpt from the same health textbook. Its topic is *regular physical activity.* The formulated main idea is, *Regular physical activity can help you have a lifetime of cardiovascular health.* Read this passage; then determine the authors' point of view by asking yourself, "What is the authors' position on the issue of regular physical activity?"

With all the benefits that come with physical activity, it amazes health professionals that so many Americans refuse to participate in regular exercise. Perhaps people feel that they do not have enough time or that they must work out strenuously. However, only twenty to sixty minutes of moderate aerobic activity three to five times each week is recommended. This is not a large price to pay for a lifetime of cardiovascular health. Find a partner and get started!

What is the authors' point of view?
_____
_____
_____
_____
_____

Source: From Wayne Payne and Dale Hahn, *Understanding Your Health,* 5th ed. Copyright © 1998 McGraw-Hill. Reprinted by permission of The McGraw-Hill Companies.

Stop and Annotate

Go back to the textbook excerpt above. Write the authors' point of view in the space provided.

In this excerpt the authors give their point of view (their position) on regular physical activity: They are in favor of regular physical activity, and they want people to exercise on a regular basis. They state what they believe people should do (engage in moderate aerobic exercise at least three times a week), and they explain why they hold this position (because it promotes cardiovascular health).

WHAT IS MEANT BY AUTHOR'S PURPOSE, AND HOW CAN YOU DETERMINE IT?

KEY TERM
purpose

An author's reason for writing.

A second critical reading skill is determining the author's purpose. Whenever authors write, they write for specific purposes. For that matter, whenever *you* write, you have a specific purpose. An author's **purpose** is simply his or her reason for writing. In other words, the author has a particular purpose he or she hopes to achieve. The author's purpose may be to *inform,* to *instruct,* to *entertain,* or to *persuade* the reader to believe something or to take a certain action.

Most textbook authors write for the purpose of informing (giving information) or instructing (explaining how to do something). However, some authors, such as movie critics, newspaper editors, and political writers, write to give their opinion or to persuade. Finally, other writers, such as humorists or certain newspaper columnists, write for the purpose of entertaining. They may entertain readers with humorous stories or with enjoyable descriptions. It is important to understand an author's purpose for writing because you will then be aware of his or her motive for writing and you will have a greater insight as to what was important in their message.

Comprehension Monitoring Question for Determining an Author's Purpose

"Why did the author write this?"

To determine an author's purpose, critical readers ask themselves this comprehension monitoring question: "Why did the author write this?" Fortunately, authors often state their purpose directly. For example, the author of a biology textbook might write, "The purpose of this section is to define and explain the types of root systems in plants" (to inform). Or the author of a newspaper editorial may state, "The citizens of our city should vote 'yes' on funding a new municipal sports arena" (to persuade). At other times, authors may not state their purposes for writing because they feel that the purpose is quite clear, and they assume that the reader will infer it.

To determine an author's purpose, notice the words the author has used and the way the information is presented:

- When the author's purpose is to *inform* (give *information,* he or she will use phrases such as *It is interesting to know that . . .* or *There are different types of . . . .*

- When the author's purpose is to *instruct,* he or she will typically give a set of directions *(instructions)* or a sequence of steps to follow.

- When the author's purpose is to *persuade,* he or she will deliberately use emotional language or words that are designed to influence your thinking and make you respond a certain way. For example, *Any reasonable person will agree that . . . , Only a fool would believe that . . . ,* or *The only intelligent choice, then, is . . . .*

- When the author's purpose is to *entertain,* he or she may tell a funny story, use wild exaggerations (hyperbole), or simply describe a pleasant event or place. For example, writers might begin, *A funny thing happened to me on the way to . . .* or *Vermont is perhaps the loveliest place to be in autumn.*

Here is an excerpt from a U.S. history textbook. Its topic is *the first people to come to America.* The formulated main idea is that *The first people probably came from Asia to America by walking across a land bridge that existed thousands of years ago.* Read this passage; then determine the authors' purpose by asking yourself, "Why did the authors write this?"

People probably first came from Asia to America during a prehistoric glacial period—either before 35,000 B.C. or about 10,000 years later—when huge amounts of the world's water froze into sheets of ice. Sea levels dropped so drastically that the Bering Strait became a broad, grassy plain. Across that land bridge between the two continents both humans and animals escaped ice-bound Siberia for ice-free Alaska. Whenever the first migration took place, the movement of Asians to America continued, even after 8000 B.C. when world temperatures rose again and the water from melting glaciers flooded back into the ocean, submerging the Bering Strait.

What is the author's purpose?

_____

_____

_____

_____

_____

_____

Source: From James West Davidson, William Geinapp, Christine Heyrmann, Mark Lytle, and Michael Stoff, *Nation of Nations,* 3rd ed. Copyright © 1998 McGraw-Hill. Reprinted by permission of The McGraw-Hill Companies.

Stop and Annotate

Go back to the textbook excerpt. Write the author's purpose in the space provided.

The authors' purpose in writing this passage is to *inform* the reader about a particular event: the way people probably first came from Asia to America. The passage consists of historical information the authors want you to know. (Asians came on foot over a land bridge that existed thousands of years ago.) Notice that the authors are not trying to instruct the reader how to do anything, nor trying to persuade you to accept their ideas nor to entertain you.

Here is a passage from a health textbook. Its topic is given in the heading: *dealing with a stalker.* The formulated main idea is, *There are steps you can take if you are being stalked.* Now read the passage and determine the authors' purpose by asking yourself, "Why did the authors write this?"

Dealing with a Stalker

Nearly every state has passed a law making stalking a crime in and of itself. But what can *you* do if you are being stalked? If someone bothers or intimidates you with phone calls, written notes or letters, or unwanted gifts, take the following steps:

• Contact your local police immediately and fill out a report.

• Report the harassment to the telephone company and ask that they install call-tracing devices and tape recorders to gather evidence against the stalker.

• Keep a detailed record, with dates, times, and exact wording of all incidents or threats, including the number of telephone calls, letters, or other harassments.

- Save all letters, answering machine tapes, and other evidence.
- Contact the local prosecutor and seek a court order prohibiting the stalker from any further contact. If the stalker violates the court order, press the prosecutor to take action, such as indicting the stalker.
- Keep the pressure on police to take the appropriate action.
- Law-enforcement officials urge against any contact with the stalker. Let the police, telephone company, postal investigators, and prosecutors handle the problem.

Source: From Wayne Payne and Dale Hahn, *Understanding Your Health,* 5th ed. Copyright © 1998 McGraw-Hill. Reprinted by permission of The McGraw-Hill Companies.

What is the authors' purpose?

_____

_____

_____

_____

_____

_____

Stop and Annotate

Go back to the textbook excerpt above. Write the authors' purpose in the space provided.

The authors' purpose in writing this passage is to *instruct* the reader what to do when dealing with a stalker. They say "take the following steps"; then they explain the things you should do if you suspect or know that you are being stalked. Notice that the authors are doing more than merely presenting information. Their main purpose is to instruct you about the appropriate actions to take. They are not writing primarily to persuade you to accept their suggestions (although they undoubtedly hope you will follow their suggestions if you ever need them). And they certainly did not write this passage to entertain you.

The next excerpt comes from a business textbook. As the heading indicates, the topic is *the information superhighway.* The stated main idea is the first sentence, *If you can navigate the information superhighway, you can be among the most successful college graduates of tomorrow.* Now read the passage and determine the authors' purpose by asking yourself, "Why did the authors write this?"

The Information Superhighway

If you can navigate the information superhighway, you can be among the most successful college graduates of tomorrow. (As you will recall, the information superhighway, or I-way, is the network of computer and telecommunications equipment that links people throughout the world into one unified communications system.) Information on almost any topic will be available. To access that information, you must be able to use computers and other telecommunications equipment. It would be a mistake to think you can escape learning such information because you plan to work as a mechanic or

What is the authors' purpose?

_____

_____

_____

_____

_____

_____

_____

farmer, or in some other job that hasn't required computer literacy in the past. Mechanics now order parts by computer and read repair manuals on computer screens. Farmers often have cellu- lar phones and even computers on their combines. These tools now link them to suppliers and enable them to schedule everything on the farm.

Source: From William G. Nickels, James M. McHugh, and Susan M. McHugh, *Understanding Business,* 4th ed. Copyright © 1999 McGraw-Hill. Reprinted by permission of The McGraw-Hill Companies.

Stop and Annotate

Go back to the textbook excerpt above. Write the authors' purpose in the space provided.

The authors' purpose in writing this passage is to *persuade* college students that to be successful in their careers they must be knowledgeable about using the information superhighway. The passage presents examples of how knowledge of computers and telecommunications equipment is needed for success in almost any job. In order to be persuasive, the authors stress that "you *must* be able to use computers and other telecommunications equipment" and that "It *would be a mistake* to think you can escape learning such information." Notice that the authors are doing more than merely presenting information. Their purpose is to convince you to accept their advice. They do not, however, instruct you as to how to become knowledgeable about computers and telecommunications devices. Nor did they write this passage merely to entertain.

WHAT IS MEANT BY AUTHOR'S INTENDED AUDIENCE, AND HOW CAN YOU DETERMINE IT?

When speakers make a presentation, they have an audience, and they adjust their presentation to the type of people in the audience. For example, suppose a doctor is asked to give a presentation on the topic of alcoholism. If her audience is other doctors, her speech will probably be very technical and contain many specialized medical terms. If, however, her audience is students in a high school biology class, then her presentation will be quite different.

KEY TERM
intended audience

People an author has in mind as his or her readers.

When authors write, they also have specific "audiences" in mind. Their audiences, of course, are the people they anticipate will be reading what they have written. An author's **intended audience** is the people the author has in mind as his or her readers. For instance, a computer scientist may decide to write a textbook for students who have no knowledge of computer programming and who will be taking an introductory-level computer programming course. The computer scientist will have these students in mind while writing. Having this particular audience in mind will influence the material the author includes, how he or she presents it, and how simple or sophisticated an approach he or she chooses. However, if that same computer scientist were writing an article for other computer scientists, the material would be presented very differently.

Why is it important to determine an author's audience? Actually, there are several reasons. First, if you are not among those in the intended audience (people knowledgeable about multimedia production, for example), you may need to do some extra work in order to understand the material. Second, if you are doing research, you can decide whether material on the topic is written for the audience you are part of (for example, those who know little or nothing about multimedia production). Third, knowing who the audience is gives you insight into the author's purpose, his or her reason for writing. This, in turn, allows you to evaluate whether or not that purpose was accomplished. For example, if you determine that an author's audience is people who disagree with him or her, then you can evaluate whether the author succeeded in presenting a persuasive case that might change readers' minds. Perhaps the most important reason for you to become aware of the importance of audience, however, is that it can make you a better writer: You will learn to shape your message to your intended audience, and this will enable you to communicate your message more effectively.

Comprehension Monitoring Question for Determining an Author's Intended Audience

"Who did the author intend to read this?

Critical readers ask themselves the comprehension monitoring question, "Who did the author intend to read this?" Sometimes an author will state who the intended audience is. Even if the author does not state who the intended audience is, you can determine the audience by considering these three things:

- *The topic* (Is it a common topic? Or is it an unusual or specialized one?)
- *The level of language used* (Is it simple? Sophisticated? Specialized?)
- *The author's purpose for writing* (Is it meant to inform? To instruct? To persuade?)

Here is the excerpt on smoking that you read earlier in this chapter. Reread this paragraph. Then determine the authors' audience by asking yourself, "Who did the authors intend to read this?"

Smoking

For years it was commonly believed that if you had smoked for many years, it was pointless to try to quit; the damage to one's health could never be reversed. However, the American Heart Association now indicates that by quitting smoking, regardless of how long or how much you have smoked, your risk of heart disease declines rapidly. For people who have smoked a pack or less of cigarettes per day, within three years after quitting smoking their heart disease risk is virtually the same as those who never smoked. Since the damage from smoking can be reversed, people who smoke should consider quitting, regardless of how long they have smoked. Of course, if you have just started to smoke, the healthy approach would be to quit now before the nicotine controls your life and damages your heart.

Who is the authors' intended audience?

_____
_____
_____
_____
_____
_____
_____
_____

Source: From Wayne Payne and Dale Hahn, *Understanding Your Health,* 5th ed. Copyright © 1998 McGraw-Hill. Reprinted by permission of The McGraw-Hill Companies.

The authors' intended audience is *everyone who smokes, including those who have just started to smoke.* In the last sentence of the paragraph, the authors use the word "you" and refer to "your life" and "your heart" since they are speaking directly to readers who smoke.

Here is another passage you read earlier. It is about the *information superhighway*. Now reread it and then determine the authors' intended audience. Ask yourself, "Who did the authors intend to read this?"

Stop and Annotate

Go back to the textbook excerpt. Write the authors' intended audience in the space provided.

The Information Superhighway

If you can navigate the information superhighway, you can be among the most successful college graduates of tomorrow. (As you will recall, the information superhighway, or I-way, is the network of computer and telecommunications equipment that links people throughout the world into one unified communications system.) Information on almost any topic will be available. To access that information, you must be able to use computers and other telecommunications equipment. It would be a mistake to think you can escape learning such information because you plan to work as a mechanic or farmer, or in some other job that hasn't required computer literacy in the past. Mechanics now order parts by computer and read repair manuals on computer screens. Farmers often have cellular phones and even computers on their combines. These tools now link them to suppliers and enable them to schedule everything on the farm.

Who is the authors' intended audience?

_____

_____

_____

_____

_____

_____

_____

Source: From William G. Nickels, James M. McHugh, and Susan M. McHugh, *Understanding Business*, 4th ed. Copyright © 1999 McGraw-Hill. Reprinted by permission of The McGraw-Hill Companies.

Stop and Annotate

Go back to the textbook excerpt. Write the authors' intended audience in the space provided.

The authors suggest their intended audience at the beginning of the paragraph: *students who want to "be among the most successful college graduates of tomorrow."* In the rest of the paragraph the authors explain what students must learn if they want to be among the most successful graduates: They must know how to use computers and telecommunications equipment.

WHAT IS MEANT BY AUTHOR'S TONE, AND HOW CAN YOU DETERMINE IT?

When people speak, their tone of voice often reveals their attitude toward whatever they are speaking about. To convey a tone, speakers rely on pitch, volume, and inflection, along with their choice of words. You can usually tell by

Words That Describe a *Humorous, Sarcastic, Ironic,* or *Satiric* Tone

(can appear in writing of many sorts, including literature and social criticism and some newspaper and magazine columns and articles)

lighthearted	not being burdened by trouble, worry, or care; happy and carefree
irreverent	disrespectful; critical of what is generally accepted or respected; showing a lack of reverence
cynical	scornful of the motives, virtue, or integrity of others; expressing scorn and bitter mockery
scornful	treating someone or something as despicable or unworthy; showing utter contempt
contemptuous	showing open disrespect or haughty disdain
mocking	treating with scorn or contempt
malicious	intended to cause harm or suffering; having wicked or mischievous intentions or motives
ironic	humorously sarcastic or mocking
sarcastic	characterized by the desire to show scorn or contempt
bitter	characterized by sharpness, severity, or cruelty
skeptical	reluctant to believe; doubting or questioning everything
disbelieving	not believing; refusing to believe

Words That Describe a *Supportive* Tone

(found in writing of many types, such as certain textbooks, inspirational writing, some magazine articles, and personal correspondence)

encouraging	showing support
supportive	showing support or assistance
enthusiastic	showing excitement
optimistic	expecting the best; having a positive outlook
approving	expressing approval or agreement
positive	being in favor of; supportive; optimistic
sympathetic	inclined to sympathy; showing pity
tolerant	showing respect for the rights or opinions or practices of others

Some *Other* Words That Can Describe Tone

authoritative	speaking in a definite and confident manner
ambivalent	having opposite feelings or attitudes at the same time
conciliatory	willing to give in on some matters
cautious	careful; not wanting to take chances; wary
arrogant	giving oneself an undue degree of importance; haughty
grim	gloomy; dismal; forbidding
humble	marked by meekness or modesty; not arrogant or prideful
apologetic	self-deprecating; humble; offering or expressing an apology or excuse

Here is the passage about dealing with a stalker that you read earlier in this chapter. To determine the tone the authors use in writing about stalkers, reread this passage and then ask yourself, "What do the authors' choice of words and style of writing reveal about their attitude toward dealing with a stalker?"

Dealing with a Stalker

Nearly every state has passed a law making stalking a crime in and of itself. But what can *you* do if you are being stalked? If someone bothers or intimidates you with phone calls, written notes or letters, or unwanted gifts, take the following steps:

• Contact your local police immediately and fill out a report.

• Report the harassment to the telephone company and ask that they install call-tracing devices and tape recorders to gather evidence against the stalker.

• Keep a detailed record, with dates, times, and exact wording of all incidents or threats, including the number of telephone calls, letters, or other harassments.

• Save all letters, answering machine tapes, and other evidence.

• Contact the local prosecutor and seek a court order prohibiting the stalker from any further contact. If the stalker violates the court order, press the prosecutor to take action, such as indicting the stalker.

• Keep the pressure on police to take the appropriate action.

• Law-enforcement officials urge against any contact with the stalker. Let the police, telephone company, postal investigators, and prosecutors handle the problem.

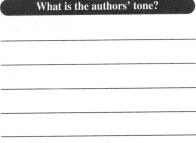

What is the authors' tone?

_____

_____

_____

_____

Source: From Wayne Payne and Dale Hahn, *Understanding Your Health,* 5th ed. Copyright © 1998 McGraw-Hill. Reprinted by permission of The McGraw-Hill Companies.

Stop and Annotate

Go back to the textbook excerpt above. Write the authors' tone in the space provided.

The authors' tone is *serious* and *unemotional.* Even though stalking can be an emotional issue, the authors do not use an emotional tone. Their tone is not upset or alarmed. They use the words "bothers" and "intimidates" instead of stronger, more emotional words such as "harasses," "torments," "terrifies," or "threatens." They then calmly suggest some "steps" you can take to deal with the problem.

Here is one more passage that you read earlier in the chapter. It is about *the benefits of regular aerobic activity.* To determine the tone the authors use in writing about the need for regular physical activity and the benefits it brings, reread the passage and ask yourself, "What do the authors' choice of words and style of writing reveal about their attitude toward the benefits of regular aerobic activity?"

With all the benefits that come with physical activity, it amazes health professionals that so many Americans refuse to participate in regular exercise.

Perhaps people feel that they do not have enough time or that they must work out strenuously. However, only twenty to sixty minutes of moderate aerobic activity three to five times each week is recommended. This is not a large price to pay for a lifetime of cardiovascular health. Find a partner and get started!

> **What is the authors' tone?**
>
> _____
>
> _____
>
> _____
>
> _____

Stop and Annotate

Go back to the textbook excerpt. Write the authors' tone in the space provided.

Source: From Wayne Payne and Dale Hahn, *Understanding Your Health,* 5th ed. Copyright © 1998 McGraw-Hill. Reprinted by permission of The McGraw-Hill Companies.

The authors' tone is *enthusiastic, encouraging,* and perhaps even *urgent.* Readers are admonished to "Find a partner and get started!" The authors use an exclamation point for added emphasis.

As you may have noticed, author's purpose, tone, point of view, and intended audience are related to each other. The chart below shows the *interrelationship* among author's purpose, tone, point of view, and intended audience.

HOW THE CRITICAL READING SKILLS ARE INTERRELATED

The author's purpose causes him or her to use a certain tone to convey a point of view to an intended audience.

- The author decides on a *purpose* (reason) for writing:

  to inform   to instruct   to persuade   to entertain

- To accomplish his purpose, he or she uses an appropriate *tone:*

  serious   formal   sincere   enthusiastic

  disapproving sympathetic   informal   humorous

  ironic, etc.

- To convey his or her main idea or *point of view* (position on an issue):

  point of view   (*in favor of* or *opposed to*) argument

- To an *intended audience:*

  the general public   a specific group   a particular person

---

The chart on the next page illustrates the application of critical reading skills to a piece of writing, a music critic's review of an imaginary CD. It is also designed to show that critical reading skills are often part of everyday reading.

EXAMPLE OF CRITICAL READING APPLIED TO A MUSIC CRITIC'S REVIEW OF A NEW CD

The controversial group *The Gate Crashers* has just released its fourth CD, *The Gate Crashers—Live!* Is it a good CD? That depends: Do you like vulgar lyrics that glorify violence? Do you mind listening to painfully bad musicians? Do you have any problem sitting through twelve tracks (65 excruciating minutes!) of mind-numbing noise? If not, then *The Gate Crashers—Live!* is a CD you'll surely want to add to your collection.

Questions	Answers
What is the author's purpose?	To persuade readers not to buy this new CD.
Who is the author's intended audience?	People who buy CDs.
What is the author's point of view?	The new Gate Crashers CD is awful.*
What is the author's tone?	Sarcastic

*Notice that this is also the author's main idea or "argument."

OTHER THINGS TO KEEP IN MIND WHEN READING CRITICALLY

Here are five helpful things you should keep in mind about critical reading:

1. You should avoid seeing the purpose of everything you read as to *inform.*

When you are determining the author's purpose, use *inform* as a last choice. Instead of really thinking about the author's purpose, you may be tempted to label the purpose of every passage as "to inform." If the author is explaining how to do something, then the purpose is to *instruct.* If the author is trying to convince readers of something, then the purpose is to *persuade.* If the author is presenting material that is simply amusing or pleasant to read, then the purpose is to *entertain.* Only when the author is just providing information is the purpose to inform.

2. If the author's purpose is to persuade you to adopt his or her point of view, you should determine which side of an issue he or she favors.

Remember that although an author may claim to be presenting unbiased information about both sides of an issue, his or her real purpose may be to persuade you to believe or support one side.

One way you can determine which side of an issue an author favors is by examining whether or not the author presents both sides of an issue, or whether the author presents good things about only

(Continued)

one side (the side he favors). You can check to see if the author has left out important information that might weaken his position. Or perhaps the author presents only negative things about the side or position he opposes.

There are times, of course, when an author does present both sides of an issue and, rather than taking a position, allows readers to make up their own minds. If the author presents both sides fairly, we say that he or she is *objective* or *unbiased*. When an author favors one side of an issue, we say he or she is *biased*.

3. Understanding the author's tone will enable you to grasp the true or intended meaning, even when the author's words may appear to be saying something different.

Although an author's tone is often obvious, there may be times when the tone is less clear and requires careful thought on your part. If you misunderstand an author's tone, you may misinterpret the message. You may think she is saying something different from what she really means. For example, if you read a short story and you miss the author's ironic tone, you will mistakenly think her meaning is the opposite of what it actually is. Or if you overlook irony, you may think authors are being serious when they are actually joking; you may think that they are calm when, in fact, they are angry, or that they are in favor of something when, in reality, they oppose it.

4. There are two forms of irony: irony in tone and irony in situations.

When authors are being ironic, they create a deliberate contrast between their apparent meaning and their intended meaning; they say one thing but mean the opposite. That is, the words are intended to express something different from their literal meaning. You use irony every day in conversation. For example, you might say, "Well, that test was a breeze!" but your ironic tone makes it clear how difficult the test actually was.

Another form of irony occurs when there is incongruity or difference between what is expected and what actually occurs. For example, it would be ironic if you got on an airplane to make a surprise visit to a friend in another city, and your friend was not there because he was making a trip to pay a surprise visit to you in your city!

5. Sarcasm and irony are not the same thing.

Students sometimes confuse sarcasm with irony. *Sarcasm* is a cutting, often ironic remark that is intended to convey contempt or ridicule. Sarcasm is always meant to hurt; irony is not. An example of a hurtful, sarcastic remark is, "That college must have bought its band uniforms at a thrift shop sale!" An example of an ironic remark is, "This winter makes last winter seem like a day at the beach" (meaning this winter is much colder than last winter).

DEVELOPING CHAPTER REVIEW CARDS

Chapter review cards are a way to select, organize, and review the important information in a textbook chapter. Preparing chapter review cards helps you organize the information so that you can learn and memorize it more easily. In other words, chapter review cards are an effective study tool.

Preparing chapter review cards for each chapter of this book will give you practice in creating these valuable study tools. Once you have learned how to make chapter review cards, you can use index cards to create them for textbook material in any of your courses and use them when you study for tests.

Now, complete the chapter review cards for this chapter by answering the questions or following the directions on each "card" below. (The boxes below represent index cards.)

Reading Critically

1. Define *critical reading.*

_____

_____

_____

2. Why is it important to be able to read critically?

_____

_____

_____

Card 1 Chapter 8: Reading Critically

Study the example in the box below to see how information you learned in this chapter about critical reading can be applied when you read. When you are sure you understand the example, complete the five exercises that follow. (You may want to refer to pages 403–404 for the definitions of some words that are often used to describe tone.)

EXAMPLE

This passage comes from a health textbook. Its topic is *sexual victimization.* Read the paragraph; notice that the paragraph's main idea is given below it. Then determine the authors' purpose and tone by asking yourself these comprehension monitoring questions: "Why did the authors write this?" and "What do the authors' choice of words and style reveal about their attitude?"

Sexual Victimization

Ideally, sexual intimacy is a mutual, enjoyable form of communication between two people. Far too often, however, relationships are approached in an aggressive, hostile manner. These sexual aggressors always have a victim, someone who is physically or psychologically traumatized. Sexual victimization occurs in many forms and in a variety of settings. Sexual victimization includes rape and sexual assault, sexual abuse of children, sexual harassment, and the commercialization of sex.

Source: From Wayne Payne and Dale Hahn, *Understanding Your Health,* 5th ed. Copyright © 1998 McGraw-Hill. Reprinted by permission of The McGraw-Hill Companies.

Main idea: *Sexual victimization occurs in many forms and in a variety of settings.*

_____ *a*   What is the authors' purpose?

     a. to inform

     b. to instruct

     c. to persuade

_____ *b*   What is the authors' tone?

     a. disapproving and bitter

     b. unemotional and straightforward

     c. nostalgic

The correct answer to the first question is a. The author's purpose is *to inform* readers about sexual victimization. *The correct answer to the second question is b.* Although this topic could be a highly emotional one, it is presented in an unemotional tone.

control, cravings and withdrawal symptoms, social isolation, marital discord, academic failure, excessive financial debt, and job termination. Certain kinds of people may prefer cyberlife to real life. If you feel yourself becoming addicted, set a time limit for how long you spend on the Internet each day, and try to stay focused on the task at hand. Many Web pages contain enticing ads intended to draw you away from your original purpose. You can reduce the amount of time you spend online if you stay focused on accomplishing your intent instead of surfing off in other directions.

Source: From Fred Hofstetter, *Multimedia Literacy.* Copyright © 1995 McGraw-Hill. Reprinted by permission of The McGraw-Hill Companies.

Main idea: *Internet Addiction Disorder (IAD) is as real a problem as alcoholism, but there are certain steps you can take to deal with the problem.*

_____ Who is the author's intended audience?

  a. people who cannot stay focused on the task at hand

  b. people who are alcoholic

  c. people who use the Internet

  d. people who spend more than an hour a day using computers

_____ What is the author's point of view?

  a. People who are alcoholic should be very careful about using the Internet.

  b. If you are addicted to the Internet, you should join a support group.

  c. If you suffer from IAD, you should seek medical help.

  d. If you sense you are becoming addicted to the Internet, you can take certain actions to prevent it.

5. This paragraph comes from a psychology textbook.

Prior to 1968, individuals who had strong objections to the death penalty were routinely barred from serving on juries in cases involving a possible death penalty. In a landmark Supreme Court ruling in 1968, however, an appeals judge commuted a death penalty to life imprisonment in the case of *Witherspoon v. Illinois* on the grounds that the jury was composed only of persons who favored the death penalty and was not, therefore, a fair and "representative" jury. In making this ruling, the judge cited a Gallup poll conducted at that time that found that only about 55 percent of the people surveyed favored the death penalty. The judge ruled that prospective jurors could be excluded only when they were so opposed to the death penalty that they would vote against it regardless of the evidence.

Source: From Benjamin B. Lahey, *Psychology: An Introduction,* 6th ed. Copyright © 1997 McGraw-Hill. Reprinted by permission of The McGraw-Hill Companies.

Main idea: *Due to a landmark Supreme Court ruling in 1968, prospective jurors can be excluded only when they are so opposed to the death penalty that they would vote against it regardless of the evidence.*

———— What is the author's purpose?

a. to inform readers of the effect of *Witherspoon v. Illinois* on jury selection

b. to instruct readers how to avoid jury duty

c. to persuade readers to oppose the death penalty

d. to inform readers about the history of the jury selection process

———— What is the author's tone?

a. sarcastic

b. sentimental

c. unemotional

d. urgent

COMPREHENSION PRACTICE: CRITICAL READING EXERCISES (2)

Study the example in the box below to see how information you learned in this chapter about critical reading can be applied when you read. When you are sure you understand the example, complete the five exercises that follow.

EXAMPLE

This excerpt comes from a speech communications textbook. Its topic is *choosing an approach for your résumé.* Read the paragraph; notice that the paragraph's main idea is given below it. Then determine the authors' purpose and tone by asking yourself these comprehension monitoring questions: "Why did the author write this?" and "Whom did the author intend to read this?"

Although you want to make yourself stand out from the crowd, when you apply for a job, you should be cautious about using unusual kinds of paper or typefaces on your résumé. A novel approach may capture the fancy of a prospective boss, but it may be a turn-off. The more you know about the field and the organization itself, the better your decision will be about the best approach. Be sure that the approach you choose is compatible with the nature of the organization.

Source: From Ronald Adler and Jeanne Elmhorst, *Communicating at Work,* 5th ed. Copyright © 1996 McGraw-Hill. Reprinted by permission of The McGraw-Hill Companies.

(Continued)

Main idea: *Be sure that the approach you choose for your résumé is compatible with the nature of the organization with which you are seeking employment.*

What is the authors' purpose?

to instruct
_____

Explanation: The authors' purpose is *to instruct* readers about the correct approach for a résumé. The author explains why it is important to choose an appropriate paper and type-face for a résumé, and advises readers to learn more about the field and the organization.

Who is the authors' intended audience?

those who will be submitting résumés when applying for jobs
_____

Explanation: It is clear from the first sentence that the authors' intended audience is those persons who will be creating and submitting résumés when applying for jobs.

Directions:

- First, read the paragraph carefully.
- Next, determine the main idea sentence of the paragraph and write it in the space provided. The main idea may be stated, or it may be implied.
- Finally, read critically and then answer the questions about the author's point of view (write a sentence that gives the author's position or opinion), purpose (*to inform, to instruct, to persuade,* or *to entertain*), intended audience and tone. (See tone words and definitions on pages 403–404.)

1.   This paragraph comes from a health textbook.

Risk Factors That Can Be Changed

Four cardiovascular risk factors are influenced, in large part, by our lifestyle choices. These risk factors are smoking, physical inactivity, high blood cholesterol level, and high blood pressure. Healthful behavior changes you make concerning these four risk factors can help you protect and strengthen your cardiovascular system.

Source: From Wayne Payne and Dale Hahn, *Understanding Your Health,* 5th ed. Copyright © 1998 McGraw-Hill. Reprinted by permission of The McGraw-Hill Companies.

Write the main idea sentence:

_____

_____

_____

Who is the authors' intended audience?

_____

_____

What is the authors' point of view?

_____

_____

What is the authors' purpose?

_____

_____

2. This paragraph comes from a communications textbook.

The Importance of a Sense of Humor

   Recognizing the humor in daily situations and occasionally being able to laugh at yourself will make you feel better not only about others but also, more importantly, about yourself. Others will enjoy being associated with you, and your ability to perform physically and to recover from injuries and illnesses will probably be enhanced. For example, any student-athlete who has experienced a career-threatening injury can attest that a positive outlook and a sense of humor were key ingredients in relation to the speed and extent of recovery. Develop your sense of humor. Learn to laugh at yourself. It's good for you!

Source: Adapted from Ronald Adler and Jeanne Elmhorst, _Communicating at Work,_ 5th ed. Copyright © 1996 McGraw-Hill. Reprinted by permission of The McGraw-Hill Companies.

Write the main idea sentence:

_____

_____

What is the authors' purpose?

_____

What is the authors' tone?

_____

_____

What is the authors' point of view?

_____

_____

3. This paragraph comes from the introduction to a computer science textbook.

   It is obvious that computers are part of everyone's life. Your future success requires a basic level of knowledge about computers and skill in using them. This book is designed to help you attain these goals. As you read and complete the assignments in this text, you will learn to involve computers in your critical thinking. As a student in the 21st century, you should understand how computers affect your life and how they are used to solve everyday problems. You should be able to talk intelligently about computers. Equally important, you should be prepared for the changes computers will bring in your life.

Source: From Timothy Trainor and Diane Krasnewich, *Computers!,* 5th ed. Copyright © 1996 McGraw-Hill. Reprinted by permission of The McGraw-Hill Companies.

Write the main idea sentence:

_____

_____

_____

_____

Who is the authors' intended audience?

_____

_____

What is the authors' point of view?

_____

_____

4.   This paragraph comes from a health textbook.

Avoiding Date Rape

The first step in avoiding date rape is to consider your partner's behaviors. Many, but not all, date rapists show one or more of the following behaviors: a disrespectful attitude toward you and others, lack of concern for your feelings, violence and hostility, obsessive jealousy, extreme competitiveness, a desire to dominate, and unnecessary physical roughness. Consider these behaviors as warning signs for possible problems in the future. Reevaluate your participation in the relationship.

Source: From Wayne Payne and Dale Hahn, *Understanding Your Health,* 5th ed. Copyright © 1998 McGraw-Hill. Reprinted by permission of The McGraw-Hill Companies.

Write the main idea sentence:

_____

_____

What is the authors' purpose?

_____

_____

What is the authors' tone?

_____

_____

5. This paragraph comes from a child development textbook.

Homelessness

For children who have no homes, the consequences of poverty are especially severe. Sadly, families are the fastest growing segment of the homeless population, about 2.5 million people, one-third of whom are single mothers and young children. Compared to most poor children, the majority of homeless children living in emergency shelters are developmentally delayed and suffer from anxiety, depression, and learning difficulties. Young girls are the most affected. While the large majority of poor children attend Head Start or other preschool education programs, only 15 percent of homeless children are enrolled. Many never get to such programs, and tragically, others are so disturbed that they are rejected even by Head Start.

Source: Adapted from Laurence Steinberg and Roberta Meyer, *Childhood.* Copyright © 1995 McGraw-Hill. Reprinted by permission of The McGraw-Hill Companies.

Write the main idea sentence:

_____

_____

_____

_____

What is the authors' purpose?

_____

_____

What is the authors' tone?

_____

_____

SELECTION 8-1
ECONOMICS

TICKET SCALPING: A BUM RAP?
From *Economics*
By Campbell McConnell and Stanley Brue

You see them at every big-name concert and every major sporting event. They're usually in the parking lot or near the stadium or the arena: scalpers. Loudly and openly—or discreetly, in venues in which scalping is prohibited—they are there to supply a ticket to any person who is willing to meet their price. Do you think scalping is bad or good? Read this economics textbook selection to see the authors' thoughts on scalping.

Some Market Transactions Get a Bad Name That Is Not Warranted

1   Tickets to athletic and artistic events are sometimes resold at higher-than-original prices—a market transaction known by the term "scalping." For example, the original buyer may resell a $50 ticket to a college bowl game for $200, $250, or more. The media often denounce scalpers for "ripping off" buyers by charging "exorbitant" prices. Scalping and extortion are synonymous in some people's minds.

2   But is scalping really immoral and unethical? We must first recognize that such ticket resales are voluntary transactions. Both buyer and seller expect to gain from the exchange. Otherwise, it would not occur! The seller must value the $200 more than seeing the event, and the buyer must value seeing the event even more than the $200. So there are no losers or victims here! Both buyer and seller benefit from the transaction. The "scalping" market simply redistributes assets (game or concert tickets) from those who value them less to those who value them more.

3   Does scalping impose losses or injury on other parties, in particular the sponsors of the event? If the sponsors are injured, it is because they initially priced tickets below the equilibrium level [the price level at which supply and demand balance]. In so doing, they suffer an economic loss in the form of less revenue and profit than they might have otherwise received. But the loss is self-inflicted because of their pricing error. That mistake is quite separate and distinct from the fact that some tickets are later resold at a higher price!

Annotation Practice Exercises

Directions: After you have read this selection, answer the critical reading questions below. This will help you gain additional insights about what you have read.

Annotation Exercise

What is the authors' purpose in writing this selection?

_____

_____

_____

_____

(Illustration by Jacques Cournoyer.)

4   What about spectators? Does scalping deteriorate the enthusiasm of the audience? Usually not! People who have the greatest interest in the event will pay the scalper's high prices. Ticket scalping also benefits the teams and performing artists, because they will appear before more dedicated audiences—ones that are more likely to buy souvenir items or CDs.

5   So is ticket scalping undesirable? Not on economic grounds! Both seller and buyer of a "scalped" ticket benefit, and a more interested audience results. Event sponsors may sacrifice revenue and profits, but that stems from their own misjudgment of the equilibrium price.

Annotation Exercise

Who is the authors' intended audience?

_____

_____

_____

Annotation Exercise

What is the authors' tone?

_____

_____

_____

Annotation Exercise

What is the authors' point of view about ticket scalping?

_____

_____

_____

_____

Source: Adapted from Campbell McConnell and Stanley Brue, *Economics,* 15th ed., p. 55. Copyright © 2002 McGraw-Hill. Reprinted by permission of The McGraw-Hill Companies.

ECONOMICS

Comprehension and Vocabulary Quiz

This quiz has four parts. Your instructor may assign some or all of them.

Comprehension

Directions: Items 1–5 test your comprehension (understanding) of the material in this selection. These questions are much like those that a content area instructor (such as an economics professor) would expect you to know after studying this selection. For each comprehension question below, use information from the selection to determine the correct answer. Refer to the selection as you answer the questions. Write your answer in the space provided.

1. The term "scalping" refers to
   a. tickets that are sold at higher prices.
   b. tickets that cost more than $200, $250, or more.
   c. tickets that are often resold at higher-than-original prices.
   d. tickets that are priced below the equilibrium level.

2. Scalping is
   a. unfair to spectators.
   b. a form of extortion.
   c. a misjudgment of the equilibrium price.
   d. a voluntary transaction.

3. Which of the following groups might suffer financially as a result of scalping?
   a. sports teams and performing artists
   b. event sponsors
   c. spectators
   d. all of the above

4. Performing artists and teams benefit from ticket scalping because
   a. profits from the sale of scalped tickets are higher.
   b. only the buyers of "scalped" tickets expect to gain from the exchange.
   c. buyers of "scalped" tickets are more dedicated and, therefore, more likely to buy more CDs or souvenir items.
   d. scalping forces event sponsors to lower their prices.

5. Scalping is acceptable in ethical terms because
   a. both the buyer and the seller gain from the exchange.
   b. it prevents extortion.
   c. the event sponsors sell more tickets.
   d. the only "victim" is the person who buys a "scalped" ticket.

Vocabulary in Context

Directions: Items 6–10 test your ability to determine the meaning of a word by using context clues. *Context clues* are words in a sentence that allow the reader to deduce (reason out) the meaning of an unfamiliar word in that sentence. Context clues also enable the reader to determine which meaning the author intends when a word has more than one meaning. For each vocabulary item below, a sentence from the selection containing an important word (*italicized, like this*) is quoted first. Next, there is an additional sentence using the word in the same sense and providing another context clue. Use the context clues from *both* sentences to deduce the meaning of the italicized word. *Be sure the answer you choose makes sense in both sentences.* If you discover that you need to use a dictionary to confirm an answer choice, remember that the meaning you select must still fit the context of *both* sentences. Write your answer in the space provided.

Pronunciation Key: ă pat   ā pay   âr care   ä father   ĕ pet   ē be   ĭ pit
ī tie   îr **pier**   ŏ pot   ō toe   ô paw   oi noise   ou **out**   ŏŏ **took**   ōō boot
ŭ cut   yōō abuse   ûr **urge**   th thin   *th* **this**   hw **which**   zh vision
ə **about**   Stress mark: ʹ

---

6. The media often *denounce* scalpers for "ripping off" buyers by charging "exorbitant" prices.

At the press conference later this morning, the mayoral candidate plans to *denounce* his opponent's campaign tactics as mean-spirited and unethical.

denounce (dĭ nouns´)

a. participate in a panel discussion
b. announce publicly to be blameworthy
c. debate in a public forum
d. openly praise

7. The media often denounce scalpers for "ripping off" buyers by charging "*exorbitant*" prices.

We didn't join the new country club because we felt the initiation fee and the monthly dues were *exorbitant.*

exorbitant (ĭg zôr´ bĭ tənt)

a. discriminatory
b. snobbish
c. excessive
d. variable

_____ **8.** Scalping and *extortion* are synonymous in some people's minds.

We are planning a protest: the prices in our school cafeteria are no better than *extortion!*

extortion (ĭk stôr′ shən)

a. exacting an excessive amount
b. an economical service
c. a giveaway
d. a sale

_____ **9.** If the sponsors are injured, it is because they initially priced tickets below the *equilibrium* level.

Even with five young children, my aunt never gets overly excited or depressed; she has a wonderful knack for maintaining emotional *equilibrium.*

equilibrium (ē qwə lĭb′ rē əm)

a. distress
b. balance
c. downswings
d. upswings

_____ **10.** Event sponsors may *sacrifice* revenue and profits, but that stems from their own misjudgment of the equilibrium price.

The Mays had hoped to sell their home for at least $75,000, but because of the recession, they had to *sacrifice* it for $60,000.

sacrifice (săk′ rə fīs)

a. give away
b. demolish; tear down
c. remodel; refurbish
d. give up; suffer a loss

Word Structure

Directions: Items 11–15 test your ability to use word-structure clues to help determine a word's meaning. *Word-structure clues* consist of roots, prefixes, and suffixes. In these exercises, you will learn the meaning of a word part (root) and use it to determine the meaning of the several other words that have the same word part. If you discover that you need to use a dictionary to confirm an answer choice, do so. Write your answer in the space provided.

In paragraph 1 of the selection you encountered the word **extortion.** This word contains the Latin root **tort,** which means "to twist," or "to bend."

Extortion literally means "twisting something away from someone." That is, it suggests wringing or wresting something from someone one who is resisting strongly. Use the meaning of *tort* and the list of prefixes on pages 60–61 to help you determine the meaning of each of the following words that contain this same root.

——————— **11.** Clowns and other performers who are **contortionists**
  a. make audiences laugh.
  b. twist and bend their bodies in extreme ways.
  c. paint on funny, exaggerated faces.
  d. wear bright, ridiculous costumes and wigs.

——————— **12.** You drive along a **tortuous** road to the top of a steep mountain. The road is
  a. winding, with many twists and turns.
  b. extremely narrow, with a single lane in either direction.
  c. hazardous because of possible rockslides.
  d. closed because of heavy snowfall.

——————— **13.** A group of mountain climbers attempts the *torturous* ascent to the summit of Mt. Everest. **Torturous** means
  a. slow and time-consuming.
  b. requiring extensive, careful planning.
  c. done at night.
  d. inflicting severe physical and mental anguish.

——————— **14.** If someone **distorts** the truth, that person
  a. twists the facts.
  b. discloses the facts fully.
  c. filters out what is fact from what is opinion.
  d. presents the facts, but adds irrelevant, unrelated information.

——————— **15.** This is an example of a famous *retort* given by a British politician to a woman who disliked him, and whom he disliked. She said, "If I were married to you, I'd put poison in your tea." His *retort* was, "Madam, if I were married to you, I'd drink it." A **retort** is a
  a. funny comment spoken in public intended to amuse others.
  b. cruel reply to a kind comment.
  c. clever, quick reply that turns the first speaker's words to his or her disadvantage.
  d. vicious, hurtful comment intended to hurt someone's feelings.

Reading Skills Application

Directions: Items 16–20 test your ability to apply certain reading skills to the material in this selection. These are the types of questions that might appear on standardized reading tests and state-mandated basic skills tests. Write your answer in the space provided.

_____   **16.** The main idea of the selection is best expressed by which of the following statements?

    a.   Ticket scalping is a form of extortion.

    b.   Ticket scalping does not deserve the "bum rap" that it gets.

    c.   Ticket scalping always imposes losses or injury on event sponsors.

    d.   Ticket scalping hurts fans, teams, and performing artists.

_____   **17.** What is the meaning of the word *grounds* as it is used in the last paragraph of the selection?

    a.   location in which a ticketed event is held

    b.   legal judgment handed down by a court

    c.   location in which ticket scalping occurs

    d.   basis for a belief, action, and performing argument

_____   **18.** In the selection, which of the following is used to support the contention a negative view of scalping is unwarranted?

    a.   a set of reasons

    b.   the authors' personal experiences

    c.   economic research data

    d.   reports from the media

_____   **19.** Which of the following represents the authors' attitude toward sponsors who lose money by scalping?

    a.   Sponsors should have the right to sue scalpers.

    b.   It is appropriate for sponsors to confront scalpers.

    c.   Sponsors should lobby for legislation prohibiting scalping.

    d.   It is the sponsors' own fault.

_____   **20.** Based on information from the selection, it can be inferred that scalping

    a.   will be made illegal.

    b.   cannot be justified morally.

    c.   is likely to continue.

    d.   hurts everyone.

SELECTION 8-2
NONFICTION

THOMAS EDISON: MAN OF INSPIRATION
From "It's Plain Hard Work That Does It"
By Charles Edison

Thomas Edison (1847–1931) was one of the most creative, hardworking, and prolific inventors in American history. During his life, he patented more than 1,000 inventions, including the incandescent light bulb. Edison originated the saying "Genius is one percent inspiration and ninety-nine percent perspiration." In these excerpts Charles Edison recounts his memories of his famous father.

1   I especially recall a freezing night in December 1914, at a time when still-unfruitful experiments on the nickel-iron-alkaline storage battery, to which Father had devoted much of ten years, had put him on a financial tightrope. Only profits from movie and record production were supporting the laboratory. On that December evening the cry of "Fire!" echoed through the plant. Spontaneous combustion had occurred in the film room. Within moments all the packing compounds, celluloid for records, film, and other flammable goods had gone up with a whoosh. Fire companies from eight towns arrived, but the heat was so intense, and the water pressure so low, that the fire hoses had no effect.

2   When I couldn't find Father, I became concerned. Was he safe? With all his assets going up in smoke, would his will be broken? He was sixty-seven, no age to begin anew. Then I saw him in the plant yard, running toward me.

3   "Where's Mom?" he shouted. "Tell her to get her friends! They'll never see a fire like *this* again!"

4   At 5:30 the next morning, with the fire barely under control, he called his employees together and announced, "We're rebuilding." One man was told to lease all the machine shops in the area. Another, to obtain a wrecking crane from the Erie Railroad. Then, almost as an afterthought, he added, "Oh, by the way. Anybody know where we can get some money?"

5   "You can always make capital out of disaster," he said. "We've just cleared out a bunch of old rubbish. We'll build bigger and better on the ruins." With that he rolled up his coat, curled up on a table, and immediately fell asleep.

*   *   *   *

(© Schenectady Museum; Hall of Electrical History Foundation/CORBIS)

> **Annotation Practice Exercises**

Directions: After you have read this selection, answer the critical reading questions on page 434. This will help you gain additional insights about what you have read.

Vocabulary in Context

Directions: Use the context clues from *both* sentences to deduce the meaning of the italicized word. *Be sure the answer you choose makes sense in both sentences.* If you discover that you need to use a dictionary to confirm an answer choice, remember that the meaning you select must still fit the context of *both* sentences. Write your answer in the space provided.

Pronunciation Key: ă pat   ā pay   âr **care**   ä father   ĕ pet   ē be   ĭ pit
ī tie   îr **pier**   ŏ pot   ō toe   ô paw   oi **noise**   ou **out**   ŏŏ **took**   ōō **boot**
ŭ **cut**   yōō abuse   ûr **urge**   th **thin**   *th* **this**   hw **which**   zh vision
ə **about**   Stress mark: ´

6. I especially recall a freezing night in December 1914, at a time when still-*unfruitful* experiments on the nickel-iron-alkaline storage battery, to which Father had devoted much of ten years, had put him on a financial tightrope.

   Heart transplant attempts proved *unfruitful* until the last half of the twentieth century when several breakthroughs occurred.

   unfruitful (ŭn frōōt´ fəl)

   a.   not popular with the general public
   b.   not producing useful results
   c.   not understood by prospective patients
   d.   not accepted by the medical profession

7. I especially recall a freezing night in December 1914, at a time when still-unfruitful experiments on the nickel-iron-alkaline storage battery, to which Father had devoted much of ten years, had put him *on a financial tightrope.*

   The Carsons had so much credit card debt that when Mr. Carson unexpectedly lost his job, it put the family *on a financial tightrope.*

   on a financial tightrope (fĭ năn´ shəl tīt´ rōp)

   a.   close to financial disaster
   b.   on a budget
   c.   spending money freely
   d.   giving financial advice

8. "You can always make *capital* out of disaster," he said.

   The new state senator benefited from the political *capital* of his father, the former governor.

   capital (kăp´ ĭ tl)

   a.   the city in which a state's government is located
   b.   an asset or advantage

c. mistakes

d. a tragic experience

_____ 9. Actually he had only six months of formal schooling, but under his mother's *tutelage* in Port Huron, Michigan, he had read such classics as *Decline and Fall of the Roman Empire* at the age of eight or nine.

In past centuries, apprentices learned their trades under the *tutelage* of master craftsmen.

tutelage (tōōt′ lĭj)

a. instruction

b. pressure

c. cruelty

d. indifference

_____ 10. After becoming a *vendor* and newsboy on the Grand Trunk Railroad, he spent whole days in the Detroit Free Library—which he read "from top to bottom."

In New York City a street *vendor* might offer customers anything from hot dogs to souvenirs.

vendor (vĕn′ dər)

a. person who displays things

b. person who collects things

c. person who buys things

d. person who sells things

Word Structure

Directions: In paragraph 7 of the selection you encountered the word **beneficial.** This word contains the Latin root **bene,** which means "good" or "well." The word *beneficial* describes something that has a good effect or, in other words, is helpful. Use the meaning of **bene** and the list of prefixes on pages 60–61 to help you determine the meaning of each of the following words that contain this same root. Write your answer in the space provided.

_____ 11. If you give a friend the "**benefit** of the doubt," you

a. continue to argue until he acknowledges that you are right.

b. supply him with a list of reasons as to why he is wrong.

c. resolve the matter by flipping a coin.

d. make a judgment in his favor even if there isn't enough evidence to support it.

Collaboration Option

Writing and Collaborating to Enhance Your Understanding

Option for collaboration: Work together in groups to complete the exercises below. Have one group member record your answers, but make sure every member of your group can explain all of your group's answers.

1. **Reacting to What You Have Read:** Describe a situation in which you were able to "make capital out of disaster," that is, you took a seemingly bad situation and made something good come of it. Describe the difficult or bad situation and the advantage that you were able to make of it.

    _____

    _____

    _____

    _____

    Edison turned his deafness into an advantage. Perhaps someone you know has succeeded in spite of some obstacle (such as not having a formal education) or having a physical handicap. Perhaps you yourself have had to overcome some handicap or obstacle. Describe the person, the obstacle or handicap, and the way in which he or she used the experience to his or her advantage.

    _____

    _____

    _____

    _____

2. **Comprehending the Selection Further:** What can you infer about Edison's character (or personality) when he says to his son, "Where's Mom? Tell her to get her friends! They'll never see a fire like *this* again!"

    _____

    _____

    _____

    What can you infer about Edison's nature from the fact that he curled up and took a nap once the fire was out and he had instructed his employees to start the rebuilding process?

    _____

    _____

_____

_____

_____

3. **Overall Main Idea of the Selection:** In one sentence tell what the author
    wants readers to understand about Thomas Edison in paragraphs 1–5. (Be
    sure to include the name "Thomas Edison" and the word "disaster" in your
    overall main idea sentence.)

_____

_____

_____

_____

In one sentence tell what the author wants readers to understand about
Thomas Edison in paragraphs 6–8. (Be sure to include the name "Thomas
Edison," the words "his deafness," and some reference to his education in
your overall main idea sentence.)

_____

_____

_____

_____

_____

Read More about It on the World Wide Web

To learn more about the topic of this selection, visit these websites or use
your favorite search engine (such as Yahoo®) to discover more about this author
and this topic on your own. Whenever you go to *any* website, it is a good idea
to evaluate it critically. Are you getting good information—that is, information
that is accurate, complete, and up-to-date? Who sponsors the website? How
easy is it to use the features of the website?

http://www.edisonian.com/

http://www.pbs.org/wgbh/amex/edison

http://edison.rutgers.edu

4   On the getaway day I try for amnesia. I do not want to know my name, where I live, or how many dire responsibilities rest on my shoulders. I detest encountering even the closest friend, for then I am reminded of who I am, and the circumstances of my life, which I want to forget for a while.

5   Every person needs to take one day away—a day in which one consciously separates the past from the future. Jobs, lovers, family, employers, and friends can exist one day without any one of us, and if our egos permit us to confess, they could exist eternally in our absence.

6   Each person deserves a day away in which no problems are confronted, no solutions searched for. Each of us needs to withdraw from the cares which will not withdraw from us. We need hours of aimless wandering or spates of time sitting on park benches, observing the mysterious world of ants and the canopy of treetops.

7   If we step away for a time, we are not, as many may think and some will accuse, being irresponsible, but rather we are preparing ourselves to more ably perform our duties and discharge our obligations.

8   When I return home, I am always surprised to find some questions I sought to evade had been answered and some entanglements I had hoped to flee had become unraveled in my absence.

9   A day away acts as a spring tonic. It can dispel rancor, transform indecision, and renew the spirit.

Annotation Practice Exercises

Directions: After you have read this selection, answer the critical reading questions below. This will help you gain additional insights about what you have read.

Annotation Exercise

Who is the author's *intended audience?*

_____

_____

_____

Annotation Exercise

What is the author's *purpose* in writing this essay?

_____

_____

Annotation Exercise

What is the author's *tone* in this selection?

_____

_____

Annotation Exercise

What is the author's *point of view* toward having a "day away" ?

_____

_____

_____

_____

4   On the getaway day I try for amnesia. I do not want to know my name, where I live, or how many dire responsibilities rest on my shoulders. I detest encountering even the closest friend, for then I am reminded of who I am, and the circumstances of my life, which I want to forget for a while.

5   Every person needs to take one day away—a day in which one consciously separates the past from the future. Jobs, lovers, family, employers, and friends can exist one day without any one of us, and if our egos permit us to confess, they could exist eternally in our absence.

6   Each person deserves a day away in which no problems are confronted, no solutions searched for. Each of us needs to withdraw from the cares which will not withdraw from us. We need hours of aimless wandering or spates of time sitting on park benches, observing the mysterious world of ants and the canopy of treetops.

7   If we step away for a time, we are not, as many may think and some will accuse, being irresponsible, but rather we are preparing ourselves to more ably perform our duties and discharge our obligations.

8   When I return home, I am always surprised to find some questions I sought to evade had been answered and some entanglements I had hoped to flee had become unraveled in my absence.

9   A day away acts as a spring tonic. It can dispel rancor, transform indecision, and renew the spirit.

Annotation Practice Exercises

Directions: After you have read this selection, answer the critical reading questions below. This will help you gain additional insights about what you have read.

Annotation Exercise

Who is the author's *intended audience?*

_____

_____

_____

Annotation Exercise

What is the author's *purpose* in writing this essay?

_____

_____

Annotation Exercise

What is the author's *tone* in this selection?

_____

_____

Annotation Exercise

What is the author's *point of view* toward having a "day away"?

_____

_____

_____

_____

SELECTION 8-3

LITERATURE

A DAY AWAY

From *Wouldn't Take Nothing for My Journey Now*
By Maya Angelou

It's hard to know where to begin when telling about Maya Angelou's fascinating life and immense talents. Early in her life she was a singer and dancer, pursuits that enabled her to tour 22 countries in Europe and Asia. She has been a civil rights activist who counted among her friends Malcolm X, Martin Luther King, Jr., and the writer James Baldwin. She has lived in Egypt and Africa. In addition to her masterful command of English, she is fluent in French, Spanish, Italian, Arabic, and West African Fanti.

Angelou is an author, poet, historian, playwright, producer, director, actor (who has made hundreds of television appearances), editor, and university professor. Her first book, an autobiography of her first 17 years of life, I Know Why the Caged Bird Sings, *won instant critical acclaim. In 1997, she had three books on the* New York Times *bestseller's list for 10 consecutive weeks. She has been a nominee for a Tony Award, an Emmy Award, the National Book Award, the Pulitzer Prize (for her first book of poetry), and she received a Grammy Award for her recording of her poetry. In January, 1993, she read at Bill Clinton's inaugural "On the Pulse of Morning," a poem she composed for the occasion at his request.*

One secret to how this remarkable woman sustains her creativity and energy (she was born in 1928) may be what she terms "a day away." In the essay that follows, Maya Angelou describes what an entire day, removed from all of the normal routine and cares, can do for us.

---

1   We often think that our affairs, great or small, must be tended continuously and in detail, or our world will disintegrate, and we will lose our places in the universe. That is not true, or if it is true, then our situations were so temporary that they would have collapsed anyway.

2   Once a year or so I give myself a day away. On the eve of my day of absence, I begin to unwrap the bonds which hold me in harness. I inform housemates, my family and close friends that I will not be reachable for twenty-four hours; then I disengage the telephone. I turn the radio dial to an all-music station, preferably one which plays the soothing golden oldies. I sit for at least an hour in a very hot tub; then I lay out my clothes in preparation for my morning escape, and knowing that nothing will disturb me, I sleep the sleep of the just.

3   On the morning I wake naturally, for I will have set no clock, nor informed my body timepiece when it should alarm. I dress in comfortable shoes and casual clothes and leave my house going no place. If I am living in a city, I wander streets, window-shop, or gaze at buildings. I enter and leave public parks, libraries, the lobbies of skyscrapers, and movie houses. I stay in no place for very long.

(© Mitchell Gerber/CORBIS)

_____

_____

_____

3. **Overall Main Idea of the Selection:** In one sentence tell what the author wants readers to understand about Thomas Edison in paragraphs 1–5. (Be sure to include the name "Thomas Edison" and the word "disaster" in your overall main idea sentence.)

_____

_____

_____

_____

In one sentence tell what the author wants readers to understand about Thomas Edison in paragraphs 6–8. (Be sure to include the name "Thomas Edison," the words "his deafness," and some reference to his education in your overall main idea sentence.)

_____

_____

_____

_____

_____

Read More about It on the World Wide Web

To learn more about the topic of this selection, visit these websites or use your favorite search engine (such as Yahoo®) to discover more about this author and this topic on your own. Whenever you go to _any_ website, it is a good idea to evaluate it critically. Are you getting good information—that is, information that is accurate, complete, and up-to-date? Who sponsors the website? How easy is it to use the features of the website?

http://www.edisonian.com/
http://www.pbs.org/wgbh/amex/edison
http://edison.rutgers.edu